Seventeenth Century
German Prose

The German Library: Volume 7
Volkmar Sander, General Editor

SEVENTEENTH CENTURY GERMAN PROSE

Edited by Lynne Tatlock
Foreword by Günter Grass

CONTINUUM • NEW YORK

1993
The Continuum Publishing Company
370 Lexington Avenue, New York, NY 10017

The German Library
is published in cooperation with Deutsches Haus,
New York University.
This volume has been supported by a grant
from the funds of Stifterverband für die Deutsche Wissenschaft.

Printed in the United States of America

Library of Congress Cataloging-in-Publication Data

Seventeenth century German prose / edited by Lynne Tatlock;
foreword by Günter Grass.
 p.   cm. — (The German library ; v. 7)
 ISBN 0-8264-0710-2 (hardcover). — ISBN 0-8264-0711-0 (pbk.)
 1. German prose literature—Early modern, 1500–1700—
Translations into English. 2. English prose literature—Translations
from German. I. Tatlock, Lynne, 1950–   . II. Series.
PT1314.S48   1993
838'.50808—dc20   91-44512
                                                          CIP

Acknowledgments will be found on page 305,
which constitutes an extension of the copyright page.

To the memory of
Stanley Loewenstein (1916–1991)

Contents

Contents

Foreword

The thing that hath been tomorrow is that which shall be yesterday. Our stories of today need not have taken place in the present. This one began more than three hundred years ago. So did many other stories. Every story set in Germany goes back that far. If I am writing down what happened in Telgte, it is because a friend, who gathered his fellow writers around him in the forty-seventh year of our century, is soon to celebrate his seventieth birthday; and yet he is older, much older than that—and we, his present-day friends, have all grown hoary white with him since those olden times.

Up from Jutland and down from Regensburg came Lauremberg and Greflinger on foot; others came on horseback or in covered wagons. While some were sailing down rivers, old Weckherlin took ship from London to Bremen. From far and near they came from all directions. A merchant, to whom due dates mean profit and loss, might well have been amazed at the punctual zeal displayed by those men of mere verbal action, especially at a time when the towns and countryside were still, or once again, ravaged, overgrown with nettles and thistles, depopulated by plague, and when all the roads were unsafe.

So much so that Moscherosch and Schneuber, who had come from Strassburg, reached their appointed destination stripped of everything they owned (except their portfolios, useless to highwaymen), Moscherosch laughing and richer by a satire, Schneuber lamenting and already dreading the horrors of the return journey. (His arse was sore from blows with the flat of the sword.)

Only because Czepko, Logau, Hofmannswaldau, and other Silesians, provided with a safe-conduct issued by Wrangel, had attached themselves to various Swedish battalions, whose foraging raids took them as far as Westphalia, were they able to reach Osnabrück undiminished; but they suffered as if in their own flesh from

the daily atrocities of the foraging parties, who showed no concern
for any poor devil's religion. No remonstrances would hold
Wrangel's horsemen in check. The student Scheffler (a discovery of
Czepko's) was almost done in while trying to shield a peasant
woman who, like her husband before her, was to be impaled before
the eyes of her children.

Johann Rist came via Hamburg from nearby Wedel on the Elbe.
A coach had brought Mülbe, the Strassburg publisher, from Lüne-
burg. The route taken by Simon Dach, whose invitations had pro-
voked all this effort, from the Kneiphof section of Königsberg, was
indeed the longest, but also the safest, for he had traveled in the
retinue of Frederick William, elector of Brandenburg. The previous
year Frederick William had become engaged to Louise of Orange,
and Dach had been privileged to recite his panegyric verses in
Amsterdam. It was then that the many letters of invitation, complete with designation of the meeting place, were written, and that,
with the elector's help, provision was made for their delivery. (The
elector's ubiquitous political agents were often required to double
as couriers.) This was how Gryphius received his invitation, though
he had been traveling for the past year with the Stettin merchant
Wilhelm Schlegel, first in Italy, then in France, and Dach's letter
was delivered to him on his return journey (in Speyer, to be exact).
He set out at once and brought Schlegel with him.

Augustus Buchner, magister of letters, arrived punctually from
Wittenberg. After declining several times, Paul Gerhardt nevertheless arrived on time. Philipp Zesen, whose letter caught up with
him in Hamburg, traveled from Amsterdam with his publisher. No
one wanted to miss the meeting. Nothing, no school, state, or court
function, could keep them away. Those who lacked funds for the
journey went looking for patrons. Those who, like Greflinger, had
found no patron, were carried to their destination by obstinacy.
And those whose obstinacy might have deterred them from starting
in time were infected with travel fever by the news that others were
already on their way. Even such men as Zesen and Rist, who
counted each other as enemies, were intent on meeting. Logau's
curiosity about the meeting proved even stronger than his scorn
for the assembled poets. Their local surroundings were too con-
stricting. No business transaction, however intricate, no love affair,
however diverting, could resist the force that drew them together.

Moreover, the peace negotiations brought increasing unrest. No one wanted to be by himself.

But eagerly as the gentlemen had responded to Dach's invitation in their hunger for literary exchange, they soon lost heart when they failed to find quarters in Oesede, the village near Osnabrück where the meeting was to be held. Though reservations had been made in plenty of time, the Black Horse, where the conferees were to have lodged, had been commandeered by the staff of Swedish War Councilor Erskein, who had recently put the demands of Wrangel's armies for indemnification before the peace conference, so adding appreciably to the cost of the peace. What rooms were not occupied by regimental secretaries and colonels in Count Königsmark's army were piled high with documents. The great hall, where they planned to meet, to carry on the discussions for which they had so fervently longed and to read their manuscripts to one another, had been turned into a storeroom. Everywhere horsemen and musketeers were lounging about. Couriers came and went. Erskein made himself inaccessible. A provost, to whom Dach presented a document showing that he had rented the Black Horse, was seized with a fit of circumfluously infectious laughter when Dach requested that his down payment be reimbursed by the Swedes. Brusquely rebuffed, Dach came back. Strong, stupid men. Their armored emptiness. Their grinning dullness. None of the Swedish officers had ever heard of the illustrious visitors. Grudgingly, they let them rest a while in the taproom. The landlord advised them to move on to the Oldenburg region, where everything, even lodging, was available.

Already the Silesians were thinking of going on to Hamburg, Gerhardt of returning to Berlin, Moscherosch and Schneuber of proceeding to Holstein with Rist; already Weckherlin had decided to take the next ship to London; already most of the travelers, not without recriminations against Dach, were threatening to let the meeting go hang, and already Dach—ordinarily the soul of equanimity—was beginning to have doubts about his plan; already they were standing in the street with their luggage, uncertain which way to turn, when—well before nightfall—the Nuremberg contingent arrived: Harsdörffer with his publisher Endter, and young Birken; they were accompanied by a red-bearded fellow who called himself Christoffel Gelnhausen and whose gangling youthfulness—he seemed to be in his middle twenties—was contradicted by his pock-

marked face. In his green doublet and plumed hat he looked like
something out of a storybook. Someone said that he had been
begotten by Count Mansfeld's soldiery on their way through—but
Gelnhausen turned out to be more real than he looked. He was in
command of a detachment of imperial horsemen and musketeers,
who were camped at the edge of town because the territory of the
towns where the peace conference was being held had been de-
clared neutral ground, barred to the military action of both parties.

When Dach had described the poets' sorry situation to the
Nurembergers, and Gelnhausen had offered his services in a long-
winded speech well larded with tropes, Harsdörffer took Dach
aside. True, he said, the fellow prates like an itinerant astrologer—
he had introduced himself to the assemblage as Jupiter's favorite,
whom, as they could see, Venus had punished in France—but he
had wit, and was better read than his clowning might lead one to
suspect. Moreover, he was serving as a secretary at the headquarters of the Schauenburg regiment, then stationed in Offenburg.
In Cologne, where the Nurembergers had arrived by ship from
Würzburg, Gelnhausen had helped them out of difficulties incurred
when Endter had attempted to sell a stack of books without a
license. Fortunately, Gelnhausen had been able to talk them clear
of clerical suspicion, which scented "heretical machinations." His
lies, said Harsdörffer, are as inspired as any romances; his eloquence reduces the very Jesuits to silence; not just the church fathers, but all the gods and their planets are at his fingertips; he is
familiar with the seamy side of life, and wherever he goes, in Cologne, in Recklinghausen, in Soest, he knows his way about. Quite
possibly, Harsdörffer concluded, he might help them.

Gerhardt warned them against dealing with a man of the imperial party. Hofmannswaldau stood dumbfounded; hadn't the fellow just quoted a passage from Opitz's translation of the *Arcadia?*
Moscherosch and Rist thought they should listen at least to the
regimental secretary's proposals, especially after Schneuber of
Strassburg had asked him about certain particulars of life in the
bustling garrison town of Offenburg and received bathhouse gossip
in reply.

In the end, Gelnhausen was given leave to explain himself to the
assembled and now desperately unquartered gentlemen. His words
seemed as trustworthy as the sheen of the double row of buttons
on his green doublet. Being a cousin of Mercury and therefore as

restlessly active as that god, he was, so he averred, bound for
Münster in any case—at the bidding of his master, an acolyte of
Mars, in other words a colonel—carrying a secret message to
Count Trauttmannsdorff, who, in his capacity as the emperor's
negotiating team, had been crammed full of wisdom by the peevish
Saturn—in order that peace might dawn at last. The trip came to
less than thirty miles. Under an almost full moon. And through
flat country. And if their lordships decided to avoid priest-ridden
Münster, they would pass through Telgte, a snug little town which,
though impoverished, had remained unscarred, since the towns-
people had managed to beat off the Hessians and had not wearied
of feeding the Königsmark regimental treasury. And since, as they
must know, Telgte had long been a place of pilgrimage, there he
would find quarters for their lordships, those pilgrims of the
Muses. For he learned early on to find lodging for all manner of
gods.

When old Weckherlin asked what they, as Protestants, had done
to deserve so much Catholic favor (after all, Gelnhausen was bearing swift tidings to the Catholic party), the regimental secretary
replied that he cared little for religion, so long as no one interfered
with his own. And that his message for Trauttmannsdorff was not
so secret as all that, since everyone knew that the Saxon regiments
in Marshal Turenne's camp had mutinied against their foreign over-
lords and dispersed. Such news ran on ahead, so there was no point
in hurrying. He therefore preferred to oblige a dozen homeless
poets, all the more so since he himself—by Apollo!—wielded the
pen, though for the present only in Colonel Schauenburg's regimental chancellery.

At that Dach accepted his offer. Whereupon Gelnhausen stopped
talking tortuous foolishness and issued orders to his horsemen and
musketeers. . . .

A discussion of the language was scheduled for after the meal.
What had wrecked it, and what might make it well again? What
rules should be laid down, and what rules would hamper the poetic
flow? How might the so-called natural language, which Buchner
disparaged as a "purely mystical concept," be nurtured with better
fare and so develop into a national language? What should pass as
High German and what place should be allotted to the dialects?
For learned and polyglot as they all were—Gryphius and Hof-

mannswaldau were eloquent in seven tongues—they all mouthed and whispered, babbled and bellowed, declaimed and postured, in some sort of regional German.

Though he had been living and teaching mathematics in Danish Zeeland ever since Wallenstein's invasion of Pomerania, Lauremberg expressed himself in his native Rostock brogue, and Rist the Holstein preacher answered him in Low German. After thirty years of residence in London, the diplomat Weckherlin still spoke an unvarnished Swabian. And into the predominantly Silesian conversation, Moscherosch mixed his Alemannic, Harsdörffer his peppery Franconian, Buchner and Gerhardt their Saxon, Greflinger his Lower Bavarian gargle, and Dach a Prussian kneaded and shaped between Memel and Pregel. Gelnhausen told his wretched bawdy tales and decanted clownish wisdom in three different dialects, for in the course of the war Stoffel had acquired the Westphalian and Alemannic stammer on top of his native Hessian.

Though they spoke a confusing variety of languages, they made themselves clearly understood, and their German was free and unfettered. But that did not detract from their prowess in linguistic theory. No line of poetry but was subjected to some rule.

GÜNTER GRASS
Translated by Ralph Manheim

Introduction

In 1967, eight years after publishing his monumental novel, *The Tin Drum,* Günter Grass wrote, "The Thirty Years' War was and probably still is the source as well as the stimulus of literature in the German language. The beginning of the German novel can be dated to 'Simplizius.'"[1] Grass's affinity to the seventeenth century, the Baroque Age as it is sometimes called, has often been noted. His petite drummer, Oskar Mazerath, has something of Johann Jacob Christoph von Grimmelshausen's picaro, Simplicissimus, and his colorful and complex prose has often been characerized as "baroque," as if he had deliberately imitated the style of the period. Grass overtly returned to the Baroque in his novel *The Flounder* (1977) where, in the chapter entitled "In the Fourth Month," he stages a meeting between Martin Opitz, the seventeenth-century arbiter of literary taste, and the great German poet of the era, Andreas Gryphius (1616–64). But if his abiding interest in seventeenth-century Germany and his debt to its literary production were at all in doubt, his short novel *The Meeting in Telgte* (1979) overtly reaffirmed it. Here Grass invented a gathering of German writers in Telgte in the duchy of Westphalia in 1647, one year before the Peace of Westphalia marked the conclusion of the Thirty Years' War. While the war continues to rage around them, these men convene to read their poetry, to discuss and normalize German poetics, and, evoking the power of the pen, to write a petition for peace.[2] Grass's imaginary seventeenth-century convocation consciously evoked the meetings of the so-called Group '47, the German writers who began meeting after World War II to consider their future role in the wake of fascism and to ponder the revitalization, indeed, cleansing of the German language after its fifteen years of servitude to the projects of National Socialism. Whereas the devastation of World War II and the shame of the holocaust had led many writers, and particularly Group '47, to express the wish to uncouple themselves from their own heritage, Grass's novel rejoins the present to the past, not to affirm it but to incorporate it. As Leonard Forster's afterword and addendum to the English language edition of Grass's novel attest, *Telgte* is best understood and more richly enjoyed with a knowledge of the seventeenth century.[3] On the other hand, Grass's writing provides the present with a lens through which to view the German seventeenth-century cultural heritage. His representation of the German past is admittedly subjective, not an attempt in the nineteenth-century German historical tradition to re-create the past "as it actually was." But in many ways *Telgte* imitates seventeenth-century forms. For example, Grass includes an emblematic frontispiece—most seventeenth-century German novels appeared with a frontispiece that in allegorical form elucidated the contents or intention—and he opens his novel with the sort of paradox beloved by seventeenth-century writers: "The thing that hath been tomorrow is that which shall be yesterday." Many of the authors included in the present anthology are resurrected in *Telgte*. I have chosen to preface this collection of German seventeenth-century prose in translation with the opening passages from Grass's novel, for I can imagine no introduction more engaging for the contemporary reader than Grass's vigorous prose and vivid portraiture.

Grass is not the only twentieth-century German writer to have sought inspiration and subject matter in the seventeenth century and specifically in Grimmelshausen's depictions of the Thirty Years' War. Grimmelshausen's female picaresque novel, *The Runagate Courage,* provided the impetus for Bertolt Brecht's *Mother Courage and Her Children,* written in 1941 during World War II. Brecht examines Courage with a critical Marxist eye, but he invented neither the figure nor her venality.[4] Furthermore, Alfred Döblin, best known to English-speaking audiences as the author of *Berlin Alexanderplatz,* turned to the Thirty Years' War in his novel *Wallenstein* (1920), as did the writer Ricarda Huch in her novel *The Great War in Germany* (1912–14) and in her historical "character study" *Wallenstein* (1915). Similarly, the nineteenth-century German novelist and journalist Gustav Freytag treated the war both in history and prose fiction, in his popular history *Pictures from the German Past* (1859–66) and in his weighty novel *The Ancestors* (1873–1981). For the Protestant and avid nationalist Freytag the Thirty Years' War marked a tragic turning point in

German history, because German unification was postponed for two more centuries. The Catholic Austrian playwright, Franz Grillparzer, less interested in German unification than his German contemporary Freytag, explored high-level events leading to the outbreak of the Thirty Years' War in his psychological drama *Fraternal Strife in Habsburg* (1872). Perhaps the most famous treatment of this war in the German traditions is that of the eighteenth-century classical writer Friedrich Schiller, who wrote both a history of the war (1791–93) as well as the dramatic trilogy *Wallenstein* (1798–99). But not only the war has preoccupied German writers. The infamous witch-hunts, like the century itself that was caught between superstition and science, credulity and skepticism, have often inspired literary treatment.

In the late eighteenth and early nineteenth centuries the so-called romantics virtually rediscovered the forgotten texts of the seventeenth century. The eighteenth-century project of Enlightenment had conditioned an uncritical condemnation of writing styles that were deemed florid, extreme, bombastic, and asymmetrical, and of contents that were often unabashedly violent, obscene, or erotic. The romantic poets not only reread and edited these texts but imitated some of their forms, as for example the mixture of poetry and prose. They also occasionally rewrote them. Achim von Arnim offered a new version of "The Soldier's Life," one of Johann Michael Moscherosch's *Visions,* as well as a condensed and bowdlerized reworking of Christian Reuter's *Schelmuffsky* combined with elements of Christian Weise's *Three Most Awful Arch-Fools in the Entire World.* Arnim's frequent collaborator, Clemens Brentano, humorously suggested that anyone who could not appreciate Reuter's novel was a philistine.[5] The enthusiasm of the Arnim–Brentano circle for Reuter's comic novel was in fact so great that the members cultivated a Schelmuffsky manner and practiced writing in the Schelmuffsky style.[6]

Romantic scholars, who were fascinated by the German past and the development of the German language, were kindred spirits to the seventeenth-century literati. The famous romantic philologists and members of the Brentano–Arnim circle, Jakob and Wilhelm Grimm, best known to English speakers as the author–compilers of *Grimms' Fairy Tales,* assembled what is to date the most authoritative historical dictionary in the German language. One finds most of the prose texts included in the present anthology among the sources the Grimms list for their work; indeed some of the specific passages included in this anthology may be found under the entries in Grimms' dictionary. In other words, these texts have become the sustenance of the German cultural heritage, not only because of their style and content, but because of the very words they employ.

The wars of the seventeenth century cannot be seen as anything but determinant in German cultural and political life. In the areas worst affected during the decades of the Thirty Years' War (1618–48), the population had been reduced by up to fifty percent as a direct consequence of warfare or secondarily as a result of plague spread by the armies.[7] The troops had plundered areas where they had long been stationed and elsewhere the costs of sustaining troops had bankrupted independent cities and principalities. For thirty years the vicissitudes of war had repeatedly disrupted commerce and communication. Most decisive for the future, the Treaty of Westphalia (1648) had left the German empire divided into sixty-one imperial cities and around three hundred states with territorial sovereignty. Within the German empire the principle *cuius regio eius religio* ruled—the religion of the ruler determined the official religion of the territory. The authority of the elected Holy Roman Emperor and the imperial diet, the ancient central authority of the loose confederation of German states, had diminished decisively and would become so diminished that in the next century Johann Wolfgang Goethe would quip in his *Urfaust* (1775) "The dear Holy Roman Empire, / How does it still hold together!" And the conclusion of the Thirty Years' War did not indicate the end of armed hostilities, even if these further conflicts were geographically more contained. In the 1670s and 1780s Louis XIV undertook a number of campaigns against the German-speaking world as well as Holland. In 1683 the Turkish army stood before the gates of Vienna, only to be routed by the army led by the future Polish king John Sobieski, and in 1697 an imperial army led by Prince Eugene of Savoy utterly defeated the Turks at Zenta on the Theiss.
  Although there were numerous unifying efforts by learned men and even learned women on behalf of explicitly German culture, the political disunity and the religious divisions promoted diverse cultural, intellectual, and political ties. The close relations between Hanover and England are, for example, well known: in 1714 the

Hanoverian elector became George I of England. The Austrian Habsburgs, on the other hand, maintained old and vexed connections with Spain. Through the marriage of Liselotte von der Pfalz to the younger brother of Louis XIV the Palatinate vainly sought to forge an alliance with France and so it went with the many German principalities as they jockeyed for position in the power politics of the times.

The physical distance of centers of publication from one another also militated against cultural and linguistic unity. While publishers undoubtedly had common interests, regulation was inconsistent. In contrast to France and England where cultural production was largely centered in a capital city, the German-speaking world counted many and diverse pockets of activity—Hamburg, Brunswick, Strasbourg, Nuremberg, Silesia (Breslau), Leipzig, Vienna, Danzig, Königsberg, and so forth. Spelling, lexicon, and grammar diverged noticeably; dialect variations abounded in printed texts.

The decentralizing political events in the seventeenth-century German-speaking world set it apart from Western Europe. Nevertheless, German intellectuals participated in many of the significant European cultural trends of the times. French, Spanish, and English sixteenth- and seventeenth-century literature was well-known among the German intelligentsia. Germany also carried on the archaeological projects of the European Renaissance. Men of letters, here as elsewhere, undertook ambitious translations of the texts of antiquity, as well as philological exercises like Erasmus's monumental etymological collection of adages *Adagiorum Chiliades* (1508). But German intellectuals were not only interested in the trends of cultural life of an explicit literary nature. The advent of the new experimental science in Europe, what an English historian, borrowing from Francis Bacon, has called "the great instauration," and the accompanying rethinking of the doings of the Real and our perception of it also had a significant impact in Germany.[8] The same German writers who were interested in the well-wrought rhyme also studied science and philosophy. Although their employ of classical themes and forms in literature and their obviously intense engagement with antiquity may lead us to think otherwise, seventeenth-century German writers were attuned to the times and to contemporary cultural production.[9]

Even as experimental science, the New Philosophy, and mathematics were calling old beliefs into question, the seventeenth century remained a credulous and superstitious age. Ghosts and demons abound in the literature, not as decoration or cheap sensationalism but as part of a system of belief. Although times were changing, the devil had for many lost little of the corporeality that he had had for Martin Luther in the previous century. Demonic possession was believed to be real, even if some medical practitioners like Johann Weyer (1515–88) had already speculated on other causes besides witchcraft for bizarre behavior. In the first half of the seventeenth century the cautioning voice of Friedrich von Spee, *Cautio Criminalis* (1631) had little effect; at the end of the century, when the craze was beginning to abate anyway, Christian Thomasius's two Latin treatises, *On the Vice of Witchcraft* and *On the Witch Trials* (1701, 1902) had a greater impact. In the meantime thousands of persons had been executed for witchcraft.[10] Some of those persecuted probably believed themselves to be practicing witches or at the very least to have had conversation with the devil, but many had simply exhibited strange behavior or failed to conform and thereby aroused the suspicions of the local authorities. Allegations that tragically led to prosecution sometimes arose merely from spite or greed. The accused were most often women. Indeed, it has been estimated that eighty percent of trial defendants were women, usually between the ages of fifty and seventy and very often impoverished.[11] According to old popular belief as well as church-sanctioned writing on witchcraft, women succumbed more readily to the machinations of the Devil.[12]

The vicious misogyny manifest in the witch trials resurfaces throughout the texts of the seventeenth century. Women were repeatedly the target of mordant and obscene satire. Johann Beer, the novelist now considered second only to Grimmelshausen, wrote not one but several scurrilous novels attacking women. In high culture, on the other hand, elaborate gallantry circumscribed women. Although they played the role of muse to male culture, they had little access to higher education. Indeed, they were barred from the university. The publishing woman writer was thus the rare exception in seventeenth-century Germany.

The tragedy of the seventeenth century, the Thirty Years' War, ostensibly resulted from divergent religious confessions. The pragmatic and rather cynical solution after thirty years of conflict hardly ended relgious strife and persecution. While the religious convictions of some major players, like the famous imperial general

Albrecht Eusebius Wenzel von Wallenstein (1583–1634), were probably a matter of expediency, and, while political marriages, as in the case of Liselotte von der Pfalz, required formal but not deeply felt conversion, religious views were strongly held and deeply pondered in the seventeenth century. Among literary figures the most famous Catholic converts are Grimmelshausen and the poet Johann Scheffler (Angelus Silesius [1624–77]). On the other hand, the Catholic Habsburgs constantly threatened the religious freedom of the Protestants in Silesia and Austria. Austrian Protestants, like the families of Johann Beer and Catharina von Greiffenberg, frequently left their homeland rather than give up their faith. In various parts of Germany Protestant sects arose, the best known of these being pietism. Religious fanaticism was also not uncommon in the century that pursued witches. One famous fanatic, the wandering religious poet Quirinus Kuhlmann (1651–89), was ultimately burned in Moscow as a heretic.

As Grass's *Telgte* demonstrates, men and women of letters in the seventeenth century wished to cultivate and reform the German language. This interest paralleled trends in other European countries but had a special urgency, indeed poignancy, in the ravaged German territories. But while political disunity certainly hampered efforts towards a standardized and refined national language, European Latinity also presented a stumbling block.

Latin was the language of the university-trained elite in the German-speaking world, indeed, throughout Europe. Students disputed orally in Latin, read Latin schoolbooks and wrote their dissertations in Latin. The vast majority of German seventeenth-century writers published in Latin, not in German. Despite Martin Luther's sixteenth-century translation of the Bible and despite the obvious cultural message of this translation, Latin ruled as the language of learning. This distinguished legacy of the universality of the Middle Ages had become an obstacle both to the development of national culture and to the democratization of that culture. Writing in the vernacular was thus a political statement, an affirmation of national culture. However, an author who wrote in the vernacular ran the risk of failing to make his mark in Europe at large. Thus Francis Bacon (1561–1626) occasionally chose to write in English, but not his major works. Remarkably, René Descartes (1596–1650) wrote many of his philosophical and mathematical treatises in French, including his seminal *Discours de la méthode*

(1637). Of course, due to the rising political power of France, French was acquiring a new status as an international language of diplomacy, warfare, and high culture, a trend that was to continue into the twentieth century. In the eighteenth century Frederick the Great, Prussian king and patron of the arts, wrote *his* essay on German literature neither in Latin nor in German but in French (*De la littérature allemande* [1780]). In the meantime in the seventeenth century, even as Gottfried Wilhelm Leibniz made his plea for treating matters of substance in German, he himself, eager to establish an international reputation, wrote in Latin or occasionally French. None of his mathematical and philosophical writings is composed in German.

Despite the topos of the power of the pen, German writers were generally not well positioned to influence affairs of state significantly. Even when they, like Gryphius, Grimmelshausen, Daniel Casper von Lohenstein, and Christian Hofmann von Hofmannswaldau, occupied positions of importance in cities; even when they, like Leibniz, served ducal families; even when they themselves, like the novelist Duke Anton Ulrich von Braunschweig (1633–1714), belonged to ruling families, their spheres of influence were sharply circumscribed. In this light the efforts to sustain and reform German culture and language might be seen as compensation for lack of political influence. Indeed, in the "Exhortation to the Germans" (1679) Leibniz explicitly defers to the ruling authorities in political matters, relinquishing any claim to insight or expertise in affairs of state, and only focuses on matters of letters. The epistles of Liselotte von der Pfalz constitute an extreme example of compensation: when she began writing her epistles from her prominent position as the sister-in-law of the French Sun King, she embarked on a private project of affirmation of self and of all things German as well as conservation of the German language. But Liselotte had virtually no influence at the French court, where she was powerless to prevent the French sack of her homeland in 1688. Not until 1788 were some of her letters published for the first time and then only in French translation. Nevertheless, despite the lack of real power, German men and women of letters took writing in German seriously and, in many cases, consciously as a national mission. They chose their words carefully as if each one mattered. And they did not necessarily undertake their writing projects in isolation.

One hedge against isolation was the German language society.

In 1617 in Weimar Prince Ludwig von Anhalt-Köthen founded the Fruit-Bearing Society otherwise known as the Order of the Palm, a language society modeled after the Florentine *Accademia della Crusca.* Other societies followed: the German-minded Association in Hamburg, the Pegnitz Shepherds or the Order of the Flowers in Nuremberg, the Order of the Elbe Swans in Lübeck, the Upright Society of the Pine Tree in Strasbourg. Members included both aristocrats and bourgeois, sometimes both men and women, both literary and nonliterary writers. Like that of the French Academy, which was not founded until nearly twenty years later, the program of these societies was to purge the national language of foreign influences, to normalize the language with the goal of rendering it pure, eloquent, and capable of treating the arts, and to promote German writing culture. The important grammars and dictionaries of the century were undertaken by members of these societies. Indeed, their ambitious and energetic members generally found an eager partner in the growing publishing industry, and new books of all kinds were to be found at the book fairs in Frankfurt and Leipzig.

Besides the linguistic and cultural program, the aims of the societies were social and ethical: the pursuit of the "old German virtues" and the worship of God. New members received a special name, a plant, and a motto. Moscherosch, for example, joined the Fruit-Bearing Society as "The Dreaming one." His plant was nightshade and his motto "lofty matters." Although their memberships grew, the language societies represented only narrow strata of the population. Unlike the French Academy, they did not evolve into a permanent institution that monitored the language. Their influence peaked in the 1640s; by the end of the century all but one of the most important of them had disappeared.[13]

At the same time, however, the German language was affirming itself in other sectors. While the Thirty Years' War had effectively hindered economic growth in some areas, it had proved to be a stimulus to the development of newspapers.[14] A credulous public longed to hear reports of the "terrible but true" events of the times: the sighting of a portentous comet, a brutal murder, a maritime disaster, a freak birth, as well as news of the war and other political events. The first newspapers—largely lists of commercial information—had appeared in the German-speaking world already in the last decade of the sixteenth century; in the course of the seventeenth-century newspapers sprung up throughout the German territories. Eventually contemporaries took note of the phenomenon in the form of polemical writing pro and contra. Some writers, ever jealous of their own sphere of influence, repudiated newspapers as a pack of lies. Others, like Kaspar Stieler, welcomed this new kind of publication as a normative and educative tool, an important source of information about an expanding world, and an entertaining pastime.

In 1624 Martin Opitz published the first German-language treatise on the poetics of German, thereby establishing himself in the seventeenth-century literary consciousness as the father of German poetry. While Opitz encouraged the writing of elegant verse, he hardly mentioned prose. If anything, prose fell under the category of rhetoric, the art of speaking, and not poetics. Indeed, prose was not generally thought of as the language of high literature. Nevertheless, it was held that, as with other kinds of writing, one acquired an elegant writing style by translating classical and foreign works into German. But writing prose was not solely the prerogative of the elite nor was it confined to literature. Indeed, despite receiving little theoretical attention, prose was ubiquitous. It was the language of the Bible, city chronicles, newspapers, sermons, the law, medicine, science, philosophy, letters, treaties, battle plans, travel reports. It was the language of the anecdote, the obscene joke, the cautionary tale. Some prose forms like the eulogy or panegyric had their origins in classical rhetoric and thus were circumscribed by thoroughly analyzed conventions of writing and speaking. Other forms, like the joke or obscene anecdote, were less self-conscious, although not without a tradition.

Many German scholars locate the birth of the German novel in the seventeenth century. Indeed, if we are to believe Grass, Grimmelshausen's *Simplicissimus* (1668) was the first German novel. *Simplicissimus* has certainly endured longer than any of the many voluminous prose fictions of the seventeenth century. It has been translated into many languages, most recently into Chinese. It occupies an undisputed place in the German canon and is at least known by title to most university-educated Germans. Nevertheless, it was most certainly not the first German novel; instead it belonged to a trend that became more pronounced as the century progressed. However, history has consigned most of the vast novelistic production of the age to oblivion or at best to the scholar's bookshelf.

In the seventeenth century new and more efficient means of printing and marketing facilitated the production of lengthy books with a broad appeal. Translations of Spanish picaresque novels and of European pastoral novels were available in Germany already in the first half of the century. In addition, new editions of German chapbooks from the previous century—*Fortunatus, Huge Schepler, Knight Oktavian, Melusine,* and the *History of Johann Faustus*— circulated. Furthermore, at the beginning of the century Germany, like the rest of Europe, was still avidly reading the most famous romance of all, the Spanish *Amadís of Gaul.* Moralists and clergy, who considered the novel a rival to the Bible and other edifying literature, repeatedly cited *Amadís* when arguing that novels dangerously overheated readers' erotic imagination, especially that of women and the young. Predictably, the moralists eventually lost the argument and novels grew in popularity.

German seventeenth-century novels are for the most part, to borrow Henry James's phrase, "large loose baggy monsters."[15] They often number over a thousand pages, have multiple plots, abound with anecdotes and passages from other works of literature, science, or philosophy, even excerpts from newspapers. Even the most enduring of the seventeenth-century German novels do not look much like what one might now identify as a novel. They include so many diverse elements that classification is difficult; one scholar, familiar with the generic chaos, has facetiously referred to the "courtly-historical satirical gallant picaresque state-heroic-romantic-baroque novel."[16] Indeed, even to speak generally of these voluminous works as prose fiction is somewhat misleading, as some of the works insist on their title pages that they are true tales (even when they are not) and still others actually contain much factual material.

Seventeenth-century prose emerges from the soil of political and social turmoil, protracted warfare, epistemological and religious controversies, a growing publishing industry, and national cultural efforts to refine German as a literary language. The present anthology attempts to give a sense of the broad range of prose writing, the many interests of the seventeenth-century intellectual, the variety of genres, fiction, and nonfiction. The authors range from the royal to the socially marginal; they represent a variety of geographical regions, from Hamburg to Strasbourg, Nuremberg to Breslau. Some of the texts included have previously appeared in English; some are here translated for the first time.

The first two essays offer examples of seventeenth-century writing about the German language. Philipp von Zesen was one of the more radical writers on this subject; in his zeal to purify the German language of what he deemed to be foreign words he suggested monstrosities, like *face-bay-window* for *nose* or *virgins' dungeon* for *convent,* that have made him the target of ridicule to this day. But he was a serious and prolific writer with a mission shared by many of his contemporaries; only his extremities put him a bit out of step. While Zesen's patriotic writing on the German language was well known to his contemporaries, the two essays in the German language by the famous philosopher Leibniz, who otherwise wrote in Latin and French, were not known; in fact the essay included in this volume was lost until the middle of the nineteenth century.

The next three selections illustrate three different kinds of writing as direct response to contemporary events. A year before the conclusion of the Thirty Years' War, Adam Olearius published the first edition of his travel report, *Description of the Recent Oriental Journey.* Olearius's work not only exemplifies the popular travel literature of the time but also early cultural anthropological writing. As is not surprising, one learns as much about Olearius's prejudices and those of his culture as one does about the Russians and Persians he describes. Stieler's treatise on newspapers is the outstanding example of writing in favor of this new form of publication. His work offers both a historical perspective on the newspaper and an analysis of its virtues as well as prescriptions for the content and writing style. The letters of Liselotte von der Pfalz have long been recognized as an important cultural document of the time. Her critical perspective as an outsider in Catholic France—a German raised as a Protestant—offers a piquant look at the Court of Louis XIV. We also see her interest in the intellectual life of the times: in philosophy, newspapers, theater, literature. As has only been recognized of late, her writing, like that of Olearius, must also be examined for what it reveals about Liselotte herself and the attitudes inculcated by her own culture.

The works of Abraham a Santa Clara, Philipp Jacob Spener,

and Catharina von Greiffenberg constitute three diverse genres of religious writing in the seventeenth century. The fiery sermons of the Augustinian monk Abraham a Santa Clara on the occasion of the Turkish siege of Vienna with their rhymes, alliterations, puns, and jokes contrast markedly with the sober and earnest programmatic prose of the leader of the pietist reform movement, Spener. The emotional, energetic, and highly personal language of Greiffenberg's quasi-mystical meditation on Christ's Passion illustrates yet another kind of religious writing.

Lohenstein's eulogy for Hofmannswaldau and Opitz's *Pastorale of the Nymph Hercynia* offer two examples of prose writing in the classical tradition. Lohenstein calls upon an entire arsenal of classical rhetoric and allusions in his praise of his deceased colleague. His elevated, indeed bombastic, style is what has come to be seen as typical of the Baroque. Shortly after publishing his translation of Sir Philip Sidney's pastoral novel *Arcadia* (1629), Opitz completed the first original German pastoral novel. Like Lohenstein's eulogy, Opitz's work is replete with generic topoi and allusions to classical mythology, and strives to achieve an elegant writing style.

Moscherosch's *German Supplement* returns to the issue of national language that opened this anthology. It also exemplifies the seventeenth-century convention of accompanying novels and satirical writings with an apologetic and cajoling explanation—usually in the form of a preface—of the intention or content of the work.

The six remaining selections are taken from seventeenth-century novels. An anthology inevitably requires regrettable omissions. The courtly novel, the historical novel, Zesen's *The Adriatic Rosemund* (sometimes labeled the first psychological novel), Eberhard Werner Happel's war novels, August Bohse's gallant novels remain unrepresented here and to this day untranslated. Forced to choose, I have favored the satiric and picaresque, what is often called the low novel. The lively prose and amusing episodes not only lend themselves more readily to excerpting, but belong to a European tradition that readers of the European novel and novella will easily recognize. Furthermore, these works have had a more enduring afterlife in the German tradition.

Weise's *Three Most Awful Arch-Fools* not only took up an old German tradition of the literature of fools, dating back, for example, to Sebastian Brant's *Ship of Fools* (1494), but they also unleashed a new vogue of so-called political novels that prescribed correct social behavior by reviewing and condemning negative examples. Johann Kuhnau is and was less well known than Weise. His *Musical Quack* operates in Weise's tradition. The passage included here was selected for its acerbic portrait of medical charlatans, frequently the objects of satire in the seventeenth century. As the undisputed great novelist of seventeenth-century Germany, Grimmelshausen rightly occupies a large space in this anthology. However, as *Simplicissimus* circulates in many translations, I have chosen also to allot space to the other Grimmelshausen novel that has had a significant impact in the twentieth century, *The Runagate Courage*. The lively Johann Beer is represented by an excerpt from his *Summer Days*. While this selection does not show Beer at his bawdiest nor in his linguistic virtuosity, it best gives a sense of the overall tone of the "Willenhag" novels, of which the *Summer Days* is the second volume: country life, the trivia of closed and somewhat marginalized communities, the play of friends, the credulity of simple folk, the uneventful days and nights that must be filled with stories, pranks, invention.

The anthology closes with excerpts from a book that eventually got its author in trouble with the law, Christian Reuter's *Schelmuffsky*. If Grass learned from Grimmelshausen, he undoubtedly also learned from Reuter. Grass's fully conscious newly born Oskar Mazerath, who would crawl back into his mother's womb had he not been promised a tin drum and had the midwife not severed the umbilical cord, surely has his literary origin in Reuter's Schelmuffsky, who, because he was so eager to see a certain rat, left his mother's womb four months early, only to be disappointed: "I didn't want to cry either because I lay there like a young piglet and didn't want anyone to see me because I was naked, thus I didn't know what to do. I was also of a will to wander back into concealment, but, the devil take me, I couldn't find the way again whence I had come."

When I consulted Albrecht Schöne's weighty German anthology of Baroque literature after having made my own selection, I found I had duplicated a number of his prose selections.[17] Schöne's work doubtlessly influenced not only Grass's *Meeting in Telgte*[18] but has generally shaped the contemporary canon of German seventeenth-century literature. But even if Schöne's anthology can be seen as the ancestor of the present one, there are many intervening progeni-

tors to whom I am more consciously indebted. I thank my friend
and teacher Hugh Powell for his valuable advice regarding the
selection of texts and for his kindly support during the project.
Furthermore, I would like to express my gratitude to Susan C.
Anderson, Jean M. Woods, and James N. Hardin, whom I consulted at different stages of the project concerning Günter Grass,
seventeenth-century women writers, and available translations. I
am grateful to my colleagues Michael Sherberg, Harriet Stone,
Egon Schwarz, James F. Poag, and especially George Pepe for their
assistance with Italian, French, obscure German locutions, and
Latin. Linda Feldman deserves special thanks for shouldering the
heavy burden of translating Opitz, Lohenstein, and Weise on fairly
short notice. I would also like to express my gratitude to the National Endowment for the Humanities, as part of the work for
this volume was completed during the tenure of a Fellowship for
University Teachers. I am especially grateful to Volkmar Sander and
Continuum for offering me the invigorating challenge of presenting
three-hundred-year-old German prose texts to contemporary English speakers. Finally, I would like to thank Joseph F. Loewenstein
for helping me to remain buoyant when the wash of German prose
threatened to drown me.

L. T.

Notes

1. Günter Grass, "Über meinen Lehrer Döblin," *Aufsätze zur Literatur*
(Darmstadt and Neuwied: Hermann Luchterhand, 1980), 67–91, here p. 75.
2. For an excellent analysis of Grass's reception and incorporation of the
seventeenth-century context in his *Telgte*, see Susan C. Anderson, *Grass and Grimmelshausen: Günter Grass's "Das Treffen in Telgte" and "Rezeptionstheorie"* (Co-
lumbia, South Carolina: Camden House, 1987). My discussion of Grass is indebted
to her work.
3. Leonard Forster, afterword, *The Meeting in Telgte*, by Günter Grass (New
York and London: Harcourt Brace Jovanovich, 1979), pp. 133–47.
4. Brecht did invent the children, however, whom Mother Courage loses to
the vicissitudes of war. Grimmelshausen, on the other hand, pointedly represents
his Courage as barren.
5. Achim von Arnim, "Philander among the Soldiers and Gypsies in the
Thirty Years' War" and "The Three Arch-Fools" in *The Winter Garden* (1809);
Clemens Brentano, "The Philistine before, in, and after History" (1811).
6. Wolfgang Hecht, *Christian Reuter* (Stuttgart: Metzler, 1966), p. 61.

7. Historians are still debating the devastation of the Thirty Years' War. Until the 1920s it was believed that two-thirds to three-fourths of the entire population of the German territories had been wiped out. It is now believed that contemporary accounts, like Grimmelshausen's *Simplicissimus,* exaggerated the destruction and horror of the war. S. H. Steinberg has even made the controversial claim that the population at the end of the war was slightly greater than in 1618. However, Gerhard Schorman maintains that, until disproven, the calculations of G. Franz are the most reliable. These estimate population losses in the hardest hit areas as over fifty percent; the surrounding areas suffered losses from thirty to fifty percent, in the secondarily affected areas the loss was from ten to thirty percent. Austria was largely unaffected. The average loss was forty percent of the rural population and thirty-three percent of the urban population. Gerhard Schorman, *Der Dreißigjährige Krieg* (Göttingen: Vandenhoeck and Ruprecht, 1985), pp. 119–20.

8. Charles Webster, *The Great Instauration: Science, Medicine, and Reform 1626–1660* (New York: Holmes & Meier, 1975).

9. Hugh Powell, *Trammels of Tradition: Aspects of German Life and Culture in the Seventeenth Century and Their Impact on the Contemporary Literature* (Tübingen: Max Niemeyer, 1988).

10. Norman Cohn offers a summary of some available statistics on the numbers executed: in the Swiss canton of Vaud, for example, 3,371 persons were tried between 1591 and 1680 and all were executed. In Southwest Germany, from 1561 to 1670, 3,229 persons were executed. Norman Cohn, *Europe's Inner Demons* (New York: Basic Books, 1975), p. 252.

11. Geoffrey Scarre, *Witchcraft and Magic in Sixteenth and Seventeenth Century Europe* (Atlantic Highlands, New Jersey: Humanities Press International, Inc., 1987), pp. 25–26.

12. By far the most notorious book on witchcraft from this period is Henricus Institor and Jacob Sprenger, *Malleus Maleficarum* (1487). Its Dominican authors originally wrote it in Latin. Later it was translated into German as the *Hexenhammer* (Hammer of witches) and reprinted many times.

13. Karl F. Otto, *Die Sprachgesellschaften des 17. Jahrhunderts* (Stuttgart: Metzler, 1972), p. 10. Otto, however, notes that additional language societies continued to be founded on into the twentieth century (68–69).

14. Else Bogel and Elger Blühm, *Die deutschen Zeitungen des 17, Jahrhunderts* (Bremen: Schünemann Universitätsverlag, 1971), pp. i–viii.

15. Henry James, preface, *The Tragic Muse,* vol. 7 of *The Novels and Tales of Henry James* (New York: Charles Schribner's Sons, 1908), p. x.

16. Giles Hoyt, "Der höfisch-historische satirische galante landstörtzerische Staats-Helden-Liebes-Barock-Roman or the Babel of Genre in the Seventeenth Century German Novel," *Colloquia Germanica* 13 (1980), pp. 323–33.

17. Albrecht Schöne, ed., *Das Zeitalter des Barock,* vol. 3 of *Die deutsche Literatur: Texte und Zeugnisse* (Munich: C. H. Beck, 1968).

18. Theodor Verweyen and Günther Witting, "Polyhistors neues Glück," *Germanisch-Romanische Monatsschrift* 30 (1980), pp. 451–65.

Philipp von Zesen

Philipp von Zesen (1619–89), son of a Lutheran pastor, attended school in Halle and studied in Wittenberg. Already a published author, in 1643 he founded the German-minded Association in Hamburg in which he was known as "The Accomplished One." In the 1640s he translated three novels, among them Mademoiselle de Scudéry's *Ibrahim* (1645). In the same year he published the first edition of his original novel *The Adriatic Rosemund,* a work that in its depiction of private matters and moods is said to anticipate the novels of the eighteenth century. In 1648 the Fruit-Bearing Society grudgingly invited Zesen to join its ranks as "The Well-Constructing One." Zesen's unconventional ideas on orthography and language rendered him a controversial figure in the Fruit-Bearing Society, and he frequently feuded with his contemporaries. As can be seen in Christian Weise's *Most Awful Arch-Fools,* Zesen's sometimes preposterous suggestions for language reform were an easy target for satire. Among his many publications are the original novel *Assenat* (1670) that treats the biblical Joseph story; books of poetry and songs; works on German poetics; polemics on German orthography; historical writings, e.g., *Crowned Majesty* (1662) on Charles II of England; a description of the city of Amsterdam (1664); books of edification, many of which are specifically addressed to women; and his language treatise *Rosen-Mând* (1651).

Perhaps hoping for financial support, Zesen dedicated *Rosen-Mând* to Queen Christine of Sweden (1626–89), who was a patron of the arts and sciences. This dialogue on the German language is based on some of the mystical, linguistic, and philosophical trends of the age. Like many of his learned contemporaries Zesen believed that German was older and more worthy than all other languages. Proof of the priority of German was to be found in its marked similarity to nature. The poet possessed the gift of releasing the authentic "meaning" of the words through the music of language; he could be aided in his art by the careful study of language, by descending into the "miraculous shaft" of language in order to discover the "pure gold," i.e., original essence, of words. For Zesen every sound had a deeper meaning, a relationship to the cosmos. From the perspective of the twentieth century such theories of language are obviously rooted in the nationalism of a beleaguered Germany, but Zesen articulates his enthusiasm for his mother tongue as a metaphysical system, not as an explicitly political polemic.

Rosen-Mând

Rosen-Mând: That Is, a Marvelous Underground Passageway to the Priceless Philosopher's Stone, Opened up in Thirty-One Conversations[1]

—Foreword

Beloved Reader,
My love for you has finally conquered your hate of me. For behold! I write out of love, I address you with love. And thus you must answer with love. I write out of love of language, out of love of you, out of love of my Fatherland. I am driven by love; I speak of love; I mix my speech with love, so that it makes you, who love love, in love so that you choose to read it. . . .

The Seventh Day of the Rose-Moone

Then the seventh day dawned, the holy day, the day of rest that the highest of the gods created so that we can rest from all earthly toil, forget all worldly voluptuousness and turn our souls, senses, and thoughts to holy worship alone, indeed praise and honor our creator with heart and mouth. Mahrhold[2] did not want to trans-

gress this holy law and refrained from—indeed on this day forgot—
all worldly pleasure, all earthly joys and all the temporal splendor
with which, without injuring holy propriety and with permissible
delight, his divine Rosemund had eagerly attended him during the
previous six days. Indeed Liebhold and Deutschlieb[3] did not want
to disturb Mahrhold in his holy worship and left him alone the
whole day, approached him not until after the evening meal and
asked him to grant them the favor of taking a half hour's stroll
with them and to take in a little evening air under the linden trees,
which, in full bloom at that time, exuded a wonderfully sweet
perfume. Mahrhold was easily persuaded because he had never
been in the habit of unreasonably refusing such a modest request,
especially not one from such dear bosom friends. And thus they
went their way along the inner city canals that were planted on
both sides with lime trees and along which beautifully adorned
houses had been built. During this stroll Deutschlieb got Mahrhold
to speak of many useful things and among others the following

Conversation.
How one should achieve the proper elegance
of High German speech; and how it is
that the German language
preceded Greek and
Latin.

D.[EUTSCHLIEB]: I have spent a fair amount time using our
mother tongue and also written a lot in it. But up until now whenever I have given my lord something of it to read that I believed to
be the best yet, he was always able to show me sometimes twenty,
thirty, or more mistakes in a single line. Either the words didn't
flow; the sentences were too long or not well put together, not well
arranged; the meaning spoiled by the words and, on account of
imprecise words, not expressed well enough; the words or the expressions un-German or contrary to nature, or not properly written. Indeed, now this, now that, was wrong. He immediately
noticed even what Argus with his hundred eyes couldn't see. Indeed, even before he had read the entire line he would begin to
count off a pile of mistakes on his fingers so that I was often
horrified. And he knew how to do this with such rhetoric and
proof that I had to confess they were genuine mistakes and I myself

would never have recognized them as such. Thus if he hadn't from time to time given me oral instruction—for which I will be grateful to him all of my days—I would have just as soon given up my writing completely since I couldn't see how I should ever achieve such perfection that he wouldn't find something to criticize. Indeed I was thinking about consigning my work to the fire so that no additional eye would ever see it.

M[AHRHOLD]: Yes, one who doesn't want to write only for the time in which one is writing, but rather for all eternity, must be very, very observant and a thousand times more so than I have been able or will ever remember to do; for it's largely on account of human weakness and failure that not everything that we once noted will strike us a second time, let alone every time. We are all human and thus we all have weaknesses and even if we lived forever as we now live and nosed through and brooded over everything day and night, we would still not reach perfection. At least I see this in myself, I who am the most fallible of all. For what I wrote only a year ago already appears to me so foreign that I can hardly believe that it is my work—and yet it is. Now I say this because between that time and the present I have from day to day gotten nearer and nearer to perfection through diligent inquiry and contemplation, indeed by exercising my mother tongue or other things, and I now see things more clearly than I did back then. Indeed, at present I am amazed that I was so dumb and blind that I couldn't do anything about this imperfection like what I could now. Nature is full of ineffable innumerable secrets that are certainly more innumerable than innumerableness itself. Thus it happens that we can neither find them nor worry them out at any one time or place. With time, with time, but also with sharp probing intellect and with great industry one can get ever closer to perfection. But one can never actually get there. For we are mortal and it is thus impossible for us to reach perfection. So those people should be booed and hissed, who right at the outset of the work claim, like all fools, that their poem or piece of writing or book or whatever that they wrote, not burning with a pure flame but in the steamy vapor of their impertinent youth, is so perfect that it couldn't be made more perfect. Under such a false and harmful delusion they provide the occasion for stinking laziness, they shelve further inquiry and let Hans get stuck on one thing.

D: But how ought one to begin if one wishes to write a good

fluent speech that is the best possible and subject to the fewest failings?

M: First, one must with diligence and mature judgment—as mature as one has been granted—repeatedly study the best High German books, like the writings of the Great Luther and especially the translation of the Holy Scripture, the imperial final decrees, and the translation of the French Amadis—these of the old texts—and, of the new ones, above all Arndt's work and then Buchner's and Opitz's and then the books written in Köthen[4] because people were especially eager to write a pure and unadulterated German there. Thereafter if one is inclined and born to poetry one can write poetry as well and thus from the beginning practice the German language and make oneself skilled in it. I advise this because poetry is more attractive than prose and everyone enjoys reading and learning it, especially because it gives the writer a great deal of freedom, which he loses when writing prose. And it is therefore easier for those who are so inclined to dash off a rhyme (I am not speaking of a proper poem, for which much more and all kinds of knowledge are required) in the German language than to write a mere letter. When he has done this and has thus made himself somewhat skillful in writing then he must himself write an entire work. Above all and almost necessarily, he must translate one book or other, which is well and elegantly written in a foreign language, into German and while writing German, pay attention to the way the sentences are put together and how the embellishment and luster of the words are applied, indeed observe how the manners of speaking that are otherwise not natural to his language can be most deftly and accurately rendered in German. From that, if he is attentive, he will get the best handle on the language and learn the most and later be able to make mature judgments about this or that case. French books lend themselves best to this, because these two languages—since half of the one emerged from the other—are closely related and similar in their manner of speaking. The father of Roman oratory, Cicero, did precisely this when he translated Xenophon's Greek *Oeconomica* and various texts of Demosthenes, Plato, Aischines, and Aratus into his mother tongue.[5] And so it happened that he became a powerful and famous orator. The Italians did the same: for many years their language was crude and unpolished until finally Dante and Petrarch in their time, and after them many more, made it rich, graceful, and famous with

their beautiful inventions, by working not only within the language
itself but also and for the most part by translating Spanish books,
especially epics. Indeed, at the time of and thanks to the efforts of
Luis Vives, Granada, Castillejo, as well as Mr. Guevara and many
others, the Spanish language that had also long been neglected was
improved and practiced.[6] What Ronsard, Mr. de Bartas, and others
achieved for French through translation and imitation is well
known.[7] Indeed the French never could have managed to give their
language such a patina if they hadn't translated Greek, Latin, Spanish, and Italian books, languages that had been polished and become famous before their own and whose speakers had recognized
the eloquent elegance and elegant eloquence of the Greeks and
imitated it in their own languages. For this reason one must translate a book into one's mother tongue. In addition one must study
Mr. Schottel's grammar book[8]—because we have no better one
nowadays—and read it with keen inquiry, or study the grammar
of the royal French translator who, as a foreigner and born Frenchman, truly lent the German language a certain renown, by not only
writing as good a grammar book as is to be had, but also by
maintaining that German is the mother of French.[9]

D: But why does one commonly tend to say that one can learn
the best High German from the genteel ladies of Leipzig?

M: Because they seldom associate with or speak—in many cases
never speak—with foreign or common people and rustics who
speak a crude, half Low Saxon language. Thus their language,
learned from good books—as a rule they read these books so that
they can acquire an elegant language that will please the young
men all the more—and from daily speech with aristocratic persons,
remains pure and elegant. For in every country there are two kinds
of languages: a high or elegant one and a low or peasant one. The
former is used at court among educated, adroit, and polite persons
and especially among ladies. The latter is in full swing among common men and country folk. Thus in Athens people spoke the most
elegant Greek; in Rome the most elegant Latin. Thus in Upper
Saxony and Meissen the most elegant High German that is used in
writing is spoken; in Tuscany the best Italian; in Castile the best
Spanish; the best Persian in Asia; the best French in Orléans and
among the courtiers and young ladies of Paris. Thus it happened
that Cicero, as a mayor of Rome eager to speak the most noble
language since he dealt with the most courtly and noble persons,

could write so elegantly. In contrast Vitruvius[10] was a master builder who constantly dealt with the common people and paid little attention to the language of courtiers and so he spoke crudely and peasantlike. The Frenchman Barclay[11] is sorely mistaken when he says that the Germans' crude pronunciation is not at all appropriate to learned persons: indeed Poliaeus[12] was also mistaken when he attributed to them an almost bestial voice. . . . Indeed all those who do that give offense, since they can't distinguish between the crude peasant and Swabian language and the pleasing language of court. If one didn't want to observe this distinction in any language then one could say the same of the French, who otherwise brag so much about the charm of their language (the language that they at least twice received from the Germans), for in many provinces they speak totally crudely and the peasants, even courtly persons in Normandy say *sching schou, la hau* etc., while the courtiers in Paris, Orléans, and other places say *cinq* or *sinq sou, la ho,* as my own ears have witnessed.[13]

D: How does it happen that our High German language is so noble and yet is so seldom learned by foreign peoples, when in contrast people tend to learn French, Italian, and Spanish?

M: There are many reasons for this. The two most important ones among them are these: that it is more difficult than others to comprehend and that it is not as polished as the others or made as famous through good and ingenious writings. The first reason, namely that German is more difficult, arises first of all from its especially serious, splendid, penetrating, and clear pronunciation, for one articulates all words according to their letters so that one can clearly perceive each and every letter and, second, it results from false orthography, so that the language is arbitrarily made difficult and confused, as it were. For people don't always consistently write the words as they are actually spoken. The second reason—that the German language is not so famous and polished—is the fault of the headstrong ways of our ancestors, even of their laziness. For one finds that good books in our language are few and far between. Whenever our ancestors put something special in a field of knowledge on paper they mostly did it in Latin in order to acquire fame throughout the world. They should have done it in their mother tongue, like the Greeks and Romans, and thus made their language renowned. But the main reason they didn't write in German was that they didn't want to trouble themselves with hammering out the unworked metal so that they could lend it the elegance that it was still lacking with regard to appropriate phraseology. Oh! If only they all had done what the great Luther did. What kind of wonderful language do you think we would have now? But they had fallen into this dangerous delusion—which must have been a clever pretense for their indolence—that Luther alone had brought the language to the perfection that was possible. Never mind that he, too, was only a human being and no god, that is, that he too was incapable of creating perfection. Never mind that he, too, so often confessed his frailties and asked, as it were, that we try to improve what he on account of human weakness could not achieve in our language. Indeed, he placed the following statement right at the beginning of the same little book in which he explained the etymologies of some German names: I am breaking a path, I have given you an instructive model so that you may do more and greater things. It's the same with Opitz: nowadays people want to see him as a god, as if he had found everything there is to it and everything that the mother of poetry hid in our language. Oh, how very wrong! He was only a human being and for this reason his human achievements could not reach such perfection that he himself, had he or others after him thought further about the matter, could not have reached greater perfection. I recently maintained that nothing, no field of knowledge, can achieve perfection for all eternity among mortals. And I say this, too, as the immortal truth, and Mr. Rist, the famous Holstein master of poetry, also admits it and everyone with a sound brain and undamaged reason must admit it.[14] In short: it would be desirable for everyone to strive as Luther did and to help his mother tongue onto her feet. Indeed if not with weapons (as did the Macedonians with Greek when they penetrated far into Asia, Syria, and Egypt, and the Romans who did not want to deal with any peoples in foreign languages and so spread Latin throughout the entire world) then they should at least through renowned, useful, and elegant High German writings make German known throughout the world.

D: It really is time for us to part since the evening is fast becoming night. But I would like nevertheless to know which language came first: German, Greek, or Latin.

M: In their debates over this question our scholars have created a lot of unnecessary work and difficulties for themselves. Actually it's easy to investigate and find out. For if one examines the old histories properly and weighs them with good understanding, one will see that Japheth's children and descendants,[15] the ancient Germans, or whatever else one calls them, spread throughout Europe and, with time, even into other parts of the world and split up into different peoples who chose particular names for themselves. Thus the original Japhethite name finally faded and in its place the German one sprung up, a name that abides and is still held to be a generic name: indeed, this collective German name was in turn divided, as it were, into countless others after the powerful German people split into distinct groups. It would appear that the children of Japheth had a language that was later called German by the greatest and most powerful people among them, the Germans. And one certainly knows that these Germans (as for example the "Askanier" who come from "Ashkenas" and the "Germanier,"[16] who were perhaps the children or brothers or cousins of those from "To-Garma") preceded the Greeks and Latin-speakers since, as I will demonstrate at length elsewhere, both of them and especially the old "Tuszier" or Tuscans whom one later called the Romans came from the "Tu-Askier" or "Tu-Askanier" or "Tu-Aschier" (with the ancient German article *tho* or *to* or *tu*), the descendants of the "Askenas" or, according to contemporary German pronunciation, the "Aschen."[17] Thus it must certainly follow that the German language preceded the Greek and Latin languages that are only dialects of German and thus descended from the German language, just as the Greek and Latin peoples are descended from the Germans. Thus the Greeks and Romans are German in origin and precisely for this reason actually have a German language or dialect. It's just that over the years, as tends to happen, they changed its name and its form. Clever Schrieck[18] almost realized this when he said that the Japhethite or European language was always passed on sequentially, following from parents to children, children's children, and so forth right down to our time. Certainly it has been somewhat changed but, nevertheless, basically and at its core, it has remained the original language. Thus even today High and Low Germans,[19] the English, the Danes, and other peoples from the Land of the Midnight Sun use it. . . .

Translated by Lynne Tatlock

Notes

1. Rosen-Mând alludes to Rosemund, the heroine of Zesen's novel *The Adriatic Rosemund* (1645), who appears once again in this work. By "Adriatic" he means Venetian. The rose was the symbol of Zesen's German-Minded Association

that was also known as the Rose Guild. The Society had been founded in a rose garden. *Mând* is the Middle High German word for moon or month. May was the Rose Month. In this work Zesen's orthography reflects his ideas for regularizing German spelling according to a phonetic system of his own devising. As modern German spelling is more or less phonetic, Zesen's spellings are not difficult for the modern German reader to interpret. An English phonetic text would, however, be unnecessarily difficult to read. For this reason I have not attempted to reproduce this aspect of Zesen's prose. The translation is based on excerpts from the following German edition: Philipp von Zesen, "Rosen-Mând," in vol. 11 of *Sämtliche Werke,* ed. Ferdinand van Ingen with the assistance of Ulrich Maché and Volker Meid (Berlin: Walter de Gruyter, 1974), pp. 79–273. The notes are original, but my introduction is greatly indebted to Ferdinand van Ingen, *Philipp von Zesen,* Realienbücher für Germanisten, vol. 96 (Stuttgart: Metzler, 1970).

2. Mahrhold is Zesen himself. In his novel *The Adriatic Rosemund* (1645) the hero is named Markhold, which is a German rendering of the Greek components of Zesen's first name, Philipp.

3. Deutschlieb is a man's name analogous to Gottlieb (Amadeus) and might be rendered as Germanophilus. However, Zesen would have disapproved as he wished to avoid foreign words. According to van Ingen, the name is probably a reference to Zesen's friend P. Bense du Puis who bore the name *Der Deutschliebende* (The German-loving one) in Zesen's language society. Later in this essay Zesen refers to his friend in a note that has been omitted in the translation. Liebhold may refer to Zesen's friend Christoph von Liebenau (van Ingen, p. 78). Liebhold is initially called Liebwährt. Liebhold might be translated as "the friend of love" or "the one who is well-disposed toward love"; Liebwährt may be rendered as "the keeper of love."

4. In praising the imperial final decrees, Zesen points out the importance of chancery German in the development of the German lanuage. In the thirteenth century the imperial chanceries began issuing writs in the vernacular instead of Latin. Under the reign of the Emperor Maximilian I (1493–1519) the first successful efforts were made to adopt a uniform written language in all the imperial chanceries. The French Amadis refers to Nicolas D'Herberay des Essarts's French translation (1540–1548) of the Spanish prose romance *Amadís de Gaula* (1508) on which the German translation (1569–1595) was based. Johann Arndt, *Little Garden of Paradise Full of Christian Virtues* (1612) and others (see note 11 to Spener's *Pia desideria*); August Buchner, *Instruction in German Poetry* (1665); Martin Opitz, *Book of German Poetry Making* (1624). Köthen was the capital of the duchy of Anhalt-Köthen, not far from the city of Leipzig, which Zesen mentions below as the place where particularly good German is spoken. In 1617 Prince Ludwig of Anhalt-Köthen had founded the Fruit-Bearing Society or the Order of the Palm in Weimar. Among its members were Andreas Gryphius, Friedrich von Logau, Johann Michael Moscherosch, Martin Opitz, and Philipp von Zesen. The efforts of Prince Ludwig and the Fruit-Bearing Society resulted in a number of grammatical studies.

5. Marcus Tullius Cicero (106–43 B.C.), Roman statesman, orator, author; Xenophon (ca. 430–ca. 355 B.C.)—his *Oeconomica* treats the management of the house and farm; Demosthenes (ca. 385–322 B.C.), Athenian orator and statesman; Plato (ca. 427–347 B.C.), Greek philosopher; Aischines (389–314 B.C.), Athenian orator; Aratus (third century B.C.), Greek poet and scholar, author of *Phenomena.*

6. Juan Luis Vives (1492–1540), Spanish humanist, philosopher, and pedagogue; Luis de Granada (1504–88), Dominican mystic who translated and authored sermons, biographies, and many books, among others *The Sinners' Guide* (1567); Cristóbal de Castillejo (ca. 1491–1556), Spanish poet and cleric; Antonio de Guevara (ca. 1480–1545), Spanish writer and Franciscan monk (see Stieler's

opening paragraph). The time to which Zesen is referring is the sixteenth century, what is now called the Spanish Golden Age, the *siglo de oro*.

7. Pierre de Ronsard (1524–85), French poet; Guillaume de Salluste Bartas (1544–90), pupil of Ronsard, French scholar and poet. One of Catharina von Greiffenberg's earliest literary undertakings was notably to translate a work by Bartas (1659).

8. Justus Georg Schottelius, *The German Art of Verse and Rhyme* (1645).

9. Two notes that are placed at the end of this section have been omitted from this translation. In one of these notes Zesen identifies P. Bense du Puis as the royal French translator. In the other note Zesen points out that the Germans call heroic prose epics *Romands* (romance) but that they should properly call them *Rolands*, which means hero. He is thinking of the hero of the *Song of Roland*.

10. Marcus Vitruvius Pollio: Roman architect and engineer who lived in the first century B.C.

11. John Barclay (1582–1621) was the son of a Scotsman and a Frenchwoman. Martin Opitz's German translation of Barclay's pastoral novel *Argenis* (Paris, 1621) appeared 1626–31.

12. Zesen probably means Polyaenus (second century A.D.), a Greek rhetorician from Macedonia.

13. *Cinq sous* means five pennies. *La ho* may be a phonetic spelling of *là haut* (up there), although this does not fit well semantically with *cinq sous*. Zesen's point is in any case that in Normandy the "s" sound is pronounced "sh" and that the "o" sound becomes the diphthong "ow."

14. Johann Rist (1607–67). A learned country parson and author of works on popular science and theology. In 1660 he founded yet another language society, *Elbschwanenorden* (the Order of the Elbe Swans). His ever-strained relations with Zesen had become a full-fledged feud three years earlier in 1648. Grass alludes to this feud in *Meeting in Telgte*.

15. Japheth was the son of Noah. Japheth's sons were Gomer, Magog, Madai, Jawan, Tubal, Meschech, and Tiras. The sons of Gomer were Ashkenaz, Riphath, and Togarmah. In the German translation of Genesis the descendants of Japheth are called the "inhabitants of the islands of the heathens" (Genesis 10:1–5).

16. With a false etymology Zesen claims that the "Askanier," a German ducal house that ruled until 1319 in the Mark Brandenburg, until 1423 in the electorate of Saxony, until 1689 in Lauenburg, and until 1918 in Anhalt are the descendants of "Aschkenas" (English: Ashkenaz), the great grandson of Noah. We note that he deliberately misspells the German. Ashkenazi of course refers to one of the two great divisions of Jews comprising the Jews of Central and Eastern Europe. The "Germanier" refers to the Teutons. In this series of false etymologies I have retained the actual words that Zesen cites rather than translating them so that Zesen's line of reasoning is clear.

17. Here again Zesen uses a false etymology. The word *Tuscan* actually derives from the word *Etruscan*, the inhabitants of ancient Etruria.

18. Adrianus Schrieck (1559–1621), Dutch philologist. The work Zesen has in mind is *Van't begin de ersten Volken van Europen en van den Orsprongh der Nederlanden* (On the beginnings of the first peoples of Europe and the origins of the Netherlands).

19. High and Low Germans are probably intended to include all German speakers. More specifically, speakers of Low German, i.e., Low Saxon, lived to the north. In the seventeenth century High German was generally understood to be the German that had evolved primarily from the Middle German dialects spoken in Franconia, Thuringia, Silesia, and Upper Saxony (where Zesen maintains the best German is spoken), i.e., that German that was, with the aid of the seventeenth-century literati, to become the standard language.

Gottfried Wilhelm Leibniz

Gottfried Wilhelm Leibniz (1646–1716), mathematician, philosopher, and man of affairs, was born and educated in Leipzig where his father was professor of moral philosophy. He was refused his doctor of law in 1666 in Leipzig on account of his youth and thereupon left for Altdorf where the degree was immediately conferred. In 1667 Leibniz entered the service of the elector of Mainz, for whom he wrote essays intended to maintain the security of the Holy Roman Empire against the threat of France, Turkey, and Russia. Beginning in 1673 Leibniz was in the employment of the dukes of Braunschweig for forty years; his headquarters was in Hanover. When Duke Ernst August was made elector in 1692 Leibniz began work on a history of the Braunschweig-Lüneburg family that continued until his death. In 1690 he was appointed librarian at Wolfenbüttel by Duke Anton of Braunschweig-Wolfenbüttel. His friendship with Electress Sophie of Hanover and her daughter Electress Sophie Charlotte of Brandenburg led to an invitation to Berlin where the Academy of Sciences, he had planned was founded in 1700. Charles VI named him imperial privy councillor in 1712. Between 1690 and 1716 he composed his chief philosophical works including his *Theodicy* (1710) and the *Monadology* (1714). His apologetic view of the universe as the best of all possible worlds is satirized in Voltaire's *Candide* (1759). Liselotte von der Pfalz bluntly pronounced of the philosopher in a letter to her aunt Electress Sophie (July 30, 1705): "From all that I hear and see of Herr Leibniz he must have very great understanding and thereby be a pleasant fellow. It's rare that learned persons are clean and don't stink and understand raillery."

Leibniz's principal philosophical and mathematical essays are composed in Latin or French, the languages with which as a German one could address the learned European community in the seventeenth century. Obviously realizing the irony of this, Leibniz wrote two essays in German advocating the use of German for writing on matters of substance. The first of these, the "Exhortation to the Germans" (1679/80?), lost until 1846, is now perhaps his most famous writing in German. His plea, although not unlike the efforts of Martin Opitz and others, differs from them in that he is not interested in a literary language but rather a scientific and philosophical language that can educate the Germans. Leibniz's essays were a sign of changing times: in Leipzig in 1687 Christian Thomasius (1655–1728) held the first university lecture in German.

Exhortation to the Germans Better to Exercise Their Intellect and Language, Including a Proposal for a German-Minded Society [1679][1]

It is certain that next to the honor of God the welfare of the Fatherland should properly be most on the mind of every virtuous person. This is both our own business (not only as a matter of preservation but also for the sake of our pleasure) as well as the duty of the community. . . . Just as general misfortune is also our peril thus the well-being of the Fatherland is our pleasure, for we thereby have all things in abundance that make life pleasant. We live beneath our grapevine and fig tree.[2] Foreigners recognize and praise our fortune and, because each person is a member of this civic body, we gain strength from its health and are affected by everything that pertains to it, through a singular ordinance of God. For to what other reason can we attribute the fact that we find few good men who do not rejoice with all their hearts in the fortune of their country and people and especially in that of their sovereign authority, or who when abroad will not open up their hearts to a fellow countryman. The bond of language, custom, and even the common name unites people in a very powerful though invisible manner and creates, as it were, a kind of kinship. A letter, a piece of news that pertains to our nation can hurt us or make us happy. Foreigners can see it immediately in our eyes. And insofar as they are intelligent they must praise our inclination. But he who expressed joy over the misfortune of his Fatherland would secretly be thought an evil and dishonest person, even by those who exploit him. No noble soul could tolerate this opinion of himself. Furthermore there are few traitors to their country who are so hardened in their wicked ways that they don't feel the constantly nagging worm [of conscience] even in the middle of the success and progress of their wicked assaults. Thus we must conclude that the love of Fatherland is not founded on the conceits of simple people but on true wisdom itself. . . .

If anyone is bound in duty to his Fatherland, it is we who live in worthy Germany. I won't mention that the heavens are temperate, that they neither burn with excessive heat nor are condemned to unbearable cold, that contagious diseases are rare with us, that we know almost nothing of the earthquakes that have terrified Asia and Italy, that our land is riddled with metals, covered with fruit, filled with game and, if we wished to acknowledge our fortune, we have practically everything at home, which serves not merely to provide for our minimal needs but also our comfort. Even if oranges don't grow here we don't have to be afraid of scorpions. And our Borsdorf apples[3] refresh more than what India can send. Why shouldn't one be able to cultivate good silk and sugar as well as splendid wines, which are no less in need of sun? If our linen were properly worked, we could forego noxious cotton.[4] In metals we have the advantage over all others in Europe and metallurgy is most highly developed here. We were the first to turn iron into steel and copper into bronze. We invented the coating of iron with tin and discovered many additional technologies so that our chemists and mining engineers have become the teachers of the world. We have rich salt mines and incomparable sulfur springs that, along with a pleasant taste, carry more than an entire pharmacy and marvelously avail nature. Our coast is punctuated with handsome cities and magnificent harbors. The interior of our country is crisscrossed with navigable waters. There are stone and marble quarries in the mountains and an abundance of wood in the forests; we have leather, smoked goods, linen in excess. Indeed, I already mentioned that it would be useful to cultivate silk here and various attempts at it are going on, about which I could say a lot.[5]

If we knew how to use the gifts of God sufficiently no country would surpass us in beauty and comfort. But we have plants sent us from abroad that cover entire fields here. We are amazed at the outward radiance of foreign countries through which we travel and don't consider that the best is always put on display. They know better than we how to hide their shortcomings. But he who looks deep inside will see their misery and will have to praise our Germany whose raw appearance contains a nourishing sap within. For its hills flow with wine and its valleys drip with fat. When the Lord gives us peace, joy dwells within our walls. Blessed is this land, when it fears the Lord and when its inhabitants love virtue. God gave the Germans strength and courage and a noble blood runs in their veins. Their honesty is untarnished and their hearts and mouths are in harmony. . . .

What is more noble than German freedom? And didn't that brave prince[6] say rightly that Germany was a free realm and surely the most free on earth? I know that some know-it-alls will ridicule me here. Their lofty intellect has advanced to the point that they hold religion to be a bridle of the mob and freedom a figment of the imagination of the simple. Now they say that the emperor has oppressed the estates, now they want to convince us that the estates burden their subjects with hard servitude. One would do right to flee such people and to hate them like those who poison the wells, for they want to destroy the source of general peace and to disturb the contentment of hearts and minds. . . . Instead of soothing our wounds with balm, they rub them with salt and vinegar. But we are, God be praised, not yet so unfortunate and our treasure is not yet lost. Our crown has not yet been taken from us, but our well-being is in our hands.

I have always thought, and I am not yet to be persuaded otherwise, that the German Reich is well ordered and it is in our power to be happy. The majesty of our emperor and the majesty of the German nation is still recognized by all peoples at church councils; at gatherings the preeminence of the emperor and his ambassadors is undisputed. He is the worldly head of Christendom and the head of the universal church. As great as is the power of His Imperial Majesty, so gentle and sweet is his reign. Gentleness is inherited in the Austrian house and Leopold[7] has forced the most incredulous and suspicious to recognize that his intentions for the Fatherland are good. . . .

Where is there a greater number of free cities than in Germany and must one not confess that trade in general, food and credit, order and good administration in certain things flourish there? One ought to read how Machiavelli in his own report, which is to be found among his works, and how Boccalini in his *Parnasso* once esteemed Germany more highly than we ourselves do.[8] I'll go even further and say that the cities that are under German princes shouldn't judge themselves less fortunate. One can ask with all the changes that have occurred whether they don't complain less about their princes than they once did about their city councils.[9] Usually princely cities are the site of the court, and as a result their sustenance has increased more than their freedom has diminished. . . .

Since it cannot be doubted that many an honest German has a true heart for his Fatherland and since with the noble peace God has given us some breathing space,[10] I hope that various useful proposals will come to light—and, with God's mercy, not be without fruit—which will aim at encouraging unanimity of hearts and minds, ensuring the common peace, healing the wounds of war, and resurrecting our dying livelihood. But since such points of deliberation demand great changes and thus actually belong before exalted heads, we won't dare to broach such things here. . . . It's easy to give advice but it's always difficult to do something about it ourselves. For this reason we want to put aside other lofty matters, as for example, a stable government, useful closer relations within the Reich, a unified currency[11] or stable means, unification or at least compatibility of the religions, furthering of justice, regulating of coinage, setting up and encouraging of commerce and manufacturing, bringing military discipline in order and whatever more of such important points and instead turn our enterprise to something that we cannot only suggest but can also carry out, something that has no place in lofty things, since a private person may well speak, but ought properly not to do anything without special impetus from on high. . . .

If we can increase the number of these people who have the desire for and love of wisdom and virtue, if we can strengthen their number, awaken the ones who sleep, if we can with new and pleasant fuel feed the fire that already has been kindled in many splendid hearts and minds, both of persons of quality as well as of more common people and no less of the lovely ladies than the stalwart men, then we judge that we have done the Fatherland one of the greatest services of which a private person is capable.

This is our plan and no one should interfere with it or obstruct it. This is the suggestion that we cannot only make but also carry out with the agreement of other well-intentioned persons. These are the studies that we promote. The German-Minded Society is intended for this.[12] Its nature will become clearer in the following.

In order that one picture all this more clearly, one must consider that the delight of the mind consists of two things: agreeable activity and pleasant thoughts. And inasmuch as at the moment activities don't really concern us, we intend only to consider here that pleasant thoughts tend to arise from the reading of books where there is delight and profit as well as from attending the meetings of such societies where one hears something beneficial and can apply it. Both of these are not so well set up in Germany as they might be and as one senses is possible when abroad, inasmuch as few upright books are available that are written in the German language and that have the right taste or sap that some other nations are so well able to discriminate in their writings.

We usually write books that are patched together with nothing but copied texts or indeed with our own inane thoughts and unfounded reasoning—there is many a worthless volume circulating that is full of these things. They have neither power nor life and their clumsy nature so often fights with healthy reason. They stick to the reader and often the purity of the intellect is blemished without our realizing it. Since, as a rule, we seldom exercise our judgment, it happens with us as it does with the nations that don't know how to judge beautiful music. Or like the learned monks of several hundred years ago when one had lost the true taste for noble knowledge and had gotten along with acorns, chaff, and bran instead of wheat, until sometime in the previous century the light was properly turned on again. Whereupon an entirely different radiance was emitted from the writings that the Italians, French, and English—and not just the scholars—made their own, indeed a radiance that streamed right into the mother tongue itself.

There are many reasons for the fact that we Germans aren't as far along as they are. I won't speak of war that disturbs all good thoughts. I also won't say much about the fact that we don't have a genuine capital city that could be taken as a font of fashion and a measure for the nation. From this lack it follows that our hearts aren't on the same path, nor our opinions united. Rather, many a good thought must wilt, so to speak, like scattered and broken blossoms. I won't mention either that well-intentioned people are hardly encouraged or rewarded and that persons of high degree don't seem to show the inclination [to improve the language], as would be desirable, taking the example of other nations. Also the religious split in our studies itself creates such a rift in Germany that whoever is familiar with it senses well enough the prodigious difference in methods of education. Reviewing all this suffices to make me venture to demonstrate that all of these obstacles are not insurmountable, since, God be praised, peace has given us a pleasant prospect, and that certainly isn't without importance: if His Majesty the Emperor were to live in a large imperial city in the middle of Germany—which would be a matter for concern only because this might indicate that Vienna were already lost—I would grant that both German might and wisdom would have their principal seat there and would then spread out from there into the provinces of the empire. Except when I consider, on the other hand, that in Italy Florence is perhaps more to be thanked for the Italian language than is Rome, I believe that this hindrance [the lack of a capital city] isn't really that important. Of course it's the inclination of persons of high rank that can awaken and defeat our hearts and minds. One knows that Leo X and Francis I poured, as it were, new life into scholarship.[13] And France owes Cardinal Richelieu a debt of gratitude that not only its power but also its eloquence have attained their present level.[14] But we can't complain on this score either in Germany and it seems that here some learned men are more at fault than lofty potentates. I won't cite the immortal names of those princes here who became members of the praiseworthy societies through which German hearts and minds were to be awakened and which certainly have produced no mean results.[15] The number of our learned men, however, who have shown interest in it [the German language] has been small, in part because some of them thought that wisdom can be cloaked in nothing but Latin and Greek or because some of them feared that their secret ignorance, masked with big words, would be revealed to the world. Fundamentally learned people have nothing to fear, but rather must take for certain that the more wisdom and knowledge are circulated among the people, the more witnesses they will find for their excellence. In contrast, those who are hidden under the cloak of Latin as if by a Homerian fog,[16] who have placed themselves among the truly learned, will in time be unmasked and shamed. This also happened in France. For after things had progressed so

far that ladies and gentlemen acquired a taste for knowledge and
learnedness in the mother tongue, inflated pedants along with their
wordy disputations [i.e., Latin] came to be despised. Well-deserving
persons, however, were all the more recognized, rewarded, and
exulted among great lords. In Germany one has attributed too
much to Latin and art, but too little to the mother tongue and
nature, which has had a bad effect both on learned persons and
on the nation itself. For the learned persons, by only writing for
learned men, all too often waste their time with useless things.
With the entire nation it has happened that those who haven't
learned Latin are, as it were, excluded from knowledge. Thus a
sure wit and perspicacious thought, mature judgment, a delicate
sensibility of [judgment], formed however willy-nilly, has not yet
become as common among our people as is palpable among foreigners whose well-practiced mother tongue, like a well-polished
glass, furthers the perspicacity of the mind and heart and gives
intellect a penetrating clarity. Since we Germans still lack this magnificent advantage, how can we be surprised that we are surpassed
in many things and especially in those things in which intellect
should show itself with a certain flair among foreigners. Thus not
only our nation is covered, as it were, by a dull cloud, but also
those who have an unusually penetrating wit. And since they seek
not at home but in their travels and in their books, among the
Italians and French, they acquire, as it were, a repugnance toward
German writings and only love and esteem what is foreign and
also will scarcely believe that our language and our people might
be capable of something better. Thus we have in such things as
concern the intellect fallen into slavery and are forced on account
of our blindness to arrange our way of living, speaking, writing,
even of thinking according to foreign whims.

Those praiseworthy persons who have taken on the cause of our
language have fought many years with the Germans' carelessness
and self-hate, but have not been victorious. Indeed the evil has
increased to the extent that the goal can no longer be attained and
mastered with rhymes and amusing pieces, however well they are
phrased. Instead, other stuff of more weight and impact is necessary. For just as a strong arm cannot throw a feather as far as a
stone, thus the most magnificent intellect can do nothing with light
weapons. Thus profit must be combined with pleasantness just as
an arrow that is supposed to be driven into the distant air by a

steel crossbow is usually both provided with feathers and crowned with metal. Since most of those who have allowed themselves to be concerned with the honor of the German language have tended mainly to be inclined to poetry, thus seldom has anything pithy been written, and since we have usually been able to find everything in a better form in other languages, it is no surprise that things have not progressed beyond our ingrained despising of our own things. It would truly be a good thing, if one knew many persons who were able to write a German poem so that it would compare favorably with the elegance of other languages. But that alone isn't enough to rescue the honor of our heroic language among foreign peoples or to overcome the envy and frivolity of the uncultivated children of our country. For those who themselves don't do good scorn the best attempts until they are convinced of the incontrovertibly useful outcome. From this follows that no improvement can be hoped for as long as we do not practice our language in the sciences and the central matters themselves. This is the only way of making it esteemed among foreigners and finally to shame the un-German-minded Germans. For our German garden mustn't have only laughing lilies and roses but also sweet apples and healthy vegetables.[17] The former soon lose their beauty and scent; the latter can be kept for use. One can therefore not be surprised that the work of many persons of high rank and other superior people did not sufficiently exalt them, for despite the name of the Fruit-Bearing [Society] they only utilized plants that bear flowers but no fruits.[18] For the flowers of the elegant inventions quickly lose their charm, as it were, right under our hands and soon become tedious, if they don't contain the nourishing sap of the immortal sciences. I don't mention this in order to blame the magnificent undertaking of our predecessors (to whom we are indebted over and over for what still remains of German purity), for I well know, that not everything can be done at the beginning, but rather I am forced to cite the above in my defense so that one sees two things at once: namely, not only why nothing sufficient was accomplished but also why there is nevertheless still hope. Otherwise one would undoubtedly immediately object that it is vanity to concern oneself further with something that such lofty spirits were unable to accomplish. After the violence of our dark destiny swept away all that we had built and it therefore would appear that we are incapable of warding off our misfortune, it would be better to let the river flow and to recommend our descendants to God than to try to curb the strong current through a vain dam, since when it is pierced nothing but an even more damaging flow ensues. I can give no better answer than that up to now the dam was made only of small stones, sand, and earth poured together, but that no large chunks of substantial boulders were provided. Thus we have not yet employed the last resort, even though it would certainly be high time, since to get around to it after a lengthy delay might be too late. . . .

I know there are some people whose intelligence and virtue I recognize and honor, who believe that we shouldn't concern ourselves with the improvement of language and that we should concern ourselves only with the matter itself: language was invented that we make outselves heard and move others. If [our audience is] familiar with our words and if the words are emphatic and moving, we don't have to concern ourselves further as to whether Opitz and Fleming would condemn them[19]—unless we were dealing with a lover of linguistic ornamentation with whom we could ruin a good cause with a poor manner of speaking. Wasn't French itself a mixture of Latin and German and thus initially very illogical? But now through much use all roughness has, as it were, been worn off. If an Englishman and a Dutchman don't worry about using Spanish, Italian, and French practically all in a single line, why should we care, especially since we so highly praise their books as beautifully written?

These arguments are not without pretense and thus I gladly confess that there are people who write well, that is, clearly and powerfully, and nevertheless interlard their writing with all kinds of languages. I also don't want my judgment concerning the writers of mishmash in general to denigrate them. For, because of a backlog of affairs, they often write in such a hurry that they hardly have time to reread what they have written and are glad if they manage to get their pressing ideas, which would otherwise vanish, down on paper. . . . I am also not so fanatically German that I would weaken the power of a pithy speech for the sake of a word that cannot be translated into German. . . .

Except that this doesn't excuse those who sin not out of necessity but rather out of carelessness, those whose words are not pressed out by an urgent message, and those who have never been forced to write books by command of the emperor. If they say that after much contemplation and biting of nails they have found no German words adequate to express their magnificent ideas, they surely reveal more the poverty of their presumed eloquence than the superiority of their ideas. I ask whether their ancestors who commanded such lofty and witty faculties would have gone silent in such cases. . . . I am often reminded that several books that I had ordered years ago, whose author was a good, honest old German although otherwise a bad man,[20] caused me to introspect and that I was ashamed of myself and our times, when I considered how everything was so clearly, emphatically, and at the same time so purely and naturally phrased, that I must often doubt that I would have been able to match him. And yet one could clearly sense that such writing flowed from his pen without a lot of reflection. What is more moving than what a few, untutored but talented people, whom I neither wish to praise nor to blame here, wrote in the German language and who have acquired a large following. I also can't believe that it's possible that the Holy Scripture could be translated more beautifully than we have in German. Whenever I read Revelations in German I am, as it were, charmed and find not only a lofty prophetic spirit in the divine thoughts but also a right heroic and, if I may say so, a Virgilian majesty in the words themselves. How our ancestors were able a hundred years ago and more to fill entire folios with pure German! For whoever says that they wrote nothing worth reading hasn't read them. Who does not perceive the difference between the golden and iron age in the imperial final decrees, when he sees that the German language and the German peace have vanished and suddenly our glory and our linguistic purism has withdrawn from us? From that time on German armies have stood at the command of foreigners against their Fatherland and German blood has been sacrificed to the foreigner's lust for territory that has been whitewashed with false promises. From time to time our language has had to bear the sign of our increasing servitude. May God convert this infliction into mercy so that those whose language has been destroyed won't also lose their German freedom.

We find in all histories that the nation and the language generally flourished simultaneously, that the power of the Greeks and Romans culminated in the case of the former when Demosthenes, in the latter when Cicero lived, that the manner of writing that now prevails in France is said to be nearly Ciceronian, precisely when the nation is so unexpectedly and nearly incredibly prospering in war and peace.

I do not believe that such a thing happens by accident, but I am rather of the opinion that, like the moon and the sea, the waxing and waning of peoples and languages are related. For as stated above, language is an accurate mirror of the intellect and thus it can be taken as certain, that where they generally begin to write well, the intellect is, as it were, a readily available product and to be had at a good price. . . . I am not speaking merely of the purity of the words, but also of the kinds of reasoning, the invention, the choice, the true clarity, the natural elegance and, in sum, the entire arrangement of speech that we lack across the board. Those who believe that the restoration of German eloquence lies in the rejection of foreign words alone are mistaken. I consider this the smallest sin and would never give anyone a hard time about a foreign word appropriately used, but the inane, unnecessary patching with foreign words that are not even understood—not merely words, but expressions, sentences and paragraphs that are completely falling apart, as it were—the totally clumsy and inappropriate combinations, the inappropriate reasons of which one would have to be ashamed if one would only think back on it: all this is what not only will destroy our language but more and more infect our souls. One should be careful or one will find that elsewhere boys of twelve often speak more reasonably with one another than young men of twenty here, and that a couple of French ladies will be able to hold a more serious, orderly, and pithy conversation about their domestic activities and affairs than a couple of imperial councillors about affairs of state. To what ought one attribute this other than that they, from their youth on, read not only artful but reflective books and their societies occupy themselves not with tasteless farces (as do we) but rather pleasant thoughts, which have arisen from reading and are gainfully employed in conversation? This is largely the cause of their advantage over us. For if the air along with the other elements did it why were these nations so long barbaric, unless the heavens have been altered in the meantime? I won't deny that the sustenance and amenities that one enjoys are a great resource, but education overcomes everything and the French rightly say: dealings make the man,[21] which can properly be understood to apply to all practices.

Just let a young person associate with those who speak so badly, let him read tasteless books and spend a lot of time in dull company. He'll show the effects of it for a long time. Shall this current nearly ubiquitous total degeneration of German eloquence not extend its effect to tender souls? One has to laugh in spite of oneself when one hears and sees how many a preacher in his pulpit and many a lawyer in his writings show off with their thieves' Latin. But one is moved to anything but laughter when one sees how impoverished their speech is, how there is neither vigor nor vitality in it, even worse, how healthy reason suffers everywhere no less than the German Priscianus.[22]

Because this evil has become a contagious national plague, as it were, how can we be surprised that the remaining noble German virtues that we still have from our forefathers are going to wrack and ruin, for what is virtue without understanding? Who does not realize that he who wants to begin hastily and blindly gets started badly in war and that the balls seem, as it were, to seek a good player? . . .[23]

If German virtue were lying in the ashes so that not a single glowing spark remained, then what I have poured out, not without considerable emotion, would not only be in vain but detrimental. For what would it serve to uncover our wounds if they were incurable or if the acrid air could make them worse. But, God be praised, our misfortune has not yet climbed the highest rung. It suffices that our eyes be opened. There is still hope for the sick person as long as he feels pain. And who knows why God punished us, whose fatherly cane was well placed, as long as we ourselves don't render our improvement impossible. And because from all the above it appears that, above all, our hearts and minds must be encouraged and the intellect awakened, inasmuch as it is the soul of all virtue and valor, it would be my humble opinion that some well-intentioned persons should come together and, under the protection of their superiors, found a German-minded society whose aim would be directed toward doing everything that would preserve or rebuild the glory of the Germans and specifically those things pertaining to understanding, learnedness, and eloquence. And inasmuch as all these are manifest principally in language that is a translator of the soul and a vessel of knowledge, it would thus be necessary, among other things, to see to it that all kinds of reflective, useful, and pleasant core texts were written in the German language, so that

the course of barbarism would be curbed and that those who simply write for the present without thought of the future would be
shamed. Many write badly only because they don't know about
the proper art of writing and up until now haven't really known
how to distinguish between good and bad books, especially since
they see that many a reader knows as little about distinguishing
between good and bad writing as the chicken knows how to distinguish a pearl from a barleycorn. Thus hopefully a light would go
on in the heads of the writers and the eyes of the readers be opened.
Since one should in this way in a short time have a selection of
splendid German texts, I am assured that courtiers and worldly
people, also ladies and whoever is talented and intellectually curious, will find joy in it. This will pour new life into our hearts and
minds, as it were. It will provide pleasant and useful material for
social gatherings, for traveling companions and for correspon-
dences, and not only as a pleasant way of passing the time, but it
will also serve to open the intellect, to mature our youth who learn
everything too late, to rouse German courage, to reject foreign
idiocy, to create our own convenience, to disseminate and increase
knowledge, to sponsor and promote truly learned and virtuous
persons and in a word serve the glory and well-being of the German
nation.

N.B. The circumstances and constitution of this society will be
described in detail.

Translated by Lynne Tatlock

Notes

1. My notes are based in part on those provided in the following edition:
Gottfried Wilhelm Leibniz, "Ermahnung an die Teutsche, ihren Verstand und
Sprache besser zu üben," in *Gottfried Wilhelm Leibniz. Politische Schriften*, ed.
Zentralinstitut für Philosophie an der Akademie der Wissenschaften der DDR, vol.
3 of *Gottfried Wilhelm Leibniz. Sämtliche Schriften und Briefe* (Berlin: Akademie-
Verlag, 1986), pp. 795–820. The translation renders excerpts from this text. Leib-
niz's essay is undated but, according to the editors of his political writings, internal
evidence suggests that it was written toward the end of 1679 (p. 797).

2. [B]ut they shall sit every man under his vine and under his fig tree, and
none shall make them afraid. (Micah 4:4).

3. One of the finest sorts of rennet apple.

4. In seventeenth-century Germany pure cotton thread was still a rare item from the tropics. The fledgling German cotton-weaving industry was centered in Augsburg, but in the following century England would take over as the undisputed leader of the cotton textile industry.

5. One hundred years later, under the reign of Frederick the Great (king of Prussia 1740–86), the silk industry was flourishing. In the year 1786 over fourteen thousand pounds of raw silk were produced in Prussia.

6. Probably Landgrave Philipp von Hessen (1504–67).

7. Leopold I (1640–1705), from 1658 to 1705 Holy Roman Emperor, second son of Emperor Ferdinand III.

8. Niccolò Machiavelli's (1469–1527) report of June 17, 1508, in *Le Opere*, vol. 6 (1877), pp. 133–34. Traiano Boccalini (1556–1613), author of *Ragguagli di Parnasso* (1612–13). The first German translation appeared in 1644.

9. For example, Erfurt had lost its independence in 1644. Magdeburg had become a part of Brandenburg in 1666 and in 1671 the House of Braunschweig-Lüneburg had subjugated the city of Braunschweig.

10. Peace of Nimwegen (1679).

11. Among Leibniz papers are a number of musings on the evils in the monetary system, fluctuating exchange rates, and the consequences for trade. In the seventeenth century the unscrupulous practice of shaving coins or in some other way depleting them of their gold and silver content was widespread. Leibniz suggests that an alternative form of currency might be devised that in and of itself had no value. See Gottfried Wilhelm Leibniz, "Geldwirtschaft," in *Gottfried Wilhelm Leibniz. Politische Schriften,* vol. 3 of *Gottfried Wilhelm Leibniz. Sämtliche Schriften und Briefe* (Berlin: Akademie-Verlag, 1986), pp. 389–411.

12. The name Leibniz proposes is nearly identical with Philipp Zesen's language society, founded in 1643. Zesen uses the word *Genossenschaft,* which I have translated as "association" and Leibniz the word *Gesellschaft.* Both words could, however, be translated as "society." Leibniz emphasizes that, unlike those of the past, his proposed society will promote scientific and philosophical as well as literary writing.

13. Pope Leo X (1475–1521) renewed the University of Rome and was the patron of Michelangelo and Rafael; Francis I of France (1494–1547) was renowned as a patron of the arts.

14. Armand-Jean du Plessis, duke of Richelieu (1585–1642), great French statesman, patron of the sciences and founder of the Académie Française.

15. Ludwig, prince of Anhalt-Köthen, Duke Wilhelm of Saxe-Weimar, and Duke August of Saxe-Weissenfels (founder and heads, respectively, of the Fruit-Bearing Society [founded 1617]), Friedrich Wilhelm, elector of Brandenburg and Johann Ernst I of Saxe-Weimar (members of the society). Further societies included the Upright Society of the Pine (1633), the German-Minded Company (1643), the Order of the Pegnitz (1644), and the Order of the Elbe Swans (1660).

16. In Homer's *Iliad* the gods frequently intervene in the battle to protect their protégés by wrapping them in a thick mist.

17. This could be an oblique reference to Zesen's Rose and Lily Guild, i.e., the earlier German-Minded Society founded in 1643.

18. In the Fruit-Bearing Society each member was assigned a plant, usually a flower, as his symbol.

19. Paul Fleming (1609–40), German poet and Holstein courtier who participated in the expedition to Russia and Persia (1633–39), described by Adam Olearius.

20. The editors of Leibniz's collected works suggest that the author in question is the German theosophical mystic Jakob Böhme (1575–1624), p. 814.

21. *"Les affaires font les hommes."*

22. Priscianus authored a grammar of Latin around A.D. 500 that became the basis of Latin instruction in the German-speaking world.

23, Leibniz mixes metaphors here as he points out the necessity of coupling virtue with intelligence. "The ball seeks the good player" is a German proverb meaning that luck seems to favor the person who knows how best to use it.

Adam Olearius

Adam Olearius (Oelschläger) (1603–71) was born the son of a tailor in Aschersleben in the principality of Anhalt. He studied philosophy, literature, mathematics, astronomy and geography, earning a degree in 1627 and becoming an assistant in the faculty of philosophy of the University of Leipzig. In 1633 he joined the service of Duke Frederick II of Holstein-Gottorp. On behalf of the duke, Olearius led two diplomatic expeditions to Persia whose goal was to secure a trade route from Persia to Holstein through Russia. The first expedition (1633–35) only went as far as Moscow. Although the second expedition (1635–39) actually reached Persia, the commercial enterprise collapsed. In 1643 Olearius was dispatched to Moscow once again as a messenger and upon his return to Holstein was made court mathematician, librarian, and counselor to Duke Frederick II. Olearius spent eight years (1639–47) preparing the material he had collected for publication. His book, *Description of the Recent Oriental Journey,* first published in Schleswig in 1647, was well received, earning him the name "the Holstein Pliny." Many foreign language editions soon followed. From 1647 until his death much of his time was spent arranging for other editions.

Olearius's work numbers among the most important European travel reports of the seventeenth century and is considered the most significant work on the history of Russia of its time. It may be considered an early example of cultural anthropological writing. Olearius, steeped in the prejudices of his time, nevertheless believed himself to be recording the experiences of the trip objectively, accurately, and completely. Although the work is indeed a storehouse of facts, the student of seventeenth-century Germany may find the text just as interesting for what it reveals about the mentality of this early German observer of foreign cultures. The following selection is from Olearius's second edition (1656) of *A New Enlarged Description of Travels to Muscovy and Persia*.

Households and Social Life

The domestic arrangements of the Russians vary according to their station. Generally they live meagerly and spend little on their homes. The magnates and the rich merchants, it is true, now live in costly palaces. These were built only in the last thirty years, however, and before that they too lived in wretched dwellings. The majority, and especially the common people, live on extremely little. Their houses are shoddy and cheap, and the interiors have few furnishings and utensils. Most have not more than three or four earthen pots and as many clay and wooden dishes. Few pewter and even fewer silver dishes, let alone cups for vodka or mead, are seen. These people are not in the habit of expending much effort on cleaning and polishing their vessels. Even the Grand Prince's pewter and silver plate, with which the ambassadors were entertained, were black and repulsive, as were some of our lazy hosts' tankards, which had not been washed for a year or more. None of the houses, whether rich or poor, displays vessels as ornaments; the walls are bare, except in the houses of the wealthy, where they are hung with mats and some icons. Very few people have featherbeds, in lieu of which they lie on benches covered with cushions, straw, mats, or their clothes; in winter they sleep on flat-topped stoves, like bake-ovens, as the non-German people in Livonia do. Side by side lie men, women, and children, as well as servants, both male and female. In some places, we found chickens and pigs under the benches and stoves.

They are not accustomed to tender dishes and dainty morsels. Their daily food consists of groats, beets, cabbages, cucumbers, and fresh or salt fish. In Moscow, they use coarse salt fish, which sometimes stinks because they are thrifty with the salt. Nevertheless, they like to eat it.[1] One can detect a fish market by the odor well before he sees or comes upon it. Because of their excellent pastures, they have good lamb, veal, and pork, but they spend little on meat; for their religion prescribes as many fast days as meat-eating days, and therefore they have become used to coarse and wretched food. They know how to prepare so many dishes of fish, pastry, and vegetables that one may forget about meat. As I have already mentioned, on one fast day the Tsar granted us forty such dishes. They have a special kind of pastry, much eaten in Butterweek, which they call a *pirog*. It is like a pie or, more exactly, a fritter, though somewhat longer; it is filled with minced fish or meat and onion, and is baked in butter, or during fasts, in vegetable oil. The taste is not unpleasant. Everyone treats a guest with these, if he means to receive him well.

They have a very common food which they call *ikra*, made of the roe of large fish, especially sturgeon and whitefish. They expel the roe from the membrane in which it is contained, salt it, and after it has stood for six to eight days, mix it with pepper and finely chopped onions. Some also add vinegar and country butter before serving it. It is not a bad dish. If one pours a bit of lemon juice over it, instead of vinegar, it gives a good appetite, and has a restorative effect. Ikra is salted on the Volga, chiefly at Astrakhan. Some of it is dried in the sun. They fill hundreds of barrels with it and then send it to other countries, especially to Italy, where it is considered a delicacy and is called *caviaro*. Certain people lease the trade from the Grand Prince for a certain sum of money.[2]

The Russians prepare a special dish when they have a hangover or feel uncomfortable. They cut cold baked lamb into small pieces, like cubes, but thinner and broader, mix them with peppers and cucumbers similarly cut, and pour over them a mixture of equal parts of vinegar and cucumber juice. They eat this with a spoon, and afterwards a drink tastes good again. They generally prepare their food with garlic and onion, so all their rooms and houses, including the sumptuous chambers of the Grand Prince's palace in the Kremlin, give off an odor offensive to us Germans. So do the Russians themselves (as one notices in speaking to them), and all the places they frequent even a little.

The drink of the common people is *kvas*—comparable to weak beer or small beer—and also beer, mead, and vodka. Every dinner must begin with vodka, and in the course of the meal other drinks are served as well. In addition to good beer, the tables of the magnates offer Spanish, Rhenish, and French wines, various kinds of mead, and double vodka. They have good beer, which the Germans in particular know how to brew and preserve, doing so in the spring. They prepare ice-cellars, in the bottom of which they place snow and ice, and above that a row of kegs; then another layer of snow, and again kegs, and so forth. Over the top they lay straw and boards, since the cellar has no roof. Thus they can bring one keg after another into use, and they may have fresh and delicious beer throughout the summer—which is quite hot. They import wine by way of Archangel. The Russians, who prefer vodka, do not like wine as well as the Germans do.

They brew excellent and very tasty mead from raspberries, blackberries, cherries, and other fruits. We enjoyed raspberry mead best of all for its bouquet and taste. They taught me how to brew it, as follows. First of all, ripe raspberries are placed in a cask. Water is poured over them, and they are left for a day or two, until the flavor and the color pass from the raspberries to the water. Then the water is decanted from the berries and mixed with pure honey (separated from the wax), one tankard of honey to two or three of the water, depending on whether one wants sweet or strong mead. Small pieces of toasted bread, spread on both sides with a little yeast, are thrown in. When fermentation has begun, the bread is removed so that the mead will not get its taste, and then it is allowed to ferment another four or five days. Some who wish to give the mead a spicy taste and aroma suspend cardamom and cinnamon, wrapped up in scraps of cloth, inside the barrel. When the mead stands in a warm place it ferments for as long as eight days; therefore, once the mead has fermented a certain period of time, the cask must be put in a cool place and the yeast withdrawn. Sometimes they pour ill-tasting vodka over raspberries, mix it, and after it has stood a day and a night, decant it and mix it with honey mead. They say that this makes a very pleasant drink. Since the vodka is counteracted by the raspberry juice, they say that its taste is no longer sensed in this drink.

They sometimes arrange banquets, at which they demonstrate their grandeur by the variety of food and drink served. However, when the magnates have feasts and invite people beneath them in rank, it is certain that they are seeking something other than their good company. Their largess serves as a baited hook, with which they gain more than they expend. For, according to their custom, guests are supposed to bring the host valuable gifts. Formerly, when a German merchant received such attentions and an invitation, he was already sensible of what this honor would cost him. It is said that the voivodes [leaders] in the cities, especially those where a lively trade is carried on, show their liberality once, twice, or three times a year, by inviting the rich merchants to banquets of this sort.

The highest mark of respect and friendship they show a guest at a feast or in the course of a visit, to convey that he is welcome and that they approve of him, is as follows. After the guest has been fed, the Russian has his wife, richly dressed, brought out to the guest to present him with a cup of vodka from her own hand. Occasionally, as a mark of particular favor to the guest, he is permitted to kiss her on the mouth. This great honor was rendered me personally by Count Lev Aleksandrovich Shliakhovskii, when I was last in Moscow, in 1643.

After a sumptuous dinner he called me away from the table and the other guests. He ushered me into another room and said that the greatest honor and favor anyone can be given in Russia is for the mistress of the house to come out and render homage to the guest as to the master. Since I, as an aide of His Excellence the prince of Holstein, was dear to him, to show his respect and reverence for the many kindnesses the prince had extended him at the time of his persecution and migration (of which more below), he wanted to do me this honor. Then his wife came forth. She had a very lovely, but berouged face, and was dressed in her wedding costume. She was accompanied by a maid who carried a bottle of vodka and a cup. Upon her entry she bowed her head first to her husband and then to me. Then she ordered a cup of vodka poured out, took a sip, and handed it to me to drink, repeating this procedure three times. Then the count invited me to kiss her. Since I was unaccustomed to such honors, I kissed only her hand, but he insisted that I kiss her mouth. Accordingly, out of respect to a higher ranking personage, I was obliged to adapt myself to their custom and accept this honor. Finally, she handed me a white satin handkerchief, embroidered with gold and silver, and embellished with a long fringe. The wives and daughters of the magnates present such handkerchiefs to a bride on her wedding day. Attached to the one given me was a little paper on which was inscribed the name of Streshnev, the uncle of the Grand Princess.

The boyars and magnates, of course, spend large sums to support their luxurious and extensive households. This they can do because they receive large salaries and have great estates worked by peasants, which provide them with large annual incomes. The merchants and artisans obtain their daily bread and income from the practice of their occupations. The merchants are shrewd and eager for profit. Within the country they trade in all varieties of goods essential for daily life. Those who have the Tsar's permission travel to neighboring countries, like Livonia, Sweden, Poland, and Persia, where they trade principally in sables and other furs, linen, flax, and Russian leather.[3] They often buy cloth from English merchants, who carry on a great commerce in Moscow,[4] at four thalers per ell, and resell it, unchanged, for three or three and a half thalers, and still make a profit. It is done in this way. They buy one or several pieces of cloth at the quoted price, engaging to pay in six months or a year. Then they sell the cloth to shopkeepers (who measure out the cloth), for cash, with which they then purchase other goods. And thus they can profit, on the average, three times or more from the turnover of their money.[5]

Since they require little for their wretched existence, in such a large community the artisans can earn enough with the labor of their hands for their food and vodka and the support of their relatives. They are very receptive and can readily imitate what they see the Germans do. In just a few years they have learned and adopted from them a great deal of which they were formerly ignorant. With such technological improvement, they sell their manufactured goods at higher prices than before. I was especially astonished by the goldsmiths, who can now produce a silver vessel as deep and tall, and quite as well shaped, as any German can make.

He who wishes to retain for himself any special knowledge or technique does not allow the Russians to observe him at work. Hans Falck, the famous gun caster, at first managed things in this way: when he made the molds for or cast his finest weapons, his Russian assistants had to leave. But it is said that now they themselves know how to cast large guns and bells.[6] I was told by several Germans from Moscow and some Russians that in the past year, in the Kremlin near the tower of Ivan the Great, an apprentice designated by Hans Falck cast a great bell, which, after being cleaned, weighed 7,700 puds [277,200 pounds]. However, after this bell had been hung in an especially prepared housing and was rung, it cracked. They say that before this happened, it had an excellent tone. Now it has been broken up, and His Tsarist Majesty wants another great bell cast at the same spot and hung as an eternal monument to his name. It is said that the works for the casting and the mold have already been built, at great expense.

Russians of high and low estate are in the habit of resting and sleeping after the noon meal. Accordingly, most of the best shops are closed at noon, and the shopkeepers and their young helpers lie down to sleep outside them. This midday rest rules out conversations with any of the magnates or merchants at that time.

The Russians determined that False Dmitri was not the Grand Prince's son, nor even a Russian by birth, because he did not take an afternoon nap like other Russians. They inferred the same from the fact that he did not often go to the bath, as the Russians do. For they attach great importance to bathing, considering it—especially at the time of marriage, after the first night—an indispensable practice. Therefore, in all towns and villages, they have many public and private baths, in which they may often be found.

To see personally how they bathe, I went incognito into a bath in Astrakhan. The bath was partitioned by planks, so that the men and women could sit separately; but they entered and left through the same door, and they wore no aprons. Some held a birch branch in front of them until they sat down in their places, others nothing at all. The women sometimes came out naked, with no timidity before others, to talk to their husbands.

They can stand great heat, for they lie on the sweating-benches and drive the heat onto their bodies with branches and leafy twigs (which was unbearable for me). When they have turned completely red and are so weakened by the heat that they can no longer bear it, they dash out, naked, and pour cold water on themselves—or in the winter, wallow in the snow and rub their skins with it, exactly as if it were soap—and then go back into the warm bath. As the bathhouses are usually located at water sites and near brooks, they are able to rush from the hot bath into the cold. If some German youth plunged into the water with the women to bathe, they were not so dismayed and indignant, as were Diana and her playmates, as to splash water on him and transform him into a deer—even if they had the power to do so. In Astrakhan it once happened that four young women came out of a bath to cool off, and plunged into an inlet of the Volga that has a flat bottom and forms a pleasant place for cold bathing. When one of our soldiers also dived into the water, they began jokingly to splash water on one another. One of them who went out too deep stepped into quicksand and began to sink. When her friends became aware of the danger, they cried out and rushed to the soldier, who was swimming by himself, and begged him to save her. Easily persuaded, the soldier sped toward her, seized her around the waist and raised her up so that she could take hold of him, and swam in with her. The women showered praise on the German and said that an angel had sent him.

We saw bathing of this kind not only in Russia but also in Livonia and Ingermanland, where the common people, and especially the Finns, in the most severe winter weather, dashed from the bathhouses into the street, rubbed themselves with snow, and then ran back again into the heat. This rapid change from hot to cold was not dangerous for them since they had been conditioned to it from their youth. Therefore, the Finns and Latvians, as well as the Russians, are people of toughness, strength, and endurance, who can bear well extremes of heat and cold. In Narva I saw with amazement how Russian and Finnish boys eight, nine, or ten years of age, dressed in their plain, light, linen cloaks, walked and stood barefooted in the snow, for half an hour, just like geese, as if they were unaware of the unbearable frost.

In general, people in Russia are healthy and long-lived. They are rarely sick, but if someone is confined to bed, the best cure among the common people, even if there is high fever, is vodka and garlic. It should be added that nowadays the great lords sometimes ask the German doctors for advice and proper medicines.[7]

We encountered good baths built inside dwellings among the Germans in Moscow, as well as among the Livonians. In these baths there were arched stone ovens in which, on an elevated grill, lie many stones. There is an aperture from the stove into the bathroom, which they close with a cover and cow dung or clay. Outside there is another aperture, smaller than the first, through which the smoke escapes. When the stones are sufficiently heated, the inner aperture is opened and the outer shut. Then, depending upon how much [steam] one wants, a certain quantity of water, sometimes infused with herbs, is poured onto the stones. In the baths, sweat- and wash-up-benches are arranged around the walls, one above the other, covered with linen cloths and cushions, stuffed with hay, and strewn with flowers and various aromatic grasses, with which the windows are also adorned. Scattered on the floor lie small finely chopped shrubs, which give off a very pleasant odor. A woman or girl is assigned to attend the bathers. When an acquaintance or a cherished guest bathes with them, he is looked after attentively, waited on, and cared for. The mistress of the house or her daughter usually brings or sends into the bath some pieces of radish sprinkled with salt, and also a well-prepared, cool drink. If this is omitted, it is considered a great fault and the mark of a bad reception. After the bath they treat the guest, according to his worthiness, with all sorts of pleasure-giving refreshments.

Such honorable hospitality and cleanliness, however, are not to be sought among the arrogant, self-interested, and dirty Russians, among whom everything is done in a slovenly and swinish fashion. One of the members of our suite, having observed the ways of the Muscovites, their life and character, recently described them in brief in the following verses:

> Churches, icons, crosses, bells,
> Painted whores and garlic smells,
> Vice and vodka everyplace—
> This is Moscow's daily face.
>
> To loiter in the market air,
> To bathe in common, bodies bare,
> To sleep by day and gorge by night,
> To belch and fart is their delight.
>
> Thieving, murdering, fornication
> Are so common in this nation,
> No one thinks a brow to raise—
> Such are Moscow's sordid days.

Although the unseemingly game of Venus is very widespread among the Russians, nevertheless they do not have public houses with prostitutes, from which the authorities receive income, as they unfortunately do in Persia and some other countries. They have ordinary marriages, and a man is permitted to have just one wife. If his wife dies, he may take another, and may even wed a third time, but he may not obtain permission for a fourth. If a priest weds people who have no right to marry, he must abandon his calling. Priests who serve at the altar absolutely must be married; but if the wife of such a priest dies, he may not remarry unless he renounces his priestly office, discards his headdress, and takes up trade or some other occupation. In arranging marriages they take into account the degree of consanguinity and do not allow weddings of close blood relatives. They also avoid connections between relatives by marriage, and do not permit the wedding of two brothers to two sisters, or even of two godparents of the same child. Their marriages are conducted in public churches with special ceremonies, and at the wedding they observe the following customs.

Young men and women are not permitted to become acquainted on their own, much less to discuss marriage together or to become engaged. Rather, in most cases, when parents have grown children whom they wish to be married, the father of the girl approaches someone whom he considers appropriate for his child, speaks either to him personally or to his parents and friends, and expresses his disposition, intention, and opinion concerning the marriage. If the offer is well received and someone wishes to see the daughter, the request is not refused, especially if the daughter is pretty. The mother or a female friend of the groom is given permission to see her. If she has no visible blemish, that is if she is neither blind nor lame, then final negotiations between the parents and friends of the two young people are initiated concerning the dowry, or *pridanoe,* as they call it, and the celebration of the marriage.

Generally, even the lesser notables raise their daughters in closed-off rooms, hidden from other people, and the groom does not see the bride before he receives her in the marriage bedroom. Thus some are deceived, and instead of a beautiful bride are given an ugly and sickly one; sometimes, instead of the daughter, some friend, or even a maidservant is substituted. Such cases are known [even] among high-ranking personages. Under the circumstances, one should not be surprised that husbands and wives often live together like cats and dogs, and that wife beating is so common in Russia.

Their weddings are elaborate, and the bride is conveyed to her new home with special pageantry. Among the progeny of leading princes and boyars these ceremonies are performed in the following manner. Two women (called *svakhi*) are assigned to the bride and groom. They serve as stewardesses, who arrange one thing and another in the wedding house. On the wedding day, the bride's svakha prepares the marriage bed in the groom's house. She is accompanied by about one hundred servants dressed in caftans, each carrying on his head something required for the marriage bed or for decorating the wedding room. The marriage bed is prepared on forty sheaves of rye, laid alongside of each other and interlaced. The groom must arrange these in advance, and set near them some vessels or casks full of wheat, barley, and oats. These are supposed to symbolize bountifulness and assist in assuring that the pair will have abundant food and provisions during their wedded life.

Late in the evening, when everything is in readiness and order, the groom and his friends set out for the bride's house. The priest who has been engaged to perform the marriage ceremony rides in the lead. The bride's friends have already gathered and they cordially receive the groom and his companions. The groom's best and closest friends are invited to the table, which bears three dishes of food, but no one eats. The head of the table is reserved for the groom; but while he remains standing, talking to the bride's friends, the place is occupied by a boy. The groom must persuade him to yield it with a gift. When the groom has taken his place, the veiled bride, magnificently dressed, is seated beside him. To prevent their seeing one another, a piece of red satin is stretched between them and held by two boys. Then the bride's svakha comes, combs her hair, parts it, plaits it into two braids, places a crown and other ornaments on her head, and then allows her to sit with her face uncovered. The crown is made of finely beaten gold or silver plate and is lined with cloth; near the ears it is somewhat curved, and from it are suspended four, six, or more strands of large pearls, which reach down well below the breast. The sleeves (which are three ells in width) and front of her outer garment are thickly studded with large pearls; so is the collar of her robe (three fingers wide and not unlike a dog's collar), which fits snugly around her neck. Such a dress costs well over a thousand thalers.

The svakha also combs the bridegroom's hair. During this time the women stand on benches and sing all sorts of obscenities. Then two handsomely dressed young people bring forth, on a tray decked with sables, a very large round cheese, and several loaves. These people, who come from the bride's house, are called *korovai-*

niki [carriers of the loaves]. The priest blesses them, and also the cheese and bread, which then are carried to the church. Next, on the table is placed a large silver dish containing square pieces of velvet and satin [large] enough for a small purse, flat square pieces of silver, and hops, barley, and oats, all mixed together. One of the svakhi covers the bride's face again, and scatters the dish's contents over the boyars and the other men. While a song is sung, the guests may help themselves to pieces of velvet and silver. Then the fathers of the bride and groom stand up and exchange the rings of the couple to be married.

After these ceremonies, the svakha ushers the bride out, seats her in a sleigh, and conducts her, with her face covered, to the church. The horse drawing the sleigh is decorated with many fox-tails at his neck and under the shaft. The groom follows immediately behind with his friends and the priest. It sometimes happens that the priest has already managed so well to taste the wedding beverages that he has to be supported on both sides on the way, to keep him from falling off the horse, and also during the church service. The sleighs are accompanied by some friends and many slaves, and many coarse indecencies are bandied about.

In the church the part of the floor where the marriage is to be performed is covered with red satin, and on top of this is placed a special piece on which the bride and groom stand. When the marriage ceremony begins, the priest first of all asks for food offerings, such as piroshki, pies, and pastries. Then large icons are held over the heads of the bride and groom, and they are blessed. The priest then takes into his hands the groom's right hand and the bride's left, and thrice asks them if they wish to have one another and to live together [in peace]. When they answer Yes, he leads them around in a circle, while singing the 128th Psalm. They sing the verses after him and dance. After the dance, pretty garlands are placed on their heads. If they are a widower and a widow, the garlands are placed not on their heads but on their shoulders. Then the priest says, "Be fruitful and multiply," and unites them with the words, "Whom God has joined together let no man part," and so forth. Throughout this ceremony all the guests in the church burn small candles. The priest is given a gilded wooden cup or a drinking glass of red wine. He drinks some of it in honor of the married couple, and the groom and bride must drink three drafts. Then the groom throws the glass to the ground and he and the bride trample it into little bits, saying, "Thus let any who wish to arouse enmity and hatred between us fall under our feet and be trampled." The women then shower them with flax and hemp seed and wish them happiness. They also pull and push the newly married bride, as if to separate her from the groom, but the two hold fast to each other. When these ceremonies are over, the groom escorts the bride to the sleigh and mounts his horse again. Six wax candles are carried alongside the sleigh, as it proceeds to the bride's new home, and again coarse jokes are told.

When they come to the wedding house, that is, to the bride-groom's house, the groom and the guests sit down at the table to eat, drink, and be merry. Meanwhile the bride quickly undresses down to her shift and gets into bed. The groom scarcely has begun to eat when he is summoned to the bride. Before him go six or eight boys with burning torches. When she learns of the groom's arrival, the bride gets out of bed, puts on a fur coat lined with sable, and welcomes her beloved with a bow of her head. The boys insert the burning torches into the casks of wheat and barley placed there earlier by the groom; then each is given a pair of sables, and they depart. The groom sits down at a covered table with the bride, whose face he now sees for the first time. They are served, among other foods, a roasted hen. The groom tears it apart, throws over his shoulder whatever breaks off first, be it a leg or a wing, and eats the rest. After the meal, which does not last long, he gets into bed with the bride. No one else is present, except for an old attendant who walks back and forth outside the room. Meanwhile the parents and friends busy themselves with all manner of tricks and charms to ensure the couple a happy wedded life. The attendant who guards the room must ask from time to time whether the deed is done. When the groom replies affirmatively, it is announced to all with trumpets and drums. The drumsticks have been poised above the drums, and now the musicians play gaily. A bathroom is then heated, wherein the bride and groom bathe in turn a few hours later. Here they are washed with water, honey, and wine; and then the groom receives as a gift from the young wife a bathrobe, embroidered at the collar with pearls, and a set of new and costly clothes.

The next two days are spent in great and extravagant eating, drinking, dancing, and every manner of amusement they can think of. They also have all sorts of music, employing among other instruments one called a psalter, which is very like a dulcimer. It is held on the lap and, like a harp, is plucked with the fingers. Inasmuch as many of the women, when unguarded by their drunken husbands, are apt to permit considerable liberties to the young men and the husbands of others, the men take advantage of such occasions to amuse themselves freely. This is our account of the marriage ceremonies and customs among the present-day boyars in Moscow.

When common people and burghers wish to celebrate a marriage, a day before the wedding the groom sends his bride new clothing, a hat, and a pair of shoes, as well as a little box containing rouge, a comb, and a mirror. On the next day, when the marriage is to take place, the priest comes with a silver cross, accompanied by two boys carrying burning wax candles. The priest blesses the boys, and then the guests, with the cross. The bride and groom then sit down at the table, and a red satin cloth is held between them. When the bride has been all prepared by the svakha, she presses her cheek to the bridegroom's, while both look into a single mirror and smile cordially to each other. Meanwhile, the svakhi approach and shower them and the guests with hops. After these ceremonies they set off for the church, where the wedding is performed in the manner described above.

After the wedding, the women are secluded in their chambers and rarely appear in company. They are more often visited by their friends than permitted to visit them.

Since the daughters of the magnates and merchants receive little or no training in housekeeping, when they are married they occupy themselves with it scarcely at all. Instead, they merely sit and sew beautiful handkerchiefs of white satin and pure linen, embroidering them with gold and silver, and make little purses for money, and the like. They may not take part in the slaughter or cooking of chickens or other animals, for they suppose that this would defile them. Therefore, they leave all such work to the servants. Because they are mistrusted, they are rarely allowed out of the house, even to go to church. These customs, however, are not strictly observed among the common people. At home the women go poorly attired except when they appear, at the order of their husbands, to render honor to a strange guest by sipping a cup of vodka to him, or when they go through the streets, to church, for example; then they are supposed to be dressed gorgeously, with their faces and throats heavily made up.

The wives of princes, boyars, and the foremost people ride in the summer in closed carriages lined with red satin, with which they also decorare their sleighs in the winter. They sit pompously in their sleighs, as if they were goddesses, with a slave girl at their feet. Alongside of it run many servants and slaves, sometimes as many as thirty or forty. The horse that draws the carriage or sleigh, like that which conveys a bride, is hung with long foxtails, producing an extremely odd sight. We saw similar ornaments on the sleighs of the great magnates, indeed even on the Grand Prince's sleigh, which sometimes displays fine black sables instead of foxtails.

Since they so rarely appear in company and are little involved in housework, young wives are idle much of the time. Occasionally they arrange recreation with their maids, for example riding on swings, which they especially like. Sometimes they lay a board over a block, and one person stands on each end; then they rock and propel one another high into the air. Sometimes they use ropes, by which they can swing themselves very high. The common people in the suburbs and villages often play such games in the streets. They also have public swings [primitive Ferris wheels], which are built in the form of a gallows, with moving parts perpendicular to it, on which two, three, or more people can ride simultaneously. They indulge in such amusements especially on holidays. Then certain youths keep seats and other essential parts in readiness and lend them out for several kopeks to anyone who wants to swing. Husbands are very willing to allow their wives such pleasures, and sometimes even help them at it.

The animosity and brawls that often arise between spouses are caused by indecent or abusive words—which come easily to their lips—addressed by the wife to the husband; or because she gets drunk more often than the husband; or because she arouses his suspicion by unusual friendliness with other married men and young swains. Often all three provocations occur at once. When, as a result, the wife is beaten with the knout or a stick, she does not take it too ill, for she is aware of her guilt, and also she sees that her neighbors and sisters who indulge in the same vices get off no better. However, I did not find that Russian wives regard frequent blows and beatings as a sign of intense love and their absence as a mark of their husbands' indifference and dissatisfaction with them, as is contended by some writers who follow Petrejus's *Russian Chronicle* (and Petrejus undoubtedly borrowed this from Herberstein or from Barclajus's work, *Icon Animorum*). Indeed, I cannot imagine their wanting what every creature naturally dreads, or their taking as a mark of love what is in fact a mark of anger and hostility. In my opinion, the well-known proverb, "Blows do not make friends," applies as well to them as to others. No person in his right mind will hate and torment his own flesh without reason. Perhaps some wives said to their husbands in jest [such things as Herberstein wrote of]. . . .[8]

They do not punish adultery by death; indeed they do not even call it adultery but simply fornication if a married man spends a night with another's wife. They only call him an adulterer who takes another's wife in marriage. If a married woman commits fornication, and it is reported and proved, she is punished with the knout and must spend several days in a monastery living on bread and water. Then she is sent home, where the master of the house beats her again for having neglected the housework.

If a pair have become tired of each other and no longer can live together in peace and harmony, the way out is for one or the other to enter a monastery. If the husband does so, leaving his wife out of reverence for God, and his wife takes another husband, then the first may be consecrated as a priest, even though he might earlier have been a shoe-maker or a tailor. A husband also has the freedom to consign his wife to a monastery if she is childless, and may marry another after six weeks. Some of the Grand Princes who were unable to obtain a male heir from their wives dispatched them to monateries and married others. The tyrant Ivan Vasil'evich [properly, Vasilii III Ivanovich] forcibly installed his wife Solomonia in a monastery, after twenty-one years of married life with her, because he could have no children by her. He then married another, Elena, the daughter of Mikhail [properly, Vasilii] Glinskii. Soon afterward, however, his first wife gave birth to a son in the monastery, an event that is related by Tilmannus Bredenbachius [*De Armeniorum moribus*, etc.] (on page 251) and by Herberstein, in greater detail (on p. 19).[9]

Likewise, if a husband can prove his wife guilty of something dishonorable, she must allow herself to be shorn and sent to a monastery. This being the case, many a husband acts more out of caprice then according to right. If he becomes angry with his wife on mere suspicion, or for some other unworthy reason, he bribes a pair of rogues, who will go to court with him and accuse the wife, testifying that they caught her in some misconduct or harlotry. Thus it comes to pass—and especially where kopeks help the plot along—that a good woman, before she knows what is afoot, must don a nun's habit and, against her will, go to a monastery, where she must remain for the rest of her life. For anyone who has once accepted this condition, and had the scissors applied to her head, may no longer leave the monastery and contract a marriage.

While we were there, a great misfortune befell a certain Pole who had adopted the Orthodox faith and married a beautiful young Russian. When he had to go off on urgent business and stayed away more than a year, the good woman, probably because her bed was cold, shared it with another, and presently delivered a baby. Hearing of her husband's impending return, she felt uncertain that she could give a satisfactory account of her housekeeping, fled to a monastery, and was shorn. When her husband arrived home and learned what had occurred, he was aggrieved most of all by the fact that his wife had let herself be consecrated a nun. He would willingly have forgiven her and taken her back, and she would have returned to him, but they could not be reunited no matter how much they wished it. In the eyes of the Patriarch and the nuns, it would have been a sin against the Holy Ghost that could never be forgiven.

Although the Russians are greatly addicted to sexual intercourse, both in and out of wedlock, still they consider it sinful and defiling. Therefore, during coitus they temporarily lay aside the little cross that they are given upon baptism and that they wear around the neck. Moreover, since coitus is not supposed to take place in the presence of holy icons, they are carefully covered. One who has engaged in sexual intercourse is not supposed to enter the church on that day unless he has washed himself well and put on clean clothes. The very pious even then will not enter the church but instead remain in the porch to pray. After a priest has been with his wife, he must wash well above and below the navel before he may enter the church, and he may not go to the altar. Women are considered more unclean than men; accordingly, they are not fully admitted when mass is celebrated, and usually stay at the rear, near the doors of the church.

Translated by Samuel H. Baron

Notes

1. Offended by Olearius's unflattering remarks about the Russians' diet, Iurii Krizhanich retorted that he himself had seen the Germans eat worm-ridden cheese with relish. Krizhanich was a Croatian priest who came to Russia in the 1660s. He wrote a defense of his fellow Slavs against the charges of foreign writers like Olearius. Included in the book is a counterattack on the Germans, a chapter entitled "On the Nature of the Germans." The introduction and notes are based on those provided by in Samuel H. Baron, trans., "Households and Social Life," *The Travels of Olearius in Seventeenth-Century Russia,* by Adam Olearius (Palo Alto, California: Stanford University Press, 1967).

2. Many grants of monopoly trade rights were made to foreigners in the seventeenth century.

3. Most of Russia's foreign trade was conducted on Russian soil, particularly in border towns and in Moscow. Russian merchants were rarely seen abroad, but foreign merchants were conspicuous in Russia. Some of them acted as the tsar's commercial agents for his trade with West European countries.

4. Even in 1647, when Olearius's first edition was published, this would have put the matter too strongly; in 1656, when the second edition appeared, it was simply untrue. From the time of Richard Chancellor's discovery of the northern route to Russia in 1553, English commerce in Russia prospered. But during and after the Time of Troubles, the English steadily lost ground, and the Dutch gained the upper hand. In 1649 the English merchants were forbidden henceforth to trade in Moscow. A convenient pretext was found in the beheading of King Charles II of England, but the pressure came from Russian merchants, who persistently sought to minimize or destroy foreign competition in the Russian market.

5. By these dealings foreign merchants were able to evade the government restriction that forbade them to engage in retail selling.

6. Foreign artisans who entered the Russian service were usually bound by contract to teach their skills to their Russian aids.

7. Ordinarily they could not apply directly to the doctors, all of whom were in the tsar's service, under the direction of a department of the government, the Aptekarskii Prikaz. They were obliged, instead, to petition the tsar for the privilege of obtaining professional medical attention.

8. Baron Sigismund von Herberstein (1486–1566), *Rerum moscoviticarum commentarii* (Notes on Muscovite things) (1549).

9. Solomonia was installed in the Pokrovskii Monastery in Suzdal in 1525. The story of her having given birth to a son is apocryphal.

Kaspar Stieler

Kaspar Stieler (1632–1707), son of an apothecary, began his study of medicine at the University of Leipzig, later transferring to Giessen and then, after being expelled from Giessen, to Königsberg in 1653 where he studied theology, law, and eloquence, but never completed a degree. In 1657 he published, *Armored Venus,* his collection of songs of love and war, anonymously. After years of rambling through Europe, now serving as soldier, now serving as tutor, he went to Jena to take up the study of law, which he soon gave up for a position as chamber secretary to Count Albert Anton of Schwarzburg-Rudolstadt. At the court of Rudolstadt Stieler carried on many activities that were to his taste: he wrote six plays, instructed the pages in letter writing, and read newspapers aloud at table. His subsequent compilations of scientific writings brought him recognition and presumably paved the way to membership in the Fruit-Bearing Society (1668) as "the Latecomer." He continued to change positions through his life, nevertheless managing to produce a string of publications. In 1691 he completed *The Genealogy and Continued Growth of the German Language,* a three-volume dictionary and grammar of the German language.

Although Stieler was certainly not the first to write about newspapers his *Newspaper's Pleasure and Profit* (1695) is the first comprehensive treatment of them. The popularity of this treatise immediately resulted in a second edition in 1697. A Latin quotation from Christian Weise's work on newspapers, *Schediasma curiosum* (Careful caprice, 1676), serves as motto for Stieler's text: "I love the new, both for the sake of pleasure and of necessity." In addition to the introduction and three books that comprise the work Stieler includes some aids to reading the newspaper: an appendix with an alphabetized list of commonly used foreign words; lists of living rulers in the German Reich and neighboring countries, important clerics, imperial generals and high officials of the empire, French generals, generals from the allied army in Brabant and the Rhine, high officers in the Piedmont and Poland, important naval officers, and ambassadors; a short description of places that have been at war and tend to appear in the newspaper; and information about important coats of arms in Germany and neighboring countries alphabetized according to the symbols used.

Newspaper's Pleasure and Profit.
The First Chapter of the First Book
which Pertains to the Entry
into or Introduction to This Work[1]

1. No one is so wooden and lifeless that he doesn't have a natural urge to know all kinds of things and to be informed about that which he didn't know previously. As Aristotle, the wise pagan, says: all men desire to know and learn something. Even children don't merely ask in their stammering speech of their parents, wet nurses, teachers, and whomever takes care of them: "What is this? What is that?" But they listen attentively when their nanny tells them a story in their cradles or on her lap and are amused and laugh about it, demand, moreover, that it be repeated until they are rocked into sweet slumber over it. Guevara talks about it very cleverly in his "Princely Clock"[2] when he says: whatever we taste and own in this life eventually brings nausea, boredom, and satiety, except for knowledge that is free of all irritation and repugnance; or when we think that we have become tired from it, our eyes may close over our reading, but the inner mind will never become dull in the knowledge and enjoyment of things. . . .

3. As far as knowledge of world events is concerned, one might say that the chasers of new tidings belong largely to the first order of people who only want to know that they know something new. They ask about it, pay attention to it, and speak of it, unconcerned

whether they have honor or profit from it. Indeed, they hurry and scurry after new tidings and can hardly wait for the day and hour when they will be printed and published. For this reason they rush to the post offices and the news shops and time hangs heavy until they learn what the king of France, the emperor, the pope and the sultan of Constantinople are doing. Which of them has won or lost the battle. Whether and where an earthquake has occurred. Whether Mount Etna and Mount Vesuvius are still burning and whether or not the returning ships have arrived in England and Holland in good shape. And all of this is of as little concern to them as knowing whether or not men or spirits live on the moon or whether there are to be found nothing but wildernesses and deserts there. It's lamentable that such would-be pundits, like the aforementioned Diogenes, roll the barrel around when they otherwise have nothing to do, just so people can see that they belong in the world among the loquacious race of men, like the maids during laundry bleaching and in the baking houses. . . .

5. They who despise newspapers across the board, and say and write many sharp and scornful things against them, do them an injustice. Indeed, as the proverb says, they throw the baby out with the bath water. . . .

Chapter 5. Of the Stuff or So-Called Contents of Newspapers

1. It has been said that everything that happens in the world, be it true or apparently true or presumably true, provides the stuff, matter, or content—the wise call it the object and, in German, the stuff put forth—of our newspapers. And all kinds of things belong there, be they spiritual or worldly, warlike or unwarlike, if they treat religious belief and practice, law and custom, medicine and natural science, world wisdom, statecraft, morals, mathematics, domesticity, or the condition of persons of high and low degree, storms, the fertility of the earth, together with everything that occurs in public or in private on land and sea. Nowhere would it be of little use to know something about these things.

2. Above all, that which gets into newspapers must be new. For newspapers are called *novellas* from the word for "recent." It

would be an odd bird who would include in the newspaper what
Alexander the Great, Mohammed, or Tafilet did many years ago.[3]
For what would such distant things have to do with our present
condition? New things are and remain pleasing. That which happened in earlier worlds belongs on the scrap heap and in no way
satisfies desiring minds—as little as if the newspaper writer were
to repeat something that had already appeared ten times, as for
example, that Don Juan of Austria is planning a trip to the Spanish
Netherlands and yet still hasn't left Madrid; when a betrothed
princess plans to go to her betrothed and is always under way but
never gets there; when a general has been dispatched and sends his
baggage on ahead and yet always stays right where he is; when
one is storming this or that fortress but not a single person ever
actually stands before its gates. Such news vexes and nauseates the
reader to such a degree that in his heart he curses the newspaper
writers who always speak of only one thing and who, changing
only a couple of circumstances, constantly recapitulate the often
said. Just as nothing old can pass for something new, this in no
way satisfies our demand for the sequel and conclusion. Certainly
I don't intend to reproach newspapers for occasionally briefly describing, according to the situation and occasion, an unknown
place that is besieged or a bridge that is being built over a small
river, or to report the name of a king, prince, or hero and what
his plans are. Indeed, I wish rather that in obscure things people
would not conceal these circumstances. Thus it is necessary to
exercise reasonable moderation and to avoid vain blabbing. When
the ambassador of a ruler is sent to foreign courts it's a good idea
to report his name so that, for example, I know that the English
ambassador to Constantinople is called My Lord Bajet and the
envoi extraordinaire to Turin is named Monsieur Aglioby. On the
other hand when the cavaliers, ordered by the elector of Bavaria
to the daughter of the king in Poland, are not named nor indeed
the bride herself, we should object. One fills entire pages with the
ceremonies that occur on the occasion of marriages by proxy—
how many horses and people rode before and after them, which
route they took, and what kind of staff the marshal carried—but
one doesn't learn how old the bride is, how she was brought to
bed, and what kind of armored knight[4] was placed there. There is
probably nothing new under the sun, but nevertheless the characters, the time, and circumstances are always new and these later

provide the opportunity for contemplation in such a way that even a small innocuous event may lead to a great event that one had never dreamed of. For this reason the newspaper authors must always be clever people who know how to distinguish the important and consequential from trifles, inasmuch as many a thing is smeared all over the newspapers that a clever pen would have had to eliminate. I could scarcely name two or three postmasters in the entire Holy Roman Empire who would be careful in such cases and would know how to separate tomfoolery from material that is worthy to appear in the newspaper.

3. These good people don't simply collect everything that comes their way out of the blue but examine and check the chits that come to them as to where they come from and whether they can be trusted. There are often scorners, would-be pundits, fabulists, and wormers[5] who sometimes out of frivolity, sometimes out of expediency scatter lies into the world and afterwards laugh about them. One must learn to recognize such fellows and to recognize their lies before one turns them over for printing. Upright and reasonable postmasters select honest, blameless, and credible men who occupy a position of trust and who receive reliable correspondence from time to time. And if they must esteem that which gets into print higher than other things, they nevertheless weigh it and are not in a hurry to reprint everything without exception. In particular they do not trust every bit of gossip that is spread in the city or country where they live because even little people tend to lie, especially regarding miracles. For example, they say that three suns stood in the heavens, that it rained on a particular stretch of grain, that a lady of state wearing a diadem with a rod in one hand and a crucifix in the other was seen in the sky in broad daylight, and all kinds of other chimeras. For precisely this reason the newspapers have such a bad name and so little credibility because they are often larded with so many fictions that they lose approbation in true things as well.

4. We have, to be sure, in discussing newspapers as to their content made mention that they consist of accounts of things that are thought to have happened. We choose, above all, the truth, which lends them value and gives the newspaper dealers a good reputation. People buy and read the newspapers precisely because they learn what is true and can be repeated. "A lie hath no feet" and it

doesn't last long [without further lies to support it], especially when it is written: the pope, the kaiser, the king of France is dead—the same people who in the week immediately following are deliberating with their counselors, traveling, giving orders at the front. Such deception in newspapers is an enormity and unleashes confusion throughout the land, especially among the overly credulous. All the same, the inclusion of an invented creature can't always be avoided and then it's a matter of seeing whether the account is probable or not: whether time and circumstances are in agreement and whether the nature of the persons described there corresponds to what the newspaper reports. When not, it will be a matter of awaiting the confirmation of the tidings, that is, whether similar reports come in from additional credible sources, regardless of whether [as a result] the event is made public somewhat later.

5. A postmaster or newspaper writer also has to see to it that he doesn't publish anything insidious or dangerous in his newspapers. One must suppress rather than publish many things. A lot of things damage the honor and reputation of a prince or a potentate. A lot of things create unrest in the land. A lot of things have a bad effect on the security of the land, a lot cause impatience, rebellion, and despair, etc. Thus a postmaster has to consider where he is and lives, who his lord and master is, which party he sides with and what one generally does or does not want to read or hear. It is not unusual in Vienna that a postmaster or a newspaper writer gets his knuckles rapped, is arrested and not freed until he comes up with a sum of money. In other places one pursues these careless and all-too-bold newspapersmiths, chases them out of the country, or takes everything from them. Apart from that, sharp counterpleas are made when they print something insidious and false and with wide ramifications. Their passage is blocked in the neighboring territories, they are arrested, and their goods confiscated. Subsequently things go very badly for such ill-bred bearers of tales and he only has himself to blame if he is disadvantaged or damaged as a result of his "mastery of poetry."

6. Satirical writings, scornful heckling, and pasquils also belong to the group of writings with which many a profit-seeking mercury-messenger can make a reputation for himself, since he knows that the common man loves to read and hear such base things. Such things agree with the scandal-mongering ear twitchers and idle

thumb twiddlers as grass agrees with a dog, so that they are chased away by their own slanderous handiwork or become involved in great liability. It's a good idea, people say, to shoot from far away. Thus in a Lutheran territory when one is secure one can certainly publish something provocative from Rome that one would have to leave out in a Catholic territory. And in this case no small caution is necessary. For he who wishes to say and write what he wants must subsequently hear and read, indeed suffer, what he doesn't want.

7. Furthermore, those who are involved with newspaper writing should guard against nasty things and obscene words and expressions, not only because as the proverb says, "Out of the abundance of the heart the mouth speaketh," and one will be judged ill on account of such crude words, but because the place where such obscenity is printed will gain little honor at home and abroad and because chaste ears are thereby noticeably irritated and, to a certain degree, violated. One should avoid them all the more because ladies and clerics sometimes see the newspapers. Naughty words and tomfoolery are also not appropriate to the Christian and there should properly be a difference between harlequins and buffoons, on the one hand, and postmasters who value their honor, on the other, inasmuch as the latter are public imperial bureaucrats, in part educated and experienced persons, for whom it's not appropriate if their written or printed paper makes people blush.

8. If a postmaster should receive something that were questionable and inasmuch as it were despicable and worthy of sharp criticism, he should determine whether it is already public and in print or who the reporter is. For in that case one can excuse oneself to some extent by citing the author and publisher. All the same, I would have to advise that one repudiate such voluptuousness, flee scandal, and preserve oneself with the good appearance of respectability and commendable seriousness, inasmuch as one's good name is a fragile thing when an evil writing unintermittently speaks and witnesses against it.

9. Even if we take account of the presumably true news items in our remarks, it should not be thought that a postmaster can give out his own inventions and ficitions as the truth and put them in among the news items, recount dreams, and try to pull the wool

over people's eyes. He mustn't know anything but that everything he includes in the newspaper happened as reported and not in another way. Thus when in doubt he has to believe things that come to him until he gets a different or better report. In which case he doesn't need to be ashamed and can simply report in the next issue that it's not continuing as it was, indeed the opposite must be proclaimed, one has received a certain news item, etc. However, if, as often happens, the lord and authority of the town were to command that the newspaper report a victory that was never achieved, an ongoing siege of this or that fortress, a planned courtship or another arrangement, it is proper for the postmaster as a subject to obey. Mr. Fritsch recounts an example from Besold concerning the duke of Maine who had him write of a victory instead of a defeat, saying that if one can insist on such a lie for a few days it could be worth thousands of guilders.[6] The reason for this is that the state often demands that unfounded things are fed to the people when it is salutary for the people. . . . Such invented news items are often of manifold use to the state and even if they do deceive friend and foe, it suffices that they to some extent elicit courage or create fear in the interested parties and thus often facilitate the concerns of the lord of the land.

10. Otherwise a postmaster must also see to it that he publishes things that are worth knowing and that Hans doesn't forever stay in the same place.[7] It is a tedious thing when a departure, a wedding, a battle, and such things that never change are repeated again and again: it suffices that I know that they entered a carriage or boarded a ship, that a wedding took place, that this or that side came up short. Those things come up once and are popular. This is as it should be. Too much repetition, however, is nauseating, just as monotonous things render the reader's desire dull and contrary. The world is large enough and presents a surplus of material that is novel. If in addition pleasant and funny events are mixed in, it brings the reader pleasure and he gladly relinquishes his penny when he experiences things that gladden his heart and give both him and his listeners joy.

11. Nevertheless, this doesn't mean that a newspaper writer ought to or can include and fill up the innocent paper with all kinds of things that take place in obscure places. For what concerns is it of mine what the Great Mogul or John the Priest is doing in the Land

of the Moors, what ministers he appoints or fires, how many wives or children he has, and in which palace they are staying. If, however, the neighboring powers start something from which particular consequences can result that will require future contemplation, as for example when two czars reign simultaneously in Moscow and the mother of one of them incites cabal and rebellion that causes the court to be split up into factions or if discord arises in the seraglio in Constantinople and one party sides with the grand vizier, the other with the mufti or the sultan on account of his mother and a rebellion in the imperial seat ensues. Thus one can include such foreign occurrences in newspapers. But not what happens in Utopia or something that neither interests nor affects anyone here.

There would be much to say about the writing of news or rather its style, which we call the manner of writing. Unfortunately it's come to such a state that our newspapers are nothing but beggars' cloaks so that if one were to cut out the colorful French, Spanish, Italian, and Latin patches there would be nothing of intelligence or enduring importance left. But it isn't a sickness that a doctor could heal or bandage. It can't be denied that all such foreign words could be translated into good German. But, because the abuse is so ingrained, one is no longer able to control it. Thus one has to let five equal four and run with the pack and think of a way of teaching these foreign words to the Germans who aren't widely traveled. To such purpose this little book has been provided with a short explanation of such un-German words and expressions. Nevertheless it's lamentable that the Germans dishonor their magnificent and rich language so that foreigners think that we couldn't break out of muteness without the help of their words, but rather must necessarily borrow from them regardless of what is to be said or written. Not a single Pole, Muscovite, Italian, or Frenchman would mix German words in his newspapers. And we are such a miserable and curious people that we adorn ourselves without difficulty with foreign feathers and are ridiculed and despised for it by many. We love our sickness and weakness. For this reason it's no wonder that no medication takes effect with us but that we always remain sick and powerless.

13. Meanwhile the style or manner of writing must remain historical, that is, it must be simple but also lively, flowing but also nimble

and meaningful. All that is precious or forced has no place there. Rhetoric can show her charm elsewhere. Metonymic or flowery speech doesn't belong in the newspapers, just as little as poetical whimsy and neologisms. One soon notices who wrote the news, a good German or a courtesan, depending on whether he sticks to the point or goes on at length with fancy talk that doesn't serve any purpose here. The best comes from Regensburg where German councillors and ambassadors are gathered, as also from the Saxon courts. The Viennese newspapers already don't sound as good. The Dutch wield a merchant's pen and should certainly not be despised if only they would refrain more from using the foreign patchwork words. Nevertheless, they all provide the impetus for elegant short stories with their accounts of circumstances that a history writer, if he's clever, can make use of later. For it's no small art to write the news so that it has a flair, and many a good report is omitted by the postmaster if it neither sings nor succeeds, especially if he has no good collector at hand who both knows how to order things and how to write.

14. Finally there is nothing more despicable than when those who are in the print shop and are charged with checking over the newspapers—these are sometimes clerics, public teachers, and beadles—publish their private concerns in the newspapers. Then one has to listen to things like how the superintendent married his daughter off to a tax collector or secretary, what guests attended the wedding, how one dined, and whether the bride rode in the coach or went on foot. Many a chancellor is so foolish that he publishes in the newspaper that his son has left for Holland and France and that he wishes him good luck and Godspeed and a happy return. Amen. If a town councillor or his cousin and brother-in-law are sent off to do something, it has to appear in the newspaper with fulsome praise and touting of the emissary who often doesn't do anything or is doing something of so little consequence that one shouldn't waste words on it. And yet there are postmasters who accept such bagatelles or paltry things and print them. This, when newspapers ought to treat things that are far removed from private matters and solely a matter of public life. For how is a city or a country helped when one knows that the cattle in one village were driven away, what the watchman in one city blows and rattles, that someone gave a good sermon and was therefore praised, that

Mopsus is marrying Nisa, that a couple of women argued and fought? These things aren't going to cause any country to go to war and such folderol that serves no one should be left out of the papers. . . .

Book II

Chapter 7. Of the Necessity and Usefulness of Newspapers in the Women's Room[8]

1. One does the female sex an injustice when one accuses all women without exception of frivolity, curiosity, and loquaciousness, and on account of [these accusations] there are fathers who forbid their daughters and husbands who forbid their wives to read newspapers: as if there were not much good to be found in them, where they too could find examples to follow and warnings that would increase their understanding and wisdom. It is agreed and proven by many worthy writings that this half of the world, when it is led to it, is just as little lacking in aptness for learning, contemplation, knowledge, and adroitness as menfolk, among whom one can find a lot of ill-bred fellows.

2. Still a difference must be made here as in other cases. Village folk, hired girls, and the daughters of common burghers are better suited to sewing and spinning than to reading newspapers. But nowadays it is no longer as it was in the old world when womenfolk remained, like snails, working at home in the house year in and year out, and instead they have acquired more freedom to circulate in society and to carry on conversations on politics and morals. Thus it is all the better that they speak of foreign affairs and recount what of their kind has been spread abroad in the newspapers than that they gossip about a neighbor, criticize her housekeeping, or talk about pride and new fashions.

3. At the beginning of the third chapter of this book we mentioned that we understood by princely persons at court the female consorts, regents, and guardians along with the princesses as well. These women have a large interest in what happens here and there. One has a father and spouse in the war; the other a brother and

cousin who are traveling. One of their men is in captivity, another sick, the third even dead. One has changed his religion, the other has become a monk. These are exalted and those are struck down by fortune. These women always have an interest in these things for they must sometimes aid, guide, and protect [their men] especially since events are nowadays so marvelously intertwined. Thus it often happens that a highborn lady's care, advice, and impetus, which would otherwise be long in coming or which would not come at all, is quickly proffered. One should not object that the newspapers would be incomprehensible to them on account of the foreign words, since these days there is rarely a princess who can't in addition to German and Latin speak a little French and Italian if pressed.

4. The consort of a prince otherwise seldom worries about matters of governing, but lets her lord take care of these things. But this is not true of a female regent and guardian who, as the Mother of the Country, must, like a regent himself, give her attention to all things so that the country entrusted to her is preserved in war and peace and that all calamity is carefully averted from it. And everything that was said in the aforementioned third chapter about princes and lords applies. We have excellent examples of women who comported themselves well in matters of state and war in Elizabeth, the queen of England; Christine, the queen of Sweden; and in the guardians of the Landgraves of Cassel.[9] Indeed Donna Olympia in Rome had a better grasp of everything that happened in and outside of Christendom than did many a great statesman.[10] No one can dispute that such important women had an interest in reading the newspaper.

5. Aristocratic women of higher and lower degree are not occupied with newspapers at the court alone, but are newspaper writers themselves, inasmuch as one can find out much more easily and quickly from them about a secret attack, a long-range plan, and events at and away from court. They know, better than the best confessor, how to get things out of the cleverest ministers at other courts or, at home, the foreign ambassadors. For this reason they concern themselves with everything. They read everything, transcribe it, and send it off. Whoever is intimate with them is well off since in the twinkling of an eye they will tell him more than he could have read in many newspapers. And these women have their

relatives and are concerned with learning how things are going with them. They are especially happy when they get good mail, which pleases the sovereign and are otherwise careful to note what is happening abroad on land and on sea. They seek their advantage when the booty that was seized is for sale at a low price.

6. What shall one say about the highborn ladies who live in the cities? A young lady in Leipzig and Halle is often more capable of saying where the armies in Germany, Hungary, and Italy are and what they are undertaking than many a learned statesman and is able to throw foreign words into her conversation so cleverly that one would swear she understood them. And even if reading the newspaper is not just as necessary and useful to them, they nevertheless amuse themselves with it and learn from it to speak in a refined and elegant manner. Even when they are read to by others, they understand it and, if necessary, also communicate some of it to their sisters.

Translated by Lynne Tatlock

Notes

1. The notes are based in part on those with which Gert Hagelweide furnishes his German edition of Stieler's treatise on newspapers. Kaspar Stieler, *Zeitungs Lust und Nutz: Vollständiger Neudruck der Originalausgabe von 1695,* ed. Gert Hagelweide (Bremen: Carl Schünemann, 1969). The translation renders passages from this edition.

2. Antonio de Guevara (ca. 1481–1544). His earliest work, a didactic novel, was entitled *Reloj de principes* (Clock of princes) and published in 1529.

3. Tafilet refers to Mawlāi d-Rashid, the ruler of Tafilelt (1660–72). He conquered Fez and Morocco.

4. Stieler probably means to indicate an effigy of some kind that served as proxy for the absent bridegroom, i.e., a symbolic consummation of the marriage.

5. See Kuhnau. Wormers claimed to cure illnesses by removing disease-causing worms. They were generally considered quacks.

6. Christoph Besold, *Thesaurus practicus Christophori Besoldi. . . .* (Christoph Besold's practical treasury) (Tübingen, 1629). Adhasver Fritsch, *Discursus de Novellarum quas vocant Neue Zeitunge / hodierno usu et abusu* (Discourse on the novellas called new tidings, their uses, and abuses) (Jena, 1676) pt. 1, ch. 3–4.

7. Stieler makes a pun here on the expression *Hans in eodem,* which is a designation for a rogue. *Eodem* means "in the same place" in Latin. Thus Stieler says both "that Hans doesn't forever stay in the same place" and "that Hans doesn't forever remain a rogue."

8. The German word *Frauenzimmer* literally means women's room but in

the seventeenth century was commonly used to refer to women themselves. The word now sounds old-fashioned.

9. Amalie Elisabeth (1602–51) and Hedwig Sophie (1623–83), who both served as guardians of their children upon the deaths of their husbands Wilhelm V (d. 1637) and Wilhelm VI of Hesse-Cassel (d. 1662).

10. Olympia Maidalchini (d. 1656), sister-in-law of Pope Innocent X.

Liselotte von der Pfalz

Elisabeth Charlotte, Duchesse d'Orléans, (1652–1722), commonly known as Liselotte von der Pfalz (Liselotte of the Palatinate), was, as the daughter of Elector Karl Ludwig of the Palatinate and Charlotte of Hesse-Cassel, raised in the Protestant religion. However, when the possibility of contracting a marriage to the only brother of Louis XIV of France arose, Liselotte was forced to convert to Catholicism in secret, so that her father might save face while engineering a politic marriage for his daughter. In 1672 Liselotte left the relatively quiet Palatinate for the French court, the center of European culture and model of absolutism. Her new husband, Philippe d'Orléans, was a homosexual who as a child had been encouraged to love fashion, parties, dancing, and other pursuits considered appropriate for the female sex so that he might never become rival to his brother. The couple managed to produce three children and after that more or less led separate lives. Liselotte found herself in a peculiar position: as a German and in her heart a Protestant she was a cultural outsider in France; as sister-in-law to the king she was an insider, privy to the secrets of one of the most powerful circles in Europe. Outwardly she represented the puissance of the French monarchy, yet she herself completely lacked power, sometimes even the means to cover her household bills. Liselotte was for obvious reasons intensely unhappy at court. She sought consolation in the letters she wrote in German to friends and relatives, especially to her aunt, Sophie of Braunschweig-Lüneburg. The need to write grew into a daily and time-consuming occupation, resulting in over five thousand letters.

Liselotte's letters were not intended for the public arena of print culture but rather for private consumption. Although a royal princess living at the most splendid court in Europe and writing about the most exalted persons in France, her language is markedly blunt and earthy. Indeed, her vocabulary bears a greater resemblance to that of popular literature, the low novel, the satire, than to the public language of the learned men who represented German high baroque culture. Liselotte's letters do not simply document court life under the Sun King but reveal much about their author. This unique example of women's writing in the seventeenth century tells us much about Liselotte's historical consciousness—her conception of self, nation, family, estate, gender roles—as well as the psychological and cultural significance of the exercise of letter writing in and of itself.

Letters of Liselotte von der Pfalz

To Duchess Sophie[1]

Saint Germain, 14 December 1676

I humbly beg Your Grace's forgiveness for having failed in my duty to write for such an eternity. . . . After I arrived here, I meant to answer every day, but every time something kept me from doing it, especially a lot of tiresome visits with which I was loaded down after my fall from the horse. But this is a story I must tell Your Grace: We had already caught a hare and flushed out a magpie and were therefore riding along slowly. I felt that my dress was not under me properly and so I stopped and bent down to straighten it out, but just at the moment when I was in that position a hare burst forth and everyone gave chase. My horse, seeing the others rush off, wanted to follow and jumped to one side, and in this way, not being firmly in the saddle, I slid all the way to one side, but I quickly grasped the pommel and kept my foot in the stirrup, hoping to lift myself back into the saddle; but as I grasped the pommel, I let go of the reins. I called out to a rider in front of me to stop my horse, but he galloped toward me so furiously that he frightened my horse, which lost no time turning to the other side and then bolted. Yet I held on as long as I saw that the other horses were close to me, and as soon as I found myself alone I slowly let go and dropped onto the green grass. This came off so well that I have not, thank God, hurt myself in the slightest. Your Grace, who so much admired our king for being such a comfort to me in the throes of my labor, will also love him for what he did in this instance, for he was the first one to reach me, looking as white as a sheet; and although I assured him that I had not hurt myself or fallen on my head, he would not rest until he had personally examined my head on all sides and finally decided that I had told him the truth; he also led me back to my room and even stayed with me for a while to see whether I might become dizzy. . . . I must say that even now the king still shows me his favor every day, for he speaks to me whenever he sees me and now calls for me every Saturday to have *medianoche*[2] with him and Madame de Montespan.[3] This is also the reason that I am now very much à la mode; whatever I say or do, whether it be good or awry, is greatly admired by the courtiers, to the point that when I decided to wear my old sable in this cold weather to keep my neck warm, everyone had one made from the same pattern, and sables have become quite the rage. This makes me laugh, for five years ago the very people who now admire and wear this fashion so laughed at me and made so much fun of me with my sable that I could no longer wear it. This is what happens at this court: if the courtiers imagine that someone is in favor, it does not matter what that person does, one can be certain that the courtiers approve of it; but if they imagine the contrary, they will think that person ridiculous, even if he has come straight from heaven. Oh how I wish it were possible for Your Grace to spend a few months here to observe this life: I am certain that Your Grace would have many a good laugh.

To Duchess Sophie

Saint Cloud, 13 April 1681

In the last few days I have received three letters from Her Grace the electress,[4] in which I am being reproached, albeit in a most polite manner, for taking so much interest in the children of the Raugräfin[5] and writing so often on their behalf. My brother has not yet replied to my letter, but the electress my mother goes into great detail about this matter. I do not write to the children themselves, for this does not help them and only irritates my brother and my mother. I shall advise Carllutz,[6] considering that Oncle[7] and Your Grace have extended him their gracious permission to call on them, to stay with them, for it appears to me from the electress's letter that my brother hates him terribly, but she also says that he likes the girls and will eventually soften toward Carllutz. . . .

I know some fine stories, one of which I simply must tell Your Grace: I heard it three or four days ago, and it happened in a Jesuit college. The Chevalier de Lorraine claims that it is his son who did this trick and that he does this sort of thing all the time. One of the pupils at the college was full of mischief of all kinds, ran around all night long, and did not sleep in his room. So the reverend fathers threatened him with a tremendous beating if he did not stay in his room at night. The boy goes to a painter and asks him to paint two saints on his buttocks, on the right cheek Saint Ignatius of Loyola and on the left Saint François Xavier, which the painter did. With that the boy tidily pulls up his breeches, goes back to his college, and starts making all kinds of trouble. When the reverend fathers catch him at it, they tell him, "This time you'll be whipped." The boy begins to struggle and plead, but they say that pleading will not do him any good. So the boy gets down on his knees and says, "O Saint Ignatius, O Saint Xavier, have pity upon me and perform a miracle for me to prove my innocence." With that the fathers pull down his breeches, and, as they lift up his shirt to beat him, the boy calls out, "I am praying with such fervor that I am certain my invocation will be heard!" When the fathers see the two painted saints, they exclaim: "A miracle! the boy whom we thought a rogue is a saint!" And with that they fall on their knees to kiss the behind and then call together all the pupils and make them come in procession to kiss the holy behind, which all of them do.

To Duchess Sophie

Saint Germain, 19 February 1682

I am well aware that by being sad one only harms oneself and does one's enemies a great favor, but there are occasions when one cannot help but take things to heart. However much I seek to arm myself by reason, I often find myself caught, for I do not have as good a mind nor as much spunk as Your Grace and therefore cannot dismiss these things right away and accommodate to the ways of the world. I just go along as best I can, thinking that if I do not seek to harm others, I should be left in peace too. But then when I see that I am being set upon from all sides I become very cross, and as I am quite impatient to begin with, all these vexations make me lose what little patience I have left. And then I have to sort everything out in my own head in order to break out of this labyrinth, and there is no advice or help anywhere because everyone here is so calculating and false that one cannot trust anyone. That makes me preoccupied and cranky, and when I am cranky my spleen swells up, and when that is swollen it sends vapors into my head, which make me sad, and when I am sad, I get sick. These are some of the causes of my recent illness, but as for describing how they came about and what has upset me so much, that cannot be entrusted to paper, for I am quite certain that my letters are being read and opened. The post office is doing me the honor . . . of resealing my letters in the most careful fashion, but our dear Madame la Dauphine[8] often receives hers in strange condition and ripped at the top; and when I see that I often think, as the Scripture says: "If they do these things in a green tree, what shall be done in the dry?" I assure Your Grace that I should by no means be bored at Hanover if I were so fortunate as to be there with Your Grace and Oncle; after all Your Grace knows that however much I hate convents I was never bored at Maubuisson as long as Your Grace was there. I also must confess one thing to Your Grace: all that glitters is not gold, and for all their boasting about the famous French liberty, all diversions here are unbelievably stiff and constrained. And besides, I have become accustomed to so many dreadful things since my arrival in this country that if I could ever return to a place where falseness does not rule everything and where lies are neither the daily fare nor approved of, I should think that I had come to a paradise. I therefore leave it to Your Grace to imagine whether I would (if I had the choice) be better off here or at Hanover. I have heard from others that Your Grace is having the entire château remodeled; I am only sorry that my room and my apartment are changed, for I flatter myself that if these remained as they were in my time, they would always remind Your Grace of her Liselotte, and that Your Grace would never have walked through my room without thinking of me. . . .

It seems that my credit with my brother is none too good these days, since he does not give Carllutz his due even though I had so earnestly begged him to do so; but I am not worried that he is angry with me for having become a Catholic, for if we were ever to see each other again, we would soon be good friends again, since I am convinced that he is fond of me in spite of himself.

To Duchess Sophie

Fontainebleau, 29 September 1683

At the last hunt, which took place at Fontainebleau, I would have suffered a grave accident if I had not quickly remembered my old tricks and jumped off my horse. A doe that had been startled by the hunt bounded straight toward me so impetuously that although I reined in my horse with all my might I was unable to stop short enough, so that in coming at me the doe hit my horse's mouth so hard that the harness, the bit, and the reins were scattered all around. My horse was frightened out of its wits, snorted like a bear, and jumped to one side. When I saw that my horse had lost the bit, I quickly placed the reins into its mouth, jumped off, and held it until my men caught up with me. If I had not been very quick about it, my horse would without fail have broken my neck. I assure Your Grace that she would have lost a faithful servant in me. This adventure has caused such excitement at court that for two days no one talked of anything else. . . .

My daughter is a true little leaf rustler; she will not learn anything, although her tongue is nimble enough and she is full of laughter and chatter. I am certain that if she were fortunate enough to converse with Your Grace and Oncle she would sometimes make them laugh, for she comes up with the funniest ideas. I must not be too familiar with her because she is not afraid of a single soul in the world except me, and without me no one can do anything with her. She is not a bit concerned about Monsieur,[9] and if he wants to scold her when I am not present, she laughs right in his face. Her governess she deceives from morning till night. I do not know what will become of this girl, her vivacity is quite shocking. If she were to put it to proper use, everything might turn out well, but I do confess that I am worried about it, for we are living in a strange country. I wish that she and her brother could swap temperaments, for while he is also bright, he is as staid and proper as a girl should be, and she is as wild as a boy. I suppose it is the nature of all Liselottes to be so wild in their youth and just hope that in time some lead will be added to the mercury; in time she may well be cured of the desire to carry on, just as I have been cured of it since I came to France. . . .

They say here that the king of Poland[10] has found many boxes full of money in the grand vizier's tent and that he has received eight million worth of spoils for himself alone. A nice box full of ducats would not do any harm to our Raugraf[11] either. . . .

Some days ago as I was washing my hands, Madame de Duras-fort told me that the late prince de Tarente always had his hands washed, and his arms too, by two of his wife's ladies-in-waiting; one of them was called Maranville and the other d'Olbreuse. Then she asked me whether it is true that the latter is now a reigning princess and has risen so high; she said that she could scarcely believe it, having heard that German princes never make misalli-ances. I confess that this question really embarrassed me for Oncle and Godfather; therefore I quickly changed the subject.

To Duchess Sophie

Versailles, 11 May 1685

. . . The king has sent his confessor to mine and this morning con-veyed a horrendous scolding to me about three points. The first is that I am too free in my speech and have said to Monsieur le Dauphin that even if I were to see him naked from the soles of his feet to the top of his head I should not be tempted by him or anyone else.[12] The second is that I permit my young ladies to have *galants*. The third is that I laughed with the Princesse de Conti[13] at her lovers. These three things, I was told, have displeased the king so much that if he had not bethought himself that I am his sister-in-law, he would have banished me from the court. To this I replied that as far as Monsieur le Dauphin is concerned, I admit that I said this to him, never thinking that it is shameful not to have temptations, and also because I had never heard that this was a necessary part of being modest. As for the other things I had freely said to him about shitting and pissing, I said that this was more the king's fault than mine, since I had heard him say a hun-dred times that one could speak of everything within the family, and that he should have given me warning if he no longer thought this was proper, since it would have been the easiest thing in the world to correct. As for the second point, that my young ladies have *galants*, I said that I never meddle in anything that goes on in my household, and that I would certainly not start with the very thing that is most difficult to handle, but that this sort of thing is not without example, since such things have always been part of court life everywhere; in short, that as long as they do not do anything that soils their honor, I cannot believe that this can harm either them or me. As for the third point about his daughter, I said that I am not her governess and therefore in no position to restrain her if she wants to have lovers, and that I could not be expected to weep when she tells me her adventures. And since I had heard the king himself speak with her about this and had seen him laugh with her, I thought that this was permitted to me as well. I added that Madame la Duchesse is my witness that I had never involved myself in any of this, and that I am deeply hurt to see myself, though innocent, treated by the king as if I had committed some terrible crime and to hear words that I do not deserve and that I was not brought up to hear. I have not said a word about this to Monsieur, for I know how his Grace is, he would only make it worse; but I must confess that I am thoroughly angry with the king for treating me like a chambermaid, which would be more befitting for his Maintenon,[14] for she was born to it, but I was not. I do not know whether the king is sorry to have lectured me in this manner, but this morning when he went to mass he gave me a friendly laugh. But I did not feel like laughing, therefore I only made my usual deep curtsy, but with an extremely surly look on my face. What will happen further in this matter, I shall report to Your Grace as soon as I know more. If I had been innocently exiled, I think I would have run away and come straight to Your Grace.

To Duchess Sophie

Fontainebleau, 8 October 1688

On Saturday we went to hunt the boar with the king. But I was in great anxiety during this hunt, for we had received news from Paris that my daughter had had a relapse. I have asked Monsieur four times to let me go to Paris to look after the poor child, but so far he has not permitted it, and all because of a cabal, for the Grancey,[15] who meddles in everything, wants me to have a new doctor, and that is something I am not willing to take from her, in order to have this new doctor appointed by Monsieur anyway, he has been sent to my daughter; so now when my doctor says white, this one says black, and the poor child has to suffer for it. Yet if I were in Paris I could examine what is most useful and would abide by that without partiality. That is why they have put it into Monsieur's head not to let me go to Paris. And so I have to watch my only daughter being put to death for the sake of a cabal, which grieves me in my soul, and I just had to unburden my heart to my dearest Ma Tante. However, I was unable to abstain from saying a few words, which Monsieur has taken very much amiss. So all I can do is to recommend my poor child to God Almighty. . . . On Monday I received more bad news about my daughter, which again made me shed bitter tears . . . That evening I had to attend the *appartement* with red eyes. On Tuesday we again went hunting with the king and returned only at nightfall; on Wednesday we again chased the stag, but I did not chase away my discontent, as Your Grace can easily imagine. . . .

I wish with all my heart that I could serve the children of the Raugräfin. I would be so glad to do it, but what can I do? I am not even allowed to take care of my own children. They will be even more to be pitied now, for this wretched war will not be helpful to them, nor to me either. . . .

That my children are not afraid of anyone but me is only too true, for Monsieur never wants to take the trouble of saying a single word of reprimand to them, and both their governor and their governess are the silliest and most stupid people one could find anywhere. The children, thank God, are not lacking in wit and therefore cannot resist laughing at those who are in charge of them, and so it falls to me to tell them what they must and must not do. So they fear me, yet withal they love me too, for they are reasonable enough to see that what I tell them is for their own good. I do not scold often, but if it has to be, I really let them have it, that makes it all the more impressive. If they follow my advice, I will bring them up to be good people, notwithstanding all the bad examples these poor children constantly have before them.

But this, too, is a text that one had better bypass in silence, and I shall therefore turn to coiffures. I am certain that if Your Grace could see the great care and trouble that the women are now taking to make themselves repulsive, Your Grace would have a good laugh. For myself, I cannot go along with these masquerades, but the coiffures are getting higher every day. I think they will finally have to make the doors taller, for otherwise these ladies will no longer be able to go in and out of the rooms. When they are wearing wimples, they look just like Melusine,[16] as I saw her painted in an old book that His Grace the late elector had in his library at Heidelberg, and I believe that the train on their dresses will eventually turn into a snake, just as she did. If this happened to the Grancey I should not wonder, for she already has a snake's and adder's tongue with which she stings me only too often. But I think it is time now to end this long epistle.

To Duchess Sophie

Versailles, 14 April 1689

I do not wish the present Palatine Elector any harm, nor do I blame him for the dreadful devastation that has been visited upon the poor Palatinate since it has come into his hands. What I cannot forgive is that the poor people of the Palatinate have been deceived in my name, for these poor, innocent people, out of affection for the late elector our father, thought that the best thing they could do would be to surrender willingly, that this would make them my subjects, and that then they would live more happily than under the present elector, since I am still of their rightful prince's blood. And yet they were not only deceived in their hope and most cruelly rewarded for their affection, but plunged into the utmost misery because of it.[17] This pains me so much that I cannot swallow it. If there were anything here that could give me pleasure I might be able, notwithstanding all the misery one encounters, to enjoy myself now and then; but the very people who are responsible for the misfortune of my fatherland also persecute me personally here, and not a day passes without bringing me new troubles. And yet I shall have to spend the rest of my life with these people. If at least they would say what it is they want, one would know how to act, but one is not told anything and whatever one says or does is considered bad. I would be better off if I were beaten in secret and if that were the end of it than I am now, constantly set upon in this manner, for this squeezes the very marrow out of one's bones and makes life altogether unbearable. I have noticed something else, too, namely that whenever the king fears that Monsieur might get angry with him, as for example when he gives military governorships to his bastards but nothing to Monsieur, or when he is planning to refuse one of Monsieur's requests, or now, when he lets Monsieur sit around here without entrusting him with the command of a single army, or in other cases of this kind, the king will flatter the Lorrainers and all of my husband's favorites but treat me very badly and show contempt for me; and since Monsieur likes them and hates me, he is being paid in this manner. This satisfies Monsieur, and he stops asking for more. . . .

To Electress Sophie

Saint Cloud, 19 March 1693

I can never hear a sermon without going to sleep; preaching is a true opium for me. Once here in France I had a bad cough and spent three nights without sleeping a wink. Then I remembered that I always sleep in church as soon as I hear preaching and nuns singing. Therefore I drove to a convent where there was to be a sermon. The nuns had barely begun to sing when I went to sleep, and I slept throughout the three-hour service; that made me feel much better. From this Your Grace can see that I am blessed with the ability to sleep in church no less than Your Grace and His late Grace my father.

To Electress Sophie

Versailles, 13 February 1695

Where in the world does one find a husband who loves only his spouse and does not have someone, be it mistresses or boys, on the side? If for this reason wives were to go in for the same behavior one could never be sure, as Godfather so rightly says, that the children of the house are the rightful heirs. Does the young duchess[18] not know that a woman's honor consists of having commerce with no one but her husband, and that for a man it is not shameful to have mistresses but shameful indeed to be a cuckold? . . .

Your Grace would not believe how coarse and unmannerly Frenchmen have become in the last twelve or thirteen years. One would be hard put to find two young men of quality who know how to behave properly either in what they say or in what they do. There are two very different causes for this: namely, all the piety at court and the debauchery among men. Because of the first, men and women are not allowed to speak to each other in public, which used to be a way to give young gentlemen polish. And secondly, because they love the boys, they no longer want to please anyone but one another, and the most popular among them is the one who knows best how to be debauched, coarse, and insolent. This habit has become so ingrained that no one knows how to live properly any longer, and they are worse than peasants behind the plow. . . .

It is a great honor to sit next to the king during the sermon, but I would be happy to cede this honor to someone else, for His Majesty will not permit me to sleep. As soon as I go to sleep, the king nudges me with his elbow and wakes me up; thus I can never really go to sleep nor really stay awake. And that gives one a headache.

To Raugräfin Luise[19]

Marly, 4 July 1698

Those who cannot imagine that things here are as bad as they really are think the king and the court are still as they used to be, but the sad fact is that everything is changed so much that if a person who had left the court since the queen's death were to return now, he would think that he had come to an altogether different world. A great deal more could be said about this, but it cannot be entrusted to paper, since all letters are read and then resealed. Ma Tante always says, "One man is the other's devil in this world," and how true that is. We do know that everything comes from God and that in His all-powerful way He has decided from all eternity how things are to be; but just as the Almighty has not consulted us beforehand, so He also does not let us know why things happen as they do; so we can only acquiesce in His holy will. I do not doubt that Karl Moritz[20] will have many a dispute with Monsieur Helmont at Hanover.[21] I wish Karl Moritz every good thing and a long life, but I doubt that for all his learnedness he can ever become as dear to me as my dear departed Carllutz was. . . .

It does not behoove me to look at other people's beauty or ugliness, considering that it has pleased God to make me so very ugly; however, I have now reached an age where one more easily finds consolation, for even if I had been beautiful, I would have become ugly by now, so it all comes to the same thing. But then I set greater store by inner than by outward beauty anyway. I already wrote to you what I think of parsons and priests who forbid comedies, so I will say nothing more about it, except to add that if these reverend gentlemen were able to see a little further than their noses, they would understand that the common people's money is not wasted on comedies. In the first place, actors are poor devils who make their living from the theater, and furthermore, comedies give pleasure, pleasure gives health, health gives strength, and strength makes people work better; so in fact they should order rather than forbid them.

To Electress Sophie

Port Royal, 26 July 1699

There is no doubt that if Monsieur were not so weak and did not permit himself to be bamboozled by the wicked characters whom he likes so much, he would be the best husband in the world; therefore he is to be pitied more than to be hated when he does one a bad turn. My son[22] is extremely intelligent, and I am certain that his conversation would not displease Your Grace; he knows a great deal, has a good memory, and can speak about the things he knows without pedantry. He is quite able to express himself in the grand manner, but his character is not elevated enough, and he prefers the company of lowly people, of painters and musicians, to that of people of rank and thinks that he must do what he sees other young people doing, even if it is contrary to his nature and his temperament; also, he thinks that he is ten times stronger than he is. This, I am afraid, will kill him some day; he never follows good advice, only bad; and although he knows perfectly well what virtue is, he thinks it is smart to despise it and to approve of vice. He is kind and will never willingly harm anyone, but he is unsure of himself. . . . Right now he is working hard for Your Grace, painting a fable, for everything he paints must have to do with history. He says he must go to Paris early in the morning to paint but, just between us, there is a young girl of sixteen, very sweet, an actress; our cavalier is quite smitten with her and has her brought to him. If he paints her little face into his Antigone, she will be pretty indeed. I have not yet seen the picture, but if he uses her face in the painting, I will let Your Grace know.

I confess that I would be happier if reincarnation were true than if I had to believe in hell or the extinction of our soul; this last idea I dislike most of all, but unfortunately it seems more likely than the other two. I think that the person who wrote the book proving that hell does not exist has done so out of compassion, in order to comfort the sinners. It is quite certain that there cannot be two eternities; the Scripture may well have said "from eternity to eternity" to express the idea of eternity more forcefully. I have great trouble believing in ghosts, for if there were something that is quite unknown to us and yet can manifest itself, one would know about it from better sources; yet ordinarily ghosts appear only to superstitious people, drunkards, or sad people troubled by their spleen, and what they say cannot be trusted. If one looks into the matter, one usually finds trickery, thievery, or amorous intrigues.

To Electress Sophie

Marly, 6 May 1700

Monsieur, thank God, has gotten over his fever, but His Grace is still quite languid and melancholy and does not take pleasure in anything. I think I know what makes him so dejected: His Grace realizes that his past life cannot go on any longer; yet all his plans and actions used to turn only on his pleasures, which are all that he cares about. Of course, he does not want to die either, yet he realizes that his wild life and his activities must come to an end. That makes His Grace very sad, and this sadness prevents him from regaining his strength; so I am quite worried about Monsieur.

My son has such a great talent for all aspects of painting that he never uses any expedients for designing and sketches everything from nature and living models. Coypel, his former teacher, says that all the painters should be glad that my son is a great lord, because if he were an ordinary fellow he would surpass them all. He can draw anything that comes into his head, his conceptions are strong, and he knows how to make the most difficult postures look easy. . . .

I cannot understand how anyone could imagine that the Song of Solomon has anything to do with God or with piety. One only has to read it to see that this is a lover carrying on. It must have gladdened the hearts of the reverend Jesuits of Regensburg to see two boys playing the lovers. I am now reading Ecclesiastes, and find it a beautiful book, but I am surprised that it was included among the books of the Bible, for it clearly shows that Solomon did not believe in an afterlife. . . .

In my youth I often deceived the good Mistress Kolb by eating at night, but we did not eat such dainty things as chocolate, tea, or coffee, but stuffed ourselves with a good cabbage salad with bacon. I remember that once at Heidelberg, while a door was being changed in my room, my bed and that of the Kolbin were moved to the room next to that of my maids. The Kolbin had forbidden me to go into the girls' room at night; I promised that I would not cross the threshold and told her that she might as well go to bed, because I was not yet sleepy and would like to look at the stars for a while. The Kolbin did not trust me and did not want to budge from her night table; finally I told her that I felt sorry for her and suggested that she go to bed leaving the curtains open so that she could see me. This she did. As soon as she was in bed, the girls opened the door and placed the plate of cabbage salad on the threshold. I pretended to drop my handkerchief, picked up the plate with it, and went straight to the window. I had just swallowed three good mouthfuls when suddenly the cannon that stood on the terrace under my window was set off because a fire had broken out in the town. The Kolbin, who was dreadfully scared of fire, jumps out of bed; I, not wanting to be caught, toss my napkin out of the window along with the silver plate and the bacon salad, so that I had nothing to wipe my mouth with. Right then I heard someone come up the wooden stairs; it was the elector our late father, who had come to see where the fire was. Seeing me with my greasy mouth and chin, he started to swear, "*Sacrement,* Liselotte, don't tell me you smear stuff on your face!" I said, "It is just some lip balm that I have put on because my lips are chapped." Papa said, "You look dirty." Suddenly I was seized with a fit of laughter; Papa and all those who were with him thought that I had gone mad to laugh so hard. The Raugräfin had also come up and passed through the girls' room; she came in saying: "What an odd smell of bacon salad in the girls' room." Then the elector saw what the joke was and said: "So that is your mouth balm, Liselotte." When I saw that the elector was in good humor, I confessed the whole thing and explained how I had gone about deceiving the governess. The elector only laughed about it, but the Kolbin did not forgive me for a long time. This is an old story, and I only tell it to show Your Grace that I know how much fun it is for young people to eat at night against the governess's will.

To Electress Sophie

Versailles, 20 April 1702

Yesterday I gave Madame de Châteauthiers a beautiful parrot, which talks amazingly well. I wanted to hear what it can say and let it into my room; my dogs became jealous and one of them, by the name of Mione, started to bark at it; the parrot kept saying: "Give me your paw." I wish Your Grace could have seen how surprised Mione was to hear the bird talk: she stopped barking, stared at it, then looked at me; and when it continued to talk, she took fright like a human being, ran away and hid under the day bed, and at that point the parrot screamed with laughter. That made me think of Herr Leibniz, since Your Grace tells me that he maintains that animals are endowed with reason, are not machines as Descartes has claimed; and that their souls are immortal.[23] In the next world I will be delighted to find not only my family and good friends but also my dear little animals. But the joke would be on me if it should mean that my soul will become as mortal as theirs and that all of us will be nothing together; therefore I would rather believe the other notion, which is much more comforting.

To Raugräfin Amalie Elisabeth

Versailles, 22 July 1702

Dearest Amelise, about my recent illness I will say nothing more; I am now, thanks be to God, in perfect health and on the day before yesterday duly received your welcome letter of the thirteenth of this month. That I keenly feel and regret Karl Moritz's death and also that I have conveyed my heartfelt sympathy to you and Luise does not deserve any thanks, it is no more than I owe you. You are doing the right and Christian thing to resign yourself to God's will, for to fight it would serve no purpose other than to make yourself ill. That women, who are usually not too happy, do not care if they die does not surprise me, but I am surprised that Karl Moritz was so glad to die. If Karl Moritz had not loved wine so much, he would have been a perfect philosopher. But for this he paid dearly, because I am convinced that drink shortened his life. That he could not be without drinking is shown by his overheated and burnt liver. I wish he could have bequeathed his good memory to me, I could certainly use it here. I know very well why no one liked Karl Eduard[24] as much as Karl Moritz. He was too sly and never ever wanted to say his opinion; I was never able to get out of him what he hated or loved, liked or disliked. I used to ask him a thousand times, "Tell me what you like to do, what you enjoy." Then he would only make a deep bow, give an embarrassed little laugh, but aside from that I could not get anything out of him; that is tiresome and makes one impatient in the long run, and so I did not like him nearly as much as Carllutz. As for Carllutz, I still cannot think of him without getting tears in my eyes. Whatever one may do to prepare for misfortune, when it comes one is still bound to feel it; and especially when one loses a close relative, the blood is bound to stir. . . .

When the French court was as it used to be, one could really learn manners here! But now that no one, except the king and Monseigneur, knows what *politesse* is, when all the young people think of nothing but sheer and disgusting debauchery, and when the most unmannerly are considered to be the cleverest of all, I would not advise anyone to let his children get into that, for instead of learning good manners they would learn nothing but bad habits here. So you are quite right in disapproving of the many Germans who now want to send their children to France. One must always have respect for those who give their blood and property for their fatherland, I certainly agree with you there. I wish you and I were men and in the war; this is a useless wish to make, but sometimes one cannot help it.

To Raugräfin Amalie Elisabeth[25]

Versailles, 18 August 1702

It is no wonder that people who rarely speak French sometimes mix up a letter. I am keeping my promise to correct your French for you, but you and Luise do not correct my German sentences, even though I think they are often in need of correction. For I rarely speak German and realize that it no longer comes as easily as it used to; so if I do not have help I am sure to forget it. Even though I read every day in my German Bible, a psalm and a chapter in the Old Testament and one in the New Testament, this is not the same as speaking every day. Nor can I learn to speak properly from the Rotzenhäuserin, for she speaks a terrible German herself; I am teaching her more than she teaches me. There is nothing shameful about not speaking a foreign language properly; one must simply speak up in order to be corrected, that is the best way to learn. Since everyone in Germany now wants to speak and write French, I am surprised that they do not watch their spelling better. Why is it that you have a French lady of honor? For they are usually of very bad nobility, and not even comparable to our German nobility; any commoner here who buys an office of *secrétaire du roi* is immediately considered a *gentilhomme,* and moreover they never have any qualms about misalliances and marry all kinds of commoners' daughters, even peasant girls, just so long as they have money, and therefore are often kin to all kinds of artisans. Ordinary nobility commands very little respect here.

To Electress Sophie

Versailles, 10 June 1706

Such reversals as have happened in the last twenty years are unheard of; the kingdoms of England and Spain have changed as swiftly as the situation in a play. I think that when future generations read the history of our time, it will look to them like a novel, and they will be unable to believe it.

To Gottfried Wilhelm Leibniz

Paris, 21 November 1715

My son is so beset with troublesome affairs that I see him only for a moment every day. He has distributed all the directorships of the academies but has kept that of the liberal arts for himself in order to refresh his mind there after his troublesome workday. If science is indeed the heavenly manna, there must be many hungry souls. In fact I fear that if this were the case I would go hungry myself, for no one could be less learned and more ignorant than I am, even though I daily seek to find within myself means to achieve serenity, but this is much more difficult for those of us afflicted with a troublesome spleen, which acts like a microscope in human beings, enlarging all of our troubles and prolonging our sadness. It seems to me that it will be difficult to find ways to keep everyone healthy, unless it is possible to find as many remedies as there are people in the world; for what cures one person will kill another, since people's insides are as varied as their faces. . . . It seems to me that so far no one has yet found the art of living longer or more happily, and I fear that we shall have to wait in the outer court for some time. . . .

You, Herr Leibniz, will never need anyone but your own name to announce yourself to my son; he knows you better than you think, for your reputation in Paris is very great. My son must believe that one can do everything at once since, as I said before, he wants to direct the *académie des sciences* himself. . . .

The nation here is hard to satisfy; people often go along with the first person who tells them something, and in the provinces with what is written to them from Paris, especially when the vermin of priests has a hand in it. What is really happening I do not know, for I am extremely concerned that it might be thought that my son is ruled by women and therefore, in order to set an example to his wife and his daughters, I have announced loudly that I will not meddle in any of his affairs. My son has also told me that he has requested his wife and his oldest daughter to follow my example. So far I have not been sorry to have taken this resolution.

To Raugräfin Luise

Paris, 31 March 1718

My children of Lorraine are pleased with me and I with them. I am also very pleased with my eldest granddaughter,[26] and I am hopeful that she will become an excellent person. For she is changed for the better in every respect; she is intelligent and has a kind heart, and she is beginning to have the desire to pray to God Almighty for the will to hate vice and love virtue—and all of this without falling into superstition. That is why I hope that God will have mercy upon her and change her heart altogether. Of her third sister[27] I do not have as good an opinion; for one thing it would not occur to her to pray, and for another she does not have a kind character, cares nothing for her mother and little for her father, except that she wants to rule him. Me she hates like the devil and also hates all of her sisters. She is deceitful in all things, often contemptuous of the truth, and dreadfully coquettish withal. In short, this girl is sure to bring us a lot of grief. I wish she were already married and living in a faraway country, so that we would not have to hear more about her. I am afraid that we will also have grief and sorrow about the second one, who is bound and determined to become a nun,[28] although the dear girl is deceiving herself, for she does not have nun's flesh at all, and I fear that the thing will no sooner be done than she will fall into deep despair, and then she would be capable of doing away with herself, for she is courageous and has no fear of death. It is a pity for this girl; she has many good traits, is most pleasing in appearance, tall, well built, with a pretty and pleasant face, a beautiful mouth, and teeth like pearls; she dances well, has a lovely voice and is a fine musician who can sing from sight anything she likes, without grimacing and very prettily; she is naturally eloquent, has a kind heart, and likes all the things she should like. She tells everyone that I am the only person she will miss. So I am very fond of her. It is not hard to like this one, she is very pleasant, and so I am quite distressed that she wants to become a nun. My fourth granddaughter is a good child, but very ugly and contrary.[29] The fifth one, by contrast, is a beautiful and pleasant child, well mannered, cheerful, and funny; I like her too. She is called Mademoiselle de Beaujolais,[30] and she will be quite intelligent some day. The sixth one, whose name is Mademoiselle de Chartres,[31] is not too bad-looking, but a horrid child; for as soon as one so much as looks at her, she starts to bawl. The duc de Chartres[32] is a nice boy and has intelligence; yet he is a bit too serious for his age and so dreadfully delicate that I cannot look at him without worrying. He must not drink a drop of iced beverage, or else he immediately gets a fever, nor must he eat fruit or anything but the things to which he is accustomed. I keep fretting that he will not last very long, and that would be a dreadful calamity for all of us and also a pity for the child who is so smart and kindhearted and who learns everything he is taught. He is not beautiful but more on the pretty than on the ugly side and resembles his mother more than his father. The child has a natural disposition to all the virtues and is not given to any vice. This makes me very fond of him. But this is enough talk of my children and grandchildren. . . .

Histories are lies, too. . . . Why, if such lies can be told about things that have happened right under our noses, how can we believe anything that happened in faraway places and many, many years ago? I therefore believe that histories (except those in the Scriptures) are no more true than novels, the difference being that the latter are longer and more fun to read.

To Karoline of Wales[33]

Saint Cloud, 18 August 1718

As long as I can remember, I have always preferred swords and guns to dolls; I would have dearly loved to have been a boy, and that almost cost me my life, because I had heard that Maria Germain had become a man by jumping.[34] That made me jump so terribly hard that it is quite a miracle that I did not break my neck a hundred times.

To Raugräfin Luise

Saint Cloud, 8 June 1719

Writing is my greatest occupation; I have no skill and desire for fancywork and nothing in the world bores me as much as sticking

in a sewing needle and pulling it out again. You made me laugh
heartily, dear Luise, by saying that my letters are like a soothing
balm upon your head. At least this balm will not melt into your
beard, as it did with Aaron. . . .

To Herr von Harling³⁵

Saint Cloud, 22 September 1720

I am quite of your opinion that the old language was more expres-
sive than the French that is spoken now. One would not want to
read *Amadis*³⁶ in present-day French; someone tried to translate
Don Quixote into it, but it was not a success. I read Philippe de
Comines³⁷ forty years ago and do not remember his book very
well; at the time his style seemed rather naive to me. . . .

Nothing is more full of lies than gazettes and newspapers. Here
in France, if one wants to do someone a nasty turn, one asks a
third person to write the news one wants to spread on a piece of
paper, wraps this around a gold coin, and addresses it "To the
gazeteer of Holland," and at the next mail one can be sure to find
everything that was on the scrap of paper in the Dutch newspapers.
I have never done this myself, but I have often seen others do it.
So these papers cannot be too reliable, because partiality is always
involved.

Translated by Elborg Forster

Notes

1. Sophie (1630–1714), duchess of Braunschweig-Lüneburg, after 1692, electress of Hanover, daughter of Elizabeth Stuart. Her oldest son, Georg Ludwig,
became King George I of England. When Karl Ludwig's marital troubles had become
particularly severe he sent his daughter to live with her aunt for four years. The
notes and introduction are based on the translator's footnotes and introduction in
Elborg Foster, trans., *A Woman's Life in the Court of the Sun King* (Baltimore:
Johns Hopkins University Press, 1984).
2. A nightly feast.
3. Françoise Athénaïs de Mortemart (1641–1717), official mistress of Louis
XIV.
4. Charlotte of Hesse-Cassel (1627–86), Liselotte's mother.
5. Luise von Degenfeld (1637–77), morganatic wife of Liselotte's father.
6. Raugraf Karl Ludwig (1658–88), Liselotte's favorite half-brother. Raugräfin Luise (1661–1733), Liselotte's half-sister, eventually became first lady-in-
waiting and a kind of secretary to her aunt Electress Sophie of Hanover. Karl

Ludwig conferred the rather odd titles Raugraf/Raugräfin first upon his morganatic wife and their children. Inasmuch as they are a vague title of honor, the titles could perhaps be simply, although not entirely accurately translated as Count/Countess.

7. Ernst August (1629–98), duke of Braunschweig-Lüneburg, after 1692, elector of Hanover.

8. Maria Anna Christine of Bavaria (1660–90), the wife of the Grand Dauphin, the only surviving son of Louis XIV and his wife, Marie-Thérèse.

9. Philippe I d'Orléans (1640–1701), Liselotte's husband, only brother of Louis XIV. Their only daughter was Elisabeth Charlotte (1674–1744), duchesse de Lorraine.

10. John III, a.k.a. Jan Sobieski (1624–96), who had raised the siege of Vienna.

11. Karl Ludwig (Carllutz) had taken part in this campaign, as had two of Duchess Sophie's sons.

12. Louis, the Grand Dauphin (1661–1711), only surviving son of Louis XIV and his wife, Marie-Thérèse. Forster notes that it is curious that no one seems to have recognized this quip as an almost-verbatim citation from Molière's *Tartuffe* (III.2).

13. Marie-Anne de Bourbon (1666–1739), daughter of Louis XIV and his mistress Madame de la Valière, who was eventually legitimized.

14. Françoise d'Aubigné, widow Scarron, marquise de Maintenon (1635–1719), mistress of Louis XIV whom he secretly married after the queen's death in 1683. Liselotte refers to her as "the old trollop," "old pruneface," "the old ragbag," etc.

15. Charlotte de Grancey, governess in the Orléans household and mistress of the chevalier de Lorraine.

16. Old French legend. Melusine was the mother of the Lusignans. Every Saturday she changed into her true form, half woman, half snake or worm. Although her husband had promised never to seek her out on Saturday he betrayed her, whereupon she lost the possibility of gaining a soul. The German version of the tale was written by Thüring von Ringoltingen (1456, printed 1471).

17. On August 12, 1688, Liselotte's half brother, Raugraf Karl Ludwig, had died of a fever. Louis XIV had then invaded the Palatinate under the pretext of conquering it for his sister-in-law. A zone of "scorched earth" was created, and the French troops committed many atrocities. The resulting war lasted until 1697.

18. Sophie Dorothea, Electress Sophie's daughter-in-law, who was caught in a scandalous adultery with Count Christoph von Koenigsmarck.

19. Raufgräfin Luise (1661–1733), Liselotte's half sister and one of her favorite correspondents.

20. Raugraf Karl Moritz (1670–1702), the last of the Raugrafen, Liselotte's half brothers.

21. Franz Mercurius van Helmont (1618–99), son of a famous Belgian chemist. During his travels he pursued cabalistic studies, and his activities caused him to be incarcerated by the Spanish Inquisition. In 1663 he found refuge at the court of Elector Karl Ludwig (Liselotte's father) in Heidelberg.

22. Philippe II d'Orléans (1674–1723), Liselotte's second son, regent of France during the minority of Louis XV.

23. Leibniz later wrote an article entitled *Commentatio de anima brutorum* (Commentary on the souls of animals). René Descartes (1596–1650), French philosopher and mathematician. In 1649 he had written *Traité des passions de l'âme* (Treatise on the passions of the soul) for Princess Elisabeth of the Palatinate, Liselotte's grandmother. Descartes compares both human beings and animals to machines in his writings.

24. Another half brother.

25. Raugräfin Amalie Elisabeth (1663–1709), one of Liselotte's half sisters.

26. Marie-Louise, duchesse de Berry (1695–1719). In this letter Liselotte speaks about her grandchildren, the regent's children.

27. Charlotte-Aglaë, Mademoiselle de Valois (1700–1761), who later married the duke of Modena.

28. Louise-Adélaïde (1698–1743), Mademoiselle de Chartres, who became Abbess of Chelles.

29. Louise-Elisabeth, Mademoiselle de Montpensier (1709–42), who married Luis of Austria, briefly king of Spain in 1724.

30. Philippine-Elisabeth, Mademoiselle de Beaujolais (1714–34).

31. Louise Diane (1716–36), who married Prince Louis de Bourbon.

32. Louis d'Orléans (1703–52).

33. Karoline of Wales (1683–1737), married to Georg August, the heir to the electorate of Hanover who later became King George II of England.

34. The case of Maria Germain of Vitry-le-François is mentioned in Montaigne's essay "On Imagination." He reports that there is a song warning girls about the danger of jumping and spreading their legs too far.

35. Eberhard Ernst Franz von Harling, captain of the guards in Liselotte's household and field marshal in the French army.

36. The most famous of the Spanish romances of chivalry; translated into French in 1540.

37. Philippe de Commynes (ca. 1447–1511), author of historical chronicles.

Abraham a Santa Clara

Abraham a Santa Clara was born Hans Ulrich Mergele on July 2, 1644, in the Duchy of Baden. In 1662 he joined the order of Barefooted Augustinians in Vienna and in 1666 became a priest. In 1677 he was appointed court preacher at the Habsburg court in Vienna. His preaching is said to have been electrifying. His sermon of repentance "Vienna, Mark It Well" (1679), a reaction to the devastating plague of 1679, numbers among his earliest printed works. Four years latter, in 1683, the Turkish advance toward Vienna provided the impulse for *Arise, Arise, You Christians* from which the following passages are taken. The years 1686–95 saw the production of his major work *Judas, the Arch-Rascal,* a highly embellished description of the life of Judas, followed by his *Healing Mish-Mash* (1704), *The World's Hooey and Pfooey* (1707), *Spiritual Haberdashery* (1710), to name a few of his more colorful titles.

The selection included here with its puns, rhymes, neologisms, anecdotes, and jokes is characteristic of Abraham a Santa Clara's flamboyant style. Friedrich Schiller borrowed from the opening passage for the rhymed sermon of the Capuchin monk in the eighth scene of *Wallenstein's Camp* (1798), the first of the three plays that comprise the dramatic trilogy *Wallenstein.* Abraham a Santa Clara, firmly convinced of the truth of his world vision, relentlessly castigates those he sees as the enemies of Christendom, but also does not spare his flock, particularly the nobility, the lash of his tongue.

Arise, Arise, You Christians, and Blame
No One for the Barbaric Attacks on Our Lands,
Other than the Copious Sins of Our Time[1]

What is the Turk? You Christians, answer without hesitation: he is a copy of the Antichrist, a vain big-bellied bailiff, an insatiable tiger, Satan incarnate, a damned world-storming aggressor. He is a cruel glutton, a vengeful beast, an unscrupulous pretender to the crown, a murderous falcon, a discontented pile of carrion. He is oriental dragon poison, an unchained hellhound, epicurean riffraff, a tyrannical monster, etc. It is true, my dear Christians. He certainly deserves these fine laudatory epithets. But one title has slipped from your memory, namely the one that Saint Thomas of Villanova gave him, when he once preached with apostolic zeal in the presence of Charles V, Holy Roman Emperor and Austrian Hannibal.[2] And just as at that time Christian potentates armed themselves for a Turkish war, he pronounced these words, not without holy gravity: *Quid prodest colligere exercitus, & colligere peccata, an nescimus, quia Turca iste, & bella flagella DEI sunt?*[3] (What good does it do to deploy entire armies and not to root out sin? Do we not know that the Turk and such wars are the scourge of God?). . . .

Whoever looks through the Holy Bible will find everywhere clearly and really, how Almighty God treats us humans all the same, how he treats us mildly and wildly as we wish it: he shows us sword or reward, and as we show ourselves to him. If we keep the commandments of God and praise his holy name, he richly grants us a golden peace, a longed-for well-being and a most satisfying prosperity. As long as we live in unbridled freedom, sin and vice increase daily, and as long as we affront his divine majesty, he will show us an iron fist, hard wars, and hostile invasions.

As long as Adam remained in the state of innocence, as long as he remained obedient to God, as long as all creatures were under his command, Melampus didn't bark at him.[4] The weasel didn't blow on him.[5] The cats, to be sure, licked in front, but did not scratch behind. The lion treated him as a lapdog treats a lady. Not a single gnat dared to land on his nose. Even more marvelous, in those days the lovely colored rose gloried in its majestic purple without thorns, without the stabbing stiletto. But as soon as Adam sinned and affronted God, from that moment the royal rose has had those hostile weapons and green daggers at her side. It is therefore certain, said Saint Basil (homily "On Paradise")[6] that the rose was covered with hostile weapons by no one but sin.

At the moment the world, especially our Europe, is in a difficult state that no physician can quickly cure. To all appearances it is the colic, commonly called the fury since it does nothing but cut and stab in Europe's body, and all the more so since almost no country is without war, none without hostile weapons. In the past years the Holy Roman Reich has practically become the Lowly Roman Reich through continous wars; the Low Countries have become even lower through nothing but war; Alsace has become Mal-sace through nothing but war; the Rhine River has become a Swine River through nothing but war and other lands have become miserable ones through nothing but war; Hungary bears a double cross in its coat of arms and to date it has borne a thousand crosses through nothing but war.

When God came to earth, there was peace on the entire earth, *toto orbe in Pace compositio [sic]*.[7] Since at the moment there is war almost everywhere in the entire orbit of the earth, the devil must have come to the world. And doesn't the little word *Mars* not only have four letters, but also already rule over the four corners of the earth? But who causes such lengthy, pitiful, painful, destructive bellicose uprisings, who? He? No she, sin.[8]

Under the reign of the Jewish king Jeroboam there was constant warfare. When Nadab wielded the scepter in Israel there was constant war. When Baasha reigned in the land of the Jews there was always war.[9] Because then too there was copious sinning. The Jews had to suffer the constant assaults, the ferocious onslaughts, the unexpected falling upon them of the Assyrians, Chaldeans, Egyptians, Romans, etc., because of their falling away from God and their faulting of Jesus.

Well known is that image that God showed the great king Nebuchadnezzar several thousand years ago, and with which all monarchies of the world were portrayed:[10] First, this same image had a golden head, by which the Babylonian monarchy was indicated.

Second, the same statue had a silver breast, which indicated the Persian monarchy. Third, this image had a brass belly that meant the Greek monarchy. Fourth and last, the statue had iron legs, half iron, half clay feet, by which the last monarchy was indicated, namely the Holy Roman monarchy, in which Leopold the First already wields the scepter—may God yet grant him a long and happy reign. God depicted this, our monarchy, with iron and clay, and we are suffering it now—unfortunately!—that nothing but iron and clay hover before our eyes. What was it other than clay a few years ago in our countries? By this I mean the raging plague that put so many thousands under the ground. What have we been seeing for so many years other than iron, that is, the constantly bloody sabers of Mars? And to all appearances we must expect even more destructive wars. Would you, my Christian fellow, see the mother who bears this evil? Then I will show you sin. Listen to the Italian who speaks a true German truth to you: *Il peccato è la calamita della calamità: chi mal fa, mal trova*[11] (Sin is the magnet that draws the sharp iron and sword of war into our lands).

When was the world ever more perverse than now? Paulus Venetus. . . .[12] writes, that on the isle of Madagascar there is the largest bird in the world, with the name of Roc, which flies an entire elephant on its back into the sky, then dashes it to the earth, killing it. A single feather of this bird is said to be ninety spans long and the quill two spans thick—one could write huge lies with it. This bird is large, but in our time there are even larger birds, who, to be sure, are not called Roc but are de-rog-atory fellows.

In the year 1520 Leo X, Roman pope, received a letter from Nidro, the Sienese archbishop, in which the latter swore up and down that a great whale had been seen there whose mouth was two fathoms wide, the eyes so huge that if one tried to dig them out at least twenty-four men could fit in the hole.[13] From this the size of the body can be estimated. That was one big fish, but now there are even fishier fools, etc.

Jerome, the great teacher of the church, writes in the life of Saint Hilarion[14] that in that land where this saint zealously served God, there was a dragon that swallowed an entire knight along with his horse. Indeed its strong breath and poison often forceably drew entire flocks of sheep along with the shepherd to it, and they were buried in its gullet. This must have been a great beast, but now there are everywhere even greater beasts.

Petrus Gillius,[15] chapter 6, writes that in Arabia on the high mountains mice have been found that are as big as our foxes, and they are usually called mountain mice. These huge mice walk upright like people and do great damage. Those are huge rodents but now there are even bigger rats.

Where is there now a country, a city, a town, where great birds are not found who without fear of God impudently practice all kinds of evil? Where are there not such beasts who tyrannically persecute the just and who often satisfy their hunger with their goods and blood? Where are there no such rats who nibble and gnaw not the morsels but the morals of the just, since many a person would prefer that his ear be cut off rather than his honear? At least he could cover the wound with a Barocka.[16] Don't we live as if the almighty God had gouty wrists and could no longer strike us? At the moment there is nothing dearer than the fear of God. Our present life is a faithful copy of those pure lives that people led before the flood. Nowadays we have an enduring May, an everlasting Wine Month,[17] but never a Christ Month, at least very seldom, for we bear the name of Christians, as the constellations in the heavens are named fish or eagle. With the latter there is no flying, with the former there is no swimming, but only a mere label.

The boat of the apostles (Matthew 8)[18] was violently driven by the raging waves and angered currents, as though Neptune played with it like a ball. Extreme danger loomed constantly before their eyes. This evil came upon them because they had a bad and unscrupulous fellow among them, namely Judas. If there was no good fortune in that place, where there were only one bad man and several saints, then how should there be good fortune in an empire or a country where there are many bad men and scarcely a single saint? God the Almighty made human beings from clay, and even if He had constructed them of dung and filth, they could not live a more filthy life than they do now. We consider Esau so evil for having wasted his birthright for a mess of pottage. Nowadays we encounter many thousands who would fritter away eternity for the sake of lesser things. And not only do we frivolously throw away eternity in so many ways, but also our earthly prosperity, for sin is verily a magot that gnaws our earthly well-being to pieces. And just as David cut off Goliath's proud head with his own sword, so

God punishes us with the saber of the enemy, which was wrought by no one else but our own sin and perverted way of living. . . .

What is sin other than a nasty and disgusting graven image that was wrought by our evil and corrupt will? The sinner is pleased by this wild figure and laughs. But mark my words, these gales of laughter will be soon be followed by wails of lamentation. These cheers will soon be followed by tears. This grin will soon be followed by chagrin: *Risus dolore miscebitur & extrema gaudii luctus occupat.*[19] We experienced it sufficiently in the year 1679. Sin carries punishment on its back, like the traveling journeymen their pack. Sin and punishment are surrounded by a single wall. Sin and punishment are bound on a single chain. And wherever sin is welcomed at table, punishment joins her. Just laugh heartily, you voluptuous children of Adam, just dance with impudent feet, like the Israelites around the calf. Just deprive the poor of what belongs to them, like Jezebel. Just bleat like a he-goat, like the two old just judges in Babylon. Just guzzle away with the drunken Holofernes. Just feast constantly with the Sodomites and don't fall behind the rich spendthrift in the splendor of your garments. But don't forget the punishment, which is inevitable; just remember that punishment holds sin by her feet, as Jacob did Esau. And did the violently raging plague then not make us wise? We are about like an organ that never wails except when one strikes it. We cried loudly to God, when he struck us with the poisonous plague. But now, since it has passed, everything is quiet, except that new sins cry to God for new punishment. The she-ass of Balaam stopped when she saw the bared sword of the angel and shall we yet continue hurrying down the street of sinners when God has everywhere shown us the bared sword.

Who brought the Saracens into the Holy Land? Who veered the Vandals into France? Who showed the Moors the way into Spain? Who gave the Lombards access into Italy? Who showed the Muscovites the way into Livonia? Who brought the Turk, this archenemy, into Asia, into Europe, into Hungary? Nobody but sin. In the ABC's *S* is followed by *T*, after sin comes the Turk.

The Turks call us dogs, to our eternal shame. And they can hardly be blamed, for, like a dog who laps up again what he has thrown up, *"Canis redit ad vomitum,"*[20] we eagerly snap after those sins that we had thrown off at the time of the plague and other dangerous uprisings. Why should we be surprised if God takes up his rod again? The Israelites had scarcely sinned when

God punished them with the dire war that King Nebuchadnezzar waged against them. Thus through the mouth of Jeroboam God called that king his servant. Although he was a godless man and an idolatrous tyrant, he nevertheless deserved the name of the servant of God, because through him, as through a servant, God punished the Israelites. Such a servant, such an instrument, such an ambassador is the Turkish tyrant. Perhaps he comes against us, driven not by lust for honor, sicked on us not out of lust for money, not out of lust for blood, but God sends him to punish our sins. He takes up this rod again and throws it into the fire. And tremble in fear, all of you, for the sins that thrive everywhere strengthen this Ottoman archenemy, *"nostris peccatis Barbari fortes siunt* [sic], *nostris vitiis Romanus superatur exercitus, non sua hostes arma, sed nostra eos peccata in nos roborant"* (Saint Jerome, book 1 of *Epitaph*).[21]

Under the reign of King Robert, France was a constant battlefield of native rebellion.[22] The kingdom was desolated by such long dissension, rebellious tumult, and bloody struggles, not unlike the Trojan horse, which carried its own armed enemy in its bowels. This state of things pained King Robert not a little. For this reason he took refuge in God, our Lord, in the city of Orléans. With eyes full of tears he sought most earnestly His divine aid. This passionate prayer soon pierced the clouds, for Christ the Lord Himself appeared to him and spoke to him with this answer: *"Roberte pacem in regno non habebis donec blasphemias & crimina notoria extirpaveris"* (Dauroult, chapter 3).[23] Thus it's hardly necessary to bring forth further arguments, nor to seek further causes, as to why such destructive wars arise, for utterly sufficient is the word of Christ, this divine incarnation of truth, when it declares that great sins are the cause of war. Inasmuch as the Ottoman saber falls upon our throats, thus this bloody impeller, impetus, inducer, inspirer, instigator, inciter, invocator, inaugurator of war is sin, which nowadays can be found in every Christian state and fate, spot and lot.

Translated by Lynne Tatlock

Notes

1. The translation is based on the following German edition: Abraham a Santa Clara, "Auff, Auff ihr Christen, und beschuldiget niemandt anderen wegen

Seventeenth Century German Prose

deß barbarischen Einfalls in euere Länder, als die gar häuffigen Sünden diser Zeit, etc.," in *Auf Auf Ihr Christen,* ed. August Sauer, Wiener Neudrucke, vol. 1 (Vienna, 1883), pp. 27–35. The notes are original.

2. Thomas de Villanueva (1488–1555) was an important preacher and court preacher of Charles V. He had been canonized in 1658.

3. What good does it do to collect an army and amass one's sins, or do we not know that the Turk and these wars are the lash of God? Abraham a Santa Clara offers a slightly different translation in the two following sentences.

4. Melampus was one of the hounds of Actaeon. When Artemis changed Actaeon into a stag he was devoured by his own hounds.

5. According to Pliny's natural history the weasel gives off a fatal odor with which it destroys the basilisk. Oskar von Hovorke and Adolf Krenfeld further report that, according to superstition, the face of the person spit at by a weasel would swell or that person would be blinded and would die. O[skar von Hovorke and A[dolf] Krenfeld, "Wiesel," *Vergleichende Volksmedizin,* 2 vols. (Stuttgart: Strecker and Schröder, 1909).

6. Bishop and doctor of the Catholic Church (ca. 329–79).

7. The entire world having been set at peace.

8. In German the words for sin and the serpent are feminine.

9. Nadab was the son of Jeroboam (1 Kings 14:20, 15:15–26). Baasha killed Nadab and reigned in his stead (1 Kings 15:27–34).

10. Nebuchadnezzar's dream (Daniel 2:31–35).

11. Sin is the magnet of calamity. Whoever does evil will find evil (Italian proverb).

12. Paolo Sarpi (1552–1623), also known as Paulus Venetus or Fra Paolo or Paulus Servita. Venetian historian and politician.

13. Giovanni de' Medici (1475–1521), son of Lorenzo the Magnificent, pope 1513–21. Of course Siena does not lie on the coast. Abraham a Santa Clara seems a bit confused here.

14. St. Jerome wrote the *Vita Hilarionis,* the life of Saint Hilarion who died in 371 in Cypress and lived for many years as a hermit in the desert between Gaza and Egypt.

15. Pierre Gilles (1490–1555), author of natural history and description of Constantinople.

16. *Barroco* (Portuguese): a rough or imperfect pearl. The author may mean to indicate the entire shell here. The term *baroque* derives from this word.

17. October.

18. Matthew 8:23–27. Jesus reproaches his disciples who are frightened by the storm—"Why are you afraid, O men of little faith?"—and calms the sea.

19. Laughter will be mixed with sorrow. The boundary of joy embraces grief.

20. The dog returns to the vomit.

21. The barbarians are strong because of our sins. The Roman army is conquered by means of our faults. It is not the enemy's arms that make him strong against us, but our sins strengthen the enemy against us.

22. Robert II, the Pious (ca. 970–1031), son of Hugh Capet.

23. "Robert, you will not have peace in your kingdom until you root out blasphemies and infamous crimes." Dauroult is Antonius d'Averoult (1553–1614), author of *Remedia spiritualia contra pestem* (Spiritual remedies against the plague).

Philipp Jacob Spener

The Lutheran theologian and prolific writer Philipp Jacob Spener (1635–1705) was born in Upper Alsace, not far from Strasbourg where he began his theological studies. In 1666 he became chief pastor of the Lutheran church in Frankfurt am Main. From 1670 on in addition to his official pastoral duties Spener sponsored the so-called *collegia pietatis,* private meetings for the purpose of cultivating holiness. Initially these meetings were attended by academically trained men who discussed the week's sermon or devotional books that Spener read aloud to them. Later women (who were not allowed to speak) and persons of humbler estate joined the meetings and Bible passages became the topic of the discussions. Spener's idea of little churches within the church, the first of the proposals articulated in *Pia desideria* (1675) and later one of the hallmarks of German pietism, stemmed directly from these *collegia pietatis.* In 1686 Spener was made first court chaplain at the Saxon court in Dresden. His vexed relations with Elector John George III of Saxony probably hastened his departure to assume the rectorship of the Church of St. Nicholas in Berlin in 1696. While in Dresden, Spener, together with August Hermann Francke (1663–1729) and Christian Thomasius (1655–1728), was influential in the founding of the University of Halle (1694). Spener was embroiled in religious controversy until his death in Berlin in 1705.

Spener's *Pia desideria* is considered the most important formulation of the program of German pietism. With the emphasis on the lay priesthood, i.e., the non-university-trained and thus the non-Latin literate, personal religious experience, subjective faith, and new styles of preaching, Spener's religious program necessarily concerns itself with language, i.e., the German vernacular. *Pia desideria* itself exemplifies the plainspoken, yet emotional spiritual language that Spener advocated. Although *Pia desideria* was originally composed as the preface to a new edition of Johann Arndt's popular sermons, the immediate and enthusiastic response throughout Germany encouraged a subsequent separate publication. It consists of a section on the shortcomings of the Lutheran church, a second one on the possibility of reform and a third containing six proposals for reform. The first three proposals are included in the following selection. The remaining three points include a recommendation for kind treatment of the heterodox and unbelievers, a proposal for the reorganization of university theological instruction with more attention to the devotional life, and the advocation of a new style of preaching.

Pia Desideria

or
Heartfelt Desire
for a God-Pleasing Reform
of the True Evangelical Church,
Together with Several Simple Christian Proposals
Looking toward This End

[Part 3]
[Proposals to Correct Conditions in the Church]

1

Thought should be given to a *more extensive use of the Word of God among us.* We know that by nature we have no good in us. If there is to be any good in us, it must be brought about by God. To this end the Word of God is the powerful means, since faith must be enkindled through the gospel, and the law provides the rules for good works and many wonderful impulses to attain them.

The more at home the Word of God is among us, the more we shall bring about faith and its fruits.

It may appear that the Word of God has sufficiently free course among us inasmuch as at various places (as in this city)[1] there is daily or frequent preaching from the pulpit. When we reflect further on the matter, however, we shall find that with respect to this first proposal, more is needed. I do not at all disapprove of the preaching of sermons in which a Christian congregation is instructed by the reading and exposition of a certain text, for I myself do this. But I find that this is not enough. In the first place, we know that "all scripture is inspired by God and profitable for teaching, for reproof, for correction, and for training in righteousness" (II Tim. 3:16). Accordingly *all* scripture, without exception, should be known by the congregation if we are all to receive the necessary benefit. If we put together all the passages of the Bible, which in the course of many years are read to a congregation in one place, they will comprise only a very small part of the Scriptures that have been given to us. The remainder is not heard by the congregation at all, or is heard only insofar as one or another verse is quoted or alluded to in sermons, without, however, offering any understanding of the entire context, which is nevertheless of the greatest importance. In the second place, the people have little opportunity to grasp the meaning of the Scripture except on the basis of those passages that may have been expounded to them, and even less do they have opportunity to become as practiced in them as edification requires. Meanwhile, although solitary reading of the Bible at home is in itself a splendid and praiseworthy thing, it does not accomplish enough for most people.

It should therefore be considered whether the church would not be well advised to introduce the people to Scripture in still other ways than through the customary sermons on the appointed lessons.[2]

This might be done, first of all, by diligent reading of the Holy Scriptures, especially of the New Testament. It would not be difficult for every housefather to keep a Bible, or at least a New Testament, handy and read from it every day or, if he cannot read, to have somebody else read. How necessary and beneficial this would be for all Christians in every station of life was splendidly and effectively demonstrated a century ago by Andrew Hyperius,[3] whose two books on this matter were quickly translated into German by George Nigrinus[4] and, after the little work had become quite unknown, were recently brought to the attention of people again in a new edition put out by Dr. Elias Veyel,[5] my esteemed former fellow student in Strasbourg and my beloved brother in Christ.

Then a second thing would be desirable in order to encourage people to read privately, namely, that where the practice can be introduced the books of the Bible be read one after another, at specified times in the public service, without further comment (unless one wished to add brief summaries). This would be intended for the edification of all, but especially of those who cannot read at all, or cannot read easily or well, or of those who do not own a copy of the Bible.

For a third thing it would perhaps not be inexpedient (and I set this down for further and more mature reflection) to reintroduce the ancient and apostolic kind of church meetings. In addition to our customary services with preaching, other assemblies would also be held in the manner in which Paul describes them in I Corinthians 14:26–40. One person would not rise to preach (although this practice would be continued at other times), but others who have been blessed with gifts and knowledge would also speak and present their pious opinions on the proposed subject to the judgment of the rest, doing all this in such a way as to avoid disorder and strife. This might conveniently be done by having several ministers (in places where a number of them live in a town) meet together or by having several members of a congregation who have a fair knowledge of God or desire to increase their knowledge meet under the leadership of a minister, take up the Holy Scriptures, read aloud from them, and fraternally discuss each verse in order to discover its simple meaning and whatever may be useful for the edification of all. Anybody who is not satisfied with his understanding of a matter should be permitted to express his doubts and seek further explanation. On the other hand, those (including the ministers) who have made more progress should be allowed the freedom to state how they understand each passage. Then all that has been contributed, insofar as it accords with the sense of the Holy Spirit in the Scriptures, should be carefully considered by the rest, especially by the ordained ministers, and applied to the edification of the whole meeting. Everything should be arranged with an eye to the glory of God, to the spiritual growth of the participants, and therefore also to their limitations. Any threat of meddlesomeness, quarrelsomeness, self-seeking, or something else of this sort should be guarded against and tactfully cut off especially by the preachers who retain leadership in these meetings.

Not a little benefit is to be hoped for from such an arrangement. Preachers would learn to know the members of their own congregations and their weakness or growth in doctrine and piety, and a bond of confidence would be established between preachers and people that would serve the best interests of both. At the same time the people would have a splendid opportunity to exercise their diligence with respect to the Word of God and modestly to ask their questions (which they do not always have the courage to discuss with their minister in private) and get answers to them. In a short time they would experience personal growth and would also become capable of giving better religious instruction to their children and servants at home. In the absence of such exercises, sermons that are delivered in continually flowing speech are not always fully and adequately comprehended because there is no time for reflection in between or because, when one does stop to reflect, much of what follows is missed (which does not happen in a discussion). On the other hand, private reading of the Bible or reading in the household, where nobody is present who may from time to time help point out the meaning and purpose of each verse, cannot provide the reader with a sufficient explanation of all that he would like to know. What is lacking in both of these instances (in public preaching and private reading) would be supplied by the proposed exercises. It would not be a great burden either to the preachers or to the people, and much would be done to fulfill the admonition of Paul in Colossians 3:16, "Let the word of Christ dwell in you richly, as you teach and admonish one another in all wisdom, and as you sing psalms and hymns and spiritual songs." In fact, such songs may be used in the proposed meetings for the praise of God and the inspiration of the participants.

This much is certain: the diligent use of the Word of God, which consists not only of listening to sermons but also of reading, meditating, and discussing (Ps. 1:2), must be the chief means for reforming something, whether this occurs in the proposed fashion or in some other appropriate way. The Word of God remains the seed from which all that is good in us must grow. If we succeed in getting the people to seek eagerly and diligently in the book of life for their joy, their spiritual life will be wonderfully strengthened and they will become altogether different people.

What did our sainted Luther seek more ardently than to induce the people to a diligent reading of the Scriptures? He even had some misgivings about allowing his books to be published, lest the people be made more slothful thereby in the reading of the Scriptures. His words in volume 1 of the Altenburg edition of his works read:

> I should gladly have seen all my books forgotten and destroyed, if only for the reason that I am afraid of the example I may give. For I see what benefit it has brought to the church that men have begun to collect many books and great libraries outside and alongside of the Holy Scriptures, and especially have begun to scramble together, without any distinction, all sorts of "fathers," "councils," and "doctors." Not only has good time been wasted and the study of the Scriptures neglected, but the pure understanding of God's Word is lost. . . . It was our intention and our hope when we began to put the Bible into German that there would be less writing and more studying and reading of the Scriptures. For all other writings should point to the Scriptures. . . . Neither fathers nor councils nor we ourselves will do so well, even when our very best is done, as the Holy Scriptures have done—that is to say, as God himself has done. . . . I only ask in all kindness that the man who at this time wishes to have my books will by no means let them be a hindrance to his own study of the Scriptures, etc.[6]

Luther also wrote similar things elsewhere.[7]

One of the principal wrongs by which papal politics became entrenched—the people were kept in ignorance, and hence complete control of their consciences was maintained—was that the papacy prohibited, and insofar as possible continues to prohibit, the reading of the Holy Scriptures. On the other hand, it was one of the major purposes of the Reformation to restore to the people the Word of God, which had lain hidden under the bench (and this Word was the most powerful means by which God blessed his work). So this will be the principal means, now that the church must be put in better condition, whereby the aversion to Scripture that many have may be overcome, neglect of its study be counteracted, and ardent zeal for it awakened.

2

Our frequently mentioned Dr. Luther would suggest another means, which is altogether compatible with the first. This second proposal is *the establishment and diligent exercise of the spiritual priesthood.* Nobody can read Luther's writings with some care without observing how earnestly the sainted man advocated this spiritual priesthood, according to which not only ministers but all Christians are made priests by their Savior, are anointed by the Holy Spirit, and are dedicated to perform spiritual-priestly acts. Peter was not addressing preachers alone when he wrote, "You are a chosen race, a royal priesthood, a holy nation, God's own people, that you may declare the wonderful deeds of Him who called you out of darkness into His marvelous light." Whoever wishes to understand and read at greater length what our Reformer's opinion on this was, and what the spiritual functions are, should read his treatise, addressed to the Bohemians, on how ministers of the church should be chosen and installed, which treatise appears in volume 2 of the Altenburg edition of Luther's works.[8] There one will see how splendidly it is demonstrated that all spiritual functions are open to all Christians without exception. Although the regular and public performance of them is entrusted to ministers appointed for this purpose, the functions may be performed by others in case of emergency. Especially should those things that are unrelated to public acts be done continually by all at home and in everyday life.

Indeed, it was by a special trick of the cursed devil that things were brought to such a pass in the papacy that all these spiritual functions were assigned solely to the clergy (to whom alone the name *spiritual,* which is in actual fact common to all Christians, was therefore arrogantly allotted) and the rest of the Christians were excluded from them, as if it were not proper for laymen diligently to study in the Word of the Lord, much less to instruct, admonish, chastise, and comfort their neighbors, or to do privately what pertains to the ministry publicly, inasmuch as all these things were supposed to belong only to the office of the minister. The consequence has been that the so-called laity has been made slothful in those things that ought to concern it; a terrible ignorance has resulted, and from this, in turn, a disorderly life. On the other hand, members of the so-called spiritual estate could do as they pleased since nobody dared look at their cards or raise the least objection. This presumptuous monopoly of the clergy, alongside the aforementioned prohibition of Bible reading, is one of the principal means by which papal Rome established its power over poor Christians and still preserves it wherever it has opportunity. The papacy could suffer no greater injury than having Luther point out that all Christians have been called to exercise spiritual functions (although not called to the *public* exercise of them, which requires appointment by a congregation with equal right) and that they are not only permitted but, if they wish to be Christians, are obligated to undertake them.

Every Christian is bound not only to offer himself and what he has, his prayer, thanksgiving, good works, alms, etc., but also industriously to study in the Word of the Lord, with the grace that is given him to teach others, especially those under his own roof, to chastise, exhort, convert, and edify them, to observe their life, pray for all, and insofar as possible be concerned about their salvation. If this is first pointed out to the people, they will take better care of themselves and apply themselves to whatever pertains to their own edification and that of their fellowmen. On the other hand, all complacence and sloth derives from the fact that this teaching is not known and practiced. Nobody thinks this has anything to do with him. Everybody imagines that just as he was himself called to his office, business, or trade, and the minister was neither called to such an occupation nor works in it, so the minister alone is called to perform spiritual acts, occupy himself with the Word of God, pray, study, teach, admonish, comfort, chastise, etc., while others should not trouble themselves with such things and, in fact, would be meddling in the minister's business if they had anything to do with them. This is not even to mention that people ought to pay attention to the minister, admonish him fraternally when he neglects something, and in general support him in all his efforts.

No damage will be done to the ministry by a proper use of this priesthood. In fact, one of the principal reasons why the ministry cannot accomplish all that it ought is that it is too weak without the help of the universal priesthood. One man is incapable of doing all that is necessary for the edification of the many persons who are generally entrusted to his pastoral care. However, if the priests do their duty, the minister, as director and oldest brother, has splendid assistance in the performance of his duties and his public and private acts, and thus his burden will not be too heavy.

More consideration ought to be given to how this whole matter, which has hardly been pursued very much since the time of Luther, may not only be made better known to the people (for which purpose the devout sermons of John Vielitz would be very useful)[9] but also be put into more extensive practice. The earlier proposal of an introductory exercise for the reading and understanding of the Scriptures should contribute not a little to this. As for me, I am very confident that if several persons in each congregation can be won for these two activities (a diligent use of the Word of God and a practice of priestly duties), together with such other things as, especially, fraternal admonition and chastisement (which have all but disappeared among us but ought to be earnestly prosecuted, and those preachers who are made to suffer in consequence should be protected as much as possible), a great deal would be gained and accomplished. Afterwards more and more would be achieved, and finally the church would be visibly reformed.

3

Connected with these two proposals is a third: the people must have impressed upon them and must accustom themselves to believing that *it is by no means enough to have knowledge of the Christian faith, for Christianity consists rather of practice.* Our dear Savior repeatedly enjoined love as the real mark of his disciples (John 13:34–35, 15:12; I John 3:10, 18, 4:7–8, 11–13, 21). In his old age dear John (according to the testimony of Jerome in his letter to the Galatians)[10] was accustomed to say hardly anything more to his disciples than "Children, love one another!" His disciples and auditors finally became so annoyed at this endless repetition that they asked him why he was always saying the same thing to them. He replied, "Because it is the Lord's command, and it suffices if this be done." Indeed, love is the whole life of the man who has faith and who through his faith is saved, and his fulfillment of the laws of God consists of love.

If we can therefore awaken a fervent love among our Christians, first toward one another and then toward all men (for these two, brotherly affection and general love, must supplement each other according to II Peter 1:7), and put this love into practice, practically all that we desire will be accomplished. For all the commandments are summed up in love (Rom. 13:9). Accordingly the people are not only to be told this incessantly, and they are not only to have the excellence of neighborly love and, on the other hand, the great danger and harm in the opposing self-love pictured impressively before their eyes (which is done well in the spiritually minded John Arndt's *True Christianity*, IV, ii, 22 *et seq.*),[11] but they must also practice such love. They must become accustomed not to lose sight of any opportunity in which they can render their neighbor a service of love, and yet while performing it they must diligently search their hearts to discover whether they are acting in true love or out of other motives. If they are offended, they should especially be on their guard, not only that they refrain from all vengefulness but also that they give up some of their rights and insistence on them for fear that their hearts may betray them and feelings of hostility may become involved. In fact, they should diligently seek opportunities to do good to their enemies in order that such self-control may hurt the old Adam, who is otherwise inclined to vengeance, and at the same time in order that love may be more deeply implanted in their hearts.

For this purpose, as well as for the sake of Christian growth in general, it may be useful if those who have earnestly resolved to walk in the way of the Lord would enter into a confidential relationship with their confessor or some other judicious and enlightened Christian and would regularly report to him how they live, what opportunities they have had to practice Christian love, and how they have employed or neglected them. This should be done with the intention of discovering what is amiss and securing such an individual's counsel and instruction as to what ought now to be done. There should be firm resolution to follow such advice at all times unless something is expected that is quite clearly contrary to God's will. If there appears to be doubt whether or not one is obligated to do this or that out of love for one's neighbor, it is always better to incline toward doing it rather than leaving it undone.

Translated by Theodore G. Tappert

Notes

1. Frankfurt am Main. Astonishing was the frequency of weekday preaching in German cities during the seventeenth century, when special preachers and series

of sermons were endowed by wealthy benefactors. The notes are based largely on those provided by the translator: Theodore G. Tappert, trans., *Pia Desideria*, by Philip Jacob Spener (Philadelphia: Fortress Press, 1964).

2. Lections of the church year.

3. Andreas Hyperius (1511–64). *De sacrae scripturae lectione ac meditatione quotidiana, omnibus omnium ordinum hominibus christianis perquam necessaria libri II* (Of the reading of and daily meditation on the Holy Scriptures, etc.) (Basel, 1561).

4. Georg Nigrinus (d. 1602). *Ein trewer und Christlicher Rath, Wie man die Heilige Schrifft teglich lesen und betrachten soll* (Faithful and Christian advice, how one ought to read and meditate on the Holy Scriptures). (Mülhausen, 1562).

5. Elias Veyel (1635–1706), Lutheran theologian. The Veyel edition was published under the same title (Ulm, 1672).

6. Martin Luther's (1483–1546) preface in vol. 1 of the Wittenberg edition of his German works (1539).

7. In Luther's *Table Talk*.

8. *De instituendis ministis Ecclesiae ad Clarissimum Senatum Pragensem Bohemiae* (Concerning the ministry, addressed to the Most Illustrious Prague Senate of Bohemia) (1523).

9. Johann Vielitz (d. 1680). *Regale Sacerdotium, Das ist: Die hochnötige und zugleich anmütige heilsame Lehre von dem Geist- und Königlichen Priesterthumb, in dreyen Puncten und Predigten* (Royal priesthood, that is: the highly necessary and at the same time pleasant salvatory teaching of the spiritual and royal priesthood, in three points and sermons) (Quedlinburg, 1640). This series of sermons was republished by Spener in 1671 and again in 1677, the latter edition together with Spener's own treatment of the spiritual priesthood.

10. Jerome, *Commentary on the Epistle to the Galatians*, 3:6.

11. Johann Arndt (1555–1621). *Wahres Christenthum* (True Christianity) (first complete edition 1609) vol. 4, no. 2, pp. 22–38. Arndt's book was said to be next to the Bible the favorite reading of Spener's early years.

Catharina Regina von Greiffenberg

Catharina Regina von Greiffenberg (1633–94) was born in Lower
Austria into a Protestant noble family. In 1629 the Edict of Restitu-
tion of Emperor Ferdinand II expelled all Protestant clergy and
teachers from Austria, leaving the Protestant landed gentry without
a church. Although for the time being the von Greiffenbergs, unlike
many of their peers, remained in Austria, in 1680 Catharina von
Greiffenberg left her homeland forever to settle in Protestant
Nuremberg. Initially educated by her mother, von Greiffenberg
studied Latin, theology, philosophy, history, and science under the
tutelage of her uncle Hans Rudolph. This "true prodigy of our
times" as her friend Sigmund von Birken (1626–81), president of
the Nuremberg Order of Flowers (1662–81), would later call her
was not only scholastically gifted but also deeply religious. She
later described how at age eighteen a light was suddenly kindled
within her, what she called the "Deoglori light." In that moment
she conceived her life's task to spread and praise the glory of God
in word and deed. Her *Spiritual Sonnets, Songs, and Poems* appeared in 1662. In 1664, after much spiritual torment, von Greiffenberg married her much older uncle and former mentor. In 1672
her first volume of meditations on Christ's passion were published,
followed by a second book in 1678 and both parts of a third book
in 1693. In 1676 von Greiffenberg (as "the Brave One") joined
and eventually chaired the literary society, the Lily Guild, that
Philipp von Zesen had founded after the seats in his Rose Guild
had been filled.

Each of the three books of von Greiffenberg's meditations on

the life and death of Christ consists of twelve meditations of vary-
ing length and each of these is introduced by an emblem, a copper
engraving with motto and explicating poem. The meditations
themselves, mixtures of prose and verse, may be seen as further
explication of the emblem, although in point of fact the emblems
were added after the texts had been written. The verses from the
New Testament are loosely quoted from Martin Luther's translation. Meditations on the passion or life of Christ in the form of
sermons, devotions, prayers, with inserted or added proverbs,
poems and songs were popular among both Catholics and Protestants of the seventeenth century, but von Greiffenberg's literary
achievement is unique. The following selection is taken from the
first meditation. There is a version of the story of the woman who
anointed Jesus in each of the Gospels, but von Greiffenberg most
closely follows the text of Mark 14:3–9.

The Most Holy and Most Healing Passion and Death of Jesus Christ. Twelve Devout Meditations: By His Most Ardent Lover and Most Zealous Admirer Catharina Regina von Greiffenberg

A woman had a jar with costly nard water.[1]

It was precious water because it served, as a sign of His incor-
ruptibility, to embalm the Most Precious One in heaven and to
anoint the Immortal One because His death was approaching. The
panacean seed of women did not reject women, refusing to be
served by them. Because he dignified them by Himself being born
of a female person, thus He also found them worthy to be the
witnesses of His death. He wanted to begin His life emerging from
this sex and to end it in its company. He knew that He had caressed
and pressed the ardor of love into them and granted fidelity to
them in particular. Thus he wished to enjoy the noble fruit of this
tree, which His right hand had planted, and to receive the sweet
scent of the love of this truehearted refresher before his suffering,
bitter as gall. Thus he testified that he respected not strength but
gentleness and that he cared more for the intimate ardor of love
than the external ostensible holiness of good works. Although its

weak realization may not correspond to it, it is the melting ardor and desire for doing good that can soften his heart.

She breaks the jar

Over him who founded the feasts of heaven and for the sake of Him who for her and us all breaks the temple of His Holy body. In order to erect the heavenly Jerusalem is this jar broken. She pours the spirits of the balm over Him who has poured the spirit of God over her. She refreshes the bearer of heavenly refreshment. O blissful woman! You who can truly prove your holy desire upon the principal object of love! It would have been no surprise if your heart and insides had melted when you saw this font of the generations before you and had the opportunity to serve Him!

Oh! That this blissful anointing had been granted to me! For love I would have spilled out my life along with the balm. But because I shall not be so fortunate as to live during the time of thy dying, then grant, O sweetest Lord Jesus, that I in my life am mindful of thy death and am prepared to let the jar of my life be broken at whatever moment pleases thee, for thy sake so that thy glory, the costly balm of paradise, be poured through the entire body of thy church.[2] O thou heavenly maker of bliss, let me break the jar of all earthly vanity to pieces, that I may smell the balm of thy wounds. Get you behind me, you bitter world-pleasure, you ash-empty honor, you stone-laden lust for money, as you are the materials from which the jar of vanity was blown! I renounce you so that on that day I cannot be rejected and in the here and now am capable of smelling the poured-out balm of the holy passion.

O thou amiable inamorato! Behold how my heart throbs, how my blood churns, how the spirits flutter, how my innermost being seethes when I contemplate thy sweet fiery passion. How gladly (Oh! Were it in my power and thy will!) would I burst my heart's jar to pour out my sap of love and praise! It hurts me, as milk a mother, and it pains me that I must keep it in. O eternal marvelous wisdom! Anoint my spirit with heavenly influx and angelic effusions. That I may grasp the desire to praise, conceived in my heart, with the power of imagination and draw it upward, and through reason and memory purify, distill and in glorious words of praise resolve it. Oh! Stoutly heat up the spirit with spirit and power that it may become fiery and flaming. Heed not, whether the fragile glass that is my brain burst from it, if only a single glorious droplet of praise is burned out of me.

But, just God, how shall praise from out of the mouth of a sinner please thee? Because I belong among their numbers and yet am desirous of thy glory. Oh! Then purify me of all my sins through thy blood whose spilling I long to glorify. O thou savior of the entire world! Heal my frailties. May thy innocent lamb's patience blot out my impatience! May thy gentle forbearance curb my precipitous haste! May thy unparalleled amicable lover conquer my bitterness and irritability! In short: may all thy virtues swallow all my vices and my hidden faults! Oh! Let me shed the angelic balm of tears of repentance before thee, like Maria, and cast off the diamond-hard jar of my heart that I be not eternally cast out.

But because repentance is a fountain into eternal life, then let me give out the balm of mercy to my poor neighbors. O Jesus! With thy gently trickled-out blood make the little fountain of my good deeds, along with eyes and heart, flow. Because thou didst not spare thy tears for me. You beloved poverty, you incarnate body of my redeemer! Should one not gladly do you good, since He, to whom one ought, with greatest joy, to make all declarations of love, accepts that which is done for Him. Get all hindrances behind me, heavenly transfixer, which hold me back from my duty. Let my hands do that to which they have consigned themselves, namely the highest good, to do all good for the poor.

There is, however, nothing so good that it is not blamed on earth. Here the most wise message of God is called mess—and by those who were disciples of Christ and in His tutelage. Oh! How often are the doings of the Holy Spirit held to be rubbish, out of lack of knowledge. Just as Hannah's heartfelt prayer was deemed drunkenness by the priest Eli.[3] The Lord works in mysterious ways. Good need not always appear to be good. Virtue must sometimes put on the mask of vice, that it may become the more perfect. It is a right noble disgrace to be despised for the sake of hidden virtue. And a magnanimous thing indeed to increase God's honor by letting one's own be decreased. All is well with the person subjected to such evil.

O foolish calculation of reason! How could the water be sold more dearly and given a more worthy poor man than the Most Dear who let himself be sold so cheaply for our good and who was transformed from the most rich to the most poor man in the world?

Let the woman be completely silent: that the eternal Word can speak words on her behalf. He who allowed the many injustices

committed against Himself to go unrefuted could not refrain from defending this woman. His endless goodness enabled Him to bear the ignominious insults to His own honor. But He cannot allow the slightest slight against His Holy ones to go uncontested. He mentioned not how Judas betrayed Him, Peter denied Him, and the Jews wished to hang and kill Him. Do not trouble me! But when this godly woman was assailed, he spoke:
Let this woman alone!
to show that He cared more for His beloved ones than for Himself. For she has done me a good deed.

O glorious advocate! Speak that way also for me when the world assails me! Say the same also for me, my omniscient guardian, leave the woman alone! Why do you trouble her? Yes, Lord Jesus! Thou didst say it, when I was troubled on account of thy inscrutable wondrous ways. Thou didst say it, my sweetest savior, when I was sometimes attacked and persecuted for the sake of heavenly things. Thou didst say it there in that holy place when I on account of thy marvelous ways was once again violently alarmed. Thou, most faithful dear heart, hadst not the heart to leave me, innocent one, unsatisfied. They had to bless against their will, they could not curse because I had thy blessing in my heart. O Jesus, blessed fruit of my heart! Stay forever on my side and say to all of my enemies and adversaries: Let the woman be! Why do you trouble her? How comforted will I wander, when thou lightest my every way with this torch and followest me. But also grant me, O gentlest dispenser of virtue, that I do nothing but what this word of grace draws in its wake. Let all that I think and do be done in and from thee to thy service and infinite glory. Oh! That I could serve thee alone with all human faculties and capacity. Indeed that I might beg of you the power of all the angels, in order to adore you sweetly like the archangels. O almighty Jesus, who has given me such great longing, give me but the slightest power to realize some of it. Oh! That all my thoughts, deeds and poetry writing might empty themselves into thy love and glory, like the rivers into the sea! That I could think of nothing but thy love and thy passion; speak of nothing but of thy wounds and wonders. Write nothing but to thy glory and its exultation, do nothing but what would be the most pleasing and sweetest to thee, O dearest treasure of my soul. Oh, yes! I join my aspirations and operations to strive for the most extreme limit of thy glory, so that thou mightst also say of me: She has done me a good deed!

Translated by Lynne Tatlock

Notes

1. In Germans as in English Mark 14:3 refers to a jar containing an oil or ointment. Greiffenberg, on the other hand, imagines a cologne or toilet water. Although not named in the Gospels, the woman who anointed Jesus has been generally understood to be the repentant sinner Mary Magdalene who was later present at the Crucifixion and at the opening of the empty tomb. For this reason European Christian art has frequently depicted Mary Magdalene holding a jar of ointment.

2. In modern German the "thou" form is used, among other things, to express intimacy and thus family members, close friends, children, and God are addressed as thou. Although Greiffenberg uses the thou form throughout, to use it throughout in the translation is to give the text a quaint sound that it would not have had in the seventeenth century and that with respect to the form of address it still does not have. As a compromise and in order to capture some of the religious ardor expressed by the use of the intimate form, I have, in keeping with the use of thou in the Psalms in the Revised Standard Edition of the English translation of the Bible, used the thou form only when Greiffenberg addresses Jesus.

3. 1 Samuel 1:9–16.

Daniel Casper von Lohenstein

Daniel Casper von Lohenstein (1635–83) was born in Silesia, attended school in Breslau (Wroclaw), and studied law in Leipzig and Tübingen. As was customary for the sons of well-to-do families his studies were followed by several lengthy journeys of education in various European countries. He eventually settled in Breslau to practice law. In the 1660s he began writing and publishing tragedies that were performed by the pupils at local schools. Literary historians often evoke the extravagant, indeed bombastic style of Lohenstein's verse tragedies as quintessentially baroque. In 1670 Lohenstein became the legal representative of the Breslau senate under Christian Hofmann von Hofmannswaldau and in 1675, after having undertaken a diplomatic mission to the Holy Roman Emperor on behalf of Breslau, he was named imperial councillor by Leopold I. He also authored a weighty courtly historical novel, entitled *The Great Field Commander Arminius or Hermann, etc.*, that appeared posthumously (1689–90).

The life of Christian Hofmann von Hofmannswaldau (1617–79) is sketched in fulsome terms in Lohenstein's eulogy, but while Lohenstein waxes eloquent on the subject of Hofmannswaldau's public service, he offers little information about his literary production. Hofmannswaldau's publications consisted, above all, of original poems—erotic and spiritual odes, sonnets, epithalamia, epitaphs and other kinds of occasional poetry, lyrical philosophical discourses—and translations of prose and poetry, notably Giovanni Battista Guarini's (1538–1612) tragicomedy *Pastor Fido*. He also published *Heroic Letters* (1673), twenty-eight invented letters in verse that consist of imaginary exchanges between famous lovers.

Lohenstein's panegyric belongs to the classical tradition of public speeches in praise of a lofty personage or city. In the seventeenth century eulogies for important public figures were not only delivered publicly but also published. They were understood as an exercise in rhetoric to be carefully wrought and polished. Although these eulogies are often highly stylized and sometimes consist principally of fulsome praise instead of biographical data, historians have found them a fruitful source of information on the seventeenth-century mentality, for example, on the perception of illness, the institution of the family, or the ethic of the self-made man. Lohenstein's florid speech in honor of Hofmannswaldau delivers the facts of the *bios* along with ample and revealing commentary. With its elaborate rhetorical figures, rich imagery, classical allusions, and convoluted sentence structure Lohenstein's eulogy exemplifies the high baroque prose style.

Panegyric upon the Burial of
Mr. Christian Hofmann von Hofmannswaldau[1]

Highborn Count of the Holy Roman Empire Semper-Frey,
Highborn and honored Counts,
Most honored Barons
Most noble, noble, stern, reputed, learned, gracious, and honorable
   gentlemen.
As well as highborn, highborn and honored, honored, most noble,
   noble, most honorable and virtuous, gracious and honorable
   ladies.

Great Pan[2] is dead! At the time of Emperor Tiberius a loud voice cried out these words from the isle of Paxos to a passing Egyptian ship's pilot, Thamus, commanding him to convey the news of the death to the Palodian coast. Upon hearing this, Thamus's hair stood on end, and everything on board trembled, especially when an unusual calm forced Thamus to carry out the order at Palodes and a pitiful cry of thousands of mourners answered him from the shore.[3]

Would that God had willed that this voice of grief had only been heard on that passing and long-since decayed Egyptian ship plying the Ionian Sea, and that the ship of state of this city had not been shaken by a Panic horror last April 18! Would that God had willed it, I said, so that I would not now have to raise my voice and cry out from the midst of this honored assembly to the Palodian strand, or rather, to the sighing city of Breslau and cosuffering Silesia: our great Pan is dead! Namely, the late most nobly born Mr. Christian von Hofmannswaldau of Arnolds-Mühle, councillor to the Holy Roman Emperor and king of Hungary and Bohemia, municipal council president[4] of the city of Breslau, as well as manager of the royal castle holding of Namslau.[5]

Let no one be surprised that I should liken this great man to Pan, whom pagan antiquity worshiped, turned into an image of all of nature, and honored with a name that means, so to speak, "everything." . . .[6]

And why shouldn't our Pan be deemed worthy of providing an image of nature as did the son of the Egyptian priest Mercury, who lived only after Moses?[7] Especially when we recall that every man is a map of this great cosmos, a miniature, or, to be more accurate, a larger world than the large world outside him. And that the soul is a precise likeness of almighty God, while its immortality is something so great that neither the star-studded heavens nor the whole of nature can encompass it in their inconceivable scope. Nor should we forget Saint Augustine, who did not hesitate to consider a fly, or even a dot-sized worm, as being a more noble creature than God's almoner, the sun.[8]

Who is more deserving of the name of Pan than the highly esteemed Mr. von Hofmannswaldau, in whom bounteous nature placed all her treasures in the same way that Theodorus, the great creator of the labyrinth of Samos, placed all his artistry in a coach-and-four that a fly could cover because it was so small?[9] Who is more deserving than he who, as the center of our city, incorporated the full scope of all that was good in us? Who is more deserving than he who, as head of the city council, united all salutary advice and arrangements for the community, just as the head of the beast unites all five senses?

Granted, I would be kicking the spokes of the wheel of Divine Providence[10] if I were to attribute the prosperity of our city until now to him alone. If, by doing this, I wished to take away from the fame and merit of those other noble council members, I would affront the modesty of our most humble friend, who gave himself the least credit even when he had done the most. But I know that among the councillors there is no one who would want to compare his achievements to those of the incomparable deceased. The example of Thebes, which was subjugated and unfortunate before and after the leadership of Epaminondas,[11] shows that occasionally a single man is greater than a whole council or a great city, and that a moon can shine more brightly than a thousand stars.

Accordingly, it should now be my duty to praise everything laudable in our most meritorious Pan. For just as Pan was said to be wedded to Echo,[12] so, too, posthumous fame is the consort of virtue, and even death cannot sunder them. Memory is the only good deed that survivors can perform for the meritorious dead, but what is praiseworthy in the deceased is too great, time too short, my tongue too unskilled, my memory too feeble, and my heart too mournful [for me adequately to memorialize him].

I do not know whether I should praise him more for being an honorable man or a loyal citizen or a clever councillor or a God-fearing Christian. I do not know which years of his life are to be preferred to others. For he was a fruitful pomegranate tree, bearing ripe fruit in spring as well as pleasant blossoms in the autumn and thus yielding usefulness and delight at every age.

Pan is said to have been the son of clever Mercury, a god of eloquence, and of chaste Penelope.[13] Deserving of the first name and of our grateful memory is the laudable father of our deceased Pan, the late highborn and stern Mr. Hans Hofmann von Hofmannswaldau, Silesian chamberlain to His Holy Roman Imperial Majesty; deserving of the second name is his beloved mother, the highborn and most virtuous Mistress Anna, née Nagel.

Truly, we must give our noble deceased the same praise Greece accorded Timotheus, namely, that, with his virtues, he overshadowed the fame of his father Konon in the same way that dawn eclipses the stars.[14]

This shadow, however, does not extinguish the fame of his ancestors. A son who puts his forbears in the shade casts far more light on his family than an artful shadow adorning a picture. On the other hand, a son quite unlike his virtuous father scatters the mold of oblivion and the dust of notoriety onto the bright honor of his courageous forefathers. He turns himself, however, into something less than the afterbirth of the mighty camels. For nobility in itself is nothing: when the figure of virtue stands alongside it, it is worth a lot; when it stands alone, it is valueless.

Our buried council president was never a nothing. Even when he was still small in stature, he amounted to a lot. For in his childhood, he learned more in an hour than others in a week, and by himself he learned more than others from their teachers, proving that a grain of natural wit is worth more than a hundred pounds of formal learning. . . .

For reasons outlined here he came to Danzig to Mochinger, the Prussian Plato.[15] From him he learned the wisdom of the world and statesmanship. He learned Italian, French, and Low German[16] as easily as if playing a game, and because of this he made himself as popular with Mochinger as Dion[17] with Plato. With his precocious achievements he demonstrated that even immature pomegranates can bear ripe fruit.

Opitz, the famous Silesian who put German poetry back on its feet,[18] esteemed his company and friendship very highly even then, as if he could foresee that our wise Pan would be worthy of wearing not just one poor spruce wreath, but rather three laurel wreaths, since the German language has him to thank that Spanish, with its reflective plume, Italy with its perspicacious one, and France with its sweet quill are no longer superior to it. For while Opitz followed the classical and foreign writers, our Mr. von Hofmannswaldau led them.

I have no reservations about praising a Breslau council president on account of his profound poetry and to compare him in this respect with Pan, who is said to have invented the sweet-sounding flutes. For the oldest wisdom of the world is entrenched in poetry, and it tainted neither the victory garments of Scipio Africanus, who composed comedies dedicated to Terence,[19] nor the royal purple of Emperor Augustus, who wrote a funeral poem for Drusus, nor that of Tiberius, Titus, and other emperors; it sullied neither the Roman consular axes of Germanicus, who sang the praises of his own victories, nor the golden eagles of his legions.[20] Even Charlemagne is reputed to be the originator of German poetry.[21] Pope Urban VIII[22] demonstrated with his sweet poems that poetry is as honorable an insignium of the highest ranks as honeybees on their coats of arms.[23]

True, being able only to write poetry is tantamount to wearing a garment made only of lace. Wisdom and serious studies must be the base, and poetry the ornamentation, if a learned man is to resemble a Corinthian column.

In order to lay this foundation, our dearly departed traveled via Lübeck and Hamburg to the Netherlands, where all arts relating to war and peace were contesting at that time for primacy. With no less utility than diligence, he acquired a fundament for wisdom in Leyden in thirteen months, under the direction of Salmasius, Voss, Boxhorn, Barlaeus, and Mestertius, wonders of the academic world then gathered in one city.[24]

Because he knew full well that profitable travel is the best school of life, where one can glean something daily from the great Book of the World, after seeing the Netherlands, and in the company of the Count of Fremonville he turned to England, learning the English language there and seeing the most remarkable oddities in Sandwich, Rochester, London, Salisbury, Bristol, Oxford. After this he turned to France, and in Paris he made the acquaintance of the great Grotius, Thuanus, the du Puy brothers, Gothofredus, Petavius, and other prominent people.[25] In this, he observed the good injunction Toxaris gave to the Greek traveler Anacharsis, namely that he should make the acquaintance of Solon. By having seen him, he would have seen everything. For Solon was Athens, indeed, all of Greece.[26] In contrast, in their travels many people only look at splendid palaces, pleasure gardens, unusual fountains, and, in a city of three million souls, seldom meet a single honest man, apart from the riding master, the fencing master, and the dancing instructor.

Nor did it suffice that he took in the greatest part of France and benefited from it. For he knew that the association with foreign peoples, the investigation of other customs, and wisdom made a man like a demigod, in the same way that the gold that had come to the old world from the new had risen in esteem from being an object of the most ignoble contempt to that of the highest praise and had become king of the metals. He traveled via Lyon to Italy, where the knowledge adopted by other peoples is supposed to be indigenous. Genoa, Pisa, and Siena held him fast for a while before he visited Rome, the marvel of the ancient and modern world. There he saw for himself the splendid ruins of time and the traces of the barbarians. Great men built new palaces from the barbarically broken marble and molten ore of antiquity, and by rejuvenating this rubble they strained to vanquish fate, as it were; [Hofmannswaldau], however, edified himself through his relations with Nau-daeus, Holstein, and other highly learned people.[27]

When his friends and he believed himself sufficiently prepared to serve the community—the cleverest people, unlike mushrooms, do not achieve full maturity overnight—he followed his father's injunction and set his course for the Fatherland, but not before familiarizing himself with, and benefiting from, the beauty of Flor-ence, the wisdom of Bologna, the marvels of Ferrara, the cleverness of Venice and the greatness encompassed by the imperial court in Vienna.

Why am I saying he did this for himself, and not for his needy Fatherland, which at this point was consumed by the fires of war and in need of him?[28] For although everything he had read of the world or seen of it piqued his insatiable curiosity, just as it did Emperor Hadrian,[29] and although he was intending to accompany the imperial ambassador, the lord of Greiffenklau, to the Turkish court, his father and important friends got him to observe the thought-provoking teaching of Apollonius: For a wise man, Greece were the world—and for Mr. von Hofmannswaldau, Breslau.

In order to immobilize him they could find no tighter a bond than his union with the most nobly born and honorable and virtu-ous lady Maria, née Webersky.[30] In their long marriage, she and her husband were like two mirrors facing each other, each of whom existed more in the other than in himself, so that now the highly distraught widow, like a turtledove, grieves just as much for what remains of her life as for her husband's death, knowing full well that the fortune and misfortune of loving spouses, like the growth of two adjacent palm trees, derives from the rise or fall of each.

To the same degree that she now sheds tears, we must praise the happiness in this marriage, partly because our dearly departed, who was worthy of even greater good fortune, had to submit to this dangerous choice only once,[31] partly because God, who created marriage while people still retained their innocence, allowed him to be fruitful and see and witness, to his great joy, how both of his sons, who turned out well and were provided for, so laudably followed in the footsteps of their father's virtues. . . .[32]

Our praiseworthy council president did truly love his sons, but the city of Breslau was really his most darling child. He placed it above everything else, his children, and himself, and thus he acted just as did Epaminondas when he reproached the Persian, Diomedon, who wanted to bribe him, saying that all the goods of the world could not hold the scales to the love for one's Fatherland.[33]

Soon after his return, [Hofmannswaldau] clearly demonstrated this love, in addition to his capabilities, by earning the favor of all people and the highest regard of the learned, so that everyone strove to imitate him yet nobody dared to better him on account of envy. After this, he was elected city councillor in the hearts of the citizens, even before fate opened up a position for him for thirty-three years. The popular desire to elect him preceded the time and actual election because, in keeping with his name,[34] he always took pains to excel in courteousness.

In the same way that tigers have their markings, wormwood its bitterness and sloes their acidity, some people come into the world with the mark of peevishness. They marry vain gall, so that they are troublesome, even with their caresses. But our gentle council president, who knew full well that in government one can accomplish more with a grain of love than with a pound of fear, was sweetness itself. He spoke to every citizen as to his equal, and addressed the least important of the common folk as if they were his children. When occasionally his office demanded some delicacy, he gilded and sweetened his rebukes as clever physicians do their bitter pills.

This kindness, like that of Miltiades,[35] took nothing away from his reputation, nor vice versa, just as little as the bitterness of the pomegranate rind takes away from the sweetness of the juice. He combined gravity and sweetness so wonderfully that it is hard to judge whether friends and citizens loved him or respected him more.

This sweetness did not just waft from his lips, or shine from his eyes, but rather, it was anchored in his heart. That is why it can be said of him in praise, as of Atticus,[36] that throughout his life he had no enmity with anyone, and preferred to forget, rather than feel, any injustice done to him, and conceal it, rather than take his revenge. Indeed, throughout his life he intentionally did not insult anybody. The famous statesman of the Pyrenees Peace in Spain, Louis de Haro,[37] boasted he had also never done anything bad to anyone. But in response to this somebody said, "Nor anything good." Only our good council president was that eager to treat everyone well, even those who did not deserve it or who had insulted him, since he knew full well that virtue can no more be stained by the good deeds done for the unworthy than the rays of the sun can be sullied from shining upon stinking manure heaps.

When he helped someone, he attended to his affairs as if to his own, and he was so diligent about the happiness of good friends that he did not pay attention to any disadvantages incurred to himself, gladly bearing, like the balsam tree, any injury, if only others were thereby helped.

Above all, he exerted all his energies in order to give support and encouragement to learned people. He was like a touchstone for all the young people returning from higher schools of education and travels. They submitted to his affable examination and were all the more willing to give an account of their studies because, with a favorable evaluation on his part, they could dare to win the approval of the entire learned world. In a word: because all his exertions were for the city and the muses, he was the communal spring in Breslau, from which the community drew beneficent advice, the troubled, consolation; the learned, good deeds. In truth, the spirit of the Roman Maecenas lived on, as it were, in him. For that reason, all patrons in Breslau should justly be called Hofmannswaldauers in the future.[38]

For as great as his good deeds were, he spent less time remembering them than the person who had benefited from them, or, at most, only for as long as the beneficiary chose to be thankful. Throughout his life, he never forgot those good deeds done for him, no matter how small they were.

And he was the perfect image of Maecenas in that he gave up many advantages that he could have justly accepted with honor in order to satisfy himself solely with his own largess that brought him nothing. For he esteemed the delighting of his soul immeasurably higher than all the chaff that the world makes so much of without producing a grain of substance.

He sought no profit from all his activities other than a good name, as against the enhancement of his wealth. In this respect, he was another Thrasybulus, who, rather than accept the properties offered him by the Militenes,[39] took only two olive branches as a crown, which no one envied because not pride, but rather the love of the citizens, had placed it upon him.

Our good-hearted Mr. von Hofmannswaldau attained his laurels of honor and his reputation for being an enemy of all self-interest no differently, and he could take pride, along with Atticus, that he had never taken interest money from another citizen, nor personally acquired whatever was for sale at the town hall. On the other hand, he also had appropriate good fortune in that no one ever took him to court, nor did he ever have to endure the courts and judges in his own personal affairs.

He demonstrated this excessive benevolence not just to individual citizens but to the whole community right into his thirty-third year of office. . . . Not only was our inestimable council president able to mete out much good to everyone, but his sharp intelligence penetrated to the heart of all dealings, and his diligence surmounted all difficulties. Thus, it was easy for him to lavish his contributions upon the city in the most important matters.

In all these instances he demonstrated a vigorous honesty. The sun moving through the constellation of the ram[40] divided day and night into halves no less equal than the exact correspondence between heart and mouth, word and deed in him. He deserved to be called another Aristides,[41] the happiness of Greece, because of the shrewdness of his counsel, because of his diligence in carrying out this counsel, because of his alertness to all danger and attack, because of his good fortune in his four missives to Our Most Gracious Emperor, and because of his sense of justice in judgments of our city.

Thus, it is no wonder that Mr. von Hofmannswaldau, who loved everyone, was so continuously and completely loved by all the people, even though the love of the people, which at the beginning wants to burn to an ash, generally runs more risk later of freezing rather than burning, and even though amongst the many thousands of people, there can easily be some dishonest ones for whom virtue stinks like the balm that drives vultures away, whereas the putrid carcass of vice attracts them.

This love, however, did not burn just in the earthen pots and hearts of the common people. Indeed, [Hofmannswaldau] attained both prestige and favor with the princes of the land, the great personages of the court, and the highly placed men of the Fatherland because of his gentle honesty and modest intelligence, which are the two most salutary conjurations of the human spirit and which, just like the magnet, also attract the hardest ore. Loredano[42] and other famous foreigners honored him with their letters. Indeed, in his honor France and Italy learned to believe that not all Germans esteemed their writings more for their weight than for their contents, or sold them by the pound.[43] In this, he again resembled Pan, who was revered most in Lyceum and Maenalus.[44] In fact, when he turned himself into a snow white ram, he is said to have had the moon herself for a lover.

[Hofmannswaldau's] loyalty earned him the favor and esteem of two Holy Roman Emperors,[45] and for this reason twenty-two years ago the presently ruling Imperial and Royal Majesty of his own accord selected him to be his councillor. And he rejoiced in receiving several testimonies of the king's pleasure, including one in the period just before his death.

Such was the standing of our council president among men, but it was even better with God, because, unlike most people, but like the leaves of the cedars of Lebanon, he always turned the uppermost reaches of his heart in adoration toward heaven. And because the fear of God is the strongest bond of friendship between God and a pious soul, he was doubtless better loved and more esteemed by God than by people, who mostly cover up their enmity with hypocrisy, just as swans cover up their black flesh with white feathers.

In the past, our most meritorious council president was all of these things; now he is no more. Our great Pan is dead! The light of our vain hope that he would have many more years of life disappeared in the early evening of April 18. After lowering his visible remains, that is, the outer shell of his body, into the belly of the all-consuming black earth, we see just as little of him as Thamus did of Pan. All of Breslau, in truth, moistens his grave with bitter tears and would gladly dig him up again with their nails. But our tears are only the unfruitful victims of melancholy, while our latter desire is but the futile smoke of a great flame of love.

Our Pan, our father, our Solomon is dead! It is true that with him alone death has received a fat hecatomb as a sacrifice.[46] But only his most insignificant aspect is dead, namely that part, the death of which the deceased had long ago foreseen. He is gone, but only from before our eyes. For his example remains a perfect model for all subsequent councillors of Breslau. His merits still live in many thousands of hearts, and all those descendants of Breslau who are not enemies of virtue and do not wish to be guilty of a detestable lack of gratitude must keep alight an inextinguishable memory of him in their chronicles, just as the Arcadians lit an eternal fire to Pan in their temples.

The learned world will heap more tributes upon him in their writings; while alive, however, he desired far fewer of them. I myself hold several tributes to him in my hands, accolades already accorded him many years ago by persons of quality. Indeed, his own literary works, which until now have been withheld from the world not out of malevolence, but out of modesty, serve as indestructible monuments to him, for sharp-witted books are not eaten by worms.

Yet even this life of posthumous fame is a pale echo, a vanishing conceit, which is perhaps appropriate for a dead grandson, but not for the deceased. The pillars of honor are burnt to ashes, the most learned books are lost, most thankful posterity falls silent, just as Erato,[47] the prophetic priestess of Pan in Arcadia, is said to have fallen silent, together with all the pagan spirits of prophecy, on the same day on which most mighty Pan died. And in the opinion of many church fathers that very day was also the day on which Thamus learned of the death of great Pan, and on which the great shepherd of our souls, Christus Jesus, is believed to have died on the cross.

After the voice of mighty God summoned him from this world, our Breslau Pan fell silent on the day that became the last of his earthly, but the first of his eternal life. But because in his Christianity he had inseparably united himself through faith and devotion with the Eternal Word, his soul undoubtedly is among the number of those thousands upon thousands of celestial singers who for all eternity honor, praise, and laud the Lamb who has overcome evil with His blood.[48] And when the thunderous voice of the mighty Judge of the World will raise up the dead and give to those God-fearing a right learned tongue, the now decaying tongue of our dearly departed will be a truly fiery harp of God. His now cold heart will be a lamp of divine love; his heavenly hymns of praise will be more astute than all earthly ones.

That your Excellency the Count, your Graces the counts and barons, and all the illustrious company assembled here wish to confirm, even after his death, their love for the deceased who can no longer respond, and wish to demonstrate their heartfelt sympathy for the highly troubled bereaved by honoring the most noble burial service with their presence today: may the bereaved take this as a genuine sign of their high favor, grace, and esteem, and may they assume a firm obligation to repay this distinction with obedient and most willing service.

Therefore we now close with less melancholy than at the beginning. For we are assured that our heavenly Mr. von Hofmannswaldau has fallen just as little as a star that seems to be falling. We know that in the end our incomparable council president will become greater, like a river that weds the ocean. Now we are taking the roses from his coat of arms[49] and strewing them on his grave. And we are giving the armorial plumes to the learned world, so that it can record with them those deeds that should be engraved in bronze and marble. But while still alive our dearly departed, through his desire and exertions, dedicated the anchor, as a fortifying image of the welfare of the community, to our city hall.

First printed in 1679.

Translated by Linda Feldman,
with Lynne Tatlock

Notes

1. Hofmann von Hofmannswaldau died suddenly on April 18, 1679. Lohenstein's eulogy was read at the funeral on April 30. This note and others pertaining to biographical details were aided by Erwin Rotermund's work on Hofmannswaldau (Erwin Rotermund: *Christian Hofmann von Hofmannswaldau* [Stuttgart: Metzler, 1963]). The translator, Linda Feldman, also suggested several useful notes.

2. In Greek mythology Pan was the Arcadian god of shepherds and flocks. He was normally depicted with goat's feet and was said to have invented the shepherd's pipe. His unexpected appearance inspired "panic" fear or horror. He was the protector of the Athenians at the battle of Marathon (490 B.C.) and consequently a cult was set up in a cave on the north side of the Acropolis. In the course of the panegyric Lohenstein will repeatedly return to the lore surrounding Pan.

3. This opening story concerning the pilot Thamus who heard a mighty voice proclaiming "Pan is dead" is from "De oraculum defectu" (On the obsolescence of oracles) in Plutarch's *Moralia*. The incident is said to take place in the time of Tiberius, the beginning of the Christian era. In the Renaissance the death of Pan was often linked to the birth or the crucifixion of Christ and the coincidence of the two events was thought to mark the end of the old world and the beginning of the new. Lohenstein returns to this allusion at the conclusion of his funeral oration.

4. Praeses.

5. Since the end of World War II Silesia has belonged to Poland. Namslau is now known as Namysłów.

124 ·   *Seventeenth Century German Prose*

6. Through a false etymology—*pan* means "all" or "universe" in Greek—
Pan came to be conceived of as the universal god.

7. Mercury was believed to be the father of Pan. It was further believed that
this same Mercury was worshiped by the Egyptians under the name of Theut or
Thoot. The Egyptian god was thought to have lived around the time of the Trojan
War. Furthermore, the Greeks thought Pan to be one and the same with the Egyptian
god Min.

8. Aurelius Augustinus (354–430), believer in the doctrine of original sin and
predestination, author of *Confessions* and *De Civitate Dei* (The city of God).

9. Theodorus of Samos was a sculptor who, as Lohenstein mentions, built
among other things the labyrinth of Samos. He was also said to have made a statue
of himself out of metal. In one hand he was holding a file and in the other a coach-
and-four. The work was so tiny that a gnat could cover it entirely.

10. Lohenstein alludes here to the then common image of fortune as a woman
holding a wheel. By kicking the spokes of the wheel he means that if he were to
exaggerate Hofmannswaldau's role, he would be blaspheming the divine ordination,
i.e., misrepresenting or interfering with it. Kicking the spokes might also be rendered
as "putting a spoke in the wheel."

11. Epaminondas, also Epaminodas, or Epameinodas (ca. 418–362 B.C.),
greatest Theban statesman and general.

12. Pan was in love with Echo who refused him. He revenged himself by
changing her into a voice that could only repeat the last words spoken to her.

13. According to some lengends Pan was the son of Penelope and Hermes
(Mercury), but Dryops is more commonly identified as his mother.

14. Timotheus: (d. ca. 354 B.C.) Athenian statesman and admiral, son of
Conon, an Athenian admiral (d. ca. 392 B.C.). Timotheus conquered Samos, defeat-
ing the Persians.

15. Johann Mochinger (1603–52), professor of eloquence and later rector at
the academic *Gymnasium* in Danzig (now Gdansk), leading pedagogue of the day.

16. Lohenstein uses the seventeenth-century word for Low German or Low
Saxon, but he may, in fact, mean Dutch. It is impossible to tell for certain from the
context. Dutch would have been a more useful language for the young scholar in
the seventeenth century.

17. Captain from Syracuse who was advised by Plato.

18. Martin Opitz (1597–1639). For further information, see the introduction
to the section on Opitz.

19. Publius Cornelius Scipio Aemilianus Africanus Numantinus. *Scipio the
Younger* (ca. 185–129 B.C.). Scipio was the son of the general Publius Cornelius
Scipio Africanus *(Scipio the Elder)* and like his father defeated Carthage. He was
also interested in the arts and in particular in the culture of Greece. Terence, or
Publius Terentius Aser (185–159 B.C.), was born in Carthage sometime after 185
and became a writer of Latin comedies.

20. Augustus (63 B.C.–A.D. 14), first Roman emperor (27 B.C.–A.D. 14); Nero
Claudius Drusus (38 B.C.–9 B.C.), younger brother of Emperor Tiberius, famous
for battles he led against the Germanic tribes; Tiberius Claudius Nero (42 B.C.–A.D.
37), Roman emperor (14–37); Titus Flavius Sabinus Vespasianus (39–81) Roman
emperor (79–81); Germanicus Caesar (15 B.C.–A.D. 19), son of Drusus and adopted
son of Tiberius, made Roman consul A.D. 12. With the phrase "the Roman consular
axes" Lohenstein refers here to the fasces, bundles of elm or birch rods from which
the head of an axe projected, fastened together by a red strap. They were the
emblem of official authority. The consuls were preceded by twelve fasces.

21. Charlemagne (742–814), Frankish king who was crowned emperor of the
Romans in 800. He was a patron of the arts and collected Germanic poetry. He

also worked on a grammar of the Frankish tongue and invented German names for the months and winds.

22. Pope Urban VIII (1568–1644), pope (1623–44), during the Thirty Years' War.

23. In Egyptian hieroglyphic language, the sign of the bee was a determinative in royal nomenclature, partly by analogy with the monarchic organization of these insects, but more because of the ideas of industry, creative activity, and wealth that are associated with the production of honey. This significance was retained in European heraldry.

24. Salmasius, Latin for Claude de Saumaise (1588–1653), French critic and scholar; Gerardus Johannes Vossius (1577–1649), philologist and polyhistorian; Barlaeus is Kaspar van Baerle (1584–1648), Latin poet, professor of philosophy in Amsterdam; Jacob Mestertius (Maesterius) (1610–58), Dutch scholar of jurisprudence. The reference to a certain Boxhorn remains obscure.

25. Hugo Grotius (1583–1645), famous Dutch writer, historian, theologian, poet, and politician; Thuanus, Latin name of François Auguste de Thou (1607–42), royal librarian; the brothers Pierre and Jacques du Puy, the founders (with de Thou) of the *Académie Putéane;* Gothofredus, probably Jacques Gothofredus (1587–1652), jurist in Paris, learned romanist (the date of death of the German historiographer Jean Philippe Abelin [d. between 1634 and 1637] whose Latin mame was Gothofredus contradicts Rotermund's belief [p. 7] that Abelin was the Gothofredus mentioned here, especially since Rotermund also claims that Lohenstein went to Paris in 1640); Petavius, Latin name of Dénis Petau (1583–1652), French philologist, chronologist, and Catholic theologian.

26. Toxaris was a Scythian philosopher and doctor in the time of Solon (ca. 640–560 B.C.), the Athenian lawgiver and king. Toxaris was reputed to have said, "Anarcharisis was not the first to go to Athens for the sake of instruction." Anacharsis was also a Scythian philosopher whose mother was said to have instilled in him the desire to see Greece.

27. Gabriel Naudaeus (1600–1653), medical scholar; Lucus Holsteinius (1596–1661) philologist.

28. Though Breslau remained relatively untouched by the Thirty Years' War, Silesia suffered greatly.

29. Hadrian (76–138), Roman emperor 117–38.

30. I.e., Maria Webersky von Webertzig.

31. Remarriage was common in the seventeenth century, when disease, war, childbirth, and spousal age differences resulted in high spousal mortality. Socioeconomic considerations tended to encourage the remarriage of the widowed partner as soon as possible.

32. In fact, Lohenstein embellishes the facts by neglecting to remind his listeners that the Hofmannswaldaus lost two other children, a son and a daughter.

33. Epaminondas, see above. Lohenstein's account here appears to be a conflation of two different stories. Diomedon (also Diomedes) was a mythological character, the king of Argos, who fought on the side of the Greeks. He was said to have rebuffed the Persians when they attempted to bribe him.

34. *Hofmann* means courtier.

35. Miltiades (sixth century B.C.), according to legend, the Oracle of Delphi told the Doloncians that they should chose the first person to be their leader who showed them hospitality after they left the temple. This man was the Athenian Miltiades.

36. Titus Pomponius Atticus (109–32 B.C.) acquired great wealth that he generously shared with his friends, one of them being the great orator Cicero.

37. Luis Méndez Haro, duke of Carpio (1598–1661), Spanish statesman re-

sponsible for the Peace of the Pyrenees (1659) under Philipp IV, which brought 150 years of hostilities between France and Spain to an end. The marriage of Louis XIV to Marie Thérèse, the eldest daughter of Philipp V, was a further result of the peace negotiations.

38. The German word for patron, *Mäzen*, is derived from the name Maecenas: Lohenstein's neologism is thus a parallelism.

39. Thrasybulus (fifth century B.C.), Athenian general, powerful and generous ruler of Mileto who, according to one legend, required as his tribute from the Militenes only the grain that was taller than the rest.

40. Aries, the first sign of the Zodiac. The first day of Aries is March 21, the vernal equinox, one of two days when the sun crosses the equator and day and night are of equal length.

41. Athenian statesman and general (died 467 B.C.), who led the Athenians at the battle of Marathon (490 B.C.).

42. Gian Francesco Loredano (1607–61), Venetian city councillor, Italian writer and translator, author of the novel *La Dianea* (1627).

43. This is a reference to the German custom of selling books unbound and by weight at the leading book fairs.

44. Lyceum *(Lykeion)*, a grove dedicated to Lycaeus; Lycaeus was both a name for Pan and Apollo. Pan was supposedly born in Arcadia on the mountain Lycaeus. Maenalus is a mountain in Arcadia sacred to Pan.

45. Leopold I (1640–1705, Holy Roman Emperor 1658–1705) and his father Ferdinand III (1608–57, Holy Roman Emperor 1637–57).

46. A hecatomb literally means an offering of one hundred oxen. It originally referred to a great public sacrifice among the ancient Greeks and Romans but came to be extended to sacrifices of other religions.

47. One of the dryads, nymphs who presided over the woods. Erato was also the name of one of the nine muses, the muse of the lyre. The name comes from the word for love, i.e., because she makes learned persons beloved, or because she notes men's love of learning.

48. Lohenstein refers to Christ here as the *Agnus Dei*, the lamb of God.

49. Hofmannswaldau's father, Johannes Hofmann (1575–1652) had been ennobled by Emperor Matthew in 1612.

Martin Opitz

Martin Opitz, literary theoretician, translator, editor, and poet, was born on December 23, 1597, in the Silesian town of Bunzlau (Boleslawiec). Already during his lifetime he was recognized as the founder of modern German literature. As was customary, Opitz was educated in Latin and early on excelled in writing Latin poetry. Nevertheless, in 1617 he published a Latin treatise in which he maintained that one could and ought to write poetry in German. Seven years later in 1624 he completed his *Book of German Poetics,* the German work that established his reputation as the leading authority on German poetics for nearly a century. He was crowned poet laureate by Emperor Ferdinand II and in 1629, as "the crowned One," became the two-hundredth member of the Fruit-Bearing Society. Opitz collaborated as librettist with Heinrich Schütz to produce the first German opera, *Dafne,* performed in 1627. In that year Opitz was given a patent of nobility with the title "von Boberfeld." Among his famous literary translations are his revised translation of Sir Philip Sidney's pastoral novel *Arcadia* and John Barclay's *Argenis.* Opitz died of the plague in 1639 at the age of forty-two, four years before the Peace of Westphalia.

Pastorale of the Nymph Hercynia (1630) was the first original German pastoral novel. It honors Opitz's patron Count Hans Ulrich von Schaffgotsch. Its setting is a valley in the *Riesengebirge* in the Sudeten area that separates Bohemia from Silesia, near the Schaffgotsch family seat. Lamenting his lost love, Opitz takes a morning walk, composing sonnets all the while. Just as he has finished carving a sonnet into the bark of a tree he unexpectedly meets three learned friends. The four discuss Opitz's sonnet, spiritual and physical love, the infidelity of women, poetic imagination, the value of travel, whereupon they encounter the nymph Hercynia. The selection below is taken from the episode in which Hercynia reveals the secrets of the region, the marvels of nature, and the history of the Schaffgotsch family. The journey into the realm of the nymphs reworks a common motif of European Renaissance literature, as found, for example, in the Cave of Montesinos episode in *Don Quixote*. The mixture of prose and poetry and praise of the author's patron are typical of the pastoral. With his *Hercynia* Opitz attempts to tailor an ancient literary model to a German literary context and, as he explains in his introduction, he seeks in his literary language a compromise between obscure foreign expressions and a purist German.

Pastorale of the Nymph Hercynia

We had almost reached the foot of the snowy mountains when we caught sight of a reclining nymph draped in a finely worked, diaphanous veil, who was leaning with her left arm against a grotto or a cave. She had done up her hair, which was adorned with a green wreath, in a foreign fashion, and under her right hand she held a vessel of the whitest marble, from which the waters of the brook sprang. While we stood there, not just startled at the sudden apparition but in the greatest indecision as to whether we should remain or flee, this most beautiful creature, or rather goddess, began to sing the following verse with a graceful voice:

> You shepherds who have come to see
> The fountain and the hills and trees:
> You shepherds, do not run in fear,
> For as a nymph my place is here.
> This streamlet with its waters flowing
> Helps set the Zacken's[1] course a-growing
> With pristine silver shining bold,
> And in its sands lie wealth and gold.
> Should friend and foe be torn by greed
> When here your flocks can freely feed?

When man first learned to pan for gold,
His teacher dealt him grief untold.
The gods grant favors to those mortals
Whose innocence keeps golden portals
So come, you shepherds, and espy
What no one else can show, but I.

We stood amazed and confounded, and we would have retired
in fright if she had not taken me by the hand with courteous humil-
ity and enjoined the others to follow. When we entered the cave,
we saw nothing but water in front of us, which reared up like a
mountain before her, so that we passed through without getting
wet. We found ourselves then in an almost cool grotto from which
not only all this water flowed, but also other streams that forced
their way through the cliffs from hidden passages and arteries.
"This," she said, "is the starting point of the rivers that water so
many fields, and sustain so many hamlets and cities. This rather
small rivulet"—she pointed to it with her snow white fingers—"is
also a part of the Zacken River that you passed on your way here,
and not far from the mountains it mingles with it. Here on the side
you see the source of the fish-laden clear Bober River, which has
sought its portal in a shadowy forest. From here it twists and turns
its way through hill and dale and, after engulfing the Zacken near
Hirschberg and greeting numerous cities, among them," she said
to me, "your precious, albeit exhausted, fatherland[2]—which is
cherished not just by you but by us nymphs as well—it finally
reaches the frontier of the land of Silesia, surrendering both its
stream and its name to the Oder, the chief and queen of the Silesian
rivers.

"Just as the gold-bearing, wild Katzbach,[3] whose spring wells
up closer to here, does in the vicinity of Parchwitz. Directly above
it, you see the emerging Queis;[4] there, at the side, the plunging
Aupa;[5] and there, where you see the smooth gravel, the Iser have
their sources. Admittedly, we have bestowed little water upon the
latter, but we have granted it many other rich gifts that can com-
pensate for the lack of water."

Out of curiosity I would have begun asking questions, but she read
them on my face. "This great river," she said, "that wells up directly
in front of you with such whirling and bubbling is the Elbe, whose
name derives from its place of birth, the high Alps[6] over us."

As we stood there amazed at these strange feats of nature and watched dumbfounded the inexhaustible flow of waters, almost losing our hearing because of the great rushing and roaring of the welling waters, she passed ahead of us through a white portal that seemed to us to be of marble. And she said, "Look upon that place that is otherwise closed to the eyes of man. In this earthen chamber I spend my time with my sisters Thalia, Arethusa, Cydippe, Opis, and the others."[7] This graceful cavern was round, like the ancient temples, and rather high. All around stood frozen crystal pillars, which extended from the green-covered earth to the ceiling, and which lit up the room with their transparent shimmering. In the midst of them the nymphs, all of them blooming and young of face, sat in a circle upon green carpets and spun and embroidered and sewed on the finest linen, and engaged in the sweetest conversations. At that point one of them was relating how the proud weaver Arachne had challenged Minerva[8] to battle, but because her work had not pleased heaven, she hanged herself and was afterwards changed into a spider, so that she had to toil and weave before the whole world as a warning against presumptuousness. "Whoever wishes to vent his pride on the immortals," said a brunette, who was supposed to be Lycorias (our guide's name, however, was Hercynia),[9] "is repaid with evil." And she told how foolish Midas challenged Apollo with his Pan's pipes and ended up not only with no thanks, but with donkey's ears, a condition that, in keeping with human nature, he wished to hide, and which he forbade his servant to make public. The servant, however, who found it impossible to keep totally silent, went to a marshy spot and entrusted his secret to the reeds, who, when the wind brushed against them, all began to cry, "Midas has donkey's ears!" The nymphs laughed, and another began, "It's probably reeds that learned people write with to disgrace those people in front of the whole world who, with their ill-considered judgments of clever and learned spirits, reveal their similarity to Midas."

Not far from them lay several lutes, violins, and other musical instruments, as well as quivers and arrows that they used when they indulged in pleasure hunting together with the forest goddesses and mountain nymphs. On the wall were different stories, inlaid so artfully with small shells and small stones that when we approached them, we considered them to be nothing less than the work of an Apollo. Among others was the story of how Saturn, who wanted to devour his son Jupiter, was instead given a stone wrapped in swaddling clothes to swallow by the mother, Rhea. Jupiter was reared by Rhea's sisters, the nymphs, and served by an eagle. Right next to it was the story of how other nymphs had brought up Bacchus near Nisa in Asia and how Jupiter had elevated them to the sky out of gratitude and turned them into the Hyades, the beautiful stars that usually presage rain. Somewhere else there was the story of how the nymphs Erato, Pemfredo, and Dino lent Perseus his wings and bag (which, however, was taken away from him by the artists of the celestial pictures,[10] through whose help he was able to cut off the head of the Medusa and finally save Andromeda, the daughter of proud Cassiopeia, from the cruel sea monster). Further, there was the story of how Syrinx, when she fled Pan, was transformed into the flute that Mercury used afterwards, and how other river nymphs were transformed into the Echinadic Isles by an outraged Achelous. And there were other matters that cannot be related here.

"Come further," Hercynia said, "and look at the lodging of Thetis, the immortal mother of the nymphs, when she passes through the hidden corridors of the earth with her seahorses and visits us. In the company of all the other Naiads, whose golden hair flew about their delicate necks and breasts, and whose thinly woven mantles swished about their nude bodies, we passed through a bronze portal and entered a costly room of great length and width. The floor was made of crystal and inlaid with famous stones depicting all kinds of serpents, fishes, and marine marvels so that at first glance we did not trust ourselves to walk upon it. At this, the nymphs all laughed; truly, a sweet sight. On the vaulted ceiling, which was inlaid over and over with lapis lazuli, and through whose two round crystal windows the pleasant day illuminated the whole space from above, it seemed nothing less than as if birds were floating in the clouds of this exquisite work, and nothing was missing, we thought, except their songs. Standing on both sides in equal numbers and at equal intervals were chairs of amber that were alternately red or yellow. In the rear, as well as near the front door, were two gilded altars. On one of them sacrifices were made to the great ocean, on the other to Thetis. Not far from either of them were two wide silver basins or bowls, each held by a silver siren, from which there sprang pleasant fountains that kept aloft a shiny metal ball and played with it. And then they dwindled, only to be swallowed up and cast aloft again. In the middle was a long table of polished stone, at which Thetis usually took food and drink.

"You shepherds," Hercynia began, "we know what heaven and the muses have bestowed on you, and we know how strong the desire for knowledge is within you. So now, while my sisters serve the immortal gods and offer the appropriate sacrifices, let me show you what the pictures and the writings on the walls contain. Be aware," she added, "that everything you have seen until now and will see hereinafter is of indigenous extraction, deposited in this soil, washed in these waters, found, and worked here. The white chalcedony, the black crystal, the violet-brown amethyst, the blue sapphire, the striped jasper, the dark red garnet, the flesh-colored carnallite, the reddish yellow deadly enemy of the hyacinth, the yellowish beryl; the multicolored agate, the yellow topaz, which you see flashing like lightning in the hand of that eagle"—and she pointed to an eagle on the blanket upon which Ganymedes sat— "the brilliant diamond, are all at home here. These pearls, this silver, this gold, can be found, flaming and granular, in seams and quartz, in the rich fields and areas here, not to speak of the tin, copper, iron, glass, and everything else that nature, the handmaid of almighty God and the good mother of people, bears." At this she led us once again to the gates, over which the following verses hung:

You blind men, mortals all, why wander on and on
In both the Indias?[11] Should your soul be forgone
To sate the flesh, your slave? You find but war and strain,
And from your brand-new world you bring a world of pain.
You plow the wild sea and you forget your land,
Seek gold that steels your heart and keep it close at hand,
And yet the blackest Moor scarce finds the diamond bright
The jasper we find bad; the Queis puts pearls to flight.
"Come to me," call the earth and nature, oh so clear.
"And where?" "To what is good," "Why stay?" "You have it
here."

Next to these verses, which were hewn into a black, stone slab, there followed on the one side many stories and pictures of the creation of the world, of the golden, silver, earthen, and finally iron ages,[12] of the giants invading heaven, of the flooding of the earth, everything in the order listed by Hesiod, Apollodorus, Hyginus, and other poets, and particularly the most profound of all the poets in his books of the *Metamorphoses* (for that reason, it is unnecessary to repeat it all here).[13] On the other side there was a map, upon which different mountains, castles, rivers, and fields could be seen. "This," she said, "is the disposition of the local villages, the greatest part of which have long been ruled by the noble Schaffgotsch[14] family, whose history, extending up to today's worthy heroes, you will behold in the following pictures and writings. Their ancient blood, their virtue, their praiseworthy deeds and particularly the tranquil peace that up to now we have enjoyed under them, as if under protective deities, have caused us to raise this monument to them. In order to give you, who are so desirous of investigating old times, a detailed account: know that just as our highland, our Flinzberg and our snow-covered mountains in this area were inhabited by natural, Ur-indigenous Germans—the Marcomanni, the Marsinger and the like—so too they named the Harz or Hercynian Forest, after whom I am named, as well as the Sudeten or Sodoeden mountains. Those people lived there up to the time when the Sarmatian Wends (and not the Vandal peoples) crossed over their Vistula or Weichsel and took over this land and the other. But that something always still remained of the German you can adduce from the fact that the name of Bohemia, which was already famous fifteen hundred years ago and long before the Wends, has not yet been blotted out, just as a part of these mountains remain the Alps or the Elbe and other such places have kept their names until now. If you Germans had been able to record your deeds with the same diligence with which you executed them, or if your bloody wars of hundreds of years ago had not wiped out those people, together with their memory and all artistry, the worthy name of the noble Schoffes (as the family used to be called) and the courage with which they defended the fatherland could be put in more detail before your eyes. In our country, we have taken note of their fame from that time, when our brooks flowed peacefully under their rule and they were the possessors of places that are partly sketched here."

After this she moved on and said, "This man, whom you see standing in his full cuirass, is the free and worthy hero Gothardt, or, as they liked to call the old people back then, Gotsche Schoff, who handed down his name to his children's children, along with great praise and acclaim, of which everyone is justly proud. We know nothing more than that his father's name was Ulrich Schoff, and that for almost three hundred years his line had been the burgrave of Kinsberg."

"Noble nymph," I began, "if a man may ask a goddess a question: why is his right fist depicted as being bloody?"

"Near Erfurt," she answered, "he distinguished himself in a sortie so well that the general, Emperor Charles IV, had him summoned immediately in order to commend him personally and to offer his hand. The former [Gotsche Schoff], however, who had just returned from scourging the enemy, wiped off his bloody fingers on his shining armor, and thus honored the emperor with this worthy fist. The emperor then knighted him and adorned his most noble coat of arms with four red stripes so that his descendants might not only know how their nobility, which in days of yore had stemmed from deeds of valor, had been augmented by more such splendid deeds, but also so that they might be heartened and encouraged to similar accomplishments by this sign as if by a live spark."

"And where does the green tree in this coat of arms come from?" I asked.

"Victorious Bolco," she answered, "the duke of Schweidnitz and Jauer, whose niece was the wife of Charles IV, loved the aforementioned Gothardt Schoff, his arms bearer, so much because of his praiseworthy behavior and many outstanding virtues that he honored him with princely grace, bestowing on him and his descendants in perpetuity the Riesenberg near here, the swelling Iser together with the surrounding Bohemian Woods, the mountain property Schmiedeberg together with all that belonged to it, as well as the fortress or mountain castle Kinast. For that reason the pine tree, or Kinast, has been portrayed on the ancestral coat of arms. This same emperor gave him Friedeberg, which you see on the map near the mountains close to the Queis, as well as the city of Greiffenberg, which is so dear to the celestial weaver Minerva, and the mountain fortress of Greiffenstein, built by Count Boleslaus, the son of Saint Hedwig's son. We see, then, that the possession of these places is a pure reward for virtue."

Translated by Linda Feldman

Notes

1. Zacken River: a small river in Lower Silesia, which empties into the Bober River at Hirschberg. The notes are those of the translator.
2. Opitz was born in Bunzlau, on the Bober River. It was heavily damaged during the Thirty Years' War of 1618–48.

3. The Katzbach is a tributary of the Oder River, which merges with it below Parchwitz in Lower Silesia.

4. The Queis is a left-bank tributary of the Bober River.

5. The Aupa is a left-bank tributary of the Elbe in Bohemia (Czechoslovakia).

6. The high mountains being referred to are not the Alps, but the Riesengebirge of Lower Silesia.

7. Thalia, one of the nine muses, is a Greek mythological figure representing the muse of comedy and pastoral poetry. In Greek mythology Arethusa was a woodland nymph who was changed into a stream by Artemis so that she could escape her pursuer, Alpheus. The name Cydippe is borrowed from a number of mythological figures. Opis was an attendant of Diana.

8. Minerva was known in Greece as Athena. In her role as the Greek goddess of Knowledge, Minerva presided over many useful and decorative arts, including weaving, needlework, and spinning. Arachne, a mere mortal, possessed such superb weaving skills that the wood nymphs would leave their groves and fountains to come and watch her at work. Her excessive and inappropriate pride in her ability, as this myth illustrates, proved to be her undoing.

9. In this text, the wood nymph of the Hercynian Forest in Lower Silesia. The name is of Celtic origin, deriving from Fergunna.

10. I.e., the divine creators of the constellations.

11. A reference to the East Indies and West Indies, i.e., North America.

12. There was a common belief in the post-Renaissance period that the end of the world would come after the iron age—the last of four ages—was over. The apocalyptic mentality of the seventh century considered the end of the world imminent.

13. The author of the *Metamorphoses* is Ovid, whose importance to Opitz's aesthetics is manifest in the frequent direct and indirect references of Ovid's works.

14. A Frankish noble family, first documented in 1174. It split into Bohemian and Silesian wings. A member of the latter, Hans Ulrich Schaffgotsch, was Opitz's patron.

Johann Michael Moscherosch

Johann Michael Moscherosch (1601–69) was born near Strasbourg where he attended both school and university. In 1624 he undertook a two-year educational journey, after which he became tutor for the sons of Count Johann Philipp II of Leiningen. In 1630 he acquired a post with the Lutheran Imperial Count Peter Ernst von Kriechingen and Püttingen. Two years later he lost half of his property to plundering French soldiers, the first of the many vicissitudes of war he was to suffer. In 1640 the first edition of his *Visions of Philander von Sittewalt* appeared, followed by four more expanded and revised editions (1642, 1643, 1644, 1650). Moscherosch continued to revise his *Visions* until 1666. In 1645 he became a member of the Fruit-Bearing Society under the title "the Dreaming One." His other well-known work *Insomnis cura parentum: Christian Bequest; or The Appropriate Care of a Loyal Father*, an educational tract, containing an introduction addressed to his third wife and written for both his sons and daughters, appeared in 1643. Moscherosch married three times and fathered many children. Not surprisingly his material existence was precarious up to the time of his death; his employment was unsteady and he could not live from his writing, although he briefly attempted to do so.

With his *Visions* Moscherosch initially set out simply to translate and somewhat rework the *Dreams* (1627) of Don Francisco Gómez de Quevedo y Villegas (1580–1645). The first of the visions are reasonably faithful to the original, but subsequent visions and later editions not only continually rework the language, making it more German, but add new material. They thus represent a significant departure from Quevedo that is keyed to the German historical-cultural context. The satirical visions hold a mirror up to the world with the intention not only of pointing out its errors but of demonstrating how it ought to be. The following selection from the edition of 1642 is not only characteristic of the author's colorful and learned language but articulates the poetics of satire and the politics of language common in the German-speaking world of the time. Although it is presented as an addendum, Moscherosch's "German Supplement" resembles the introduction, nearly ubiquitous in seventeenth-century novels, that served the author/publisher as a forum in which to anticipate and defend against potential criticism. Like these introductions Moscherosch's "Supplement" is a key source of information on the poetics of prose fiction in the seventeenth century.

MARVELOUS AND TRUE VISIONS OF PHILANDER VON SITTEWALT IN WHICH THE NATURE OF THE ENTIRE WORLD, THE ACTIONS OF ALL PEOPLE ARE CLOTHED IN THEIR NATURAL COLORS OF VANITY, VIOLENCE, HYPOCRISY, FOLLY: DISPLAYED PUBLICLY AS IF IN A MIRROR AND SEEN BY MANY. IMPRINTED FOR THE SECOND TIME, CHECKED, EXPANDED, IMPROVED BY PHILANDER HIMSELF.[1]

Philander's German Supplement [2]

Dear German reader. Just as nothing urges the pious to do good more than the love of virtue (for where there is virtue, the reward follows automatically), so nothing keeps the wicked from evil better than fear of punishment.

For those who are given to vice and indulge in evil will find the final reckoning just as dangerous and bitter as their folly initially seemed to them pleasant and sweet.

To be sure, these people know of virtue and the good, but in no way other than by word of mouth. They practice virtue in nothing but a superficial way, and they adorn themselves with it and extort great respect and holy fear from others. But nevertheless the paint can't last any longer than the moment when, through the dispensation of the Most High, an unexpected gust of wind blows the facade away, the scoundrel is revealed and bedizened hypocrisy can be recognized by those who love honor.

To be sure, a simpleton finds it difficult to distinguish this finery and false paint from the truth. The single reliable touchstone, the plumb line according to which one can measure the substance of men, is *the word of God.*

Thus it comes to pass: because the godless will not recognize their wicked ways, will not see their monstrousness, will not hear anything of punishment, they flee and fear the holy word of God and all that which belongs to spiritual medicine as the devil flees the cross, like a headstrong horse that one can subdue only after one has lured it with caresses and whistles into a stall with hobbles and thereafter, binding it on all fours, held it fast.

A wanton desperate disease, since one not only despises all curative means but violently pushes them away from himself.

Nevertheless, if the conscientious doctor doesn't want the infected person to perish helplessly, but rather that he take the bitter medicine, he must coat the bitter pills with gold and silver, prepare the heartbreaking little drink with sugar and cinnamon so that both take on a more pleasant appearance and acquire a sweeter taste.

Noble truth is to all human beings a distasteful medicine. There are few who can swallow it uncoated and unsweetened, who can chew it without wrinkling their noses and feeling nausea. Who wouldn't become impatient? Or who would listen gladly while someone points out all his faults to him? The peasants won't stand for it—not to mention the lords—unless it occurs by imagining invented characters as in a fairy tale. Just as long as one doesn't call *them* by name, but says it about someone else, then they don't find it repugnant when one seeks out and punishes vice.

Thus one must mask and disguise noble truth if one wants it to come through without peril. One must protect and accompany it with poesy. Indeed (to say how it is in and of itself) one must in many places conceal it within a courteous lie if it is to be accepted and preserved. Those are the gilt, sweetened bitter medicines.

These visions and tales are of such a kind: in the beginning they were not only written among the endless bloody screaming and shouting of soldiers and sent overland with the uncertain mail, but also printed in great haste and, because of my absence during the proofreading, were rather neglected.[3] Therefore, since too much haste is never without harm and premature birth is not without deformity, I have by special request looked them over and now wish to present them to you for the second time. He who has sense can, without my reminding him, adequately recognize what I have done this time.

We are dangerously and mortally debased in our corrupted nature, but we don't want to listen to advice or be helped. We avoid the medicine, we don't want to hear or read anything about it, for if we heard or read it we would be ashamed of it and would have to turn away from damnable folly. And since we, like recalcitrant horses, pull away and balk, I have sweetened, covered, and gilded the hated medicine of bitter truth with such jesting and joking (which one would rather hear) so that the nausea and repulsion the needy patient feels are removed from him, and so that during the funny talk he gets so much in his body that his stomach, which is coated with the gall of roguery and the slime of hypocrisy, is cleansed, and the evil hot blood of violence and thievery is purified and driven out without him noticing, as it were.

Seria sic discentem inter ridenda juuabunt.[4]

We are so peevishly and so very foolishly sick that sometimes, when the doctor can't behave as foolishly as our own folly, we can't believe that he is skilled enough to help us.

A certain arch-fantastic had so firmly convinced himself that he was a ghost, that he would neither eat nor drink nor dress himself nor frequent human society. Not a single doctor knew a means of helping him; for the fantastic's belief that spirits don't eat or drink was so strong that it was to be feared that he would starve to death.[5] Finally, an experienced and wise doctor came along and used a different trick: he dressed himself and two other colleagues up in white linen clothes as dead spirits. They went by night with lights into his chamber, sat down together, whispered together and acted as if they were true ghosts. Finally, when they got to the sick man who had watched them for a good while and he asked them who they were and what they wanted, the doctor answered that they were ghosts who roamed about at night with lanterns. The sick man, upon hearing that, replied that he also had been a ghost for some time and if they wouldn't mind he would like to join their company. The doctor wanted to resist him a little and knew how to comport himself in speaking and gestures so that it finally seemed to the sick man that his companions were more like the spirits than he himself.

When the doctor had just about accustomed the sick man to the company, he told the others to bring him something to eat and drink. This amazed the sick man since, as far as he knew, spirits neither ate nor drank. "I would be sorry to hear that," said the doctor. "I've been a spirit for many years and have traveled in many lands. Who would have forced it on me if I hadn't eaten? Wherever I was I always observed that the spirits ate and drank at night together and amused themselves." Thus he managed to get the sick man to begin taking some food. And thus they did the same the second and third night and so on until the crazy man was eventually cured of the foolish sickness by the wise doctor.

And that is the purpose of this work. Certainly the noble and learned Warmund von der Tannen set this forth and demonstrated it with courteous words in the introduction.[6] And if there hadn't been other things to make you mindful of it in this second edition this superfluous explanation wouldn't have been necessary.

By nature I find lots of laughter repugnant; I also hate long faces. Farces and foolish company horrify me. But there is a time for jest. This physician sometimes frowned, sometimes laughed and had amazing dealings with his patient, telling him this and that until he won him over and finally imperceptibly brought him to health. Use whatever works as long as it is not contrary to God.

An unfriendly idiot, who initially imagined from these visions and thought to say in his praise that Philander must surely be a droll fellow, found himself mistaken in his opinions when he spoke with me. For many years such joy and delight have been stretched very thin with me on account of the incredible affliction I have suffered. Thus whenever I want to laugh I can hardly do so without thinking of misfortune and the evil times, and I have to temper my joy with a sigh. I laugh too, but not more than is my portion, as if Portia were my sister and Cato my father.[7] And when I joke it's, above all, to tell someone with laughter what I otherwise couldn't tell him. Official duties that must be conducted with proper gravity are to be exempted from all this.

The highly learned Mr. Konrad von Rittershausen,[8] etc., writes of the equally learned Mr. Willibald Pirckheimer, etc., *vir ille non solum, ubi opus erat, grauis & seuerus; verum etiam in loco & opportune jucundus, comis, hilaris, jocosus.*[9] (He was not there only when it was a matter of need, gravity, and seriousness, but also when the time and place demanded that he be friendly, funny, joyful, and amusing).

If it was praiseworthy of such an exalted person, it can't be blameworthy of me—without trying to exalt myself with this comparison—if I, dutiful and serious in my actions, joke—but of course without provoking anger and scandal—in my writing.

Heavens, how would it have suited if I had told and written these visions, in which mankind commits such great folly and acts so silly, with a sour face?

If I wanted to describe an ass and said that he dragged along behind him on two little wheels a sword four ells long in a leather holster an ell wide that hung down below the knee and that he, the churl, came mincing in on an equally long cudgel on all fours, what sense would that make?

If I wanted to describe an upright, honest, God-, honor-, and Fatherland-loving German and I said, He was raised every month in a different cheese-shaped hut, rattled in on tub-wide cow-footed high-heeled shoes and boots, had an Italian head, a Spanish beard, a Greek heart, a Dutch soul, Hebrew hands, English feet, and a French belly, how would that suit?

Truly the wise man says: If a painter painted a fool and gave him the form and color of a clever person, that wouldn't be a masterpiece. He is a master who paints a fool most foolishly.

And that is one of the reasons why I interlard these visions with Greek and Italian, with Latin verses and words here and there, something I would ordinarily properly criticize in a native German. Our fashionable virtues are to be sketched and painted in no other way than with fashionable colors.[10] Otherwise, in my opinion, we have paid homage long enough to foreign tongues.

The folly of many Germans is pitiful. I think that if one were to open up the heart of a little fashion-crazy German—there are plenty of those who are ashamed of their own Fatherland—and would examine it, one would see that ⅝ of it is French, ⅛ Spanish, ⅛ Italian, and not even ⅛ of it would be found to be German.

It is time, indeed high time, for two splendid loyal patriots, the noble, highly intelligent, most courteous Georg Philipp Harsdörffer of Nuremberg and the highly learned, industrious, most witty Justus Georgius Schottel of Einbeck,[11] to step forward and time for their ill-bred compatriots to be made mindful of their duty and natural debt toward the Fatherland. Truly without their loyal help a large part, indeed the pièce de résistance of our German heroic language, the best of it, would have lagged behind. May God bless their work for the good of our dear Fatherland and make them more popular. For he who writes this way does not merely brood over paltry things but promotes the main thing in and of itself and needs not fear envy. Rather, he has truly conquered Master Know-It-All with all his army.

And oh, eternal fame and praise to the princes, lords, and authorities who do not only shine upon these heroic exercises with their grace and favor, but also with whose means the work can actually be mercifully continued.

The times and the years destroy all things. All things pass and fall into oblivion and we think of them no more. The quill alone, the noble quill survives, and its yield remains as long as the earth endures. Princes and lords can make of a poor man an exceedingly wealthy one, but misfortune, thieves, and plundering soldiers can take everything away from him again. Thus in a few years such riches, wherever they may have landed, are forgotten. The pen makes a person live and be loved as long as heaven and earth do not perish. That is, I reveal in writing that person's generosity and merciful deeds and what good he did for me here in this place or rather for our common Fatherland, so that as far away as India, indeed, at the end of the world, one may read and praise him. Indeed the eternal reward will not fail to come after our time on earth. Princes and lords are nothing after their deaths if the pen is not willing; and everything that they are after life they have from the pen and those who wield it. For what one inscribes abides. That which is spent on the liberal arts is not lost. It yields fruit that sprouts eternally, blooms eternally, ripens eternally, is enjoyed eternally: *quod in literas confertur Immortale est.*[12]

> They who with their diligence and parts
> Do practice the liberal arts
> Which language and elegance give;
> Until the earth we cherish
> Itself in flames does perish
> They shall in language and arts live.

But

They who prefer another
To the language of their mother
They suffer retaliation,
All kinds of deprivation
They must yield their goods to a foreign land
When they otherwise could have a free hand.

רי למביז:[13]

Translated by Lynne Tatlock

Notes

1. The text has been translated from Wolfgang Harms's German edition, Johann Michael Moscherosch, *Wunderliche und Wahrhafftige Gesichte Philanders von Sittewalt,* ed. Wolfgang Harms (Stuttgart: Philipp Reclam, 1986). The notes and introduction are based in part on Harms's notes and afterword. Sittewalt is an anagram of Moscherosch's birthplace Wilstädt (Wilstaett).

2. The "German Supplement" follows the Latin epilogue to the first part of the second edition of the *Visions* of Philander von Sittewalt.

3. This relates directly to Moscherosch's circumstances in Finstingen from 1636 to 1642 where he began writing the *Visions.*

4. Serious things will thus under cheerfulness please the learning person.

5. The man's idée fixe is somewhat reminiscent of Don Quixote's beliefs about knights-errant (pt. 1, ch. 20): since knights-errant do not eat regularly in books of chivalry, Don Quixote concludes that they can go for weeks at a time without food and he himself is prepared to act accordingly.

6. Jesaias Rompler von Löwenhalt bore this name as member of the Upright Society of the Pine Tree, a language society that was founded in Strasbourg in 1633. The introduction contains a poem in rhymed couplets signed "Wahrmund [sic] von der Tannen" that speaks of the didactic aims of the book.

7. Portia (d. 43 B.C.), Cato's daughter and wife of Brutus, a passionate republican who according to legend committed suicide after her husband's downfall. Marcus Porcius Cato (d. 46 B.C.), a passionate republican who sided with Pompey against Caesar and committed suicide when the republican cause was lost. Cato is a model for Moscherosch. Cato's son fell in the battle of Philippi.

8. Konrad von Rittershausen (1560–1613), philologist and important judicial scholar at the university in Altdorf (near Nuremberg).

9. "That man was not only serious and sober when it was necessary but he was also joyful, pleasant, happy, good-humored as the situation required." The following sentence in the text more or less translates the Latin. Willibald Pirckheimer (1470–1530), Nuremberg humanist.

10. I.e., Moscherosch himself will have a chance to show off his own knowledge of foreign tongues and cultures while criticizing the Germans for aping foreigners.

11. Georg Philipp Harsdörffer (1607–58), author of among other things *Conversational Games for Women* (pt. 1, 1641); Justus Georg Schottel [a.k.a. Schottelius] (1612–76), tutor at the court of Wolfenbüttel and author of poetological works.

12. What is brought together in literature is immortal.

13. Daj la-merin (Enough for the experts, a formal closing).

Christian Weise

Christian Weise (1642–1708) studied in Leipzig and taught at the *Gymnasium* in the Saxon town of Weissenfels. In 1678 he became the rector of the *Gymnasium* in Zittau, the town of his birth. He authored countless school plays that were performed by pupils throughout Saxony as well as literary treatises, an essay touting newspapers, practical guides for social success, and occasional poetry. His *Short Report on the Political Nibbler, Namely How Such Books Should Be Read* (1680) defends the increasingly popular prose genre, the novel, against its detractors and explains with the aid of the *Affektenlehre* (teaching of emotions) how effective novels are to be written. The *Affektenlehre* assumes that certain emotions are common to all human beings. Weise cites four of these to which the novel can powerfully appeal: the desire for good fortune, the desire to know (curiosity), the desire to find fault in others, and the desire to act as judge and thus to enjoy the rewards or punishment meted out to others. Weise himself wrote three novels: *The Three Most Awful Arch-Fools in the Entire World* (1672), *The Three Cleverest People in the Entire World* (1675), and *The Political Nibbler* (1678). These works have been termed *political novels* insofar as their purpose is to instruct the reader in politic and polite social behavior, the behavior appropriate to the ambitious bourgeois in the absolutist state. Weise's works unleashed a vogue as reflected by such curious titles as *The Political Stockfish, The Political Mousetrap,* and *The Political Chimney Sweep.*

The following selection includes two chapters from the *Most Awful Arch-Fools.* The premise of Weise's novel is that Florindo, in order to secure his inheritance, must travel throughout the world in search of the three greatest fools who are then to be painted and hung in the family castle. Under the guidance of his tutor Gelanor, and, accompanied by Eurylas, the steward, and a painter, he sets out on an educational journey during which he meets a series of persons who exhibit various kinds of foolish behaviors. And neither he nor his traveling companions are themselves entirely free from folly. Untimately we learn that the most awful fools are those who jeopardize eternal salvation for the sake of temporal things, those who ruin their health, and those who detroy their good names.

The Three Most Awful Arch-Fools in the Entire World

Chapter 11

The others agreed, and insofar as the old superstitions are still powerful, there is no doubt that the ears of the honorable bungler must have burned. While they were talking, a fellow came and asked if anyone in the group needed a secretary. Gelanor, who in the past had often been in need of such services, took him to his quarters and told him that, as a test, he should compose a letter (for he was more than a copier)[1] paying compliments to a good friend who had recently married, and offering apologies at not being able to attend the celebration; as compensation, his friend was to accept a modest present. In a flash, the secretary was hunched over the inkwell, and within an hour and a half he had composed the following gorgeous letter:

My most gentle and perfectly loving Friend:
    I have learned that your youth, so suddenly desirous of pleasure, has been caught up in the gleaming and eye-pleasing laugh of most lovely Fenus,[2] and so I have left your most praiseworthy letter of invitation near the daylighter,[3] so that the lights of my head[4] do not lose sight of the thought of the imminent merrymaking. Before the torch of heaven[5] promenades many times around the zodiac, the sweetness of most amiable Libinne,[6] welling up to the surface, will refreshingly fill your life with bliss. And even Zizero [Cicero]

himself would have to fall silent, and appropriate words of congratulations would fail Fergil [Virgil] and Horaz [Horace] as well as Ofid [Ovid]. Given these little facts, I should be silent, so as not to expose, in comparison with the eloquence befitting the heroic language, my all too artless and apparently none-too-eloquent writing skills, nor reveal, to speak more reasonably, the defects of my oblivious spirit. In the meantime, the impatience of the eagerly rising inclinations of my heart is so great that, having decided to record with all its shortcomings the lack of words worthy enough to direct at the heaven of eternity, and begging to be excused for my lack of ability, and hoping to be granted the privilege of your favor, I wish to commend myself, with constantly and unwaveringly increasing readiness to serve

my heart's ruler, as
his faithful and obedient servant
N. N.

Penned hastily on the
10th of the Month of Roses[7]
in the year of our Lord 1656

At the very bottom was written: "Christoff Ziriacks[8] Fogelbauer, certified freeman, and confirmed arch-regal and public clerk."

Gelanor read through the letter and did not know what to make of it. He asked the honorable little Ziriacks what he had intended with these confused antics, and why he had so wretchedly spoiled the whole style of writing. The clerk was not slow to respond. "It must be deplored," he said, "that this art has so many detractors. We ought to thank heaven with folded hands that now, thanks to their indescribably great exertions, many distinguished men have helped the heroic German language back to its former immaculateness. And these fine men reap for their bitter labor nothing but mockery and contempt. Yet the final outcome is in the hands of gray eternity.

"Does my lord," he continued, "believe that I write confusedly?" But no!: the clerk said he looked only at the new books, and reflected upon the difference between Bad German and High German. He maintained he turned only to the writings of the many world-famous poets and thought of how diligently they had acted in mustering out impure words from the heroic language, creating in their stead beautiful, pure, and natural ones. "Why," he asked, "should I bestow upon the Latin authors the honor of saying *Fenster* in an effort to please them? I prefer to invent the German word *Tageleuchter* [daylighter]. And if somebody asks me what a daylighter is called at night, my response is still a daylighter, just as a nightgown is still called a nightgown by day, and your Sunday best is still called your Sunday best during the week. And the same applies to other words. Moreover, if someone is surprised at the new spelling, to him I say: he does not yet understand German. C is not a German letter, nor is V, nor is Y, and the same goes for Q. Why should I write incorrectly when I now know better? Even assuming that the custom had gone the other way, it does not follow that the multitude of the erring would therefore have to do the right thing."⁹

Gelanor listened very patiently as the good bungler wallowed in his foolishness. Finally he began, as follows: "My dear young man is one of those who wants to pull his fatherland back up on its feet. Oh, come to your senses, and don't be taken in so much by this silliness. What you just claimed is written in High German is so lofty that, truly, no goat could ever lick it away. But this is not the danger.

"High German must be understandable and must not go against the nature of the language itself. Moreover, could any vanity be greater than imagining that one word is better than another? A word is a word, that is, a mere sound that means nothing in itself, and that only becomes linked to a meaning after usage and custom confirm it. Therefore, one must allow custom to predominate. A table is called a table because it was liked and used this way by the Germans of the past. And likewise a window, a pistol, an organ, etc., came to be called as they now are by present-day Germans.

"I also have to ask: Isn't the sole purpose of all languages to enable people to understand each other? Now, no one will deny that the very words that you are abolishing are better understood by people than your new tomfoolery. Let's take an example. What if a soldier wanted to called his *lieutenant* a *place-holder,* and his *quartermaster* a *living-and accommodation master?* Or if someone wanted to have the *pistols* and asked for the *riding-puffers?* Or if he wanted to send someone to the *corps de garde* and said he should go to the *watch-gathering?* Who would understand him, with his newly coined words?

"And, to be honest, your inventions come across as being just as stupid. It will take a long time for people to guess what you are trying to say. And what gives *you* the authority to reshape the language used by counts and lords according to your pleasure? And the situation is even more wretched in the case of those miserable letters of the alphabet! They are expelled without good cause and banished from the ABC's, which presumably will be known in the future as the ABD's! Let's say they had not been used by the classical writers. My goodness, what kind of rules were the old masters of slapstick who propagated German spelling for centuries supposed to give us? And why shouldn't we hold on to them after numerous centuries have written that way peacefully and harmoniously? Besides, what sort of cleverness lurks behind any decision to use the new or the old way? For you are all reading ruffians[10] and paper wasters. If you were serious about being useful to the world, you wouldn't cling to the peel while leaving the core untouched. If you love antiquity so much, why don't you rewarm all the old-fashioned expressions? I have an old courtesy book, which Peter of Dresden, who composed the song "In dulci jubilo," used with his lady love circa 1400. If you really think that everything in it can be used again, I will gladly see at last what High German really is." Master Ziriacks's expression grew surly, from which Gelanor deduced that he would have little desire to enter his service. He therefore gave him a half thaler as a writing fee and reflected that all talk is in vain if a person has really succumbed so deeply to sweet foolishness.

Chapter 20

Beyond that the members of the group experienced nothing unusual until they departed, when an old man joined them together with a young person of about twenty-five or twenty-six years. Now, they did not know what to think of this young man. For sporadically, he jumped off the wagon and went on foot. And then he puckered his lips and whistled a saraband like a canary. And then he took a comb out of his pocket and combed himself. And then he began to sing tira, tira, tira, soldier tira.[11] And then, with a voice as high as a capon's he sang:

> Sweet shepherdess, shall we now espouse
> To deceive the guard of a jealous spouse?
> If his honor's gone, as he thinks it is,
> We should place the horns that he fears are his.[12]

Then he drew a pistol out of his little bag and tinkered with it. Then he fastened his armbands differently. Then the ribbon with which he had bound his hair close to the ears came undone. Then he took his hat and whirled it a number of times on his finger. When they arrived at the inn, and the other passengers took out their knives and forks, he dug into the salad with all five fingers, and performed other disgusting tricks. Finally he denounced the quality of the bread, saying it was not fully baked and that beautiful bread was baked in France. Then the old man said to him: "Oh, you wretched devil! This bread has been longer in the oven than you in France."

At that the others realized that the young fellow was a traveled Monsieur[13] and that he had behaved this miserably so that others would notice he had been to France. In addition, they observed that the good man had perhaps taken the mail coach through Paris just like the passenger who once complained that going to Paris had been of no help to him, because it had been so dark there that you could not distinguish one house from the next. And when the others inquired, they learned that the coach with him on board had gone through Paris right at midnight, when the moon was in the last quarter. But no one excused the youth's thinking more graciously than Gelanor, since he had reason to be dissolute. Someone who has tried living abroad for many years can easily demonstrate through his actions that he is no stay-at-home. But a person who has experienced something that quickly can easily be lost in the crowd if he doesn't tell everybody full blast about where he has been.

After the meal Gelanor engaged the old man in conversation and found he was not a bad sort. The old man complained about the young "Frenchman," saying he couldn't get him to do anything that he enjoyed and that he would stick to. Every day he wanted to be something different: first a scholar, and then a merchant, and then a soldier and then a courtier, and he had continued with such changes up to his twenty-fifth year. Recently he had as much as disappeared so that no one knew where he was. Finally, after two months he had reappeared, as could still be seen, in the shape of a Frenchman. Now he wanted to become a tutor in some noble household, but this wish would also not last long. Eurylas said the strange fellow deserved to be vexed a little, a proposal to which the old man agreed. Accordingly, when they were all sitting together again in the coach, they began to talk about how this windbag was constant only in the matter of his inconstancy. The youth apologized and was able to discuss the reasons for this very reasonably and with deliberation. Then, when Eurylas asked why he had not continued his studies, he related his whole life story.

"In truth," he said, "I was supposed to study and become a lawyer, but then I considered how easily it could happen that I might win a dispute against an aristocrat, who would later bear a grudge against me and trap me with his cold iron.

"Or what if I had an appointment in winter, and stumbled with my horse on the ice, so that my leg in the boot broke, and no one was at hand and I died like a dog? Or what if I was invited by a client and had to travel by night and some will-o'-the-wisp led me into water? No, no, I don't want that to happen to me!

"The profession of merchant appealed to me, but after a few weeks it occurred to me—just think about it!—what if you gave a credit of ten thousand Reichsthalers worth of goods to a merchant in another city, and there was an earthquake, and the city with all its inhabitants was annihilated? How would you get paid? Or what if you were unable to rent a store: where would you want to exhibit your goods? Or what if you got a package from some infected location, so that unpacking it was the death of you? No, no, plainly to such a dangerous profession!

"After that, I wanted to take up husbandry, so that with time I would be able to lease a noble property. But then I reflected how easily it could happen that your wife was so busy with the butter and cheese that she might give the child to a peasant woman to take care of, and the dumb old crow might carry it around the farmyard, and then a stork would swoop down to build its nest on the chimney, and drop a stone on the roof tiles, so that thirty of them fell down. Whose heart, if not my own, would be broken if the child's skull were split in two? Or what if the inattentive Cinderella laid the child by the door and the pigs came and ate—if you'll pardon my saying so—who knows what parts of his body up? Or what if a thief broke into the henhouse in winter, and put boots on the cows, so that no traces could be found? Oh no, I had no desire to put myself in such danger!

"Thus, I thought once more about studying and wanted to become a physician. In just two weeks I thought better of it. How easily a retort could have shattered, embedding splinters in my face! Or how easily the maid might let a cat into the laboratory, who might knock over a thousand thalers worth of glassware in one fell swoop. Or how easy it would be for a bandit to knock me off, if I wanted to become a doctor in Padua. As a result my plans changed and I wanted to become a brewer. But then I thought: what if I had to brew a batch of beer, and a dog fell into the vat by accident, so that the beer was spoiled to my detriment? Or what if my wife had the casks filled with a little fresh spring water and as a joke a neighbor shook some cut-up straw, so that people soon found pure fodder in their beer? Wouldn't such an occurrence be accounted to my honor?!"

It would take too long to recount everything here. The following was the content of his narration: After this, he had wanted to become a painter, and then a priest, and then a goldsmith, and then a secretary, and then a courtier, and then a scribbler, but he had been frightened off each time by such considerations. Eurylas joined him in conversation, and asked why he did not think what could happen to him as a court tutor: Didn't he know that nobles on their estates did not value the tutor any more than the overseer? If his master were to call out, "Come here, Hofmeister, you, etc.," wouldn't it be possible that a misunderstanding could arise?[14] The German "Frenchman" thought it over a little, and finally came up with the solution that he would have himself called governor, as is done in France. Eurylas objected that this was a bad omen, for just as a Spanish governor seldom governed for more than three years, some people might decide that he might not last much more than three weeks.[15] His advice to the young man would be to start a small business with doves, for inasmuch as a pair was worth six groschen, if he sold a thousand, he would most certainly have twenty thalers and twenty groschen.

The old man laughed at this, and reprimanded his cousin not only for living so dissolutely, but also for telling his life story without any inhibitions. It was the height of foolishness not to cling steadfastly to any plan, and Seneca[16] had spoken well when he said that the foolish man begins to live each day. Moreover, he said the young man had allowed himself to be dissuaded by causes that were more laughable than alarming. Applying such standards, no one would be able to remain in this world, since we are exposed to danger everywhere. He said that the next time the young man should consider that a pious prayer, and a merciful God, could put an end to all frightful matters.

Translated by Linda Feldman

Notes

1. A *Copiste* specialized in the copying of documents or artwork. A secretary, on the other hand, performed a variety of clerical chores, some of which, as here, included independent work. The notes are largely those of the translator.

2. Fenus = Venus. See also Zizero for Cicero, Horaz for Horace, and Ofid for Ovid. Weise is satirizing the efforts of the seventeenth-century language societies, to free the German language of foreign influences and restore it to what they believed to be its original state of purity. One such effort, supported by Philipp von Zesen, consisted of ridding the language of the so-called Latin letters *c, q, v,* and *y,* and substituting them with the "less-foreign" letters of *z, k, f,* and *i,* as illustrated in these classical references.

3. Daylighter = window. The secretary, as a linguistic chauvinist, invents his own word for window since the German word *Fenster* is derive from the Latin word *fenestra.*

4. Lights of my head = eyes. Weise is parodying the exaggerated imagery of Baroque writing.

5. Torch of heaven = sun.

6. I.e.,Venus. *Libinne* is one of Zesen's invented words. It is constructed from the German word for love *Liebe* plus the German feminine agent suffix *in.*

7. Weise alludes to Zesen's *Rosen-Mând* (1651) here, emphasizing once again that Ziriacks's writing style parodies that of Zesen.

8. It is surely no coincidence that the name Ziriacks is more or less the same name borne by the impudent clerk Cyriacus in book 2 chapter 29 of *Simplicissimus.* When Cyriacus is unable to spell Simplicius Simplicissimus he declares that there must be a devil in hell by that name and Simplicissimus replies that there must also be one named Cyriacus.—Ed.

9. The clerk is suggesting that no matter what the custom is, many people will still not carry it out correctly.

10. Reading ruffians = German *Lesebengel,* a popular term of mockery applied to students of famous professors.

11. Although the sound *tira* is musically suggestive, the phrase actually means "the soldier fired [his gun]" (from French *tirer*).

12. Horns were the signifier of the cuckolded spouse.

13. Courteous form of address for a gentleman in France. Weise is using the French term here to ridicule the prestige allotted to French culture in the seventeenth century.

14. Hofmeister, in its dual meanings of tutor and foreman, serves as the pivot for the author's pun.

15. In France the word *governor* designated a tutor; in Spain, a provincial governor.

16. Lucius Annaeus Seneca (4? B.C.–A.D. 65), Roman philosopher, political leader, and author of tragedies.

Johann Kuhnau

Johann Kuhnau (1660–1722), musician, composer, and writer, was Johann Sebastian Bach's immediate predecessor as organist (1684) and cantor (1701) of the Church of St. Thomas in Leipzig. He attended the *Gymnasium* in Zittau where Christian Weise was rector. There he became the first singer in the school choir and acted in two of Weise's school plays. He later studied law and practiced as a lawyer. In 1700 Kuhnau became the musical director of the University of Leipzig. Besides his writings on music and his musical compositions Kuhnau wrote three novels, *The Forger of His Own Misfortune* (1695), *The Musical Quack* (1700), and *On the Clever and Foolish Use of the Five Senses, First Part on Feeling* (1698), and a comedy (1701). His novels satirize foolish behaviors, clearly exhibiting the influence of Weise's so-called political novels.

The Musical Quack centers on the antics of the charlatan musician Caraffa whose name, though it sounds Italian, is a corruption of the German *Theuer-Affe,* "dear ape," i.e., "fool," the name his father gave him. Caraffa who loves to brag of his musical accomplishments always manages to find an excuse for not playing when he is asked to perform. Ultimately he must be unmasked and reformed. The following satirical passage, taken from *The Musical Quack,* contributes little to the central plot of the novel but offers an example of another kind of quack, the peddler of miracle tonics. Kuhnau's quacks are self-made men in a negative sense; they create themselves purely with language. Kuhnau's vigorous, even violent language strikes a tone that will be muffled in the more decorous novels in the following centuries.

The Musical Quack[1]

Chapter 3

[A group of musicians has been rehearsing.]

Just as they were about to hand out another piece, a hullabaloo arose below in the marketplace, and when the company ran to the window they saw that not far from their door below a physician had mounted the podium that had been erected there. He was wearing an old violet plush fur coat that was trimmed with silver and gold lace. He carried a long black cordovan sword-belt with red fringe in which hung a rapier four ells long and sewn into a piece of leather that was serving as the sheath. His wig looked as though it had been wound around his head like flax on a distaff. He wore a hat of such large dimension and with such a narrow rim that it seemed as though a large cooking pot had been overturned on his pate. Around his neck he had wrapped black crepe. In addition sacks containing his remedies hung over his shoulders front and back. Because at first not a single person was to be seen standing around listening to him and he was of a mind to attract people all the same, he began chatting with his marmot: "My dear beastie!" he shouted. "How's it going, haven't you slept just about long enough? You mustn't think that you are still on Mount Mons, since you have slept from St. Gallen to St. Johann[2] and since I took you along when I dug up my splendid cipolla.[3] No, no, you must look more lively now. What, you're not talking? Indeed you can't. If you could speak, you would ask me: 'My dear doctor! My dear oculist, stonecutter,[4] and bonesetter! What kind of worthy tricks have you bought with you to Germany? Is it worth your while to stand here in the public marketplace and beckon the people to you?' To this I would answer: 'Of course, my dear marmot, I have brought the superb Balsam Mundi, or the magnificent balm, consisting of seventy ingredients, each of which itself performs miracles.' If you further asked: 'My dear Doctor, what's this balm good for?' I would give you the answer: 'I cure all the injuries and frailties of mankind with it, be they internal or external, whether they derive from cold or heat, from winter or summer, from day or night.' But should you further ask: 'How have you tested it?' Answer: 'I recently brought back to life one, who was already lying in his grave. A master mason and a slater who fell together from a church tower and broke in two were made whole again and restored to complete health with it.'"

Thus he spoke to his marmot. When, however, he saw that a number of people had gathered, for two peasants with chickens and geese coops, two harpists or porters, a washerwoman, four beggars, three carters, a pease porridge seller, two potato diggers, and a harrow maker were standing around, this Aesculapius[5] directed his speech toward said listeners, stroked his spade beard[6] and began to declaim: "To each well-disposed soul as befits his rank! If it is our duty not to be silent on the subject of God's works and the good deeds that he does for mankind, then I must say: here stands a highly experienced man, a man who has been licensed and certified by the greatest potentates of the world, a physician and surgeon, oculist, stonecutter, and bonesetter, esteemed by all. 'In truth,' you will say. 'You're talking yourself up a lot, but we don't know you. Who are you anyway? Are you perhaps the famous Hanging Michael or the worthy Batty Matt? Or are you the well-traveled Italian Niclas[7] with the long hunting knife?'" "But I am," he said, "none of these. Or you ask further, 'Are you not the incomparable Toffel, the wormer,[8] with the thick goiter and the black ruff?' And I am one and the same. Just see that my name is already so famous in this world, that both learned and untutored, noble and ignoble, citizens and peasants know of it. If finally you ask, 'What kind of secrets did you bring along and what kind of miracles do you perform among the sick?' I will answer thus: 'I have brought the best Balsamum mundi. I cure the colic and complaints of the womb, constipations of the body, diarrhea, kidney stones, gout and rheumatism, consumption, jaundice and dropsy, dizziness, ringing in the ears, all kinds of fevers, chills, temperatures, the daily, two-, three-, four,- indeed five-day fever: I administer it to the womenfolk, I make them pregnant and help them give birth. I increase men's virility with it. In sum there is not a sickness in the world that can't be cured with this Balsamum mundi. For two pennies the box I give you the balm of the world along with printed instructions in German, as to how each patient is to use it internally or externally. Kind and gentle souls! It's but a pittance, a paltry sum of money, a brandy's worth, you'll have gobbled or sopped up more in half an hour than you give me for this magnificent medicine, which can save you from all frailties, indeed from death. Don't delay: For once I am gone, you're done for and you won't be able to get such a balm, even if you bought everything in the pharmacy. Buy it now and you'll have it when you need it. And I won't give you only this balm, but I'll make you a present of three pieces of the excellent cipolla root that grows on the river Fluvius between St. Veit and Swallowtail.[9] It's a root that one carries to guard against the old sorceress, the devil's witches and gypsies. Take it in a little brandy wine, and it will drive the fatigue out of your limbs. You, my gentle souls! You have lazy farmhands and maids, who always complain about fatigue when they are supposed to work. Give them just one of these roots and at once they will be bright and ready for work. Look, I use three pieces of it, one for the farmhand, the other for the maid and because little Betty, the nanny, mustn't be forgotten, she shall have the third piece.'"

And with all this he put together the packets he sold the people: He got a big response and so many tied up hankies and gloves flew up onto the platform that he couldn't distribute enough to the people for the money.

Chapter 4

The musicians in listening to this quack through the open window had forgotten to proceed in their musical exercise. And although they would have liked to begin another new piece, the clamor on the marketplace was so great they would have gotten small pleasure from their soft music. So they parted, since some had to go home and because in addition to their music they performed other duties and had to attend to them. They asked that Signor Caraffa grant them the honor of his presence at the next gathering since the fair would be over and it would be quiet outside.

A number of the other musicians stood on the marketplace a while longer and then they saw a woman climbing onto a table across from the doctor. They could recognize the bird immediately by its feathers. For since she wore necklaces of strung teeth around her arms and neck, one could conclude that she was a tooth-drawer.[10] And indeed she began to extol her red tooth powder, her salve and oil: "Look, gentlemen!" she said, "I extract teeth painlessly. If, however, you want to keep your teeth, I have a special oil for pain. If you simply dip a little cotton in it and put it on the pain, it will vanish in the twinkling of an eye. I am also selling a red tooth powder that no doctor in the world knows how to prepare. It removes all stench and filth from your teeth.

"Dear people, you sometimes have to speak with highborn people, or to broach something with the person you are attached to or to invite people over. You must, however, depart unheard or even having been given your walking papers. How does it come to this? Answer: Your bad breath disgusts people and many a person would rather stick his nose into the worst soldier's latrine at the city gate than be blown upon for a single moment by the dog-breeze that comes out of your throat. Now, many doctors and grand people are of the opinion that such a nasty stench comes from the stomach or the blood. But believe me, the teeth alone are the cause: if you brush and flush them with my excellent powder not only will all stench and filth dissolve, but when you speak, your breath will waft toward those around you as sweetly as if they were standing in a carnation or rose garden at eventide in spring, caressed by a gentle breeze. And then you can get what you want from people."

One of the musicians who was standing there was on the verge of giving her a penny, but the others held him back and asked him if he wanted to give these people his money for their trickery and boasting. So he stuck his penny back into his purse and left with the others. When practically no one remained in front of the woman's table and she thought that the doctor across the way had lured her audience completely away (for our musicians had to pass by him if they wanted to go home), then what invectives could be heard! I don't think that there are enough words in the most comprehensive dictionary to describe the most awful rascals and mudslingers that this woman could pull out one after another as though they were strung on a string. So that the titles of honor that she conferred on the doctor could be understood by everyone and since no more people were with her she ran in among the people who were standing around the doctor's podium. "You people," she cried, "are surely not so simple that you trust a charlatan who does not deserve the sun to shine upon him. He calls himself a surgeon but he cures wounds in such a fashion that he leaves his stolen scissors in them and another must cut this hole open again and look for the lost tool. He claims to be an oculist, but he's one of those who like the devilish crows peck out people's eyes. Instead of making them see he makes them blind. He pretends to be a lithotomist, but he isn't even capable of gelding a pig. Pooh on you, you dirty dog. You betrayer of country and folk! You rascal! You thief! You snot-nose, you worthless scoundrel! You braggart, you liar, you rascal, for whom a grave in the air has been ordered, indeed who already wears the noose under his black crepe!"

Because of the noise the doctor hadn't properly understood that this panegyric was being delivered in his honor. When he saw how the woman came nearer and began to commend him with such lofty titles right before his eyes, he retorted: "What kind of storm has been stirred up so unexpectedly? Isn't it the old witch across the way doing it? Isn't it the procuress who was banned from Hamburg a few years ago who is now pretending to be a tooth-drawer, who calls peasants to her who have nothing but teeth made of ox-bone in their throats and takes them out so that her audience will think that she can pull teeth painlessly." "Well, you bald old coot," the wench answered. "Who are you? Aren't you the de-praved tailor, who was kicked out of the guild by the honest craft because you couldn't put a patch on a pair of pants without your disgraceful bunch of threads sticking out everywhere? You've done well to run with the gypsies and to become a doctor so that you can hide your shortcomings and your clumsy patchwork among the gravediggers." "Well, you dirty old dog!" the doctor replied. "If you are no longer able to fetch brick by night from the old church wall in your village, then I'd like to see what you make your red tooth powder from, hah?" "Well, you cursed rascal!" retorted the toothdrawer. "If a heavy excise tax is placed on suet then I'd like to see how you will manage with your world-salve or balm." "Hah! You extract of all the furies of hell!" returned the quack. "If you don't skedaddle immediately, I'll use this cane to smooth out the wrinkles, which the Father of Evil smeared all over your face with his face cream." "You scum of all the worthless ragamuffins!" the old woman continued. "Wherever you dare to descend I will make so many bumps on your cursed goiter that it will get thinner before Master Hangman can begin treatment."

When the braying of her trumpet became even more penetrating, the brawl really got started. The fellow sprang down from the podium, gave her a half a dozen lumps on her head so that one would have thought that she would bite the dust from it. But before he knew it she grabbed him from behind by his natural wig, so that as he tried to get free of her, a goodly part of it along with the Polish plait[11] he had placed on his head remained in her hand. He grabbed her and tried to sling her into the puddle by the rostrum. But she held onto his black ruff and his beard so tightly that he fell into the puddle as well. Then you could have seen such a nice fight: now the quack was on top, now the toothdrawer. It's easy to guess how brightly the two of them shone after they climbed out of this bath. They hardly wished one another a good bath,[12] for they fell upon one another again and rolled around in the filth—there was no lack of it because of the rain and the traffic—so that their clothes and especially the old woman's chemise were covered over and over with a new sugarcoating. Whereupon they finally took leave of one another after exchanging many titles of honor and friendly glances, so that all the audience also left the marketplace.

I don't know whether this squabble came before the authorities and the quack along with the old cat was punished for such awful goings-on. But it is certain that this action had given both of them much to profit from for a long time. The woman's head was so bruised that it would have had to have been made of ox-horn if it hadn't felt the blows for a quarter of a year more. On the other hand, the old bag had plowed the fellow's face with her naturally sharp plowshares so that he couldn't show his face for many a day.

Translated by Lynne Tatlock

Notes

1. This translation renders chapter 3 and 4 of the following German edition: Johann Kuhnau, *Der Musicalische Quack-Salber*, ed. Kurt Benndorf, Deutsche Litteraturdenkmale des 18. and 19. Jahrhunderts, nos. 83–88, ed. August Sauer (Berlin: B. Behr, 1900). While the notes are original, the introduction is indebted to

James Hardin's two articles: "Eine Johann Kuhnau Bibliographie," *Daphnis* 10 (1981): pp. 325–43 and "Johann Kuhnau's *Der Schmied seines eigenen Unglückes* and the 'Political' Novel," *Daphnis* 13 (1984): pp. 445–64.

2. St. Gallen is in Northeastern Switzerland. St. Johann (in the original "Johanne") could be the town located about thirty miles southwest of Salzburg.

3. Cipolla = onion (Ital.).

4. I.e., lithotomist.

5. Greek god of medicine, son of Apollo.

6. A short, pointed beard. In English such beards have come to be called Vandyke beards since they are associated with the portraits painted by Sir Anthony Vandyke (1599–1641).

7. In German as in English the name is associated with the devil as well as with St. Nicholas. The mythical St. Nicholas was buried in Bari, Italy, after his body was stolen from somewhere in the Middle East and brought to Italy.

8. Wormer refers to a certain kind of medicine that claimed to cure the patient by drawing the worms causing the illness, a medical practice that was considered by some to be mere quackery.

9. As noted above, *cipolla* is Italian for onion. *Fluvius* means river in Latin. *Swallowtail* is invented. Although there are several towns named Sankt Veit, the name is probably intended to allude to St. Vitus's dance, the nervous disorder chorea (Greek for "dance"), which took its name from the dancing madness that spread from Germany to the rest of Europe in the thirteenth century.

10. In a vision entitled "Death-Host" in Moscherosch's *Philander von Sittewalt* the narrator also describes toothdrawers, or literally "tooth breakers," as recognizable by the chains of teeth they wear around their necks. In this vision the members of the medical profession file past the narrator; death brings up the rear. The toothdrawers and quacks who sell potions march nearer death because they have caused even more deaths than have the doctors.

11. A matted, filthy condition of the hair due to disease: *plica polonica*. Here it refers to the quack's wig.

12. The attendant of the public bath normally wished the bather a good bath.

Johann Jacob Christoph von Grimmelshausen

Johann Jacob Christoph von Grimmelshausen (1621–76) was born in Gelnhausen in Hesse. Although descended from nobility, his family had long practiced bourgeois trades. The hostilities of the Thirty Years' War forced the family to flee Gelnhausen and Grimmelshausen is thought, like his literary alter ego Simplicissimus, to have been carried off by Croatians. In 1637 he reappears in Westphalia as a member of the imperial forces. After years of service as a soldier in 1648 he became secretary to the imperial field commander Johann Burckhard von Elter and around that time converted to Catholicism. Thereafter he married and took up service as steward for a noble family in southwest Germany. Later he served as steward to a wealthy physician and in 1667, became mayor of the village of Renchen near Strasbourg. In 1666 the first of his literary works appeared and two years later, the first edition of *Simplicissimus Deutsch*. The success of *Simplicissimus* undoubtedly provided an impetus to continue writing; a string of works, known as the *Simplician Writings*, followed.

Simplicissimus Deutsch, the undisputed prose masterpiece of German seventeenth-century literature, consists of five books plus the *Continuatio*. It is prefaced by an emblematic copper etching of a chimera—part goat, fish, bird, human—with an accompanying eight-line poem. This emblem, known as the phoenix copper, is now understood to incorporate the purpose of the book. Within the text itself the narrator, Simplicissimus, recounts his tempestuous life, a life profoundly marked by the upheavals of the Thirty

Years' War. Simplicissimus progresses from naive observer of the world's vices to active participant in them. Although he eventually discovers his noble lineage, he is so burdened by his sinfulness and the terrible state of humankind that he chooses to conclude his life as a hermit on a desert island, hoping for redemption through God's mercy. As the rhyme accompanying the phoenix copper indicates, Simplicissimus attains the peace of the island only after many vicissitudes: "Like the phoenix I was of fire born, / I flew through the air, yet was not forlorn. / I wandered through water, I traveled o'er land, / Through my ramblings I came to understand / Much that saddened me, little to rejoice in. / What was that? I recorded it herein / That the reader might, just like me, / live, far from folly, in harmony." Like the chimera who initially speaks for our hero, Simplicissimus's narrative combines many diverse elements; it is now farcical, now allegorical, now picaresque, now encyclopedic, now satirical, now chiliastic.

Simplicius Simplicissimus

Book 1

Chapter 1: *Simplicius's peasant origin and rustic education*

In our day and age, which some think to be the last, a disease is current among commoners, a disease which—once it has enabled its victims to put a few coins in their purses, to dress in the latest foolish fashion, in a suit with a thousand silk ribbons, or by some good fortune to gain valor and renown—makes them claim that they are knights and noblemen of ancient family, though it is often found out and diligent research reveals only that their forbears were chimney sweeps, laborers; hod-carriers, pushers of wheelbarrows, and that their cousins were mule-drivers, gamblers, vagabonds, and mountebanks, their brothers flatfeet and constables, their sisters seamstresses, laundresses, or even whores, their mothers procurers or even witches and, truth to tell, their whole families with their thirty-two ancestors as filthy and polluted as a gang of thieves and cutthroats. As a matter of fact, these would-be noblemen are often as black as if they had been born and raised in New Guinea.

I don't like to compare myself to these people, though—to come right out with it—I have often thought I must have some grand seigneur or at least an ordinary, run-of-the-mill nobleman for an ancestor, for by nature I am inclined toward the business of nobility, if only I had the necessary tools and investment capital for it. But joking aside, my origin and education might be compared to that of a prince (if only you don't stress the differences too much). My "knan"—that's what they call a father in the Spessart[1]—owned a palace as good as the next man's. A king as mighty as the great Alexander himself would not have been able to build it with his own two hands. It was well chinked with adobe, and instead of being covered with barren slate, cold lead, or red copper, it was thatched with straw, on which grows noble grain. In order not to show off his ancient nobility (which went back as far as Adam) and his wealth, he had the wall about his castle made not of fieldstone picked by the wayside, or of indifferently manufactured brick—no, he used oak planking, from a noble and useful tree on which grow pork sausages and juicy hams, and which requires more than a hundred years to reach its full height. Where is the monarch to imitate that? Where is the sovereign wanting to do likewise? The rooms, halls, and chambers had been tinted black by smoke—only because black is the most durable color in the world, and paintings in that color need more time to acquire perfection than even the most skillful painters give their best work. The tapestries were of the most delicate texture in the world, for they were made by a creature who in antiquity vied in spinning with Minerva herself.[2] His windows were dedicated to St. Noglass for no other reason than that he knew windows woven of hemp and flax took more time and trouble than the most precious Venetian glass. His station in life made him think that everything produced with a lot of trouble was for that very reason more precious; and whatever is precious is most becoming to nobility.

Instead of page boys, lackeys, and stable boys, he had sheep, rams, and pigs, each neatly dressed in its own uniform. They often waited on me in the fields until, tired of their service, I drove them off and home. His armory was sufficiently and neatly furnished with plows, mattocks, axes, picks, shovels, manure forks, and hay rakes. He drilled and exercised with these weapons daily; hoeing and weeding was his military discipline, as in peacetime among the Romans. Hitching up the oxen was his captaincy; taking manure to the field, his science of fortification; plowing, his campaigning; splitting firewood, his troop movements and maneuvers; and cleaning out the stables, his war games and most noble diversion. With these activities he made war on the whole earth—as far as his resources went—and thereby obtained rich harvest every fall. I mention all this only by the way and without boasting, for I don't think I was any better than my knan, whose residence was situated in a pleasant spot, the Spessart Hills (a place hardly anybody has ever heard of). Only brevity keeps me from telling you about my knan's family, and mentioning his name and ancestry here and now. Suffice it to say that I was born in the Spessart.

Just as my knan's household was aristocratic, so my upbringing was similarly superior; in my tenth year I had already absorbed all the rudiments of the above-mentioned exercises, drills, and maneuvers. In book learning, on the other hand, I was equal to the famous Amplistidus, of whom Suidas reports that he could not count beyond five. My father was much too bright for organized studies and observed herein the usage of the times, that is, people don't think much of useless knowledge, because you can hire flunkies for that kind of drudgery. In addition, I was an excellent musician on the bagpipes, on which I could produce splendid dirges. Musically I equaled Orpheus, but I excelled on the bagpipes while he handled merely the harp.

Concerning theology, there was no one like me in all Christendumb; I had heard of neither God nor man, heaven nor hell, angel nor devil, and I did not even know the difference between good and evil. You can easily imagine that with such theology I lived like our first parents in paradise; they also knew nothing of sickness, death, or dying, not to mention resurrection. Oh, aristocratic (or asinine) life in which one does not worry about medicine either! My studies in the law (and all the other arts and sciences in the world) were similar. I was so perfect and excellent in ignorance that I could not possibly have known that I knew nothing at all. Once more I say, Oh, happy life!

But my knan did not want me to enjoy such bliss any longer. He thought I should live and act in accordance with my aristocratic birth. So he started to draw me toward higher things and to assign me more difficult lessons.

Chapter 2: *The first rung on the ladder of success which Simplicius climbed, together with praise of shepherds and appended excellent advice*

He endowed me with the office most dignified not only in his household but in the whole world, namely, the ancient appointment of herdsman. He entrusted me first with the hogs, then with the goats, and finally with the whole flock of sheep, and had me mind pasture and protect them from the wolf, particularly with my pipes, the sound of which, according to Strabo, helped to fatten the lambs and sheep of Arcadia. At that time I resembled David, but instead of bagpipes he had only a harp; that was not a bad start for me, for I took the omen to mean that in time I too might be world famous. Since the beginning of time prominent men have started as herdsmen; in Holy Writ we read of Abel, Abraham, Isaac, Jacob and his sons, and Moses (who had to mind his brother-in-law's sheep before he became the leader and legislator of six hundred thousand Israelites).

Someone may object here that the aforementioned were devout and holy men, not peasant lads from the Spessart who did not know God. I grant you it is so; but my innocence had to make up for my other shortcomings. Examples can be found among the ancient heathens as well; among the Romans there were noble families who without doubt were called Bubulcus (ox herd), Statilius Taurus (bull), Pomponius Vitulus (calf), Vitellius (baby beef), Annius Capra (goat), and others who were so named because they handled such critters, and probably herded them too.

But to get back to my own flock, you must know that I was as unacquainted with the wolf as I was with my own ignorance. For that reason my father was all the more specific with his instruction. He said, "Boy, pay attention! Don't let no sheep stray too far, and play on yer bagpipes so the wolf don't come and cause a lot of damage. He's a kind of four-legged rascal and thief who gobbles up men and animules. And if you don't watch good I'll tan yer hide." With equal graciousness I replied, "I ain't never seen a wolf." "Go on, ya muttonhead," he answered, "you'll stay stupid all your life. I wonder what'll become of ya. You're a big lunk already, not knowing that a wolf is a big four-legged rascal." He gave me some more instructions, and finally he got mad and walked off grumbling. He surmised that my crude understanding, which had not yet been sufficiently refined by his instruction, could not grasp his subtle teachings. . . .

Chapter 4: *Simplicius's residence is taken by storm, plundered, and destroyed; warriors make a mess of it*

Though I hadn't intended to take the peace-loving reader into my father's home and farm along with these merry cavalrymen, the orderly progress of my tale requires me to make known to posterity the sort of abysmal and unheard-of cruelties occasionally perpetrated in our German war and to testify by my own example that all these evils were necessarily required for our own good by the kindness of our Lord. For, my kind reader, who would have told me that there's a God in heaven if the warriors hadn't destroyed my knan's house, if they hadn't forced me to be among the people who taught me well enough? Shortly before this event I could neither know nor imagine but that my knan, mother, and Ursula, myself and the hired hands were the only men on earth, for no people or habitations were known to me except my knan's residence where I went in and out daily. But I soon found out where people come from, and that they have no permanent abode, but often have to move on again before they can look around. I had been human in shape alone, and a Christian in name only; in reality I was an animal! But the Almighty looked upon my ignorance with forgiving eyes, and wanted me to come to the recognition of both him and myself. And though he had a thousand different ways for this purpose, undoubtedly he wanted to use as an example to others the manner in which my knan and mother were punished for my negligent upbringing.

The first thing these horsemen did in the nice black rooms of the house was to put in their horses. Then everyone took up a special job, one having to do with death and destruction. Although some began butchering, heating water, and rendering lard, as if to prepare for a banquet, others raced through the house, ransacking

upstairs and down; not even the privy chamber was safe, as if the
golden fleece of Colchis might be hidden there. Still others bundled
up big packs of cloth, household goods, and clothes, as if they
wanted to hold a rummage sale somewhere. What they did not
intend to take along they broke and spoiled. Some ran their swords
into the hay and straw, as if there hadn't been hogs enough to stick.
Some shook the feathers out of beds and put bacon slabs, hams,
and other stuff in the ticking, as if they might sleep better on these.
Others knocked down the hearth and broke the windows, as if
announcing an everlasting summer. They flattened out copper and
pewter dishes and baled the ruined goods. They burned up bed-
steads, tables, chairs, and benches, though there were yards and
yards of dry firewood outside the kitchen. Jars and crocks, pots
and casseroles all were broken, either because they preferred their
meat broiled or because they thought they'd eat only one meal with
us. In the barn, the hired girl was handled so roughly that she was
unable to walk away, I am ashamed to report. They stretched the
hired man out flat on the ground, stuck a wooden wedge in his
mouth to keep it open, and emptied a milk bucket full of stinking
manure drippings down his throat; they called it a Swedish cock-
tail. He didn't relish it and made a very wry face. By this means
they forced him to take a raiding party to some other place where
they carried off men and cattle and brought them to our farm.
Among these were my knan, mother, and Ursula.

Then they used thumbscrews, which they cleverly made out of
their pistols, to torture the peasants, as if they wanted to burn
witches. Though he had confessed to nothing as yet, they put one
of the captured hayseeds in the bake-oven and lighted a fire in it.
They put a rope around someone else's head and tightened it like
a tourniquet until blood came out of his mouth, nose and ears. In
short, every soldier had his favorite method of making life miserable for peasants, and every peasant had his own misery. My knan
was, as I thought, particularly lucky because he confessed with a
laugh what others were forced to say in pain and martyrdom. No
doubt because he was the head of the household, he was shown
special consideration; they put him close to a fire, tied him by his
hands and legs, and rubbed damp salt on the bottoms of his feet.
Our old nanny goat had to lick it off and this so tickled my knan
that he could have burst laughing. This seemed so clever and entertaining to me—I had never seen or heard my knan laugh so long—

that I joined him in laughter, to keep him company or perhaps to cover up my ignorance. In the midst of such glee he told them the whereabouts of hidden treasure much richer in gold, pearls, and jewelry than might have been expected on a farm.

I can't say much about the captured wives, hired girls, and daughters because the soldiers didn't let me watch their doings. But I do remember hearing pitiful screams from various dark corners and I guess that my mother and our Ursula had it no better than the rest. Amid all this horror I was busy turning a roasting spit and didn't worry about anything, for I didn't know the meaning of it. In the afternoon I helped water the horses and that way got to see our hired girl in the barn. She looked wondrously messed up and at first I didn't recognize her. In a sickly voice she said, "Boy, get out of this place, or the soldiers will take you with them. Try to get away; you can see they are up to no good!" That is all she could say.

Chapter 5: *How Simplicius uses his legs and is frightened by rotten trees*

Suddenly I began noticing the misery about me and started thinking about how to get out of it as soon as I could. But where should I go? My mind was much too shallow to give me a suggestion, but toward evening I succeeded in escaping to the woods and I didn't even leave my beloved bagpipe behind. But what now? I didn't know the roads any better than I knew the lanes through the frozen sea to Nova Zembla. There was some safety in the pitch-dark night that covered me, but to my dim wit it wasn't half dark enough. So I hid in thick bushes where I could hear the screams of the tortured peasants and the song of the nightingales, shut my eyes, and fell fast asleep. But when the morning star rose brightly in the east I saw my knan's house go up in flames, and no one was there to put out the fire.

In hopes of finding someone I knew, I crept out of hiding, but at once five cavalrymen saw me, and one shouted, "Boy, come here, or by God I'll drill you so the smoke will come out of your ears!" Since I didn't know what the soldier wanted, I stopped in my tracks, forgetting to shut my mouth, and stared at them as a cat looks at a new barn door. They wouldn't have become angry with me if a bog hadn't kept them from getting at me. One of them fired his carbine at me, and I was so scared by the flash and the noise (made more frightening by a multiple echo) that I fell to the ground and lay there for dead. As a matter of fact, I never moved a muscle. And when the horsemen rode off, thinking I was dead, I did not feel like sitting up or looking about me all day.

When night came around once more, I got up and walked a long way into the woods, until in the distance I saw a rotten tree sending out an eerie light. That frightened me again. I turned on my heels and kept walking till I saw another such tree, and I ran from this one too. I spent the whole night like this, running from one rotten tree to another. Finally daylight came to my aid by bidding the trees to stop being luminous, but this was no great help, for my heart was full of fear, my legs full of tiredness, my empty stomach full of hunger, my mouth full of thirst, my brain full of silly notions, and my eyes full of sleep. I kept on walking without knowing where I was headed. The farther I walked, the farther I went away from people and into the forest. At that time (though I didn't know it) I felt the effects of ignorance and unreason; if a dumb beast had been in my shoes, it would have known better what to do than I. But when night came a third time, I had enough sense to crawl into a hollow tree (taking good care of my beloved bagpipe, too), and I firmly resolved to sleep all night.

Chapter 6: *This chapter is so short and so devout that Simplicius faints over it*

I had hardly made myself comfortable for sleeping when I heard a voice saying, "O great love shown to us ungrateful men! O my only solace, my hope, my treasure, my God!" and more in this vein that I could not altogether understand.

These words might well encourage, console, and gladden the heart of a Christian in the shape I was in at that time. But—oh, ignorance and simplicity!—it was all Greek to me and I couldn't make head or tail of it. But when I heard that the speaker's hunger and thirst would be appeased, my own unendurable hunger and my stomach, which from lack of food had become the size of a walnut, advised me to invite myself too. So I told myself to be courageous, crawled out of the tree, and approached the voice.

I saw a tall man with long gray and black hair that hung disheveled down to his shoulders; his tousled beard was the size of a cheese. His face, though haggard and sallow, was kind, and his long cloak was patched and mended with more than a thousand snippets of different materials. Around his throat and body he wore a heavy iron chain. To my eyes he looked so frightening and ghastly that I started trembling like a wet dog. But my fear was increased by the fact that he was hugging a crucifix about six feet high. Since I didn't know him, I could not but imagine that this old man must be the wolf of which my knan had recently warned me.

In my fear I whipped out my bagpipe (which I had rescued from the cavalrymen as my only treasure), blew it up, and started to make a horrendous sound to drive off this wolf. The anchorite was caught up in astonishment. No doubt he thought a devilish ghost had come to trouble him, like the great St. Anthony,[3] and to disturb his meditation. As soon as he had recovered a little he reviled me, his tempter in the hollow tree (for I had retreated to it once more); he was even bold enough to come right up to me and rail at the fiend of men. "Hah!" he said, "you are just the one to trouble the God-fearing. . . ." I did not understand another word, for his approach frightened me so much that I fainted dead away.

Chapter 7: *Simplicius is given a friendly welcome in a poor inn*

I don't know how I came to, but I was out of the tree, my head was in the old man's lap, and he had opened my jacket. When I had recovered a little, seeing the hermit so close to me, I screamed as if he were about to rip the heart from my chest. But he said, "Son, be still; I won't hurt you; calm yourself," and so on. But the more he comforted and soothed, the more I shouted, "You'll eat me!" "Now, now, my son," he said, "be quiet; I won't eat you." I carried on this sort of wrangling for some time until I managed to come with him into his hut. Here Poverty herself was marshal, Hunger was cook, and Want was the manager. Here my stomach was given some greens and a drink of water, and my mind, which was altogether confused, was straightened out and corrected by the old man's comforting friendliness. Soon Sleep tempted me to pay her tribute. When the hermit saw this he left the hut, for only

one person could sleep in it. About midnight I awoke again and
heard him sing the following song, which I later learned:

> Come, nightingale, O balm of night,
> Come, let your voice cheerful and bright
> Sing out in lovely rapture.
> The other birds have gone to sleep,
> But you a tuneful vigil keep,
> Your Maker's praise to capture.
>
> > Loudly raise your brilliant voice
> >   And rejoice.
> >   Show you love
> > God who is in heaven above.
>
> Although the sunshine now has left
> And we of daylight are bereft,
> Yet we may now compete
> To praise his mercy, praise his might,
> Nor darkness hinder us nor night
> To offer praise replete.
>
> > Therefore raise your brilliant voice
> >   And rejoice.
> >   Show you love
> > God who is in heaven above.
>
> True Echo with her wild reply
> Wants also to be heard close by
> When your praise is ringing.
> She bids us to avoid all sloth,
> That we be active, never loth
> She joins in happy singing.
>
> > Therefore raise your brilliant voice, etc.
>
> The stars which in the sky are found
> In praise of God do still abound
> And show their veneration.
> The songless owl with ugly screech
> Does yet a noble lesson teach:
> Praise God in every nation!
>
> > Therefore raise your brilliant voice, etc.

O come then, sweetest bird of night,
Inspire with your song's delight.
In bed let us not linger.
Instead let's sing to God in praise
Till Dawn the somber pall doth raise
From woods with rosy finger.

Loudly raise your brilliant voice
And rejoice.
Show you love
God who is in heaven above.

While this song went on, it seemed almost as if the nightingale, the owl, and Echo had joined in, and if I had ever heard the morning star sing, or could have imitated its melody on my bagpipe, I would have slipped out of the hut to join in, because this harmony seemed so lovely.

But I fell asleep again, and did not wake up until late in the day. When the hermit stood in front of me and said, "Get up, little one, I'll give you something to eat and show you the way out of the woods, so you get back to your people in the village before night falls," I asked him, "What's that, 'people,' 'village'?" He said, "Have you never been in a village? Don't you know what 'men' or 'people' are?" "No," I said, "I've been nowhere but here; but tell me, what are 'people,' 'men,' and 'village'?" "God preserve us!" answered the hermit. "Are you foolish or bright?" "I am ma and pa's boy. My name is neither Foolish nor Bright." The hermit gave a sigh, crossed himself, and said, "My dear child, for God's sake I'd like to keep you here and teach you." The next chapter will tell of our dialogue.

Chapter 8: *How Simplicius uses elevated speech and
thereby gives evidence of his excellent qualities*

HERMIT: What is your name?
SIMPLEX: My name is Boy.
HERM: I can see you're not a girl. But how did your father and mother call you?
SIM: I never had a father and mother.

HERM: Then who gave you that shirt?

SIM: My mither, of course.

HERM: How did your "mither" call you, then?

SIM: She called me "boy," also "rascal," "jackass," "clumsy lout," "stupid fool," and "jailbird."

HERM: Who was your mother's husband?

SIM: Nobody.

HERM. But with whom did your mother sleep at night?

SIM: With my knan.

HERM: How did your knan call you?

SIM: He called me "boy."

HERM: What was your knan's name?

SIM: Why, "knan"!

HERM: But how did your mother call him?

SIM: "Knan," and sometimes "boss."

HERM: Did she ever call him anything else?

SIM: Yes, she did.

HERM: What?

SIM: "Belch," "roughneck," "boozehound," and several other names when she was riled.

HERM: You are an ignoramus not to know your own name or that of your family.

SIM: Well, smarty, you don't know it either!

HERM: Do you know how to pray?

SIM: Naw, Annie and mither did all the praying at the house.

HERM: I'm asking you if you know the Lord's Prayer.

SIM: Sure.

HERM: Let me hear it.

SIM: Our dear father, who art heaven hallowed be name, kingdom come your will done heaven on earth, give us debts as we forgive debtors. Lead us never in no evil attempts, but save us from the kingdom and the power and the glory. Emma.

HERM: Didn't you ever go to church?

SIM: Sure. I'm a good climber and stole a whole shirtful of churries.

HERM: I didn't say *cherries* but *church*.

SIM: Ha, ha, you mean the little blue ones?

HERM: Heaven help me! Don't you know anything of our Lord God?

SIM: You bet! He hung in the corner behind the kitchen door. Mither brought him home from the fair and fastened him up there.

HERM: Oh dear Lord! Only now I see the great benefice of grace in thy presence and how man is nothing if he does not know thee. Listen, Simpleton—for I cannot call you anything else—when you say the Lord's prayer you must speak thus: "Our Father, who art in heaven, hallowed be thy name. Thy kingdom come, thy will be done, on earth as it is in heaven. Give us this day our daily bread."

SIM: Cheese, too?

HERM: Alas, dear child, be silent and learn. You need that more than cheese. Your mother was right when she called you clumsy. Boys like you should not interrupt an old man, but be silent, listen, and learn. If only I knew where your parents lived, I'd be glad to take you to them and teach them how to bring up children.

SIM: I don't know where to go. Our house burned down; my mither ran off and come back with Ursula; my knan ran off too; the hired girl was sick and lay in the barn. She told me to run away and not to hang around.

HERM: Who burned down the house?

SIM: Well, iron men came riding on animals as big as oxen, but without horns; these men stuck the sheep and cows and hogs, broke the windows and the oven; then I ran off, and later the house burned down.

HERM: Where was your knan?

SIM: Well, the iron men tied him up; then our old nanny goat licked his feet; this made him laugh and he gave the iron men lots of silver coins, yellow ones too, and nice shiny things and strings of white marbles.

HERM: When did this happen?

SIM: When I was supposed to herd the sheep. They wanted to steal my bagpipe too.

HERM: When were you supposed to herd the sheep?

SIM: Don't you get it? When the iron men came. Later our tousleheaded Annie told me to run away; otherwise the warriors would take me along. She meant the iron men, and I ran away and came here.

HERM: Where do you want to go now?

SIM: I sure don't know. I want to stay here.

HERM: It isn't good to keep you here, neither for you nor for me. Eat, and then I'll take you to some people.

SIM: Well, tell me what this "people" is.

HERM: People are humans like you and me. Your knan and mither and your Annie are humans. And when some of them get together, they are called "people."

SIM: Hoho!

HERM: Now go and eat!

This was the conversation we had together. The hermit often looked at me and sighed from the bottom of his heart; I don't know whether he pitied me in my excessive simplemindedness, or for a reason I discovered only some years later.

Chapter 9: *Simplicius turns from a mere beast into a Christian*

I stopped chatting and started eating. This lasted only until I had had enough and the old man asked me to go away. Then I chose the tenderest words my peasant vocabulary afforded and used them all to persuade the hermit to keep me with him. Surely he thought it would be hard to keep me around, but still he decided to put up with me, more to instruct me in Christianity than to let me help him in his old age. His greatest worry was that my tender youth might not long endure his severe and frugal way of living.

My trial period lasted about three weeks. It was spring and I worked so well in the garden that the anchorite took a special liking to me, not so much because of the work I did (I was used to it), but rather because he saw I was eager to hear his instruction and my heart was apt to benefit from it.

He started his teaching with the fall of Lucifer. From there he proceeded to the garden of Eden, and when we with our parents were run out of it, he passed through the law of Moses and taught me, through God's Ten Commandments (and their interpretation) to tell virtues from vices, to do good and avoid evil. Finally he got around to the Gospels and told me of Christ's birth, suffering, death, and resurrection. He concluded with doomsday and pictured heaven and hell as I could best grasp and understand it, clearly but not with too much detail. When he had finished one story he started another; my questions guided our progress, and he could not possibly have been a better teacher. I loved my teacher and the instruction so much that sometimes I couldn't sleep because of them. The hermit was successful in teaching me mainly because the smooth tablet of my mind was altogether blank; when he started writing on it, he did not have to crowd out or erase anything. Nevertheless, compared to other folks there still was plenty of simplicity in me, and for this reason the hermit called me "Simplicius," since neither of us knew my real name.

I learned from him how to pray, and when he had decided to let me stay, the two of us built me a hut. It was just like his, made of logs, brush, and dirt, and shaped almost like a soldier's tent or (to use a different comparison) like a turnip cellar on a farm, hardly big enough for me to sit upright. My bed was made of dry leaves and grass; it was the same size as the hut, and I can't decide whether to call this sort of shelter a covered bed or a hovel.

Chapter 10: *How he learned to read and write in a wild forest*

The first time I saw the hermit reading the Bible, I could not imagine with whom he was carrying on his secretive and, as I thought, very serious conversation. I saw his lips move and heard his mumbling, but I saw and heard no one with whom he was talking. And though I knew nothing of reading and writing, I noticed by his eyes that he was carrying on with something inside the book. I paid close attention to the bok, and after he had put it aside I took hold of it, opened it, and happening on the first chapter of the Book of Job, with a beautifully colored illustration, I asked the picture some strange questions. But when no answer was forthcoming I became impatient and—just as the hermit came up behind me—I said, "You little rascals, can't you open your mouths anymore? Only a moment ago you were gossiping with my father." (That is what I had to call the hermit.) "I can see very well that you are driving the sheep home for your poor knan and that you too have set the house on fire. Wait, wait, I can still put out the fire so it won't do any more damage." With those words I got up to get a bucket of water, because I felt something had to be done. "Where are you going, Simplex?" said the hermit, whom I hadn't noticed behind me. "Oh, father," I said, "these soldiers have sheep and want to drive them off. They took them from the poor man you were just talking with. His house is on fire too, and if I don't help put it out it'll burn to the ground." And I pointed with my finger to what I saw. "Don't rush off," said the hermit, "there is no danger." I answered politely, "But are you blind? *You* see about the sheep and *I'll* get the water." "Boy," said the hermit, "these pictures are not reality. They are made to give us an idea of events long past." I answered, "But you were talking with them a while ago. Why shouldn't they be real?"

Contrary to his habit, the hermit laughed at my childish simplicity or simpleminded childishness and said, "Dear child, these pictures cannot talk. But I can tell from these black lines what they mean. It's called 'reading,' and when I read, you think I am talking with the pictures, but it's not so." I answered, "Since I am a human being like you, I should also be able to read the black lines. How am I to take your words? Dear father, tell me what to make of this." Then he said, "All right then, son, I shall teach you and you'll be able to talk with the pictures just as I can, but it will take time, and both of us will have to try hard."

On birch bark, he wrote the letters as they appear in print, and when I had learned them, I learned how to spell, then how to read and write; and since I imitated the printed letters I could write better than my teacher. . . .

Chapter 12: *A pretty way of experiencing a blessed death and getting buried at next to no cost*

I had spent about two years and had just become used to my hard life when my best friend on earth took his mattock, gave me a shovel, and led me by the hand into the garden where we usually said our prayers. "Well, Simplex, dear child," he said, "since the time has come when I must depart the earth, pay my debt to nature, and leave this world behind, and as I see the future events of your life approaching, knowing well that you will not stay long in this lovely place, I have done my best to strengthen you in the way of virtue by giving you instruction. By means of this you are to guide your life as by a compass, to attain eternal life."

These words made my eyes water, and I said, "Dear father, do you want to leave me alone in this forest? Shall I . . ." That is all I could utter; my heart was so troubled for love of the hermit that I fainted at his feet. He picked me up, consoled me as best he could, and pointed out my mistakes by asking if I wanted to rebel against the order instituted by the Almighty. "Don't you know," he continued, "that neither heaven nor hell is able to do that? Nor you, son! Do you ask me to tarry longer in this vale of tears? Ah no, my son, let me depart, for I will be kept here in this misery neither by your tears nor by my own desire. I am called away by God's express will, and I prepare joyfully to obey his command. Instead of crying foolishly, pay attention to my last words. They are: know yourself, the longer you live the more so. And if you grow as old as Methuselah, do not give up trying. Most men were lost because they did not know who or what they were, what they could have become or had to become." Then he advised me to stay away from bad company, because the damage done by evil companions was inexpressible. He gave me an example of it by saying: "If you put a drop of sweet wine into a crockful of vinegar, the wine turns to vinegar, but if you put a drop of vinegar into sweet wine, the vinegar will go unnoticed." "Dearest son," he said, "most of all, remain steadfast. Do not let the sweat of carrying the cross discourage you from finishing a good work, for whoever perseveres to the end shall be saved. But if against my expectation you should fall because of weakness of the flesh, do not stubbornly wallow in sin, but quickly arise through honest repentance!"

These three admonitions—to know oneself, to avoid evil companions, and to remain steadfast—this pious man considered good and necessary because he had practiced them and he had not gone wrong. After he had come to know himself, he fled not only bad companions but the whole world; he persisted till the end, and in his end he was doubtless saved—how, I shall soon tell.

After he had finished speaking, he started digging his own grave with the mattock. I helped him as best I could and as he had requested, but I couldn't imagine his purpose. Then he said, "My dear and only true son—for I have begotten no creature but you to praise our Creator—when my soul has gone to its resting place, pay your due respect to my body. Cover me with the same dirt we have just now dug out of this pit." Then he embraced me, kissed me, and pressed me much harder to his chest than I thought a man like him could. "Dear child," he said, "I commend you to God's protection and die joyfully, for I think he will protect you." But I could not help crying and bawling; I clung to the chains he wore about his neck, thinking I might thus keep him from getting away. But he said, "My son, let go of me so I can see if the grave we have dug is long enough." He unfastened the chains, took off his cloak, and, lying down in the grave like someone going to sleep, he said, "Great God, take back the soul that thou hast given me. Into thy hands, O Lord, I commend my spirit," and so on. Then he gently closed his lips and eyes while I stood there like a stick, not believing that his dear soul had left the body, because I had seen him in such seizures before.

As was my custom in these situations, I stayed a few hours by him and prayed. But when my very dear hermit did not make any effort to get out of the grave, I climbed down to shake, kiss, and stroke him. But life had left him; grim, relentless death had robbed Simplex of his company. I sprinkled the lifeless body (maybe I should say I embalmed it) with my tears and after I had run to and fro for some time and torn my hair, I started to bury him, more with sighing than with shovels of dirt. And when I had hardly covered his face, I climbed down and uncovered it, to see it and kiss it once more. I carried on like this all day, until I had finished the funeral in this manner, altogether alone. Anyway, bier, coffin, shroud, candles, pallbearers, mourners, and clergy were not available to help the dead man into his grave. . . .

Chapter 15: *Simplicius is raided, and has a wondrous dream about peasants and how it goes in time of war*

When I got back home, I found that all my firewood, my household goods, and all the frugal food I had saved and harvested all summer for the coming winter were completely gone. "What now?" I thought. At that moment, need taught me to pray. I called on all my modest wit to decide what would be best for me. But since my experience was limited and indifferent, I could not reach a good decision. The best I could do was to commend myself to God and to put my trust in him; otherwise I would surely have despaired and perished. Moreover, the predicaments of the injured parson and the five miserably wounded peasants that I had witnessed that day were before me all the time, and I thought not so much about food and survival as about the hatred that existed between soldiers and peasants. But in my simplicity I could not help thinking that since Adam's creation there must surely be not one but two kinds of people on earth—wild ones and tame ones— who cruelly chase each other like unreasoning animals. I was cold and troubled, and with such thoughts I fell asleep, on an empty stomach.

Then, as in a dream, I saw how all the trees standing around the place where I lived were suddenly changing and taking on an utterly different appearance. On top of each tree sat a cavalier; and instead of bearing leaves the branches were decorated with all sorts of men. Some of these fellows had long pikes, others muskets, pistols, halberds, small flags, and drums and fifes. The sight was a pleasure to look at, for everything was neatly divided by rank. The root was made up of lowly people like day laborers, craftsmen, peasants, and such, who nevertheless gave the tree its strength and imparted vigor anew when it had been lost. In fact, to their own great disadvantage and even peril they made up for the deficiency caused by the fallen leaves. They were complaining about those sitting in the tree; and they had good cause, for the whole load rested on them and pressed them so hard that all their money was being squeezed out of their pockets and even out of the strongboxes that they had secured with seven locks. But if money was not forthcoming, certain commissioners curried them with combs (a process called military execution), and because of this there issued sighs from their hearts, tears from their eyes, blood from their nails, and marrow from their bones. Yet among them there were some jokers called funny birds who were little troubled by it all. They took everything easy, and in their misery they came up with all sorts of raillery so that they needed no consolation.

Chapter 16: *Omissions and commissions of modern soldiers, and how hard it is for a common soldier to get a commission*

The roots of these trees had sheer wretchedness to contend with, but the men on the lowest branches had to endure even greater trouble, hardship, and discomfort. And though the branch-dwellers were jollier, they were also more defiant, tyrannical, and for the most part ungodly; and they constituted at all times an unsupportable burden for the roots. About them there appeared these lines:

> Hunger, thirst, and poverty,
> Heat and cold and tyranny,
> Whence, whatever, where the ache,
> Mercenaries give and take.

These words were all the less equivocal because they described the men's work perfectly; for their entire activity consisted of hard drinking, suffering hunger and thirst, whoring and pederasty, rattling dice and gambling, overeating and overdrinking, killing and being killed, harassing and being harassed, hunting down and being hunted down, frightening and being frightened, causing misery and suffering it, beating and being beaten—in a few words, spoiling and harming, and being despoiled and harmed in turn. And neither winter nor summer, rain nor wind, mountain nor valley, fields nor swamps, ditches, passes, seas, walls, water, fire, nor ramparts, danger to their own bodies, souls, consciences, nay, nor even loss of life, heaven, or any other things of whatsoever name kept them from it. On the contrary, they continued eagerly in their works until after a while they gave up the ghost, died, and croaked in battles, sieges, storms, campaigns, and even in their quarters (where soldiers enjoy paradise on earth, especially when they run into fat peasants)—except only a few oldsters who (unless they had stashed away stolen or extorted goods) made the very best panhandlers and beggars. Right above these troubled people sat some old chicken thieves who had squatted and suffered a few years on the lowest branches and who had been lucky enough to escape death till now. These looked a little more serious and respectable than the lowest bunch, for they had climbed up one level. But above them there were some still a little higher, and they also aspired to grandeur. Being the lowest in the chain of command, they were called jacket-dusters: they beat the pikemen and musketeers and with their abuse and cursing dusted their backs and heads. Above these, the tree had a kind of break or separation, a smooth section without branches that was greased with the soap of envy so that no one (unless he was of the nobility) could climb up, no matter how smart or skillful he was. This section was polished more smoothly than a marble column or a steel mirror.

Above this place sat those with flags or ensigns, some young, some older. The young ones had been given a boost by their cousins. The old ones had climbed up under their own power, either by means of a silver ladder called bribery, or else by means of a rope which luck had let them catch because there were no better men present just then. A little further up sat still higher ones, and they also had their afflictions, cares, and troubles. They did, however, enjoy the advantage of being able to line their purses most conveniently with a liner they were cutting out of the roots; and for this they were using a knife known as forced contributions. The situation became most pleasant, to the point where a commissioner happened along and emptied a tubful of money above the tree to refresh it. Then those on top caught almost all of the rain as it dropped, while practically nothing trickled down below. For this reason more of the lower squatters died of hunger than were killed by the enemy. The upper echelons were troubled by neither danger.

There was constant wrangling and climbing in this tree, for everyone wanted to sit in the highest, happiest place. And yet, there were some lazy, devil-may-care louts who hardly tried for a better position and who sleepily did what they had to do. The lowest men were hoping for the fall of the uppermost so that they might sit in their seats. The struggle was fiercest and least rewarding in the slippery section, for whoever had a good sergeant did not want to lose him through promotion. So they found impoverished noblemen, ex-pages, poor cousins, and other starvelings, and made ensigns out of them, and these were taking the bread out of the mouths of meritorious old soldiers. . . .

Chapter 18: *Simplicius takes his first leap into the world, and has bad luck*

I did not feel like listening any longer to this argument; and, turning to the trees again, I saw that they were moving and colliding. The men came tumbling down lickety-split, and the noise of falling and cracking up was all around me. One man lost an arm, another a leg, a third even a head. While I was still staring, it seemed as if all the trees were only one tree and on its top sat Mars, the war god. He was covering all of Europe with the branches of this tree; but seemingly he could have covered the whole world, except that the sharp north winds of envy and hate, distrust and jealousy, pride and avarice were blowing through the tree and making it thin and transparent.

Awakened by the roaring and raging of noxious winds and by the destruction of the tree, I found myself alone in my hut. Therefore I started thinking again, pondering inside my little brainpan what in the world I was to do. To stay in the woods was impossible, for I had been robbed of everything and could maintain myself no longer. Nothing was left except a few books that lay scattered pell-mell here and there. While I was picking them up with tears in my eyes, and calling on God to guide my steps where I was meant to go, by chance I found a letter the hermit had written while he was still alive. It read: "Dear Simplici, when you find this letter, leave the woods at once and save the parson and yourself from present hardship, for he has done me much good. God, whom you should ever have before you and to whom you should pray, will take you to the place most suitable for you. However, always keep him in mind and always try to serve him as if you were still with me in the woods. Keep this always in mind and follow these, my last words, and you will be able to live. Farewell!"

I kissed this letter and the hermit's grave many thousand times, and without tarrying longer I started out to look for people until I should find them. I continued walking straight ahead for two days, and when night overtook me I looked for a hollow tree to sleep in. My only food was the beechnuts I picked up on the way. On the third day, not far from Gelnhausen,[4] I came upon a plain. There I enjoyed, as it were, a meal like a wedding banquet, for everywhere in the fields lay sheaves of wheat the peasants had not been able to carry off, having been chased away after the important battle of Nördlingen.[5] Their loss was my gain. I made a bed of some of the sheaves, for it was cruelly cold, and rubbed out some grain and ate it. It was most delicious food, because I hadn't tasted anything like it in a long time.

Chapter 19: *How Hanau is conquered by Simplicius, and Simplicius by Hanau*

At daybreak, I fed myself on wheat again, and then walked toward Gelnhausen, where I found the city gates wide open. One or

two gates had been burned; some still were barricaded with manure. I walked in, but though I saw no living people, the streets
were littered with corpses, some stripped of all their clothes. This
miserable sight frightened me, as you can well imagine. In my
simplemindedness I could not think what kind of disaster might
have left the place in such a shambles. After a while I found out
that imperial troops had surprised some of Prince Bernhard of
Weimar's[6] men, and this is how they had been treated. I had hardly
gone a stone's throw or two into town when I had seen enough of
it. So I turned around, took my way through the fields, and came
to a busy highway that took me to the lordly fortress of Hanau.[7]
As soon as I saw the first guard I wanted to run like a rabbit, but
two musketeers stopped me and took me to their guardhouse.

But before I go on I must tell the reader about my droll appearance at that time, for my dress was very strange, and wondrously
disgusting; the governor later had me painted that way. To begin
with, my hair had not been cut in four years, either in the Greek,
German, or French fashion, nor had it been curled or combed.
Rather it reposed on my head in its natural dishevelment, covered
with more than a year's dust for powder (*poudre* or puff-stuff or
whatever the name of this foolish material that's made for male or
female fools), and my waxen, pallid face peered out from under it
like a hoot owl about to light out at a mouse. And as I went
bareheaded all the time and my hair was naturally curly, I looked
as if I wore a Turkish turban. The rest of my outfit matched my
coiffure perfectly, for I wore the hermit's cloak, if cloak it could
still be called, since the original cloth from which it was cut had
altogether disappeared and there was nothing left but the shape
of it, barely held together by more than a thousand snippets of
multicolored cloth meticulously joined and patched. Over this
worn and multifariously mended cloak I wore the hair shirt. In
place of a shoulder wrap (because I had cut off the sleeves and was
using them for stockings), my body was girded with iron chains
crossing neatly in front and back, as they usually paint St. William.
I looked almost like one of those persons who has been caught by
Turks and goes begging for his friends. My shoes were carved from
a piece of wood and tied on with ribbons of basswood bark; my
feet looked as red as if I wore a pair of red Spanish stockings or
had colored my skin with brazilwood dye. I think if at that time

some mountebank, quack, or vagrant had owned me, and adver-
tised me as a Mongol from Siberia or an Eskimo, he would have
found plenty of fools willing to pay a farthing to see me. Though
anybody with brains could easily see from my lean and hungry
look and my neglected exterior that I had not run away from a
cook shop or a lady's drawing room, much less from some great
man's household, still I was closely questioned by the guard; and as
the soldiers stared at me, so I stared at the crazy attire of the officer
whose questions I had to answer. I did not know whether he was a
"he" or a "she," for he wore his hair and beard long *à la française*;
on either side of his face long braids hung down like ponytails, and
his beard was so miserably dressed and botched that between his
mouth and his nose only a few scraggly hairs showed. I was no less
puzzled by his wide trousers; to me, they looked more like a skirt
than a pair of men's pants. I thought to myself, if he's a man he ought
to have a regular beard, for this dandy isn't as young anymore as he
pretends. But if he is a woman, why does the old harlot have so many
hairs straggling about her face? Surely it must be a woman, I thought,
for an honest man won't have his beard ruined in such a deplorable
way. Even billy goats won't set foot in a strange herd when their
beards have been clipped—they are that bashful. And though I was
in doubt, not knowing the current fashion, I finally decided he was a
man and a woman at the same time.

This male woman (or female man) had me searched thoroughly,
but found nothing on me save a little book made of birch bark in
which I had written my daily prayers; in it lay the slip of paper
that the pious hermit (as reported above) had left me as a memento
and a good-bye present. He took it away. But since I did not want
to lose it, I knelt before him, took hold of his knees and said, "Alas,
dear Mr. Hermaphrodite, leave the prayer book with me!" "You
fool," he answered, "who in hell told you my name was Herman
Phrodite?" I had noticed right away that this joker couldn't read
or write, and he gave the book to two soldiers and ordered them
to take me to the governor.

Well, they led me through town and everybody came out to stare
at me like a sea monster and made a big fuss over me. Some thought
I was a spy; others, an idiot; still others, a bogey, a ghost, a spook,
or an apparition of some kind of evil omen. A few thought I was

a fool, and they might have been nearest the mark—if I hadn't had knowledge of God.

Chapter 20: *How he was saved from prison and torture*

When I was led before the governor, he asked me where I came from. I replied that I did not know. He continued, "Where do you want to go? And what do you do for a living?" I kept answering, I didn't know. He asked, "Where's your home?" And when I answered again that I didn't know, his expression changed, whether from anger or astonishment I can't say. But since everybody likes to suspect the worst, especially when the enemy is close by (Gelnhausen had been taken only recently, and a regiment of dragoons had been lost there), the governor agreed with those who thought me a traitor and a spy. He ordered me searched. But when he heard from the soldiers who had brought me in that it had already been done, and that they had found only the small book they had handed over, he read a few lines in it and asked me who had given me the book. I answered that it had always been mine, for I had made it up myself and written it. He asked, "But why on birch bark?" I answered, "Because the bark of other trees won't do for the prupose." "You rascal," he said, "I am asking you why you did not write on paper." "Well," I said, "we didn't have any in the woods." The governor asked, "Where? In what woods?" I answered again, in the same vein, that I didn't know.

Then the governor turned to several of the officers in attendance and said, "This fellow is either a bad egg or a simpleton. Well, he can't be a simpleton because he can write so well." And as he thumbed through the book to show them my beautiful handwriting, the hermit's letter fell out. He had it picked up, but I turned pale because I considered this my dearest possession and treasure, and almost like a holy relic to me. The governor noticed and again suspected me of treason, especially when he opened the letter and read it, for he said, "I have seen this hand and know it was written by a famous soldier, but I can't remember who it is." The contents puzzled him, too, for he said, "This is undoubtedly some kind of code no one else understands except the one with whom it was arranged." Then he asked me my name and when I answered, "Simplicius," he said, "Well, well, I know your kind! Get him out of here and put his hands and feet in chains. Mabe he'll talk differently then." The two soldiers went with me to my newly appointed hotel, that is, the hoosegow, and there turned me over to the warden, who according to orders decorated my hands and feet with bonds of iron, as if it weren't enough to carry the hermit's chain I had around me.

This first reception was not enough for the world. Next came hangmen and executioners with their instruments of torture who (although I was satisfied with my innocence) made my miserable life altogether hell. "Oh, my God!" I said to myself, "this serves me right. Simplicius left God's service and joined the world so that this caricature of a Christian could get his just reward. I had it coming with my irresponsible actions. Oh, unhappy Simplici, where does your ingratitude take you? Behold, God had hardly got you into his service and cognizance when you quit him and turned your back on him. Couldn't you have kept on eating acorns and beans in order to serve your Creator without hindrance? Didn't you know that your faithful hermit and teacher fled the world and chose the wilderness? Oh, you bump on a log! You left the woods hoping to satisfy your shameful desires and see the world. But now look; while you think to feast your eyes, you must needs perish in this dangerous labyrinth. Could you not have imagined, you numbskull, that your late predecessor would not have exchanged the joys of the world for the hard life in the loneliness of the woods if he had been confident of obtaining true peace, real quiet, and the salvation of his eternal soul in the world? You benighted Simplici, now you get the reward for your vain thoughts and insolent foolishness! You can't complain of injustice and protest your innocence, because you rushed to this martyrdom and the death that's sure to follow, and all the misery ahead is of your own making."

Thus I accused myself, begged forgiveness of God, and commended my soul to him. Meanwhile we were approaching the jail for common thieves, and when my need was greatest, God's help was nearest. For when I was surrounded by police and stood waiting (together with a multitude of people) for the jail to open, the parson whose village had lately been robbed and burned wanted to see what was the matter. His lodging was close by and he too was under arrest. When he looked out of the window and saw me he shouted wildly, "Oh, Simplici, is it you?!" When I heard and saw him, I couldn't help raising both hands toward him and crying,

"Oh, father! Oh, father! Oh, father!" He asked what I had done. I answered that I didn't know; they had surely brought me here because I had escaped from the forest. But when he found out from the onlookers that I was considered a traitor, he begged them to stop until he had reported to the governor. Such would be good for his and my release, especially since he knew me better than anyone else.

Chapter 21: *Fickle Fortune throws a friendly glance in Simplicius's direction*

He was permitted to see the governor, and half an hour later I, too, was summoned and told to go to the servants room, where there were two tailors, a shoemaker with a pair of shoes, a haberdasher with hats and hose, and someone else with all sorts of cloth to dress me up at once. They got me out of my ragged and patched coat, and took off the chain and the hair shirt so the tailors could measure me. Then a soldier barber came in with strong cleansers and scented soap, and just as he was about to start on me, another order arrived that scared me out of a year's growth. Though I worried, it didn't mean anything; it said I was to put my old weeds right back on, for a portrait artist was on his way with the tools of his profession—to wit, minium and cinnabar for my eyelids; lacquer, indigo, and azure for my coral-colored lips; orpiment and oxide of lead for my white teeth (which I bared from hunger); and carbon black and burnt sienna and lots of other colors for my weather-beaten coat. He also had a whole handful of brushes. This fellow now started squinting, drawing outlines, and putting the first coat of paint on; he tilted his head in order to compare his work exactly with my shape. Now he changed my eyes, now my hair, now my nostrils and everything he had not done right the first time, until in the end he had produced the spitting image of what Simplicius had once been, and I was quite shocked at my own ghastly appearance. Only then was the barber allowed to work on me. He washed my hair and snipped at it for at least an hour and a half. Finally he dressed it according to the latest fashion, for I had hair enough and to spare. After that he put me in a bathtub and scrubbed from my emaciated body the dirt accumulated over the last three or four years. He had hardly finished when I was given a white shirt, shoes and stockings, also a turndown collar and a hat with a feather in it. The trousers were beautifully finished, and trimmed with galloons all over. Now the only thing missing was the jacket, and the tailors were hurrying to finish it. The cook came in with a thick soup and the kitchen maid brought me a drink. There sat Mr. Simplicius like a young count, all dressed up and waited on. I enjoyed the food regardless of my uncertain future, for I had never heard of the hangman's meal! For this reason my magnificent beginning pleased me so much that I can hardly express it, let alone glory in it adequately. As a matter of fact, I don't think I've ever felt better, any time before or since.

When the coat was ready I put it on, but I made a pitiful appearance and looked like a scarecrow, for the tailors had intentionally made the coat too big, hoping I would soon grow in all directions, a hope I amply justified, for with the governor's good vittles I put on weight so fast you could almost see it. My rustic dress with its chain and other accessories was put in the museum among the rarities and oddities; my life-size portrait was hung next to it.

After supper my lord (that was me) was put into a bed the like of which I had never seen, neither at the hermit's or at home. But there was a roar and a rumble within me all night long so that I could not sleep, perhaps either because my insides did not know yet what was good for them or because they were upset about these newfangled vittles they had taken on. One way or the other, I stayed in bed (for it was cold) until the sun was shining again, and thought over the strange experiences of the last few days and how the good Lord helped me through and led me to such a good place.

Chapter 22: *The identity of the hermit whose generosity Simplicius enjoyed*

That same morning the governor's marshal ordered me to go to the preacher and find out what his master had decided about me. A soldier escorted me to the minister, who had me sit down in his study. "Dear Simplex," he said, "the hermit with whom you stayed in the woods is not only the governor's brother-in-law, but has been his dearest friend and protector in the wars. As the governor deigned to tell me, this man never lacked the heroic courage of a soldier or the godliness and reverence of a monk, two virtues rarely found together. His religious sense and the late troubles so marred his worldly happiness that he disdained and gave up his nobility and great estates in Scotland (which was his home), for all worldly business appeared to him stale, vain, and reprehensible. To say it in a few words, he hoped to exchange his present high estate for an even brighter future glory, because his high mind was disgusted with all temporal splendor, and his thoughts and intentions were set on such a plain and pitiful life as you saw in the woods where you kept him company till he died. In my opinion, he was brought to this pass by reading too many popish books about the lives of the ancient hermits, or possibly also by his untoward luck.

"But I do not want to conceal from you how he happened to come to the Spessart Hills to fulfill his wish for a poor hermit's life, so you can tell others about it sometime. The second night after the bloody battle of Höchst[8] had been lost he came all alone to my parsonage, toward morning, when my wife and children had just dropped off to sleep. (We had been kept awake all of the previous night and half of this one by the commotion caused by refugees and their pursuers.) First there was a timid knock at the door which got louder until he awakened me and my exhausted servants, and when I opened the door after a short, polite exchange of words, I saw him dismount his steed. His costly dress was as much covered with the blood of his enemies as decorated with gold and silver. And since he was still brandishing his sword I became frightened. But when he put it in the scabbard, and uttered nothing but polite speech, I wondered why such a great gentleman was asking lodging of such a poor parson. Because of his splendid personal appearance, I addressed him as General von Mansfeld, but he answered that only as far as misfortune was concerned could he be compared to him, indeed take precedence over him. He complained of three things, to wit: (1) the loss of his highly pregnant wife; (2) the lost battle; and (3) the fact that, unlike other good soldiers, he had not been favored to give his life for his faith. I wanted to comfort him, but I soon saw that his magnanimity needed no consolation. So I shared with him what was in the house and had a soldier's bed made up of fresh straw, because—though he needed rest badly—he wanted to sleep in no other. The first thing next morning he gave me his horse and his money (of which he had quite a bit with him, in gold) and handed out precious rings among my wife, children, and the servants. I did not know what to make of him and could not adjust to him quickly, for soldiers usually take sooner than give. For that reason I was worried about accepting his precious gifts and insisted I had not deserved such of him, nor knew how to deserve them. Besides, I said, if such riches, and particularly the expensive horse (which could not well be hidden), were found at my place, many people would conclude I had robbed or even helped to kill him. He said not to worry about that; he would give me a letter of donation in his own handwriting; he did not intend to wear his shirt, much less the clothes on his back, when leaving the parsonage. And then he acquainted me with his intention of becoming a hermit. I did my utmost to dissuade him, for it seemed to me such action smacked of popishness, and reminded him that he could better serve the gospel with his sword. But in vain, for he talked so much and so long with me that he wore me down, and I furnished him with the books, pictures, and utensils you saw at his place, though he wanted in return for everything he had given me, only the wool blanket on which he had slept during the night. From this he had a cloak made. I also had to exchange my wagon chain, which he wore from then on, for a golden one on which he had been wearing his beloved wife's picture; thus, he kept neither money nor valuables. My hired man took him to the loneliest spot in the woods and helped him build his hut there. How he spent his life there and how you helped him, you know yourself, and better than I.

"When the Battle of Nördlingen was lost a while ago, and I was stripped clean and robbed of my shirt, as you know I fled to this place for safety because my most valuable things were here already. And when my money was about to give out, I took three rings and the gold chain with the picture on it that I had received from the hermit (the ring with his initials was among the lot) and went to a Jew to make them into money. On account of their high value and good workmanship, he offered them to the governor, who straightway recognized the coat of arms and the picture, sent for me, and asked how I got the jewelry. I told him the truth, showed him the hermit's letter of donation (in his own hand) and told him the whole story—how he had lived and died in the woods. But he refused to believe me, and threatened to arrest me until he found out the facts. While the governor was preparing to send out soldiers to look at the hermit's place and to have you brought here, I saw you being led to prison. As the governor no longer has cause to doubt my words, because I referred to the place where the hermit used to live, to you, and to other witnesses, but especially to my sexton, who often let you and him into church before daybreak; and since the note he found in your prayer book gives excellent proof not only of the truth but also of the late hermit's holiness— the governor wants to do you and me as much good as he can, for the sake of his departed brother-in-law, and take good care of us. You have only to make up your mind what you want him to do for you. Do you want to study at a university? He will pay all expenses. Do you want to learn a trade? He'll apprentice you. Do you want to stay with him? He'll treat you like his own son, for he said that if even a dog came straying in from his late brother-in-law's, he'd take care of him too."

I replied that anything the governor wanted to do with me would be a pleasure, and I would be sure to like it.

Chapter 23: *Simplicius becomes a page.* *How the hermit's wife was lost*

The minister had me wait in his lodgings until ten o'clock before going with me to see the governor to tell him of my resolve. The reason was that then he might eat with him, since the governor was very hospitable. For at that time Hanau was surrounded, and the common man had a hard time of it, especially the refugees in the fortress; thus, a few of the better ones did not mind picking up from the streets some frozen turnip peels thrown out by the rich. The parson was lucky enough to get a seat opposite the governor. But I waited for food, plate in hand, as the majordomo told me to; I did it with the gracefulness of a jackass playing chess or a hog performing on the harp. But the preacher made up through his conversation what my own clumsiness jeopardized. He said I had been reared in the wilderness, had never been among people, and must therefore be considered excused because I was ignorant of how to behave. My loyalty to the hermit and my endurance of the hard life were admirable, so much so that not only should my clumsiness be excused, but I should even be given preference over the finest nobleman's son. He further told how the hermit had thoroughly enjoyed my company, because—as he had often said—I was the very image of his dearly beloved's face, and because he had often admired my perseverance and unswerving intention of staying with him, and many other virtues he had praised in me. In fine, he could hardly stress enough how, shortly before his death, the hermit had warmly commended me to him, the minister, and how he had confessed he loved me like his own child.

This speech tickled my ears so well that it seemed to me I had received from it reward and pleasure enough for all I had ever endured at the hermit's. The governor asked whether his late brother-in-law hadn't known that he was in command at Hanau. "Certainly," answered the preacher, "I told him so myself. But he took it (with a joyous face and a little smile) as coldly as if he had never known a Ramsay. As I think of it now, I still have to marvel at the man's constancy and firm resolve, how he could endure not only renouncing the world, but even forgetting his best friend, who was so close by!" The eyes of the governor (who wasn't a bit effeminate, but rather a tough heroic soldier) filled with tears. He said, "Had I known he was still alive and where to look for him, I would have had him brought here even against his will, that I might repay his good deeds. But since luck was against me, I will take care of his son Simplicius and thus show him my gratitude after his death." "Alas!" he continued, "the upright man had good cause to mourn his pregnant wife, for she was captured by a band of imperial cavalry who were in pursuit. That was in the Spessart Hills too. When I found out about it, not knowing but that my brother-in-law had been killed at Höchst, I immediately sent a trumpeter to the enemy to inquire about my sister and to ransom her. But I found out only that the group of cavalry had been broken up by peasants in the Spessart, and that my sister had been separated from them and become lost. To this hour I don't know what happened to her."

This and similar matters, concerning my hermit and his beloved, a lovely couple lamented all the more as they had been married but a single year, were the table talk of the governor and the preacher. But I became the governor's page boy, and such a fellow as the people (especially the peasants, when they wanted me to announce them) called Master Young, though one seldom sees a young one who is a master (but many masters that used to be young ones). . . .

Book 2

Chapter 4: *About the man who provides the money, the military service that Simplicius rendered to the Crown of Sweden, and how he received the name "Simplicissimus"*

While they were all having a good time and were about to continue yesterday's celebration, a guardsman handed a letter to the governor and announced that a commissioner, sent by the Swedish war council to inspect the garrison and look over the fortress, was at the gate. This spoiled all the fun, and the diners' enjoyment collapsed like a bagpipe when the air escapes. Musicians and guests dispersed like clouds of tobacco smoke that leave only a faint smell behind. My master, with his adjutant (who carried the keys) and a committee of officers (carrying lights), trundled toward the gate to let in the so-and-so of an inspector. My master wished Old Nick would break the visitor's neck in a thousand pieces before he ever entered the fortress! But when he let the commissioner in, welcoming him at the inner drawbridge, he almost held his stirrup to show his sincere devotion. In fact, the respect mutually displayed soon grew so monstrous that the inspector dismounted and walked to his lodgings. Each of them wanted to show his politeness by getting on the left side of the other, etc. Alas, I wondered, what is this strangely false spirit that rules men by making a fool of either one through the folly of the other?

As we approached the main guard, the sentry shouted, "Who goes there?"—though he saw it was the governor. He didn't answer because he wished to allow the commissioner the honor of replying. So the sentry shouted a second time, twice as loud. Then the inspector answered, "The man who pays you!" As we passed, I, being one of the last ones, heard the sentry (who was a green recruit, a well-to-do young farmer from the Vogelsberg) mutter these words, "I'll bet you are a liar. 'Man who pays!' A filcher and a robber who grabs my money, that's what you are. You've stolen so much money from me, I wish lightning would strike you dead before you leave this town."

At this point, I got the notion that our gentleman in the velvet jacket must be a holy man, not only because curses did not harm him, but also because even the people who hated him showed him honor, love, and respect. That same night he was entertained like a prince, made blind with drink, and put into a magnificent bed.

The inspection on the following day was a crazy affair. Even I, so simpleminded, was smart enough to hoodwink and outwit our smart inspector (and for this sort of job they don't usually employ innocent children). I was too small to pass for a musketeer, so I took about an hour to become a drummer boy. They gave me a borrowed uniform (my page-boy pantaloons would not do for this) and a borrowed drum—probably because I was borrowed myself!—and that is how I passed the inspection. But since they didn't think I could remember an assumed name to which I could answer at roll call, I kept "Simplicius." To this the governor himself added the family name and had me mustered in as "Simplicius Simplicissimus." He made me the first of my family, like a harlot's child, though in his own opinion I greatly resembled his sister. I later kept this name—until I found out the correct one—and under it I played my role quite well, doing a considerable favor to the governor and only slight harm to the Crown of Sweden. And that's all the military service I ever rendered the Crown, and its enemies have no cause to hate me for it.

Chapter 5: *Simplicius is taken to hell by four devils and treated to Spanish wine*

When the commissioner had left, the minister secretly asked me to come to his rooms. He said, "O Simplici, I take pity on your youth, and your future misfortune moves me to sympathy. Listen, my child, and find out for certain that your master has decided to rob you of your reason and make you into a fool. He has already ordered you a costume. Tomorrow you will have to attend the kind of school in which you are to lose your reason. They'll probably grill you in such a way that you become a buffoon, unless God and natural means prevent it. But since being deprived of reason is a dubious and troublesome matter, I have decided to help you with advice and other good and necessary remedies and therapies—all for faithful Christian charity and the sake of the hermit's piety and your own innocence. Therefore follow my advice and swallow this powder. It will strengthen your mind and memory, that you may overcome every attempt without hurting your reason. Here I also give you an ointment. Put it on your temples, the nape of your neck, and your nostrils. And use these remedies before you go to bed, for you may be gotten out of bed at any hour. But look out and be sure that no one discovers anything about my warning or these remedies; otherwise both of us might be the worse for it. And when they give you their damnable treatment, don't believe everything they want you to believe but act as if you do. Don't talk much or your teachers will find out they are sawing deadwood and they'll make your troubles worse, though I don't know what they will do to you. When you have put on the fool's cap and bells, come back and we'll discuss your situation again. Meanwhile I will pray to God that he save your health and your mind." Then he gave me the powder and the ointment, and I walked home.

The matter proceeded as the parson had said. I was in my first sleep when four big fellows, dressed up like frightful devils, came into my room and stopped before my bed. They jumped around like mountebanks and Shrovetide fools. One had a red-hot poker, the other carried a torch; the other two whisked me out of bed, danced with me awhile, and forced my clothes on me. I acted as if I thought they were real, natural devils, let out some piteous wails, and made gestures of fear, but they announced I would have to leave with them. They tied a towel around my head, that I might not see or hear or scream. By various roundabout ways, upstairs and down, they led me, trembling like an aspen, into a cellar where a big fire was burning. After they had taken off the towel they began toasting me in Spanish wine and malmsey. It wasn't hard for them to persuade me I had died and gone to the pit of hell, because I purposely pretended to believe everything they were making up. "Go right on drinking," they said, "for you'll be with us forever anyway. But if you don't want to be a regular fellow who joins in, you'll go into that fire!" Those poor devils tried to disguise their voices so I couldn't recognize them, but I noted right away that they were the governor's quartermaster sergeants. Of course I didn't let on I knew; rather I laughed up my sleeve that these bruisers, who wanted to make a fool out of me, instead must be my fools. I drank my share of the Spanish wine, but they outdid me because such heavenly nectar is seldom given to such fellows, and I swear they got full before I did. When the time seemed right, I staggered about as I had recently seen my master's guests do. Finally I no longer wanted to drink, only to sleep, but with the poker that was always kept in the fire they chased and pursued me into all the corners of the cellar. They seemed to have become foolish themselves, for they wanted me to drink, not sleep. And when I fell down in the chase (as I did often, on purpose), they picked me up and made as if to throw me into the fire. They kept me awake like a falcon in training, and it was a great trouble and hardship to me.

I might have outlasted them in drinking and waking, but they took turns, and in the end I would have come out the worse for wear. I spent three days and two nights in the smoky cellar, which had no light but that shed by the fire. My head started to hurt and throb as if it was about to burst, and I had to think of something to rid myself of these tortures and torturers. I did as does the fox who urinates in the dogs' eyes when he sees no hope of escaping them. When nature urged me to defecate, I stuck three fingers down my throat, and filled my pants and beslobbered my clothes all at the same time. The stench was so unbearable that even the devils could stay with me no longer. They wrapped me in a bedsheet and beat me so miserably that my innards and my soul almost left me. From this treatment I fainted and lost the use of my senses. I lay there like a corpse and don't know what else was done to me, I was so far gone.

Chapter 6: *Simplicius goes to heaven and is changed into a calf*

When I came to again, I was no longer with the devils in the cellar vault but in a beautiful room, in the hands of three of the ugliest old women the earth has ever seen. At first, when I opened my eyes, I thought they were natural spirits of hell. (If I had read the heathen poets, I would have thought of the Eumenides.) One of them had eyes like two will-o'-the-wisps and between them a

long bony hawk nose whose tip reached her lower lip. I saw only
two teeth in her mouth. They were so long, round, and thick that
either could compare with a ring finger in shape, and with gold in
color; there was bone enough for a whole mouthful of teeth, but
it was badly distributed. Her face looked like Spanish leather and
her hoary hair hung strangely disheveled about her head, for she
had just been hauled out of bed. I don't know how to compare her
two long breasts, except maybe with two cow bladders about half
blown up. At the end of each dangled a dun-colored plug half a
finger long. Truly this was a frightening sight that might have been,
at best, a good remedy for the mad love of lustful bucks. The other
two were just about as ugly; they had flat monkey noses and their
dresses weren't quite so sloppy. When I regained my senses a little
more, I saw that one was our dishwasher; the other two, the wives
of the two quartermaster sergeants.

I acted as if all my limbs had been cut off so that I couldn't
move. As a matter of fact, I didn't feel like dancing. These three
old hags undressed me naked as a grape and cleansed me of all
filth like a little baby. This did me no end of good, and during their
work they showed much patience and sympathy. I almost revealed
to them how well I had caught on to everything.

But I thought, No, Simplici! Do not confide in an old crone.
Rather remember you will have glory enough if you, a child, can
pull the wool over the eyes of three experienced old hags with
whose help one might catch the very devil in an open field. Let this
be a sign of your future success.

When they had finished with me they laid me in a marvelous
bed where I fell asleep without being rocked. They left, taking the
dirty clothes and the washtub with them. As I figure, I slept more
than twenty-four hours without interruption, and when I woke up
two beautiful winged boys stood by the bed. They were magnificently dressed in white nightshirts, taffeta sashes, pearls, jewels,
golden chains, and other precious jewelry. One carried a gold-
plated washbasin full of cookies, candy, marzipan, and other good-
ies; the other held a gold-plated cup. They claimed to be angels
and wished to convince me that I was now in heaven, since I had
happily gotten out of purgatory and escaped the devil and his dam.
For that reason I was to ask for whatever I wanted; everything I
wished either was on hand or could be sent for. I was bothered by
thirst and when I saw the cup before me I asked only for a drink,

which was gladly given to me. However, I drank not wine but a sleeping potion, and fell asleep again as soon as the potion got warm inside me.

The next day I awoke—otherwise I'd be sleeping yet!—and found myself no longer in bed, or in the previous room, or with my angels, or in heaven—but in my old goose-pen. It was as dark and scary as the previous cellar; moreover, I wore a suit made of calfskin with the rough side out. My trousers were in the Polish (or Swabian) style and the jacket was even crazier. On my head was a cap like a monk's cowl; it was pulled way down and had a large pair of donkey's ears. I had to laugh at my misfortune, for I saw by the nest and the feathers what sort of bird I was to represent. Only then did I begin to take stock and to think of my welfare. And as I had reason to thank God for not letting me lose my mind, I also ardently begged him to keep, rule, lead, and guide me. I determined to play the fool as much as I could, and at the same time to bide my time and see what else fate had in store for me.

Chapter 7: *How Simplicius behaved in this bestial state*

I could have escaped from the pen by means of the hole the crazy ensign had cut in the door. But because I wished to seem a fool, I didn't, but acted like a hungry calf calling for its mother. My mooing was soon heard by those who were supposed to watch me, for two soldiers came and asked who was in the goose-pen. I answered, "You fools, don't you hear it's a calf?!" They opened the pen, took me out, and acted surprised to hear a calf talking. (But they did this like an actor newly hired and clumsy, who has trouble impersonating the character he is supposed to act. I felt like helping them get into the spirit.) They wondered what to do with me and agreed to give me as a present to the governor, who would give them more for me, since I could talk, than would the butcher.

They asked me how I was doing. I said, "Badly enough." They wanted to know why, and I said, "Because it seems to be customary here to put honest calves in goose-pens. You boys ought to know that if I am to become an honorable ox I must be raised like a respectable critter." After this brief discussion they took me across the street toward the governor's quarters. A mob of boys followed me; they all took to mooing just like me, and a blind man would have thought, judging by the noise, that a herd of cattle was being driven by. But on sight it looked like a bunch of fools, some younger than others.

Well, the two soldiers presented me to the governor as if they had just captured me in a military raid. He gave them a tip and promised me the best treatment ever. I had my own thoughts about it—namely, "All that glitters isn't gold"—but I said, "Sir, do not have us calves confined in goose-pens if you want us to grow up into regular critters." The governor comforted me, thinking he was terribly bright to have made such a cunning fool of me. But my thoughts were, Just wait! I've passed the baptism of fire and have been hardened by it. Now we'll see who can best act the other fellow's part.

Just then a peasant who had been run off his farm by soldiers drove his cattle to the watering trough. When I saw him, I left the governor and rushed mooing and bawling to the cows, as if I wanted to suck. But when I got close, the cows were frightened by me worse than by a wolf. In fact, they stampeded as if a nestful of hornets had gotten loose among them, and their owner couldn't keep them together anymore. It was lots of fun. In no time at all, a mob of people gathered who were all looking at my foolishness, and when my master managed to stop laughing a little, he said, "One fool makes a hundred more!" I thought, Pinch yourself, sir, for it is yourself you are talking about.

Since from then on everyone called me the Calf, I in turn gave everybody a special nickname or mock name. Most people (but especially my master) thought them very suitable, for I named everyone as his character seemed to require. To put it in a nutshell, many people thought I was a witless fool, and I thought of people as foolish nitwits. As I see it, this is still the way of the world; everyone is content with his brains, and imagines he is the most intelligent of all. But as the Latin saying goes, "All the world is full of fools."

My pastime with the peasant's cows helped to make the short forenoon even shorter, for it was the time around winter solstice. At the noon meal I waited on table as usual, but I also had a little fun. When I was supposed to eat, I would take no human food or drink. I demanded grass—which was not available at that season. My master sent to the butcher's for two calfskins and ordered them slipped on two little boys. He seated the boys with me at the table and asked us not to be bashful when the food came. Our first course was a tossed green salad. The governor even had a real calf brought in and it was given lettuce sprinkled with salt. First I put on a cold stare as if to express surprise, but under the circumstances I thought I had better join in the game. When some onlookers saw me so disconcerted, they said, "It is nothing new to see calves eat meat, fish, cheese, butter, and other foods. Why, calves even get drunk now and then! These critters know a good thing when they taste it. It's even reached the point where there is hardly any difference between calves and humans. So why should you be the only one to hold out and not join in the fun?"

I was pursuaded the more quickly to start eating because I was hungry, and not because I had seen men more piggish than swine, fiercer than lions, more lecherous than billy goats, more jealous than dogs, more headstrong than horses, more stubborn than jackasses, more given to drink than cattle, slyer than foxes, more voracious than wolves, sillier than monkeys, and more venomous than snakes and toads. All of these animals enjoy human food. Yet men differ from them in shape and do not often retain the innocence of a calf.

So I fed myself, along with my fellow calves, as my appetite required, and if a stranger had chanced to see us together at the table he would surely have thought old Circe had returned to change men into animals, an art my master knew and practiced.

My dinner was exactly like my lunch, and as my fellow calves had to eat with me, so they had to sleep with me—unless my master allowed me sleep in the cow barn. I insisted on this because I wanted to fool those who thought they were making a fool of me. And I concluded that God, who is full of loving kindness, provides each man with enough intelligence for self-preservation, whatever job he has been given; and the notion many folks have, that they alone are smart, is foolish, for there are people living on the other side of the mountain too, and the doctor's degree is no one's monopoly.

Chapter 8: *Of some people's retentive memories and of others' forgetfulness*

When I awoke in the morning my two vealified companions were gone. So I got up, and when the adjutant went for the key to open up the town gate, I sneaked out of the house and went to the minister. I told him everything, how I had survived hell as well as heaven. When he saw that I felt guilty about deceiving so many people, particularly my master, by playing the fool, he said, "That is something you must not worry about. The foolish world wants to be fooled. Use what intelligence they have left you; use it for your own advantage and thank God you came out on top—that's not given to everyone. Imagine you have been reborn like the phoenix, through fire, from unreason to reason and thus to a new life. But keep in mind that you aren't out of the woods yet. At the risk of losing your mind, you slipped into this jester's outfit, but the times are so strange that no one knows if you can slip out of it without risking your life. Anybody can dash into hell, but to get out again takes sweat and toil. You aren't half the man you think you are, when it comes to escaping imminent danger. For that you'll need more brains and caution than you had when you couldn't tell bright from foolish. Put yourself into God's hands, pray diligently, remain humble, and await future changes with patience."

His lecture was purposely much different in tone, and I thought he had seen by the size of my head that I considered myself quite a big shot because I was so good at tricks and tomfoolery. In turn I read in his face that he was put out with me—and what good *was* I to him? Accordingly, I changed my tune and thanked him heartily for giving me such wonderful remedies for preserving my mind, and made an impossible promise to repay him everything. This tickled him and changed his mood. He praised his remedies and told me that Simonides Melicus had invented a technique (perfected by Metrodorus Sceptius) by which people could repeat word for word everything they had heard or read. This could not have been done, he said, without mind-building drugs of the kind he had given me.

Well, dear parson, I thought, in the books you lent the hermit I read it quite differently—but I was smart enough not to say so. For to tell the truth, it wasn't until I was supposed to have turned foolish that I became careful in my speech. The parson droned on about how Cyrus had been able to call any of his thirty thousand soldiers by name and gave many other examples of mnemonics. Finally he said, "I am telling you all this so that you will really believe a man's memory can be improved and strengthened by drugs, just as it can be weakened or even erased by them." And he launched into at least a dozen more examples.

Then he gave me some more medicine and instructions. When I left the house, about a hundred boys again followed me, all bellowing like calves. My master, who had just gotten up, came to the window, saw all these fools in a drove, and had a good laugh. . . .

Chapter 17: *How Simplicius rode to dance with the witches*

Occasionally on my travels through the woods I met some peasants, but they always ran away from me. I don't know if the war had made them fearful, had perhaps robbed them of their homes, or whether the raiders had broadcast their encounter with me, so that the peasants who saw me thought the fiend himself was walking in their part of the woods.

Once when I had been lost in the forest for several days and was afraid my rations would run out, I was glad to hear two woodcutters. I followed the sound of the axes, and when I saw them I took a handful of ducats out of the purse, sneaked up close to them, showed them this attractive gold, and said, "Gentlemen, if you will take care of me I'll give you this handful of gold." But the minute they saw me and my gold they took to their heels, leaving behind them axes, wedges, and hammers, as well as their lunch of cheese and bread. This I picked up, put it in my knapsack, and got lost in the woods again, almost despairing of ever getting back among people.

After much thinking I reached this conclusion: Who knows what will become of you? But you have money, and if you put it in a safe place with reliable people, you can live on it for a long time. Thus it occurred to me that I should hide it. From the donkey's ears that made people run I made two armbands, combined all my ducats, sewed them inside the armbands, and fastened them on above my elbow. When I had thus secured my treasure I again entered a peasant's house and took from their supplies what I needed and could lay my hands on; and though I was still quite simpleminded I had enough sense never to return to a place where I had once stolen the least bit. For this reason I was very lucky in my thefts and never got caught.

Once, toward the end of May, I again wanted to get some food in my usual (though forbidden) manner. I had made my way to a farmstead and gotten into the inner sanctum of the kitchen. When I heard people were still up, I opened wide a door leading out to the yard, to provide a way out in case of necessity. (N.B. I never went where they kept dogs.) I was waiting quietly for everyone to go to bed when I noticed a slit in a little serving window to the next room. I sidled up to it, to see if the people were going to bed. But my hope came to nothing, for instead of undressing they had just gotten dressed, and instead of a candle they had a bluish flame burning on a bench. They were greasing sticks, brooms, forks, chairs, and benches, and, one after the other, were riding out the window on them. I was greatly surprised and rather horrified. But since I was used to greater horrors and had neither heard nor read of ghosts, I did not worry too much.

When everyone was gone and it was quiet, I went into the room to look for whatever I could take along. I sat down astride a bench and had hardly touched the wood when I rode—no, whizzed—on this bench straight out the window. My gun and knapsack stayed behind as carfare! Sitting down, taking off, and landing took place in one instant, it seemed, and all at once I was in a big crowd of people who were all doing a strange dance, the like of which I had never seen. Holding each other by the hand, they had formed many circles, one within another, their backs toward the center, as the three graces are sometimes pictured. The innermost ring consisted of seven or eight persons; the second had twice as many; the third more than the first two, and so on, so that there were over two hundred people in the outer ring. Since one circle danced clockwise and the next counterclockwise, I could not distinguish exactly how many circles there were, or what occupied the center around which they all revolved. The way the heads all reeled past one another looked awfully funny.

And the music was as weird as the dance. I think everyone was singing the tune while dancing, making an extraordinary harmony. The bench that took me there set me down by the musicians who were standing outside the circles. Instead of clarinets, flutes, and whistles, they were busily playing on vipers, asps, and chicken snakes. Some were holding cats and blowing in their bungholes; when they fingered the tails, the sound was like a bagpipe. Others ran a bow across a horse's head as if it were a fiddle, and still others played on a cow's skeleton (like you sometimes find in a pasture) as on a harp. An old gaffer was holding a bitch, cranking her tail, and fingering her tits! Then there were devils using their noses for trumpets, and the echo resounded through the woods. When this dance came to an end, the whole hellish mob started racing, shouting, reeling, roaring, howling, raging, and raving as if everyone had gone stark raving mad. It is easy to imagine how frightened I was.

While this noise was going on, a chap came toward me, carrying on his hip a giant toad, big as a drum. Its entrails hung out the rear and were stuffed in at the front again. It looked so repulsive that it just about turned my stomach. "Lookee, Simplex," he said, "I know you are a good luteplayer. Let's hear something!" I practically keeled over when I heard him address me by my name. I could not answer and felt as if I were in a deep dream. In my heart I prayed to God Almighty that he help me out of my dream and let me wake up. The chap with the toad looked me straight in the eye and flicked his nose in and out like a turkey; then he struck me such a blow on the chest that I couldn't breathe. I started shouting to God, "Jesus Christ!"

This strong word was no sooner out of my mouth than the whole army disappeared. In no time at all it was pitch-dark, and I felt so bad I crossed myself at least a hundred times.

Chapter 18: *Why it is unlikely that Simplicius is telling tall tales*

Since there are people—some of them learned and influential—who don't believe that witches and ghosts exist, let alone fly through the air, there are bound to be those who will say at this point that Simplicius is pulling the wool over their eyes. Well, I don't want to argue with these people. Nowadays four-flushing is a very common practice, and I don't deny that I know how, for otherwise I would be something of a stick-in-the-mud.

But people who doubt that witches ride through the air should remember that Simon Magus was raised on high by an evil spirit and did not fall down until St. Peter had prayed. In book 3 of his *History of Northern Nations* (chapter 1, p. 19), Olavus Magnus[9] tells us that Hadingus, king of Denmark, who had been expelled from his kingdom by rebels, returned home on the spirit of Othonus, who had disguised himself as a horse. It is well known from the *History of Doctor Faustus*[10] that he and others (though they were not sorcerers) traveled through the air from one place to another. I myself knew a woman and her maid (both are dead now); this maid was polishing her mistress's shoes, and when she had finished one and set it down by the fire to do the other, the polished one slipped up the chimney in no time. But this story was kept quiet.

I have reported all this only because I want to let you know how witches and wizards have at times actually traveled to their conventions, and not because I want you to believe that *I* traveled that way. It's all the same to me whether you believe it or not; but whoever prefers to be skeptical, let him figure out a better way to get me from Hersfeld or Fulda—I don't know myself exactly where in the woods I was hanging out—to Magdeburg in such a short time. . . .

Chapter 25: *Simplicius is metamorphosed from a youth into a virgin and acquires several wooers*

This true story proves that one cannot reject all predictions, as do some smart alecks who think they know everything and believe in nothing. It also shows that a man can hardly avoid the end that was set for him, even though his downfall is foretold by prophecy. As to whether it is necessary, useful, and good to have one's horoscope cast, I only say this: Old Heartbrother told me so many things, but I have often wished, and still wish, that he hadn't. I have never been able to avoid the bad things he predicted, and the ones still ahead are turning my hair gray—and all in vain, for presumably, like all the rest, they will happen whether or not I look out for them. Concerning the good forecasts, I hold that they are more deceptive and will not help a person as much as the bad predictions.

What good did it do me that old Heartbrother swore to high heaven I was the son of noble parents, while I knew of no other parents than my knan and mither, who were crude peasants in the Spessart? Or, to cite another example, what good did it do Wallenstein, duke of Friedland, to be told he would be crowned king while violins played? Everybody knows how *he* was rocked to sleep at Eger.[11] Let other people ponder these matters. I'll get back to my story now.

When I had lost both my Heartbrothers, as I have told, I became disgusted with the camp at Magdeburg; I grew sick and tired of my jester's garb and my foolery, and I no longer cared to be the butt of everyone's jokes. I wanted to be free of all this, even if it cost me life and limb. And because there was no better opportunity, I went about it in a thoroughly irresponsible way.

Oliver, who had become my tutor when old Heartbrother died, allowed me to go foraging with the soldiers. Now, when we came to a large village and everyone went into the houses to see what he might take along, I sneaked off to see if I could find some peasant clothes I might slip into. But what I was looking for did not turn up and I had to be satisfied with a woman's dress. Finding myself alone, I changed into it, threw my suit into a privy, and imagined that now I was out of trouble. In my new outfit I started walking across the street toward some officers' wives; I was very careful to take little steps. But I had hardly left the house when some of the foraging party saw me and I speeded up my gait. When they shouted, "Stop!" I ran all the faster and reached the officers' wives before they did. I implored the ladies, for the sake of honor and virtue, to save my virginity from these lusting goats. Not only was my wish granted, but a captain's wife hired me as her maid and I stayed with her until our men had captured Werberschanze, Havelberg, and Perleberg.

The captain's wife, who was no longer a spring chicken, though she wasn't too old either, took such a liking to my pretty face and straight body that finally, after much hemming and hawing and beating vainly about the bush, she told me in plain language where the shoe was pinching her. But at that time I was still very conscientious; I acted as if I had not understood and gave no indications but those from which one might conclude that I was a shamefaced maiden.

The captain and his man were sick and confined to the same hospital. He asked his wife to have me dressed better, so that they need not be ashamed of my ugly peasant dress. Doing more than she had been told, she dressed me up like a French doll, and this fed the fire in all three of them. In fact, the ardor of the captain and his man grew so that they hotly begged of me what I could not give them and what I was most elegantly refusing the lady.

Finally, the captain determined to create a situation that would enable him to get by force what he couldn't possibly have. His wife got wind of it, and because she hoped ultimately to wear down my scruples, she blocked his every move so that he thought he'd go crazy. The one I really felt sorry for was our man, the poor fellow, for master and mistress could cool their ardor with each other, but this poor chap had nobody. Therefore, one night when man and wife were sleeping, the hired man stood by the wagon where I slept, with fiery tears poured out his love for me, and asked for my pity. But I proved harder than any stone and let him know that I intended to keep my virginity until I got married. When he offered marriage a thousand times and yet heard only that it was impossible for me to marry him, he despaired (or at least acted that way), pulled out his sword, put the point to his chest and the handle against the wagon, and let on he wanted to kill himself. I thought, the devil pushes a man to suicide. I comforted him and said I would give him my decision in the morning. This satisfied him and he went to sleep. But I stayed awake all the longer and contemplated my dilemma. I sensed that my situation would come to no good end; the captain's wife was becoming more and more impatient, the captain more daring in his approach, and the man more desperate in his love. I did not know what to do.

Often I had to help my mistress catch a flea, but of course this was to get me to see and touch her lily white breasts and her whole body. And because I was flesh and blood, this sort of thing was getting more difficult for me. If the woman left me in peace, the captain pestered me, and if I had a night of peace from these two, the manservant was after me. Thus my female clothing was much harder to wear than the fool's cap. At that point (but much too late) I thought of the deceased Heartbrother's prophecy and warning, and I imagined I was right in the middle of that danger to life and limb he had predicted for me. The dress held me captive; I could not escape in it, and the captain would have crushed every bone in my body if he had surprised me catching fleas on his pretty wife. What was I to do? I decided to make a clean breast of it to the manservant next morning. I assumed his ardor would cool, and if I gave him some of my ducats he might help me back into men's clothing and thus out of trouble. This would have worked well if luck had been with me, but it wasn't.

My foolish lover got up right after midnight in order to hear my consent. He started rattling and rocking the wagon just after I had fallen into a deep sleep (for I had lain awake worrying for some time). In a loud voice he called out, "Sabina, Sabina, get up and keep your promise!" But he woke up the captain before me because his tent was close to the wagon. Undoubtedly the captain was livid and green with envy, but he did not come out to interfere; he only got up in order to see how the deal would come out. The manservant woke me up and urged me either to come out of the wagon or to let him in. I gave him a scolding and asked if he thought I was a whore; my promise was based on marriage and without that he could never have me. He asked why I didn't get up; it was beginning to get light and I could make an early start with the breakfast. He would fetch water and firewood and make a fire for me. I answered, "If you want to do that, I can sleep that much longer. You go ahead. I'll be there soon." But since the fool would not leave me in peace, I got up, more to do my work than to be kind to him, especially since yesterday's mood of despair seemed to have left him. I could easily pass for a soldier's hired girl, for I had learned from the Croats how to cook, bake, and launder, and no finer work was required. Whatever I could not do, like arranging the captain's wife's hair, she gladly overlooked, for she knew very well I had never learned it.

When I climbed out of the wagon my lover became so enflamed by the sight of my white arms that he could not refrain from kissing me, and I didn't put up much resistance. The captain, who was looking on, could not stand it and came running with drawn sword to dispatch my lover. But he took to his heels and forgot to come back. The captain said to me, "You bloody whore! I'll teach you. . . ." He couldn't say *what* because of his anger. He started beating me as if he were insane. I began screaming and he had to stop to avoid causing an alarm, for the Saxon and the imperial armies were encamped close to each other since the Swedes, under General Banér, were approaching.

Chapter 26: *How Simplicius is considered a traitor and a warlock*

When daylight came and both armies began to break camp, my master abandoned me to the stable boys. They were a bunch of brutes and the trouble I had with them was bad enough. They chased me toward a clump of bushes where they hoped to satisfy their animal lust, as is the custom of these children spawned by the devil when a woman is turned over to them. Many other lads ran out just to watch this pitiful sport, and among these was John, the manservant. He had kept an eye on me, and seeing that things were gettting rough, he wanted to save me by main force even if it cost his head. He got some help by saying I was his fiancée. His friends felt sorry for both of us and wanted to do what they could. But the stable boys, who claimed prior rights and did not want to give up their quarry, took a different view and set force against force. So a fight started and help came running to either side; the situation almost resembled a tournament where everyone does his best for the sake of a beautiful lady.

The riotous noise brought in the constable, who arrived just as they were dragging me back and forth and tearing the clothes off me. And then they saw I was no woman. The appearance of the constable calmed everybody, for he was feared worse than the devil, and those who had been fighting evaporated. He got the essential information quickly, and while I was hoping he would get me out of distress, he arrested me because it was most unusual and highly suspicious for a man in women's clothing to be found inside an army camp. On the way to the general provost marshal, the constable and one of his men led me past the different regiments (who were all ready to march). But when we passed my colonel's regiment he recognized me, talked to me, and gave me some clothes, and I was handed over to our old provost who put me in handcuffs and chains.

I found it hard to walk that way, and I would have starved if Oliver, the secretary, had not given me something to eat. I did not dare show my ducats, which I had managed to conceal until now, for surely I would have lost them and drawn even greater suspicion on myself. In the evening Oliver told me why I was given such severe treatment. Our regimental magistrate had received orders to question me at once and to communicate the results to the provost marshal. They thought not only that I was a scout or spy, but also that I knew witchcraft, for shortly after I disappeared from the colonel, some witches had been burned, who had confessed (and died for it) to seeing me at one of their meetings, at which they had deliberated about drying up the river Elbe so that Magdeburg could be captured sooner.

The regimental magistrate was given a list of seven questions to ask me, but I wanted to tell him my whole story so that the strange circumstances of my life might explain everything neatly and put my answers to the questions in proper context. But the magistrate was not that curious; he was tired and grouchy from marching and wanted only brief answers. When he had finished writing them down he said, "Hm, yes, you are the kind whose tongue needs loosening on the rack." My thought was, "May God help me if things go his addlepated way." Early next morning the provost marshal sent our constable an order to keep me under arrest because he intended to examine me personally, as soon as the armies stopped moving. Doubtless I would have been tortured if God had not destined it differently. While under arrest I thought constantly of the parson at Hanau and of the late Heartbrother, for both had predicted my fortune after my escape from the fool's cap. I also pondered how difficult—maybe downright impossible—it was for a poor girl to go on living in these military times and keep her virginity.

Chapter 27: *How the provost weathered the battle of Wittstock* [12]

We had hardly pitched camp that night when I was taken to the provost marshal. He had my previous answers in front of him and started examining me. I told him how things had come about, but he did not believe me. It *was* hard for the provost marshal to tell whether he was dealing with a fool or a clever scoundrel, for although questions and answers came tripping off my tongue, the whole business was most strange. The provost marshal asked the constable whether anything unusual, like written documents, had been found on me. The constable answered, "No, why bother to frisk him? The camp police brought him in almost naked." But, alas, that wasn't good enough. The provost had to frisk me in everyone's presence, and since he did this most thoroughly, he found the two donkey's ears that were wrapped around my arms and contained my ducats. Then they said, "Do we need any other proof? This traitor undertook some big job. Why else would a man put on fool's clothing or a woman's dress? It's best to put him on the rack tomorrow or, as he is probably guilty, burn him; since he admits keeping company with sorcerers, he doesn't deserve anything else."

You can easily imagine how I felt. I knew I was innocent and trusted in God, but I also saw the danger, and deplored the loss of my ducats, which had disappeared into the provost marshal's pockets. But before they could give me the third degree, Banér's[13] army and ours started fighting. First they fought for position and then for the heavy artillery, which we promptly lost. Our constable, that clever puppy maker,[14] stayed pretty far behind the battle lines, with his helpers and the prisoners, and yet we were so close behind our own brigade that we could recognize the individual soldiers by their clothing. When a Swedish squadron clashed with ours, we were in danger of death no less than the fighters, for the air was so full of whizzing bullets that you might think they were fighting exclusively for our personal benefit.

Those who were afraid ducked and cringed, but those with experience and courage let the bullets pass without turning pale. In the battle itself each man tried to prevent his own death by killing the man approaching him. An awful music was performed by the cruel shots, the clashing of armor plates, the splintering of pikestaffs, the screams of the attackers as well as the wounded, by the blare of trumpets, the roll of drums, and the shrill sound of fifes. Heavy dust and dense smoke covered the scene, as if to hide the ghastly sight of the wounded and dead. From the darkness one heard the pitiful moaning of the dying and the joyful shouting of those still full of courage. As time went on, even the horses seemed to become more energetic in the defense of their masters. A few of them fell down dead beneath their riders. They had received wounds through no fault of their own and in recompense for faithful service. For similar reasons, others fell on their masters, and thus, while dying, enjoyed the honor of being supported by those whom they had carried while alive. Still others, in rage and anger, ran away, leaving mankind behind, and for the first time sought their freedom in the open fields. The earth that is accustomed to covering the dead was, herself, now covered by corpses. In one place lay heads that had lost their masters, and elsewhere lay bodies without heads. Out of some bodies entrails hung in a cruel and ghastly manner. The heads of others had been crushed and the brains spattered all over. Here one saw lifeless bodies robbed of their blood; there, some still alive and gory with the blood of others. Here lay severed arms with the fingers still twitching as if they itched to get back into the melee. There some fellows who had shed or spilled not one drop of blood were taking to their heels. In one place lay thighs separated from the burden of their bodies; yet they had become heavier than ever they were in life. In another place mortally wounded men were praying for speedy death, while others were begging for mercy and asking quarter. To sum it all up: it was one pitiful, miserable sight.

The Swedes soon drove our people before them and scattered them in quick pursuit. On this occasion our Mr. Constable and his prisoners also decided to flee, though we—never having fought—did not deserve any hostility; but the constable threatened to kill us if we didn't join him. At that moment young Heartbrother came galloping up with five other horsemen and greeted the constable with a shot from his pistol. "Look at you, you old son of a bitch," he shouted. "Do you still feel like producing puppies? I'll repay you for your trouble!" But the shot didn't hurt the constable any more than it would a steel anvil. "Ho-ho!? Is this the kind you are?" shouted Heartbrother. "I don't want to have made this trip for nothing. You puppy-maker, you'll die even if your soul is sewed to your guts." Then Heartbrother ordered one of the constable's own soldiers to kill him with an ax, if *he* didn't want to get killed.

This is how the constable got his comeuppance. When Heartbrother recognized me, he took off my chains and handcuffs, put me on his horse, and had his man take me to safety.

Chapter 28: *Concerning a great battle in which the triumphant conqueror is taken prisoner in the very act of being victorious*

Though my savior's man removed me from further danger, his master rode into it, for reasons of honor and a desire for spoils. He was surrounded and taken prisoner. When the victorious Swedes had divided their loot and buried their dead, and Heartbrother was missing, his captain inherited me, the horses, and the man. I had to become the captain's stable boy for no other pay than the promise that he would "set me up," i.e., buy me a mount

218 · Seventeenth Century German Prose

and an outfit, if I did well and when I had grown a little older. For
the time being, I had to be content and patient.

Soon after that my captain was promoted to lieutenant colonel.
It was my job to do what David did long ago for King Saul; I had
to sing and play the lute. On the march I had to carry his cuirass
for him—a job I hated. Though this piece of equipment was invented to protect against the enemy's thrusts, I found the very
opposite to be true, for under the protection of the cuirass the little
crawlers that fed on me could persecute me all the better; beneath
it they had free passage, fun, and frolic. It seemed I was wearing
this piece of armor for *their* protection, not mine, because I
couldn't possibly get at them with my hands. I thought of all sorts
of strategic devices for eradicating this armada, but I had neither
the time nor the opportunity to stamp them out by fire (as is done
by baking them in an oven), water, or poison (mercury would do
it!). Nor did I have the money to get rid of them by buying all new
shirts or a set of new clothes. I had to live with them at the expense
of my life's blood. When they were nibbling and irritating me too
much, I'd whip out my pistol as if to exchange shots with them,
but I only took the ramrod and pushed them away from their food.
After a while I put a piece of fur on the end of the rod, tied it with
sticky tape, and, reaching under the cuirass with this louse catcher,
I nabbed them by the dozen and hurled them to the ground from
high on horseback. But still, it didn't really help.

One time my lieutenant colonel was ordered to ride to Westphalia[15] on a special mission. If he had then had as many men as I had
lice, he would have frightened the whole world. But since he hadn't,
he had to proceed carefully and hide in a forest between Hamm and
Soest. At that time my pedicular enemies had reached the height of
their glory. They were plaguing me so much with their undermining
tactics that I thought they would soon take up quarters between
my skin and flesh. No wonder the Brazilians eat lice—anger and
the spirit of revenge drives them to it! One time, when part of the
cavalrymen were feeding their horses, while others slept or kept a
lookout, I could no longer stand the annoyance and stepped aside
under a tree to do battle with my enemy. Though others put on
their armor when they fight, for this battle I took mine off and
started such a murder and massacre that my swords (both thumbs)
were dripping blood, and corpses (or dead skins) fell everywhere.

The ones I didn't kill I chased out into the cold world and let them take a walk under the tree. I thought of a ditty I had heard:

> And when the slaughter started, my nails they all got red.
> One louse said to her neighbor, "O lousy, we'll be dead!"

When I think of the slaughter my skin still itches. I continued so furiously that I did not notice some imperials charging my lieutenant colonel until they were close upon me, relieved the poor lice, and captured me. My manly courage, with which I had lately slain many thousands, did not impress the imperials. I was given to a dragoon and the best thing about me that he got was my lieutenant colonel's cuirass; he sold it to his commander at Soest (where they were quartered) for a stiff price. I had to be the dragoon's stable boy, and he became my sixth master in this war. . . .

Chapter 30: *How the Hunter prospered when he began soldiering. Any young soldier can learn a lot from this chapter*

Because the commander at Soest needed a stable boy and I seemed to be the kind he liked, he was reluctant to see me become a soldier. He said he'd get me yet, for I wasn't old enough to pass for a man. Then he argued with my captain about it, sent for me, and said, "Listen, Hunterboy, you ought to be my servant!" I asked what I was to do in this position. He answered, "Help wait on the horses." "Sir," I replied, "we are far apart in this matter. I'd rather have a master in whose service the horses wait on me; but since I can't have that kind of a job, I'll stay a soldier." He said, "Your beard is too soft yet." "Oh no," I said, "I feel strong enough to outdo a man of eighty. It's not the beard that kills another man; otherwise billy goats would sell at a higher price." He said, "If your courage is as good as your tongue, I'll let it pass." I answered, "This you can find out in the next battle"; and so I let him know I wished to be a stable boy no longer.

Next I performed an autopsy on the dragoon's old pants. With their contents I bought a good horse and the best pistols I could find. Everything had to be spick-and-span, and because I liked the name "Hunterboy" I also had a new green suit made. I gave the old one to my stable boy, for I had outgrown it. So my boy and I rode side by side, and no longer could anyone consider me poor stuff. I was bold enough to decorate my hat with an outrageous plume, like an officer's, and soon I had plenty of enemies who were jealous of me. We exchanged angry words and finally came to blows. But as soon as I had shown a few of them what I had learned from the furrier in Paradise, and that I could repay every thrust in kind, they not only left me in peace but even sought my friendship.

I frequently volunteered to go raiding, either on foot or on horseback, for I was well mounted and faster on foot than many others. When we got involved with the enemy, it was neck or nothing with me, and I always wanted to be one of the first.

This activity soon made me well known and so famous among friend and foe that both sides reckoned with me, especially since the most dangerous tasks were given to me and I was put in charge of whole groups of raiders. About that time I started helping myself to everything, and whenever I got hold of something special I gave my officers such a big share of it that they helped me out and looked the other way when I raided off limits. General Götz[16] had left three enemy garrisons in Westphalia, one each at Dorsten, Lippstadt, and Coesfeld. I annoyed them no end, for I was at them with small groups of raiders almost every day, now here, now there; and I took valuable loot. Because I came out on top everywhere, the people grew to think I could make myself invisible and was bulletproof, like iron or steel. Therefore, I was feared like the plague, and thirty of the enemy's men were not ashamed to run like rabbits when they knew me to be nearby with only fifteen men. It got to the point that I was sent to exact "contributions" from towns or to see that they paid what they owed. This benefited my purse and my name; officers and fellow soldiers loved their Hunterboy; the most prominent enemy raiders shook in their boots, and the peasants were kept on my side by love or fear. I punished my enemies and richly rewarded those who had done me the least favor; I spent almost half my plunder on rewards and information.

For this reason no enemy raiders proceeded, no convoy or expedition by the enemy took place that I didn't know of. I then guessed their intentions and made my plans accordingly. And since, with a little luck, I had for the most part anticipated well, everyone was surprised at my youthful success, and many officers and experienced soldiers, even on the enemy side, wanted to see me. Furthermore, I treated my prisoners with great consideration so that they often cost me more than I gained through them; and whenever I was able to show some courtesy to an enemy, especially to officers, I always did so, if it could be done without violating my duty and loyalty.

With this sort of behavior I would soon have been commissioned as an officer if my youth hadn't prevented it. For if one wanted to command a squadron at my age one had to be of ancient nobility; moreover, my captain could not promote me because at the moment there were no positions vacant in his company. He did not want to lose me, for in me he would have lost more than a milch cow. But he did make me a sergeant.

The honor of being preferred over older soldiers—though it was a slight thing—and the praise I received daily encouraged me to even greater achievements. I lay awake at night thinking of what I could do to make myself even greater, more renowned, and more admirable. I worried over lack of opportunity to show my skill with weapons, and often wished for the Trojan War or the Siege of Ostend, but, fool that I was, I did not consider that every gray goose gets caught at last. But when a rash young soldier has luck and pluck and money, that's how it goes. Pride and arrogance are sure to arise in him. Because of my arrogance I kept two hostlers instead of a stable boy. By giving them expensive clothes and horses, I incurred the envy of all the officers who begrudged me what they lacked the energy to go out and get. . . .

Book 3

Chapter 3: *The great god Jupiter is caught and discloses the designs of the gods*

I soon found this out, and I changed my former ungodly life and strove for pious virtue. I went on raids as before, but I was so kind and discreet to friend and foe alike that everyone I dealt with thought me different from what they had heard of me. Then, too, I stopped throwing away my money and collected many pretty ducats and jewels, some of which I cached in hollow trees near Soest because that's what the famous lady soothsayer of Soest suggested. She said I had more enemies in my own regiment and in town than outside or in the enemy's garrison, and that they were all after my money. And while the news was spreading that the Hunter had skipped the country, I was right on the backs of those who were tickled about it. And before one place really found out that I had struck at another, that same place had reason to feel I was still present, for I got around like a whirlwind, was now here, now there, and more rumors spread about me than had in the days when the other fellow impersonated me.

One time, near Dorsten, I lay in ambush with twenty-five shooting irons and waited for a convoy of several carts. According to my custom I was on lookout because we were close to the enemy. Who came along but a single man, neatly dressed, talking to himself and carrying on a strange argument with his fancy walking-cane. He seemed to say, "Unless the great Numen interposes, I'll punish the world." From this I suspected he might be a great prince, traveling incognito, who wished to learn how his subjects live and who had resolved to punish those that did not live according to his wishes. I thought, if this man is of the enemy, he'll fetch a good ransom; if not, I ought to treat him so politely and impress him so favorably that I'll have a friend in a high place for the rest of my born days. So I jumped out of the bushes, with my gun cocked, and said, "You will please walk ahead of me into the bushes, sir, unless you want to be treated as an enemy." He answered very seriously, "I am not accustomed to such treatment." I urged him on politely and said, "You will not regret doing the inevitable just this once." When I had taken him to my men and replaced the lookout, I asked who he was. He answered very magnanimously that it would probably matter little to me, if I didn't know already that he was a great god. I thought he might perhaps know me or be a nobleman from Soest pulling my leg, for the Soesters are sometimes kidded about the great god and his golden apron, a huge crucifix they have in their church. But I soon caught on; I had caught not a nobleman but an arch-nut who had studied too many things too hard and had gone off the deep end particularly on the subject of poetry. When he warmed up a little, he claimed to be Jupiter.

By now I wished I hadn't made this catch, but since I had the fool I had to keep him until we moved on. And as time hung heavy on my hands anyway, I thought I'd tune up this instrument and enjoy the sounds it made. So I said to him, "How is it, my dear Zeus, that your divinity leaves its heavenly throne to descend upon us here? Forgive my question, O Jupiter; you might consider it frivolous, but we too are related to gods, being sylvan folk born of fauns and nymphs, and you can speak frankly to us." "By the river Styx," answered Jupiter, "if you were Pan's own son you wouldn't find out a thing about this, but since you resemble my cupbearer Ganymede to a T, I'll tell you that a big hue and cry about the viciousness of the world has penetrated through the clouds to me, and the council of the gods has given me permission to destroy the earth by flood, as in the days of Lycaon.

"But since in my heart I harbor an unaccountable love of the human race and prefer to use kindness rather than severity, I am presently perambulating here in order to explore human behavior. And though I find everything worse than I had expected, I am not about to terminate the human race unconditionally and peremptorily; rather, I'll punish the guilty and try to educate the rest."

I had a hard time keeping a straight face, but I said, "Alas, exalted Jupiter, your care and trouble will presumably be in vain if you don't annihilate people as before, by water or even fire. For if you send a war, all the bad, refractory rascals will get busy killing the peaceable, pious people; if you send hard times, it will mean good business for usurers and wholesalers who have a corner on the market; if you send sickness and death, the misers and survivors will have their heyday since they'll inherit a lot. You will have to eradicate the whole rotten bunch if you want to punish them."

Chapter 4: *Concerning the German hero who will overcome the whole world and make peace among all nations*

Jupiter answered, "You speak of this problem like a human, forgetting that we gods can devise means to punish only the bad and to preserve the good. I shall create a German hero who will accomplish all with the edge of his sword. He will kill all the bad people and preserve and foster the good." I said, "Such a hero would need soldiers; where soldiers are involved there is war, and where there is war the innocent must suffer with the guilty!" "You terrestrial gods are just like people on earth; you understand practically nothing! I shall send a hero who needs no soldiers and yet can reform the world. In the hour of his birth I shall give him a body stronger and more handsome than that of Hercules; he will be equipped with abundant foresight, wisdom, and understanding. Venus herself will give him an ingratiating face so that he will surpass Narcissus, Adonis, and my own Ganymede; she will endow him (in addition to all his virtues) with a peculiar charm, grace, and personality so that he will become popular with everybody. Mercury will present him with incomparable sense and reason, and the inconstant Moon will encourage rather than hinder him, for he will give him great speed. Pallas Athene will raise him on Parnassus, and at the astrologically right time Vulcan will forge his weapons, particularly the sword with which to strike down the godless and subdue the whole world—without the help of a single person fighting as a soldier. He'll need no help. Every large city will tremble at his presence and every fortress that is otherwise impregnable will fall to his power in the first quarter of an hour. Ultimately he will rule over the greatest sovereigns on earth and set up such a government over land and sea that men as well as gods will love it and praise it."

I said, "How can destruction of the godless and power over the whole world be achieved without strong-armed action? O Jupiter, I frankly confess that I can understand these matters even less than a mortal." Jupiter answered, "I'm not surprised, for you don't understand the wondrous power the hero's sword will have. Vulcan will make it of the same material of which he makes my thunderbolts, and he'll give it such virtue that my magnificent German hero can deprive whole armadas of their heads with one stroke through the air, although the men may be behind a mountain and an hour's distance away. The poor fellows will have to lie down headless before they even know what hit them. Whenever he comes to a town or a fortress, he'll use one of Tamerlane's tricks,[17] raising a white flag as a sign that he comes in the interests of peace and the common welfare. If the people come out, well and good; if not, he'll draw his sword, and by virtue of its special power he'll cut off the heads of all warlocks and witches in that town and display a red flag. But if no one presents himself after that, then in the same manner he'll dispatch all murdererers, usurers, thieves, rogues, adulterers, whores, and pimps and run up a black flag.

Finally, if the ones still left in town don't come to him and act repentant, he'll want to eradicate the whole city as disobedient and obstinate. But he will execute only the ones who kept the others from yielding sooner. Thus he will go from one town to another, giving to each the countryside around it, to be governed in peace. From each town in all of Germany he will summon the two wisest and most learned men, make a parliament of these, unite the towns forever, abolish serfdom and tariffs, imposts, interests, mortgages, and dues throughout Germany, and take such measures that all memory of servitude, contribution, confiscation of money, warring, or onetime special taxes will be lost among the people, who will be more blessed than the inhabitants of the Elysian fields.

"Then," Jupiter continued, "I shall descend frequently with the whole crowd of the gods to revel among the Germans and their vines and fig trees. I shall relocate Helicon inside Germany and transplant the Muses there. The three Graces will awaken a thousand merriments in the Germans. I shall bless Germany more abundantly with all sorts of luxuries than Arabia felix, Mesopotamia, and the country around Damascus. I shall forswear use of the Greek tongue and speak only German, and, in a word, prove such a Germanophile that I shall yield to them (as previously to the Romans) dominance over the whole world."

I said, "Your Highness Jupiter, what will the masters and princes say when the future German hero illegally takes away what is theirs? Won't they resist by force or at least protest to men and gods against this seizure?" Jupiter answered, "My hero will bother very little with them. He will divide all the mighty into three groups. Those who live in sin and evil he will punish like commoners, for no earthly power can resist his sword. The others will be given the choice of staying in the country or leaving it. Those who love their land and elect to stay in it will have to live like other common people. But the private life of the Germans will become much happier and more enjoyable than is the life of kings at present. All Germans will be like Fabricius who refused to share the kingdom of Pyrrhus because he loved his fatherland and his virtue and honor too dearly.[18] Those will constitute the second group. The third group, the ones who want to stay rulers, our hero will lead by way of Hungary and Italy into Moldavia, Wallachia, Macedonia, Thrace, Greece, and even across the Hellespont into Asia. Having obtained these countries for them, he will there deposit and make into kings all the military cuthroats of Germany. Then he will capture Constantinople in one single day, will lay in front of their behinds the heads of those Turks who won't convert to Christianity, and reestablish the Roman Empire.

"Returning to Germany, he (with the two members of parliament summoned from each of the German cities, who will be called the leaders and fathers of the German fatherland) will construct a city right in the middle of Germany. This city will be larger than Manoah in America, contain more gold than Jerusalem in the days of Solomon. Its ramparts will compare to the Tyrolean Alps; its moats, to the straits between Spain and Africa. In the city he will build a temple of diamonds, rubies, emeralds, and sapphires; and in the museums that will be built he will collect the rarest objects from all over the world and the rich gifts that will be sent him by the kings of China and Persia, the Great Mogul of the East Indies, the Great Khan of Tartary, Prester John in Africa, and the Great Czar in Moscow. The Turkish emperor would send him even-more—if our hero hadn't taken his realm away from him and given it as a fief to the Roman emperor."

I asked Jove what the Christian kings would do in this emergency. He answered, "The ones in England, Sweden, and Denmark (because they are of German blood and family), and the ones in Spain, France, and Portugal (because the ancient Germans once conquered and ruled these countries) will volunteer to receive their crowns, kingdoms, and lands as fiefs from the German nation. Then there will be a constant and everlasting peace among all nations of the world—as in the days of the Emperor Augustus."

Translated by George Schulz-Behrend

Notes

1. A sparsely inhabited, wooded hill country north of the Main River and south of the Kinzig River. Grimmelshausen himself came from this area. The notes are based largely on those provided by the translator in: George Schulz-Behrend, trans., *Simplicius Simplicissimus,* by Johann Jacob Christoph von Grimmelshausen (Indianapolis: Bobbs-Merrill Company, Inc., 1965).

2. Arachne, a Lydian woman, wove in competition with the goddess Minerva (Athena). When Minerva ripped the cloth, Arachne hanged herself in despair and was changed into a spider.

3. St. Anthony (ca. 250–350), father of monastic life, the earliest Christian anchorite. Plagued by demons as a young man, he retreated to the solitude of the desert.

4. Grimmelshausen's birthplace, a town on the Kinzig River.

5. On September 6, 1634, the Swedish under Duke Bernhard of Saxe-Weimar and Count Horn were defeated by the imperial forces at Nördlingen.

6. Duke Bernhard of Saxe-Weimar (1604–39) was one of the most famous generals of the Thirty Years' War. When the king of Sweden, Gustavus Adolphus (1594–1632), was killed in the battle of Lützen, Bernhard took charge and saved the day for the Protestants.

7. Hanau is east of Gelnhausen on the Main River, not far from Frankfurt. The commander of the fortress, James Ramsay (1589–1638), a Scot in Swedish service, is a historical figure.

8. The battle near Höchst (now a suburb of Frankfurt) took place on June 10, 1622. The imperial general Count Johann Iserclaes Tilly (1559–1632) defeated "Crazy Christian," duke of Braunschweig (Brunswick), who fought for Protestantism in the service of Frederick V of the Pfalz (Palatinate), the so-called Winter King of Bohemia (the grandfather of Liselotte von der Pfalz).

9. Olaus Mangus (1490–1557), Swedish ecclesiastic and author; his *History* was published in Rome in 1555.

10. Chapbook published in 1587 in Frankfurt am Main; source for both Christopher Marlowe's *Tragical History of Doctor Faustus* (1588) and Johann Wolfgang Goethe's play *Faust I and II* (1808, 1832).

11. Albrecht Eusebius Wenzel von Wallenstein (1583–1634), the greatest general on the Catholic side, was murdered in the town hall of Eger, Bohemia, on February 25, 1634.

12. The battle of Wittstock (Brandenburg) took place on September 24, 1636. It is uncertain whether Grimmelshausen actually delivers an eyewitness report here.

13. Johan Banér (1596–1641), Swedish general, one of the most important generals of the Thirty Years' War.

14. In an earlier episode (book 2, chapter 22) the constable, an amateur magician, had conjured up numerous puppies that emerged from various openings in his audience's clothing.

15. Westphalia, a district in northwestern Germany, is partly hilly, partly good, level farmland. Various industries flourished there even in the seventeenth century. The towns mentioned were centers of military activities.

16. Count von Götz (d. 1645), Austrian (imperial) field marshal.

17. Tamerlane or Timur (ca. 1336–1405), a renowned Mongolian conqueror, usually pictured as the incarnation of deceitfulness and atrocity.

18. Gaius Fabricius Lucinus was regarded as a model of ancient Roman simplicity and integrity. After the defeat of Heraclea (280 b.c.) he had been sent to negotiate with Pyrrhus for the release of Roman prisoners and had spurned the enemy's bribes.

*　*　*

Johann Jacob Christoph von Grimmelshausen *(cont'd.)*

Two years after the publication of Grimmelshausen's highly successful *Simplicissimus* a short novel appeared entitled *To Spite Sim-*

228 · *Seventeenth Century German Prose*

plicius; *Detailed and Wondrously Strange Life History of the Life of the Arch-Deceiver and Runagate Courage.* The *Runagate Courage* was one of twelve publications belonging to what have come to be called the *Simplician Writings.* Not until the nineteenth century was it discovered that the alleged author, Philarchus Grossus von Trommenheim, and German Schleifheim von Sulsfort, the author of *Simplicissimus,* were anagrams for Johann Jacob Christoph von Grimmelshausen. As the title indicates, the impetus for the book is ostensibly Courage's desire for revenge against Simplicissimus, who in his autobiography had disparaged a woman he had met at a spa, namely Courage herself, with whom he had had an affair. Courage is determined to make a fool of him by recounting her own life story. Here she reveals that the child Simplicissimus thought to be theirs was in actuality the bastard child of her maid. Furthermore, she regales her readers with her triumphs over one of her husbands, the henpecked Hopalong, Simplicissimus's pal.

The *Runagate Courage* belongs to the tradition of the European picaresque novel, but, although she belongs to the company of female rogues, the Spanish pícaras Celestina and Justina, Moll Flanders, and Manon Lescault, the literary figure Courage did not become world-famous until the appearance of Bertolt Brecht's play *Mother Courage and Her Children* in 1939. Brecht's Mother Courage owes much of her venality to her predecessor, Brecht having recognized that Grimmelshausen's creation ruthlessly turned the vicissitudes of the Thirty Years' War into profit, while ironically remaining herself a victim of war. Nevertheless Brecht departs significantly from his model. Unlike Mother Courage, Grimmelshausen's Courage is barren; as the narrator pointedly explains, her purse not her belly expands. We follow her story from her earliest days as a ravishingly beautiful young woman, who soon learns to satisfy both her lust and her greed, to her days among the despised and marginalized gypsies. Although Courage enjoys moments of triumph and wealth, is frequently able to revenge herself on her male adversaries, she is punished again and again for her behavior that is both unchristian and inappropriate to her gender. Courage's female body as the site of the world's viciousness is a not-unusual motif of the misogynous literature of the century that ruthlessly pursued and executed so-called witches onto whom society had projected its ills.

Chapter 2: *Maid Libushka*[1] *(hereafter called* Courage) *enters the war, calls herself Janco, and must for a time serve as a valet de chambre, whereby it is reported how she acted and what other strange things happened to her*

Those who know how the Slavonic peoples treat their serfs might possibly think that I was bred and born of a Bohemian nobleman and a peasant's daughter. But knowing and thinking are two different things. I think a lot of things too, but I still do not know. If I were to say that I had known who my parents were, I should be lying, and it would not be the first time; but this I do know: that I was brought up tenderly enough in Prachatitz,[2] kept in school, and instructed more carefully than a girl of humble birth in sewing, knitting, embroidery, and other such lady's work. Ample money for my board came from my father, but just what place it came from I still did not know; and my mother wrote often and inquired about my welfare, though I never met face-to-face either. When the Bavarian prince[3] marched with Bucquoy into Bohemia to drive the new king[4] out again, I was an impertinent thing of thirteen years who was beginning to have all kinds of fancies and conceits about where I might have come from; and that was my greatest concern, because I could not ask, and on my own I could not get to the bottom of it at all. I was guarded from common folk as a beautiful painting is protected from dust; my nurse kept constant watch over me, and because I was not allowed to play with other girls my age, look you, the bees which curiosity hatched in my bonnet increased in number, and they were the only things I concerned myself about anyway.

Now when the duke of Bavaria separated from Bucquoy, the Bavarian moved before Budweis[5] and the latter before Prachatitz. Budweis soon surrendered and was very wise to do so, but Prachatitz held out and felt the might of imperial arms, which dealt cruelly with the zealots. Now as soon as my nurse got wind of the way things were going, she said to me right away: "Maid Libushka, if you wish to keep your maidenhead, you must let me shear your head and put you in men's clothes; if not, I would not give the buckle off a chastity belt for your honor, which has been commended so earnestly to my care."

I thought: "What strange talk is this?" But she fetched shears and cut off my golden hair on the right side, but she left the other side be, so that in every way my hair was like the most elegant men were wearing it then.

"There, my daughter," she said, "if you escape this tumult with your honor intact, you will still have enough hair to adorn you, and in a year the rest will grow back in too."

I was quick to let her console me, for from childhood on it was my nature to like things best when they were all topsy-turvy, and when she had dressed me in breeches and a doublet she taught me to take longer strides and what other mannerisms I should affect. Thus we waited for the imperial army to invade the city, my nurse with fear and trembling, to be sure, but I was lusting to see what new and uncommon carnival this might turn out to be. I soon found out; but I will not delay my tale by recounting how the men of the captured city were slaughtered by the conquerors, the women raped, and the city itself plundered, since such things were so common in the recent, long-continuing war that everyone has a tale to tell about them. But I am bound to report, if indeed I am to tell my whole history, that a German trooper took me along as his boy, to take care of his horses and to help him forage, that is, steal. I called myself Janco, and I could speak German pretty well, but, as is the custom with all us Bohemians, I did not let on that I did; otherwise, I was slender and pretty and had a noble air; and I only wish that whoever does not believe me had seen me fifty years ago, because he would surely have to attest that it was so.

Now when this first master of mine brought me to the company, his captain of horse, who was truly a brave and handsome young gentleman, asked him what he intended to do with me. He answered: "What other troopers do with their boys: have him steal and take care of my horses; I hear that for this the Bohemians are said to be the best. They say it is certain that when a Bohemian takes oakum out of a house a German will surely not find any flax in it."

"But," answered my captain of horse, "what if he works this Bohemian craft on you first and rides off with your horses as proof?"

"I'll keep my eye on him, all right," said the trooper, "till I get him out of his own backyard."

"Farm boys who have been brought up with horses," answered the captain of horse, "make much better stable boys than town boys who cannot learn in a city how to take care of a horse. Besides, it seems to me that this lad is of a good family and much too daintily brought up to take care of a trooper's horses."

I pricked up my ears mightily, without letting on that I understood anything of their discourse, because they were speaking German; my greatest concern was that I might be turned out and chased back to the plundered city of Prachatitz, because I had not yet had my fill of the drums and pipes, the cannon and trumpets, sounds that made my heart leap for joy. Finally it came to pass, I know not whether for good or ill, that the captain of horse kept me for himself, to wait upon his person as a page and valet de chambre; to the trooper, however, he gave another Bohemian clodhopper for a boy, because the trooper insisted on having a thief from our nation.

Well, I fitted quite nicely into my new role in this masquerade. I was able to fawn over my captain of horse so cunningly, keep his clothes so clean, do up his white linen so nicely, and care for his person so well that he could not but regard me as the epitome of a good valet de chambre; and because I also had a great liking for arms, I took care of his in such manner that my master and his servants could rely on them, and therefore I soon got him to give me a sword and to dub me fit for military service by giving me a cuff on the ear. That I behaved so sturdily in this could not but surprise everyone, and they all thought it a sign of incomparable intelligence that I learned to speak German so quickly, because no one knew that I had been obliged to learn it from childhood on. Next, I tried my best to rid myself of all my feminine ways and to acquire masculine ones instead; I purposely learned to curse like a trooper and to drink like a tinker besides. I drank many a cup to everlasting friendship with those whom I thought my equals, and whenever I wished to swear that something I said was true, I did it with rogues' and thieves' curses, so that no one might remark wherein I had fallen short at birth or what, for that matter, I had not brought along into the world with me at all.

Chapter 3: *While serving with a resolute captain of horse, Janco exchanges his noble hymen for the nomen Courage*

My captain of horse, as noted above, was a handsome young gentleman, a good horseman, a good swordsman, a good dancer, a cavalier, and a soldier, and uncommonly fond of the chase; in particular, to course the hare with hounds was his greatest joy. He had no more beard on his face than I, and if he had worn lady's dress not one in a thousand but would have taken him for a beautiful maiden. But where am I off to? I must tell my history. After Budweis and Prachatitz had fallen, both armies marched before Pilsen, which resisted bravely, to be sure, but afterwards received its punishment too, with pitiable slaughter and hangings; from there they moved on Rakonitz, where there occurred the first action on the open field which I had ever seen; and at that time I wished I were a man, so I could go to war all my life; for everything that happened was so merry that my heart leaped for joy, and this desire was increased by the battle on the White Hill[6] near Prague, because our side won a great victory and lost few men. At this time my captain of horse took much booty, but I did not let him use me as a page or valet, much less as a girl, but as a soldier who has sworn to go against the enemy and earns his pay by doing so.

After the encounter, the duke of Bavaria marched into Austria, the prince elector of Saxony[7] into Lusatia and our General Bucquoy into Moravia, to force the rebels against the emperor to renew their allegiance to him; and while the latter was having himself cured of injuries that he had received before Rakonitz, during this same lull between battles that we were enjoying on his account, look you, I received a wound in my heart, which was pierced by the charm of my captain of horse, for I observed in him only those qualities that I have recounted above and paid no heed to the fact that he could neither read nor write and was altogether such a crude person that I can swear on my faith that I never heard or saw him in prayer. And even if wise King Alphonsus[8] himself had called him a beautiful *bestia*, it would not have quenched my ardor, which, however, I thought to keep secret, because what little maidenly modesty I had left cautioned me to do so; but this I was able to do only with the greatest impatience, so that in spite of my youth, which made me not yet fit for any man, I often wished I could take the place of those whom I and others at times procured for him.

In the beginning I was in no small measure kept from a violent and dangerous outburst of passion by the fact that my beloved was born of a noble and renowned family, which made me imagine that he would wed no one who did not even know her own parents; and I could not make up my mind to become his mistress, because every day with the army I saw so many whores turned over to the rabble. Now although this war and strife that was going on inside me tortured me dreadfully, I was nevertheless at the same time lusty and gay, indeed I was of such a nature that my spirits were dampened by neither the desire within me nor the work and unrest of war without. To be sure, I did not have anything to do but wait upon my captain of horse, but love taught me to accomplish that with such industry and zeal that my master would have sworn a thousand oaths that there was no more faithful servant on earth than I; in all engagements, no matter how sharp they may have been, I never moved from his side or left his back unguarded, though I was not obliged to serve him thus; and on top of that, I was always willing to do anything at all that I knew would please him. Thus, he could have read from my face easily enough that I honored and worshiped him with far greater devotion than that of a common servant if only my clothes had not deceived him. In the meantime, the more time passed, the bigger my bosom grew and the more the shoe pinched me, in such manner that I did not trust myself to conceal much longer either my bosom, which would soon show without, or the fire that was raging within it.

After we had stormed Iglau, subdued Trebitz, brought Znaim to its knees, bent Bruenn and Olmuetz[9] under the yoke, and forced most of the other cities to submit to us, I shared in a good deal of the booty, which my captain of horse gave me as a gift in return for my faithful services and with which I equipped myself excellently well, got myself the best possible mount, stuffed my own purse, and at times drank a measure of wine with other soldiers at the sutler's.

Once I was making merry with a few of them who out of envy directed abusive words at me, and there was one in particular among them who was hostile toward me and who reviled and scorned the Bohemian nation quite to excess. This fool represented to me that the Bohemians had mistaken the rotten maggoty carcass of a dog for a stinking cheese and had gulped it down; and he even mocked me as if I personally had been present at the feast; therefore both of us came to cursewords, from cursewords to blows, and from blows to scuffling and wrestling, during which work my adversary whisked his hand inside my trousers to seize me by that equipment which I, after all, did not possess, which futile but murderous hold vexed me much more than if he had not found himself empty-handed; and for this very reason I became that much more enraged, indeed nearly half out of my senses, as it were, so that I summoned up all my strength and agility and defended myself by scratching, biting, hitting, and kicking in such a way that I brought my enemy down and so used his face that it resembled a devil's mask more than a human countenance; I should have throttled him too, in fact, if the rest of the company had not torn me from him and made peace. I got off with nothing but a black eye and could well imagine that this evil customer had become quite aware of my true sex, and I believe too that he would have revealed it, if he had not been afraid either that he would receive more blows, or that in addition to those already received he would be made a laughingstock for letting a girl beat him; and because I was worried that he still might gossip, look you, I departed.

When I got to our quarters my captain of horse was not at home, but in the company of other officers, with whom he was making merry and where he learned, before I came before him, what kind of battle I had fought. He loved me, knowing me to be a resolute young fellow, and for that reason my reprimand was that much less harsh; however, he did not forbear to lecture me because of what I had done. But just when the sermon was at its best and he asked me why I had thrashed my adversary so horribly, I answered: "Because he made a grab for my courage, which place no man's hands have touched." (For I wished to express myself delicately and did not wish to call it by as crude a name as the Suabians use for their penknives, which, if I were master, would not be called such a vulgar word either, but would have to be called "lewd scabbards."[10] And because my virginity, all this notwithstanding, was breathing its last, particularly since I could not but hazard that my adversary would betray me anyway, look you, I bared my snow white bosom and showed the captain of horse my firm, appealing breasts: "Look, sir!" I said, "here you see before you a maiden who donned men's clothing in Prachatitz to save her honor from the soldiers; and since God and fortune have placed her in your hands, she therefore beseeches you and hopes that you, as an honorable gentleman, will protect her and keep intact the honor which she has preserved." And after I had brought forth that, I began to weep so pitiably that one would have staked his life that everything I said was in dead earnest.

Although the captain of horse was greatly astounded, to be sure, he could not but laugh at how I had described with a new name many of the colors which were to be found on my escutcheon. He consoled me most kindly and promised with high-flown words to protect my honor like his own life; but with his deeds he soon showed that he would be the first to rob me of my maidenhead; and I myself liked his unchaste groping better than his honorable promises; however, I defended myself valiantly; not, of course, to escape him or to flee his lustful advances, but to really excite him and to make him even more lustful; and the trick succeeded so well in every way that I allowed nothing to happen till he promised, or might the devil fetch him, to wed me, despite the fact that I could well imagine that he had no more intention of keeping his promise than of cutting his own throat. And now, look you, my dear Simplex! You may have thought up till now that in Sauerbrunnen you were the first to skim the sweet cream off the top.[11] Oh no, you booby, you were cheated, it was gone, perhaps even before you were born, wherefore, since you were tardy, you were justly entitled to and received nothing but the whey. But that is only child's play compared to the other ways I have led you on and cheated you, all of which you shall learn from me too, in its proper place.

[The name Courage sticks, although no one knows its true origin. Courage manages to persuade the captain of the horse to marry her, but is soon widowed. Several husbands and many battles later she meets a certain musketeer who becomes enamored of her.]

Chapter 15: *Under what conditions they promise each other to live unmarried in marriage*

If I had had an honest bone in my body, I could have arranged my affairs differently at that time and steered a more honorable course, for my adopted mother, with two of my remaining horses and a bit of cash money, ascertained my whereabouts and advised me to get out of the war and to my money in Prague or to the

estates of my husband, the late captain of infantry, to live in peace
and quiet as a householder; but there was no talking either rhyme
or reason to my heedless youth, but rather the stronger the brew
the better I liked the beer. I and my aforementioned mother were
staying with a sutler[12] of the same regiment in which my husband
who had fallen at Hoya[13] had been a captain of infantry, where
they paid me due respect on his account; and I believe too that I
would have gotten another good officer as husband if we had
stayed quiet and lain in quarters anywhere. But because our forces
of twenty thousand men, consisting of three columns, were
marching to Italy with all haste and were obliged to break through
Graubünden,[14] which presented many obstacles, look you, few
with any brains thought of marrying, and therefore I too remained
a widow much longer; on top of that, some did not have the heart
to speak to me of marriage, and others had other reasons to forbear
to do so, and they thought me too reputable to expect anything
from me out of wedlock, because I had kept faith with my former
husband, so that one and all thought me more virtuous than I was.

But while I was poorly served by this long fast, on the other
hand that musketeer who had come to my aid during the engagement with the two above-mentioned troopers had become so smitten with me and was making such a fool of himself over me that
he had no peace, neither night nor day, and undertook many a
march on my account, whenever he had time or was off duty. I
well saw what was going on with him and where the shoe was
pinching him; but because he did not have the courage to reveal
his wishes to Courage, I felt as much contempt as pity for him.
But by and by I changed my proud mind, which in the beginning
was set on being nothing but an officer's lady; for when I observed
the sutler's trade and saw daily with my own eyes what profits
always came his way, while many an honest officer was obliged to
pull in his belt, I began to ponder how I might start and institute
such a sutlery myself. I made an estimate of the money and property that I had with me and found them quite sufficient, because I
still had a considerable number of gold coins sewn into my bodice.
Only the honor, or the disgrace, namely, that from the wife of a
captain of infantry I should sink to the rank of a sutler woman,
held me back; but when I remembered that at this time I was no
longer the wife of a captain and perhaps would not attain to such
a rank again either, look you, then the die was cast, and I was

already seeing myself in my mind's eye serving up wine and beer at double the price and haggling worse than a fifty- or sixty-year-old Jew.

Just at this time, namely, when we had arrived in Italy, having traversed the *Alpes,* or high mountains, with our three-pronged imperial army, my gallant's passion reached the highest peak, without his having yet spoken a single word to me about it. Once, under the pretext of drinking a measure of wine, he came to my sutler's tent, looking pale and disconsolate, as if he had but recently had a baby without having either father, milk, or pap for it, nor knowing where to come by them. His sad glances and his ardent sighs were the best language he spoke to me, and when I asked him what he desired, he took heart and answered me immediately as follows: "Oh, my most beloved captain's lady (for he dared not call me Courage), if I should tell you my desire, I should either arouse your ire, so that you would straightway deprive me of your lovely presence and never again ever deign to look upon me, or you would reprove me for my transgression, either of which would most assuredly mean certain death for me." And thereupon he again became as silent as a grave.

I answered: "If either of them can mean certain death for you then each of them can also revive you; and because I am indebted to you for having saved me from my ravishers when we lay in Vierlanden,[15] between Hamburg and Lübeck, I therefore gladly grant you the privilege of looking upon me till you are hale and hearty once more."

"Oh most esteemed lady!" he answered. "The very opposite is true, for when I looked upon you for the first time, the sickness began which will be the death of me if I should no longer look upon you. Truly a wonderful and strange state which I have fallen into in recompense for having saved my most esteemed lady from the danger which had befallen her."

I said I should be guilty of great ingratitude if I had thus rewarded good with evil.

"That I do not say," answered my musketeer.

I replied: "What then are you complaining of?"

"Of myself, of my unhappiness," he answered, "and of my fate, or perhaps of my impertinence, or of my fancy, or of I myself know not what. I cannot say that the captain's lady is ungrateful, because for the trifling trouble I took in driving off the trooper who was yet alive and threatening her honor I was sufficiently rewarded by the legacy of the trooper whom my most esteemed lady had already so gloriously deprived of his life, so that he should not shamefully deprive her of her honor. My sovereign mistress," he said further, "I am in such a perturbed state, which so perturbs me that I can neither explain my perturbation, nor my desires, nor my guilt or indebtedness or your own, much less my own guiltlessness, or anything at all which might help me. Behold, most beauteous lady, I am dying because fortune and my low estate do not grant me the joy of showing your Highness how happy I should esteem myself to be your most humble servant."

I stood there like a fool, because I had heard from a lowly and still very young musketeer such a speech, all mixed up and, as he said, proceeding from a perturbed mind; nevertheless it seemed to me to reveal a lively spirit and an ingenious mind that was worthy of my love and that seemed to me would be profitable for me to use in good faith in the sutlery with which my belly was teeming at that time. Therefore I made short shrift of the poor booby and said to him: "My friend, first you call me your sovereign mistress; secondly, you call yourself my servant, if you only could be that; thirdly, you lament that without me you must die: now from these I recognize the great love which you perhaps bear me. Now just tell me how I may requite this love, for towards one who has saved me from my ravishers I do not wish to be found wanting in gratitude."

"With love," said my gallant, "and if I be found worthy of it I should count myself the happiest man in the whole world."

I answered: "You have yourself confessed, first of all, that to stay with me your estate is lower than you would wish it to be, and whatever else you have given me to understand in your long-winded discourse. But what is to be done to help you, to free me from any accusation of ingratitude and you from your suffering?"

He answered that for his part the decision should be mine, particularly since he held me to be not an earthly creature but a goddess from whom he was prepared to gladly accept the sentence of either life or death, *servitut* or liberty, indeed anything and everything which it pleased me to command. And this he indicated to me with such gestures that I could well perceive that I had a monkey on a chain who would rather choke to death in his willingness to serve me than live in freedom without me.

I pursued what I had begun and did not hesitate to fish in troubled waters; and why shouldn't I have, since after all the devil himself undertakes to get completely into his nets those who are in the state in which my beau found himself? I do not say this so that an honest Christian should find an example in me and copy the actions of the evil fiend just because I was imitating him at that time, but so that Simplicius, to whom alone I am dedicating this, my life history, may see what kind of lady he loved when he loved me. And listen closely, Simplex, and you will find out that I repaid you for that fine trick you played on me in Sauerbrunnen, so that for every pound you gave you got a hundredweight in return. But this gallant of mine I cajoled into agreeing to and promising to hold to, the following points.

First of all, he was to obtain a discharge from his regiment, for otherwise he could not be my servant, since I did not wish to be the wife of a musketeer.

Then, secondly, he was to live with me and show toward me all the love and faithfulness that a husband is wont to show toward his wife, as I should toward him in return.

However, thirdly, this union was not to be confirmed in the Christian church till I first found myself with child by him.

Till then, fourthly, I was to have and hold authority in every way and form, not only over the provisions but also over my own body, indeed even over my *serviteur* himself, in just the way a husband usually has jurisdiction over his wife.

In consequence, fifthly, he was not to have the power to hinder or prevent it, much less look askance at it, if I should converse with other men or do anything of the sort that commonly causes husbands to wax wroth.

And because, sixthly, I was of a mind to play the role of a sutler woman, he was of course to be the head of this enterprise and direct it like a faithful and diligent householder, by day and by night, but let me have the last word, particularly about the money and himself, and obey patiently, and even change his ways and improve himself if I were to reprimand him for his laziness. *In summa,* he was to be considered and looked upon by one and all as the master and was to have this title and honor too, but toward me observe every one of the above-mentioned duties in every respect. And all this we both signed and sealed.

And so that he might remember his duty toward me at all times, he was to suffer, as a seventh point, that I call him by a special name, which name was to be formed from the first words of the command by which I should the first time order him to do something.

Now when he had agreed to all these points and had sworn to hold to them, I confirmed it with a kiss, but for the time being permitted him no further liberties. Soon afterwards he brought me his discharge; I, for my part, got down to work and arranged with another infantry regiment for everything that a sutler should have and began to ply the Jew's trade as if I had been at it all my life.[16]

Chapter 16: *How Hopalong and Courage kept house with each other*

My young man showed excellent promise in everything for which I had taken him on and was using him; thus he also kept to the above-mentioned articles so nicely and proved himself so obedient that I did not have the least cause to complain of him. Indeed, when he could divine what might be my desire he was straightway eager to fulfill it; for he was so besotted in his love for me that he neither heard with his ears wide open nor saw with his eyes wide open what he had in me and I in him; but rather he believed that he had the most gentle, most faithful, most reasonable, and most modest sweetheart on earth, in which belief my adopted mother, whom he held in high regard on my account, was able to strengthen him and help me. She was much slyer than a fox, much greedier than a wolf, and I cannot say whether she was more proficient in the art of making money or in the art of pandering. If I had a lewd plan of that sort in mind and felt a bit of apprehension (for I wished to be regarded as very gentle and modest), I had only to confide it to her and it was as good as assured that my wish would be carried out; for her conscience could encompass as much as the thighs of the Rhodesian Colossus, which were spread so far apart that the largest ship could sail in between them without striking sail.

Once I had great lust to enjoy a young man of nobility who was a cornet at that time and had recently given me to understand that he loved me; at just that time when this desire arose in me, we had made camp near a village, for which reason everyone, including my rabble, left the camp to fetch wood and water; but my sutler was busying himself about the wagon, having just pitched my tent and put our horses with the others in the pasture close to us. Now because I had revealed my wishes to my mother, she arranged for this same cornet to be at hand, though not at the proper time; and when he came the first thing I asked him in the presence of my husband was whether he had any money. And when he answered, "Yes," for he thought that I was already asking a *salva venia*[17] for whore's wages, I said to my sutler: "Hop along and catch our piebald! The cornet here would like to ride him and bargain for him for cash."

Now while my good sutler obediently went to carry out this first command of mine, the old crone kept watch while we made the sale with each other and paid each other off valiantly. But since it was not as easy for my sutler to catch the horse as it was for the cornet to catch the sutler's woman, he came back to the tent all tired out and as impatient as the cornet pretended to be on account of the long wait. Because of this story said cornet later composed a song called "The Piebald," beginning with the words: "Oh, what inexpressible torture . . . &c," with which later on Germany was burdened for several years, because no one knew where it had originated. My sutler, however, received on the strength of our marriage contract the name "Hopalong," and this is the same Hopalong whom you, Simplicissime, repeatedly praise as a good fellow in your life history.[18] You must know too that all those little tricks which you and he practiced, both in Westphalia and at Phillipsburg, and many more besides he learned from none other than me and my old mother; for when I paired up with him he was simpler than a sheep, and when he left us he was more cunning than any lynx or archrogue can be.

But to tell the truth, he did not come by such science for nothing, but first had to pay me a proper apprentice fee. Once, while he was still all simplicity, he and I and my mother were discoursing on the deceit and malice of women, and he was impudent enough to maintain that no woman could ever deceive him, however cunning she might be. Now though he was clearly demonstrating his simplicity sufficiently by saying this, it nevertheless appeared to me that such talk was too disparaging and insulting to the dexterity of myself and all clever women, and therefore I told him candidly that I deemed myself capable of deceiving him nine times before morning soup, if only I wished to. He, on the other hand, was audacious enough to say that if I should be able to do so he would be my slave for his whole life long, and even dared me to do it, but with the proviso that if during such a span of time I could not practice any of the nine deceptions I should then let him lead me to the altar and be wedded to him. Now after we had thus made our wager I came to him early the next morning with the soup dish, in which lay the bread, and in the other hand the knife and the whetstone, with the request that he sharpen the knife a little so that I could cut the bread for the soup. He took the knife and the stone from me, and because he had no water he licked the whetstone to moisten it. Then I said: "Well, by God, that's twice already!"

He was surprised and asked what I meant by that. I, for my part, asked him if he could no longer remember our wager of yesterday. He answered: "Yes," and asked whether and how then I had already deceived him.

I answered: "First of all, I dulled the knife so that you would be obliged to sharpen it again; secondly, I rubbed the whetstone on a place you can easily imagine and then gave it to you to slobber over with your tongue."

"Oho!" he said. "If it has gone this far already, just hush and stop; I gladly declare you the winner and do not wish to hear about the rest of the tricks.

So now I had in my Hopalong a slave; by night, when I had nothing else better, he was my mate, by day my servant, and when people were watching, my lord and master in every respect. He even submitted so nicely to this arrangement and to my humor that I could not have wished for any better husband in all my life, and I should have been more than glad to marry him too, if I had not worried that he might thereby shake off the reins of obedience and, in asserting the mastery over me that would then be rightfully his, pay me back a hundredfold for whatever I had done to him while we were still unmarried and what he had doubtless been obliged to suffer at times with much vexation. In the meantime we lived together as harmoniously, but not as saintly, as the angels. My mother served as the sutler's woman in my stead, I as the beautiful cook or maidservant whom mine host keeps in the loft to attract many guests. My Hopalong, on the other hand, was master and servant or whatever else I wished him to be. He was obliged to pay me strict obedience and to follow the counsel of my mother; for the rest, all my rabble, of whom I had more than many a captain of infantry, obeyed him as their master. We had slovenly commissary butchers with the regiment who were wont to rather drink up their money instead of making it; therefore I weaseled my way into their profession through bribery and kept two butchers of my own for the price of one, so that I alone received preference and by and by ruined the others, because I could provide every guest, no matter where he came from, with a piece of any kind of meat he wished, no matter whether it be raw, boiled, roasted, or live.

When it came to stealing, robbing, and plundering (and what beautiful booty could not be found in full and rich Italy!), then not only Hopalong together with my rabble were obliged to risk their necks to fetch it in, but Courage herself went back to the old ways she had practiced in Germany, and by thus fighting against the enemy with soldier's arms and against my friends in camp with a Jew's weapons and keeping up my guard even during the friendliest sort of engagement, my purse grew so fat that I was obliged to send a bill of exchange of a thousand crowns to Prague almost every month, without myself or mine ever suffering want; for I diligently saw to it that my mother, my Hopalong, my other rabble, and particularly my horses always had plenty of food, clothing, and feed, even if I myself should have been obliged to go hungry and naked and live under the open sky, by day and by night. They, for their part, were obliged to earn me a profit and not to slack, neither day nor night, in this labor, even if they should have lost life and limb at it.

Chapter 17: *What a ridiculous prank was played on Courage and how she avenged herself*

Look you, Simplice, thus I was already the concubine and teacher of your companion, Hopalong, when you were perhaps still herding your daddy's swine and before you were clever enough to be other peoples' fool, and yet you dare to imagine that you deceived me in Sauerbrunnen! After the first siege of Mantua[19] we were assigned our winter quarters in a merry little town where I began to have a pretty good number of customers. There was not a banquet or a feast at which Courage was not present, and where she appeared the Italian *puttane*[20] counted for naught; for to the Italians I was fair game and something new, with the Germans I could speak their language, and towards both nations I was far too friendly, besides still being exceeding beautiful; also I was neither so very arrogant nor expensive, and no one had to worry about trickery with me, while by contrast the Italian women were full of deceit. These qualities of mine were responsible for my unhitching many good fellows from the carts of the Italian whores, which gentlemen forsook them and visited me instead, which did not endear me to them. Once I was invited to supper by a distinguished gentleman who had formerly been attached to the most famous *puttana*, but had forsaken her for me. Of this meat she in turn thought to deprive me and to that end had a furrier's wife put something in the food I ate during said meal, which made my belly swell up as if it were about to burst; indeed, the belly vapors so oppressed me that in the end they forced the gate, causing such lovely music to be heard during the meal that I was sore ashamed; and once they had found the gate, they passed through it one after the other with such enthusiasm that it kept on thundering as if several regiments at once were firing off a salvo. Now when I therefore arose from the table to run away, this physical activity really started it in earnest: At every step at least one escaped me, or ten, though in truth they followed upon one another so swiftly that no one could count them, and I believe that if I had been able to keep them in good order and properly spaced I could have beaten for two whole hours by the clock a better tattoo than the best drummer. But this way it only lasted for about a half an hour, during which time both guests and stewards suffered more torment from laughing than I did from my continued trumpeting.

This prank I reckoned a great affront to myself and was about to bolt for shame and ill humor; my host felt the same way, since he had invited me for a different purpose than to hear this beautiful music, swearing by all that is holy that he would avenge this affront, if only he could find out what peppercorn-ant-eggs cook had struck up this *harmonia* inside me. But because I was in doubt as to whether he himself might not have contrived the whole sorry business, look you, I sat in such a sulk as if I intended to kill everyone with the lightning flashes of my angry eyes, till I finally learned from a guest sitting next to me that the above-mentioned furrier's wife knew how to practice such medicine; and because he had seen her below stairs, he reasoned that she had somehow been engaged by some jealous lady to make me repugnant to this or that gentleman by means of this prank, particularly since she was known to have done the very same thing to a rich merchant, who had lost favor with his ladylove because of such music, because he had played it in her presence and in the presence of other respectable people. Thereupon I was satisfied and deliberated on swift revenge, which, however, must not be public or inhuman, because we were obliged (despite the fact that we were occupying enemy territory) to keep good order in our quarters.

Now after I had ascertained the truth, namely that it had happened just as the above-mentioned table companion had suspected I inquired as exactly as I could about the comings and goings, the ways and habits of that lady who had played this prank on me, and when I was shown the window from which she was wont to give nightly audience to those who wished to visit her, I revealed the grievance I nursed her to two officers; they, if they wished to further enjoy my favors at all, were obliged to promise me to execute my revenge, and as a matter of fact, in such and no other wise as I prescribed to them; for it seemed to me that it would be just, since she had vexed me only with the vapors, that I should pay her back with nothing less than the muck itself. And this happened in the following way: I had a bull's bladder filled with the worst kind of ordure that can be found in the upside-down chimneys by Master Arsehole's sweeps. This was tied to a stick or sort of flexible pole that is commonly used to knock nuts off trees or to clean the soot out of chimneys, and in the dark of night, while one of my cohorts was paying court to the *puttana,* who was as usual at her audience window up above, the other smashed her in the face with it with such force that the bladder burst, and the muck bespattered her nose, eyes, mouth, and bosom, together with all her ornaments and jewelry, after which prank both the suitor as well as the *executor* ran off, leaving the whore at the window to wail as long as she wished.

The wife of the furrier I paid back this way: Her husband was wont to collect and save every hair, even if it came from a cat, as carefully as if he had shorn if off the golden ram fleece of the Island of Colchis, so much so that he did not throw away a shred of skin, whether it be beaver, hare, or lamb, till he had first plucked it clean of all hair or wool. And then when he had a few pounds together the hatter gave him money for it, which indeed supplied his house with a few crumbs, and even though it was a trifling sum and went slowly, it still amounted to a bit in time. This I learned from another furrier who was lining a fur coat for me that same winter; therefore I got as much of such wool and hair as I needed and used it in the privy for a certain purpose. When it was ready, or to explain more closely, when these bits and pieces had been well salved and were as full of a certain material as the bottles and tins of a quacksalver are,[21] I had one of my boys scatter them around the furrier's privy, or *secret* as it is called, which was open a good ways above the ground. Now when this penny-pinching householder saw the clumps of hair and wool lying below, inside and out, and took them to be his own, he could not but imagine that his wife had spoiled and dishonored them thus. He therefore began to rage at her as if she had already destroyed and lost Mantua and Casale[22] to the enemy, and because she denied everything as stubbornly as a witch and even answered spitefully, he beat her till she was as soft as leather, even though he was gentle in preparing the skins of other wild and ravenous beasts, not to mention the native cat skins, all of which pleased me so well that I should not have taken a dozen crowns instead.

Now the only one left was the apothecary whom I suspected of having prepared the recipe through which I had been obliged to raise on high such a variable voice from the nether regions; for he kept songbirds that ate feed that is supposed to have the effect of causing such a clamor as I have described. But because he was well liked both by officers and noncommissioned officers, particularly since we must needs use his services every day for our sick, who could not stand the Italian air,[23] and also because I myself must worry that I might have to take his cure any day, I dared not rub him the wrong way too openly; nevertheless, I could not and would not stomach so many airy sprites, who, to be sure, had long since scattered into thin air, but cast about for a revenge to wreak, even though others had been obliged to put up with the reek of the airy sprites once I had stomached them. He had a small vaulted cellar under his house in which he kept all kinds of wares that, because of their nature, must be kept in such a place. Into this cellar I directed water from a fountain in a nearby square by tying one end of a long ox gut to the fountain and hanging the other end down inside the cellar window and letting the water run through it the whole long winter night, so that the next morning the cellar was full to overflowing. There one saw several casks of Malvoisier and Spanish wine and anything that was light swimming about; but everything that could not float lay ruined under six feet of water; and because I had the gut removed before break of day, everyone thought the next morning either that a spring had welled up in the cellar or that this trick had been played on the apothecary through sorcery. But I knew better, and because I had planned and executed everything so well I laughed up my sleeve while the apothecary lamented his spoiled *materialia*. And at that time I was glad that the name "Courage" had taken such deep root, otherwise the scalawags would no doubt have called me the General Fartress, because I do it better than anyone else.

Chapter 18: *About the quite too overweening godlessness of unscrupulous Courage*

The profits that came my way through such varied trades were so to my liking that the longer I plied these trades the more profit I desired; and since it was already all the same to me whether I made my profit by honest or dishonest means, I began not to care either whether the business might better be pursued with God's help or Mammon's. Finally I cared little through what kind of advantage, what kind of holds, with what kind of conscience, and by what kind of manipulations I prospered, just as long as I became rich. My Hopalong was obliged to play the horse trader, and what he did not know he was obliged to learn from me, since in his profession I practiced a thousand different roguish, thieving, and fraudulent tricks. No ware, neither of gold, silver, jewelry, much less of tin, copper, cloth, clothing, or whatever else it might be, no matter whether it be legitimate booty, robbed or even stolen, was too dear or too cheap for me to trade for; and whenever someone did not know where to go to turn what he had into silver, no matter whether he had come by it by fair means or foul, he was sure to find an outlet with me as easily as with any Jew, and Jews are more loyal to thieves to safeguard them than they are to the magistrate in helping to punish them. Therefore my two wagons resembled too much a general market not to contain much more than mere expensive *victualia,* and for just that reason I, for my part, was also able to supply any soldier, no matter whether he be high or low in rank, with anything he needed for cash in hand. On the other hand, I was obliged to make gifts and to grease many a palm to protect myself and my affairs: the provost was "my dear father," his old *mère*[24] (his old woman, I meant to say) was "my dear mother," the colonel's lady "milady," and the colonel himself "milord," and all of them protected me from anything which might have endangered me or my band or my business.

Once an old chicken thief, I meant to say "an old soldier," who had been carrying a musket long before the Bohemian fracas brought me some sort of something in a little sealed glass flask that did not rightly look like a spider or like a scorpion either; I took it to be no insect or living thing, because the flask had no air in it by which the imprisoned thing could have maintained its life, and I thought rather that it must be some sort of artful device made by an excellent master craftsman who had fashioned it to present the likeness of I know not what kind of perpetual motion, because it stirred and crawled about in the flask without rest. I prized it highly, and because the old man offered to sell it to me I asked, "How much?" He offered me the piece of trash for two crowns, which I forthwith paid him too, and then offered him a measure of wine in the bargain; but he said that full payment had been made, which surprised me in such an old tippler and caused me to ask him why he was refusing the drink, which, after all, I gave to anyone with whom I made a sale, however small.

"Oh, Madam Courage," he answered. "It is different with this than with other wares; it has a certain price at which it must be bought and sold, for which reason Madam must be careful when she in turn sells it, for she must needs sell it for less than she paid for it."

I said: "That way I should have little profit from it."

He answered: "Let that be your worry. As far as I am concerned, I have already owned it for thirty years or more and have never suffered any loss by it, though I bought it for three crowns and sold it again for two."

This was so much nonsense to me, and I could make neither head nor tail of it and perhaps did not wish to either; for I was fair drunk and was expecting to entertain several emissaries of Venus; therefore it worried me but little; or (dear Reader, you tell me how I should put it) I knew not what to make of the bag of bones. He did not seem to me man enough to deceive Courage, and being accustomed to the fact that others who looked smarter than this old man often sold me something for one ducat that was worth a hundred made me so sure of myself that I pocketed the treasure I had bought.

Next morning, when I had slept off my drunk, I found my purchase in the pocket of my breeches (for you must know that I always wore breeches under my skirt); I remembered straightway in what manner I had bought the thing and put therefore with the rest of my rare and lovely possessions, such as rings, jewels, and the like, to save it for the day when I should perhaps come upon a connoisseur who could inform me of its nature. But when I happened to put my hand in my pocket sometime during the day, I found it not where I had put it for safekeeping but instead in my pocket again, which astounded me more than it frightened me; and my curiosity to know what it actually was caused me to look about diligently for the old man who had sold it to me; and when I found him I asked him what he had sold me, told him besides what wondrous thing had happened with it, and begged him not to keep from me any information concerning its nature, power, effect, talents, and all the details about its properties.

He answered: "Madam Courage, it is a servant-spirit which brings great good fortune to that person who buys it and keeps it with him. It shows where hidden things are located, it procures sufficient partners for any kind of business transaction and increases prosperity, it makes its owner loved by his friends and feared by his foes. Anyone who has it and relies on it, it makes as shotfree as steel armor, and it protects from imprisonment; it brings good fortune, victory, and conquest over the enemy and makes it necessary that almost everyone love its owner."

In summa, the old lynx told me such a pack of tales that I thought I was more fortunate than Fortunatus[25] with his little sack and his wishing cap. But because I could well imagine that the so-called servant-spirit would not give such gifts for nothing, I asked the old man what I must do in return to please the thing, for I had heard that those sorcerers who rob other people with the aid of a mandrake are obliged to give the so-called mandrake weekly baths and other care. The old man answered that this was not at all necessary here; there was a very great difference between a mandrake and such a thing as I had bought from him. I said that no doubt it would not be willing to be my servant and fool for nothing; he should simply reveal to me boldly, and in confidence whether I might own it without any danger at all and also without rewarding it all while I enjoyed its considerable services without making any pact with it and serving it in return.

"Madam Courage," answered the old man, "you know enough already, namely, that you must sell it for less (when you have tired of its services) than you paid for it, which I did not hide from you at the time you bought it from me." And with that the old man went his way.

My Bohemian mother was at that time my most intimate counselor, my father confessor, my favorite, my best friend and my *Zabud Salomonis:*[26] I confided everything to her and therefore also what had happened to me with the treasure I had bought.

"Hah!" she answered. "It is a *stirpitus flammiarum*[27] which can perform everything that the man who sold it to you told you; but whosoever has it when he dies must, as I have been told, travel with it to that other world, which, to judge by its name, must without doubt be hell, where there is said to be fire and flame everywhere; and just for this reason it will let the owner sell it only for less than he paid for it, so that the last one who buys it must fall prey to it. And you, dear daughter, are in great danger, because you are the last one who can sell it; for what fool will buy it from you if he cannot sell it himself, but knows for sure that he is buying his eternal damnation from you?"

I could well appreciate that my trade had been a bad one, but my frivolity, my blooming youth, hope for a long life, and the universal godlessness of the world caused me to regard it lightly. I thought: "You will enjoy this help, this assistance, and this fortunate advantage a long as you can. In the meantime you will surely find a thoughtless fellow somewhere in this world who, either when he is drunk or because of poverty, desperation, blind hope for great good fortune, or because of avarice, lewdness, anger, lust for revenge, or something like that, will take this guest off your hands for the price asked."

Accordingly, I availed myself of its help in every way and form, as had been described to me by the old man and also by my nurse, or adopted Bohemian mother. I remarked its effect daily too; for where another sutler was dispensing one barrel of wine I was selling three or four; once a customer tasted my food and drink he did not forbear to come back a second time. Whatever man I looked at and wished to enjoy was straightway ready and willing to serve me with most submissive devotion, indeed to revere me just like a goddess; when I came to a billet where the householder had fled or to some inn or deserted dwelling or other where no one else could live (particularly since the sutlers and commissary butchers were not generally lodged in palaces), then I straightway found where the loot was hidden and was able, I know not by what inner voice, to find such treasures as had not seen the light of day for many, perhaps a hundred, years. On the other hand, I cannot deny that there were some who cared nothing for Courage, but rather despised, in fact persecuted, rather than honored her, without a doubt because they were illuminated by a greater *lumen* than the *flamine* with which I was possessed. This did put me on my guard and taught me to philosophize and ponder, after considerable thought, how come? what for? and so on. But I was already so drowned in rapaciousness and all the vices that attend it that I left everything as it was, rather than prepare the foundation on which my eternal salvation rested, as it indeed still does today. All this, Simplice, I am telling you in excessive detail to crown your glory, because you have bragged in your biography that you enjoyed a lady in Sauerbrunnen whom you really did not even know yet.

In the meantime, as time went by, my pile of money grew larger, indeed so large that even with all my means I was afraid.

Listen, Simplice, I must remind you of something else. If you had been worth anything when we played at dalliance with one another in Sauerbrunnen, you would have been even more impervious to my wiles than those who stood under God's protection when I still owned the *Spirit. famil.*

Translated by Robert L. Hiller and John C. Osborne

Notes

1. Libussa is the name of the legendary founder of Prague. The notes are based largely on those provided by the translators in: Robert L. Hiller and John C. Osborne, trans., *The Runagate Courage,* by Johann Jacob Christoph von Grimmelshausen (Lincoln: University of Nebraska Press, 1965).

2. In the Bohemian Forest.

3. Duke Maximilian Emanuel of Bavaria (1573–1651). Karl Bonaventura of Longueval, count of Bucquoy (1571–1621), a general of the Emperor Ferdinand.

4. Frederick V, prince elector of the Pfalz (Palatinate), the so-called Winter King, grandfather of Liselotte von der Pfalz.

5. The united armies first took Budweis (on the river Moldau in southern Bohemia) on September 11, 1620. Maximilian then moved against Wodnian, Bucquoy against Prachatitz, which was taken after heavy resistance. Almost 1,500 people were slain in the city.

6. White Hill is in the vicinity of Prague where the duke of Bavaria and Bucquoy defeated the Winter King on November 8, 1620. The story therefore begins in this year and Courage must have been born in 1607.

7. John George, elector of Saxony (1611–56).

8. Alfonso X, king of León and Castile (1252–84), called the Wise, philosopher and astronomer who devised the planetary tables that bore his name.

9. Iglau, Trebitz, Znaim, Bruenn, and Olmuetz are cities in Moravia that were taken by Bucquoy in 1621.

10. Hans Speyer translates the German *unzüchtige Messer* (naughty knives) as scabbard in order to avoid the misinterpretation that Grimmelshausen was suggesting the male organ. The vulgar German word meaning penknife to which Grimmelshausen alludes also means female organ. Hans Jacob Christoph von Grimmelshausen, *Courage, the Adventuress,* trans. Hans Speyer (Princeton: Princeton University Press, 1964), 100.

11. Courage refers to their meeting at a spa *(Sauerbrunnen)* which is first described in *Simplicissimus* (book 5, chapter 6). Simplicissimus's slighting remarks concerning the woman who was *mehr mobilis als nobilis* (more loose than noble), namely, Courage herself, prompts her to write her life story. In her version of the story she manages to saddle Simplicissimus with the bastard child of her maid (chapter 24) by claiming that it is theirs.

12. A provisioner to the army who traveled with it.

13. Hoya on the Weser River.

14. Alpine region in Switzerland.

15. A marshy region southeast of Hamburg.

16. *Mit dem Judenspieß laufen,* proverbial phrase to be found frequently in Grimmelshausen's works. Its connotation was "demanding an excessively high rent, interest, or price."

17. With your indulgence.

18. The German is *Springinsfeld,* literally "jump in the field," and corresponds to the first three words of the order that Courage gave to her servant. Hopalong first appears in Grimmelshausen's *Simplicissimus* (book 2, chapter 31) as Simplicissimus's partner in crime in Westphalia. He reappears in another novel of 1670— Courage was also first published in 1670—that bears his name *Der setzame Springinsfeld* (The strange Hopalong). Courage is determined to use the story of her ill treatment of Hopalong as yet another means of taking revenge on Simplicissimus. For example, the name Hopalong, which in the earlier novel appears simply to be an appropriate name for a carefree, roguish fellow, is now seen to originate in Courage's enslavement of Simplicissimus's buddy. In *The Strange Hopalong,* Hopalong in turn fulminates against Courage, "that crazy gypsy," "the image of the whore of Babylon" (chapter 5).

19. Mantua was besieged in the winter of 1629–30.

20. Prostitutes (Italian).

21. It was believed that the patient's excrement was a potent antidote.

22. At the time an important fortress on the Po River.

23. According to Speyer, Italian air is an allusion to syphilis (169).

24. The German is *Merr*. Also a play on the French *mère* (mother) and the German *Mähre* (mare).

25. Hero of one of the best-loved German chapbooks of the sixteenth century. His good fortune was the result of his acquisition of a little bag that was never empty of gold pieces and a wishing hat that could transport him in an instant to any place he wished to go.

26. ". . . and Zabud, the son of Nathan was principal officer, and the king's [Solomon's] friend" (I Kings 4:5).

27. The Latin *spiritus familaris* is so altered by this malapropism of Courage's Bohemian mother that it resembles the German *stirb* (die) and *Flamme* (flame, fire). She bases her interpretation of the "thing" on this similarity—whoever dies in possession of it will be condemned to the flames.

Johann Beer

Johann Beer was born in 1655 to a Protestant family, living in Upper Austria. As a result of the religious politics of the Catholic rulers the Beer family emigrated around 1668 to the then predominantly Protestant city of Regensburg where Beer received instruction in Latin, music, mathematics, and philosophy. In 1676, after a few months of study in Leipzig, he accepted a position with the court orchestra of Duke August of Saxe-Weissenfels. Upon the death of the duke in 1680 the court of Saxe Weissenfels was moved from Halle to the small town of Weissenfels where Beer acquired a reputation as an excellent musician and composer. He became concertmaster in 1685. In 1700 Beer was fatally wounded during a shooting contest. For over two hundred years after his untimely death Beer was known only as a seventeenth-century composer and musician. Not until 1932 was Richard Alewyn able to identify Beer as the author of over twenty anonymously published novels. Beer was familiar with the popular prose fiction of his day: chapbooks, novellas, courtly novels, political novels in the manner of Christian Weise, and picaresque novels, those of Spanish origin as well as Grimmelshausen's *Simplicissimus*. His novels rework much of this literary material, now imitating it, now satirizing it, now transforming it. Beer's language is frequently scatological, sexual innuendoes abound, and women are mercilessly satirized. His vigorous prose is particularly noteworthy for its language parodies, e.g., of university Latin, and its hilarious neologisms.

Beer's double novel *The German Winter Nights* (1682) and *Amusing Days of Summer* (1683) is considered his most important literary work. The two volumes treat a group of friends, country squires, and their wives, who enjoy celebrating together, playing pranks, and telling stories. Although the characters can hardly be considered psychological portraits, it is nevertheless clear from the description of the friends, provided by the narrator at the outset of the *Days of Summer* and included in the following selection, that besides recounting piquant stories Beer is interested in at least a rough delineation of character. The central narrator is Willenhag, but embedded in his account of day-to-day occurrences are scores of autobiographical anecdotes related by his friends, traveling students, old soldiers, etc., stories that, as he explains, he has determined to record. Harmless gossip is the glue of Willenhag's little society of friends that rejoices in its remoteness from courtly life and values tales of human interest rather than of high politics.

The Summer Tales

Necessary Enlightenment for and General Introduction to the Following History

It was a hot summer, and the heavy rays of the sun drove many people from their occupations. The wayfarer had to make frequent pause for rest under shade trees and spent the greater part of his trip parched with thirst. The harvester had no other refreshment than the sweat rolling down his cheeks, and those ordinarily found poring over books were now seen spending their time idly in the woods. It was in such summer weather that several noblemen banded together in order to pass their days in the most cheerful manner possible. So that their names and propensities will not remain a secret we'll sketch them here, to whet the appetite, so to speak.

The first one is Gottfrid, a young nobleman endowed with all the traits that one can expect from his class. He was sole heir to the entire estate of his late parents, and even though he occasionally appeared to be an amorous fellow, his singular meditativeness and devotion to a solitary life seemed to indicate otherwise. He preferred the pen to the sword and was quite eloquent in matters that served the common good.

The second is named Friderich and is a Scot by birth, but few Germans were his equals in honesty. He was likewise of a meditative nature but at the same time drawn to the company of women in such a way that both qualities were well balanced, a man whom any nation would like to have as its citizen. He was considered one of the most devout men in the country. Although he was married and lived in the travail of the world, in his heart he still cherished sparks of a spiritual nature.

The third is called Dietrich. Though poor, he is an honest man of nobility who has been around in the world and who enjoys travel. His person is objectionable to no one save those who hate German honesty. He's been a student at many schools, and his peasants were never taxed unreasonably.

The fourth is Philipp of Oberstein, a man of exceedingly good humor who hardly knows melancholy. He always esteemed courtiers more than scholars and is happily married, for he and his wife are of one mind.

The fifth is called Wilhelm of Abstorff, of an old German family and a man whose good works are worthy of his venerable name. A man of means, but not too open-handed, and yet no one could rightly call him stingy.

The sixth goes by the name of Sempronio. He is fond of military life, and that's where he sought his fortune. Otherwise a man who could get along with the most disagreeable curmudgeon.

The seventh is a brother of Gottfrid and his name is Christoph. And these two, just as they were not dissimilar in appearance, resembled one another in disposition as well. The latter, however, was fonder of travel.

The eighth is my old father Alexander. And if I were inclined to emulate those who find glory in tracing their ancestry, I could easily trace mine back several hundred years. But in order not to bore the sympathetic reader with my own self-esteem, I, as the author, will merely announce that he is an aged man and nearly ninety years old.

The ninth was a barrister from the city of Ollingen,[1] a parasite who manipulated the law to his own advantage. In company he was not overpolite, and of a nature wonderfully suited to poke fun at.

The tenth is myself, charged with the task of writing this modest history; my name is Wolffgang von Willenhag.

May these words serve the kind reader as a foretaste and necessary introduction to the story. No artificial contrivances or denoue-
ments are to be found in this tale; rather, that which was written
was designed as a memento for our descendants so that they too
will entertain such friendship toward one another as have we. For
everyone's land and fortune prospers in good harmony, but everything is destroyed and lost in mistrust, enmity, and hatred. That's
why we wove a bond of confident trust and thereby not only made
our lives more pleasant but also kept our enemies at bay.

It would be superfluous to indicate here the names of whatever
other persons are mentioned now and then. Besides, the text will
specify whether this or that one was single or married. It is only
important that our first decision had been to take a trip, but because the sun as well as other matters prevented that, some of us
thought we should pass the time with pretty music under the shel-
tering foliage in spite of the fact that this was quite expensive. We
even followed this suggestion for a while and often gathered out
of doors since our castles were not very far apart from one another.
Later though we realized the senselessness of this, for not only did
such carousal diminish our vigor, it also caused us to neglect our
duties at home. Sometimes we played at jousting, but that wouldn't
do either, as it was harmful to the horses. Finally the decision was
taken to ban worldly pleasures from our hearts for a while; most
of the company decided to go into the cool and shady woods to
try a taste of the hermit's life. It was the pious Friedrich who
swayed us to do so, he whom I mentioned earlier as one of the
most reverent in all the land. Having come to this conclusion we
celebrated with fine music and a great meal in Philipp's castle at
Oberstein, after which feast the noble company dispersed everywhere into the surrounding forests. My short preface is then the
first portal through which I proceed to the main work.

At this point I want to ask the praiseworthy company in whose
honor this narrative was gladly rendered, as well as the kind reader
who takes up this book, to accept everything related here with an
open mind. In a basket filled with fruit, there surely will be one or
the other rotten pear among the good ones. But I don't want to
serve it to anyone. Should someone take it himself, that is his fault.
Expressam saepe imaginem nostram in alienis personis videmus:[2]
(We often see our own praise and shame in other people). What I
put down here was not written to shame anyone; occasionally I

even sewed with a gentle thread when I should have used heavy cord. I don't pretend to proffer a rule book for the conduct of one's life, but only to record the opinions we had at the time. After all, in these troubled times one is well served by a cheerful book that is at the same time not harmful, for pleasure that injures is forbidden, and books that vex innocent minds belong in the fire rather than in the hands of men.

Therefore, everything was taken down with fitting prudence, as much as I could remember. Students occasionally drafted the content of the text; I rendered their sketches in my style, not because it is better but because I don't want to serve two dishes from one bowl. No one should be offended because a vice is ascribed to this or that person. We all know that weeds grow even in the most beautiful gardens and that gold is often mixed with filth and mire. Even the sunny sky is ocasionally darkened, and the clearest rivers become muddy sometimes: Such are the inconstant ways of men too, as the following story will sufficiently reveal, which, to be sure, I did not work out with ornate eloquence but wrote down in words understandable to all.

Book 3.
Chapter 5.
An amusing comedy is played at Ocheim.[3]

A little later the students sent me a message that their preparations were complete and we arose from dinner without further ado. The room chosen for the theater didn't hold many people so that a guard was posted at the door to let in only those he didn't know. The idea was that visitors could come in unaccosted while the local members of the peasant-profession were turned away since they don't care for theater anyway and just sit there with their mouths agape, laughing when others laugh.

Actus Primus: Scena Prima
Julio and Poco.

JULIO: The love that's burning my heart is a most violent pain, but if it stopped I'd die.

POCO: I really don't know which is the right way to Straubing.[4] Sir, whatever your name, which way to Pfada?

JULIO: It saddens my heart that I cannot assuage the desires of my infatuated hopes.

POCO: Yes, that's just the way I feel, I can't find the right way. Tell me, should I go this way, or should I go over that stile?

JULIO: Oh, I beg you, my thoughts, don't torture me. Is it such a great victory for you to take your own abode by storm?

POCO: Sir, I've never stormed an abode in my life. I'm not a soldier but a tailor. What's the right way to Straubing?

JULIO: It's true, she loves me ... but maybe she doesn't. So I just don't know, am I going astray or not?

POCO: I don't know whether I'm on the right way either. A pox on those people who pointed this way from across the field! Tell me, where do I go from here?

JULIO: My patience will console me. If she abandons me, very well. What can one do against the cruelty of a beautiful woman? But do you know, oh Julio, where you should turn?

POCO: No, indeed I don't, and if I did I wouldn't ask you.

JULIO. Yes, yes, be it resolved: grief shall be my food and a rain of tears my abode.

POCO: Yes, dear sir, exactly. From Grievesfurt[5] I'm going to Stadtroda.[6]

JULIO. What do I care about her hate! Generosity is a rock that shatters the sturdiest ships, yet my burden is becoming heavier and heavier.

POCO. My sack isn't exactly light either. Sir, tell me, where to?

JULIO. Oh, merciless Clio! I sigh, but you don't hear me. I call, and you cover your ears!

POCO. Yes, that's what I mean: if I don't get to town soon, they'll lock the gate.

JULIO. Your voice that bewitched me has lost its former sweetness. The sirens' song is dangerous; now you change into a bird of prey just when I thought you a white swan.

POCO: Sir, you guessed it. That's where I'll stay the night, at the White Swan, that's the inn for tailors.

JULIO: Oh, how illusory are the thoughts of man! I'd have wagered a thousand thalers on her constancy; now I wouldn't bet you four pennies.

POCO: Yes, kind sir, I agree, that is too much. I can't afford four pennies for a meal.

JULIO: Oh Clio! I see you before me, but where are you going?

POCO. To Straubing.

JULIO. Stay, my beauty, and sit in the shade with me!

POCO. No sire, I cannot. I must be on my way.

JULIO. But I see you are running away.

POCO: I wish I could, if only I knew the way!

JULIO: All is lost now! Everything's going awry just when I thought I had set it right.

POCO: Many thanks to you, sir! I'll take the road to the right.

(Exit Poco)

[The play contains two other humorous scenes.]

Just at this point the scenery collapsed and the play had to be ended. To the accompaniment of music, the spectators left roaring with laughter.

Chapter 6. Philipp muses about the play.
Two highwaymen receive an unpleasant
welcome at castle Ocheim.

As short as these scenes had been, everyone still had his own interpretation. "You rascals," said Philipp to us, "you thought this thing out very cleverly. Now listen to what I make of it. In the first scene you made it clear that a man in love is not always in his right mind nor his own master so that he can't even give information to someone who asks him for directions. The second scene taught me that one should avoid stubbornness and quarreling about rights of precedence because in the tailor and the weaver we can see that every fool defends his eccentricities. From the third scene we learned that we can't confide anything to simpleminded servant girls because they are most likely to spill it all when they try hardest to hide it and they can't even hide their own disgrace. These three main points are what I derived from your comedy. I don't care whether others grasped or even noticed your intentions. . . ."

There were other opinions too. Some understood that they had been criticized and insulted as is often the case at gatherings when one person claims to be wiser than the next. But basically good Philipp has chosen the best interpretation since we hadn't intended these three scenes as an insult or affront to the spectators—we had no reason to do so—but to entertain and instruct. We could easily have found material for a grand opera at the castle of Ichtelhausen[7] because we didn't lack the one prerequisite, time.

This is how the wedding festivities at Ocheim went. Dietrich told us that in the near future several ladies from the other side of the mountain would be on their way to Grundstett to ask the Weather Picture[8] some questions. Wearing the same disguise that had fooled us and telling their fortunes, he had persuaded them to go there very soon, on the third of the following month. This gave us another opportunity to ask about our horses, and he promised to send them to Oberstein without delay. "I'm not asking anything for oats and hay," he said, "but you can't blame me for expecting some remuneration for the trouble I took to educate you. But I beg you not to tell anybody about this business with the ladies. There are some among them who are probably going to ask about their lovers. So don't say anything. I'm going to remember everything they ask me because the tube in the wall goes through a tunnel to the back of the altar, and there I can hear everything as clearly as you can hear me now. And then you should get busy and write another comedy like the one today. I'll have it put on at my castle and you'll see what a time we'll have." And with those words he slapped Friderich and me on the back. He remarked by the by that he would let Philipp's wife, who was in on the hoax, stand beside him behind the picture so that she could hear all the questions too and see to it that everything went well, that is to say, most ridiculously.

We asked him who the little sexton had been and why there was such a terrible stench beneath the tiles we had stretched out on, and what sort of mechanism had turned the eyes of the picture back and forth and stuck out its tongue. "Gentlemen," he said, "I stood behind it. Those were my eyes and my tongue. We had put untanned goatskins under the tiles, and the little man was my page disguised for this task. While you were on the floor, I left the chapel through a side door, stopped the clock, and hurried off with the page. On the way I stopped at Philipp's and told his wife the whole story; otherwise you might have thought I was a thief stealing your horses under the pretext of a prank. This way I taught you the useful lesson that gullibility can plunge you not only into spiritual but also worldly misfortune. Enough said."

This and similar conversations carried us pleasurably through dinner. But all these contrived vanities made me feel uneasy in spite of the anticipation of the fun of seeing the ladies at the Weather Picture, and I wished in my heart that my Sophia, who was ill with a terrible tootache, and I were back home at my castle so I could take up the hermit's life again. I then talked to the village pastor, not a very learned man but pious and wise, about this and that and about how blind people are who spend their lives in luxury, for it is difficult to believe there can be two heavens in succession.

Even before dinner was over Philipp and I went to bed because I was still tired out from yesterday when we both had tipped our glasses too enthusiastically. Our wives slept together in another room because Philipp's wife had sprained her leg while dancing and my Sophia was suffering from her toothache, perhaps the worst of all ailments.

After we left Friderich didn't last much longer either, and that pleased his mother-in-law, old Lady Ocheim, since it meant she could save a lot of bread, wine, beer, and candles. Our early departure also left many glasses and mugs in one piece that otherwise would probably have been broken. The lawyer and some others stayed up a while longer, some with chess, others with cards while the students played sonatas that lulled us pleasantly to sleep.

Suddenly I woke up and didn't know why. A second later a pebble hit the chamber window; another before that probably had awakened me. I got up to see what was going on and when I opened the window, a man called out: "Monsieur, doesn't Barthel of the Heath[9] live here?" I thought that here was a chance I could get to the bottom of things and said: "Yes, he's here sleeping in this room." "Let me in, sir. My comrade and I don't know where else to go and then we'll tell all about how we attacked the lawyer and roughed him up."

I was delighted with this development, for I realized that these were the highwaymen who had assaulted lawyer Bleifuss and caused him to cry out: "Help! Help!" You fools, I thought, you've gone far astray and yet come to the right place. And I passed the word around quickly but quietly; they were let in through the gate in the dark and taken into a room they couldn't get out of. I cannot describe how the lawyer snorted and puffed up with anger when he found out who they were. From a big pile of wood he picked the biggest sticks to beat the ruffians as they well deserved! Meantime all the others who enjoyed manhandling got dressed and made ready.

Wilhelm was able to imitate Barthel's voice and he went into the pitch-black room where the robbers were waiting and said: "Are you the ones who beat up the lawyer?" "Yes, we are," said one of them, "we did as you told us." Then Wilhelm opened the door and said: "Hand me a light in here!" This was the signal for us to sneak in on stocking feet. And he continued: "How did the rascal behave when you trapped him, and where did you attack him?" "In just this forest," said one of them, "we lay in wait for him as you told us and finally he came. We attacked, pulled him off the horse, and gave him a damn good thrashing." At this the lawyer almost burst with anger. "Was he so cowardly that he didn't defend himself?" Wilhelm continued. "That's a joke!" said the other. "That buffoon defend himself? He kept asking us to spare his life."

Now the lawyer could not hold back any longer and screamed: "You're lying, you bastards! Wait, I'll. . . !" At this point I put my hand over his mouth, but it dawned on the rascals that something was up because the lawyer's voice seemed familiar to them. "Barthel," they said, "who was that?" "You'll see soon enough," answered Wilhelm and had two big torches brought in; at the same time several servants were furnished with stout clubs and whips.

This turn of events upset the two fellows, and having realized their error, they took the offensive drawing their swords in desperation. But Philipp and the others, especially the lawyer, beat the weapons out of their hands with long cudgels and knocked them to the ground. "Enough," said Wilhelm, "no one is to touch them! Tell me, who hired you to waylay this lawyer?" They said nothing.

He went on: "I ask you once again: who put you up to this?" They were silent. "All right," he said, "if you don't answer we'll beat it out of you!" At those words they fell upon the two, one with his bare hands, another with a club, a third with slippers, and they mauled them so badly that they were covered with blood and sweat and reeled around the room, almost unconscious. The ladies, awakened and frightened out of their wits by the uproar and supposing that we ourselves had got into a fight, came running downstairs half-naked and barefooted. Even Friderich, sword bared, appeared along with Amalia, but when he found how matters stood he laughed and went back to bed. The compassionate womenfolk, however, brought salves and smelling salts to help the two men, and I didn't feel good about it at all because it looked much as if the lawyer had crushed one of their skulls.

Chapter 7. Dietrich himself is outmaneuvered at the Weather Picture in Grundstett, along with the ladies he had wanted to deceive.

The two men were chained, and the women, still in tears, persuaded us to put down our clubs. Only the lawyer wanted to continue this game until we finally consoled him with the prospect of legal recourse. We threw them into a stable and had them guarded by three peasants, and all of us went back to bed so that the ladies wouldn't be put to any more trouble.

The next morning we learned that our prisoners were two journeymen who had just happened upon Barthel of the Heath on the road. Barthel had ordered them to lie in wait for the lawyer after giving a detailed description of him, and asked them to come to his castle afterwards for their reward. But they had been so confused that misfortune led them here. The lawyer couldn't remember how he had offended Barthel, but he knew only too well that he had taken sides against his party at the court of Ollingen, and apparently this had caused bad blood. Since Barthel was now a fugitive from the law, the lawyer planned to have a court order issued to auction off his goods and claim a considerable part of them for himself in compensation for the wrong he had suffered. With this in mind he took the two men with him and left.

[The company disperses. Friderich and Wolffgang accompany Philipp to Oberstein before they ride on to Ichtelhausen.]

We reached Oberstein safely, only two days away from Ichtelhausen and conferred as to what should be done to get our revenge on Dietrich. Since he had returned the horses to Oberstein, we felt free to pay him back in his own coin.

"We'll have to go to Grundstett a day before he does," said Philipp. "Let's make a hole in the church ceiling right about the place where he'll stand, and while he and my wife are busy bilking the curious ladies, we'll pour a barrel of water and horse droppings on his head." I found this an excellent suggestion. So we parted

from good Philipp at Oberstein and traveled together to Ichtelhausen, where I reinstalled Friderich with his subjects and spent
one day, after which we rejoined Philipp at Grundstett in good
time.

There we sent our horses into a neighboring village and quietly,
without being noticed, went up to the loft of the church with a
barrel of water. Philipp's wife knew nothing of our plan; we had
told her that we would hide in various places in the church. Because
she had made such fun of us and never said a word about the
whole scheme, she was to be punished along with good brother
Dietrich.

We were ready and in our appointed places when she and Dietrich crept behind the altar. Then his crafty page arrived after we
had heard the two pistol shots. Because I forgot to do so earlier, I
must say something about those shots now. A servant was posted
on an island; he shot a pistol and if the travelers turned around,
he was not to shoot again. If they didn't, he fired the second shot
and that was how Dietrich behind the Weather Picture could determine whether they had looked back or not.

The page-sexton meanwhile had played his part in front of the
church and brought the ladies in at last, giving them directions, as
he had us, by which they were much impressed. He left, and the
ladies spread a big rug on the floor so that the red tile wouldn't
ruin their dresses. But there was still a horrid stench from below,
and I'd have given a pretty penny to know what they were thinking.
There were perhaps fifteen of them lying there quiet and immov-
able in a row—it was a ludicrous sight!

The women fared no differently than we had. The page called
through the same window as Dietrich had before and said:
"They're gone!" And shortly after he continued: "Oh, you fools!
You fools!" That ended the half hour, and one by one they asked
their questions through the tube, Dietrich wrote them down on a
writing tablet while Philipp's wife looked through the picture and
stuck out her tongue as far as she could. After the first one had
asked her question, Dietrich said from behind the altar: "The second should ask too, then the third, etc., and I will answer in the
order you asked, for you did not look back on the way." So they
took turns until all had finished. "Now," said Dietrich, "I'll answer
you." As he was opening his mouth wide, we poured the water on
the hoaxers' heads and at the same time fired two pistol shots with

the result that no one could clear out of the church fast enough. The noble ladies scurried as far as they could to the door, screaming for help.

Philipp's wife was so frightened that she almost fainted and Dietrich so startled that he couldn't make up his mind whether to run backward or forward while we kept on pouring. Some bits of brick in the water gave him a couple of bumps on the head. The page was still waiting in front of the church with the ladies' horses, unaware of what was going on, and so Dietrich's hoax was revealed and thwarted at the same time. Philipp called down from a dormer window, "We paid you back, didn't we?" "You bastards!" he said, "I jumped out of my skin!" Then we came down and laughed at the ladies too for having fallen for this con game. If they had known how we had fared, they needn't have been as ashamed as they were. I firmly believe that if a vagrant or a real crook were to hear about this scheme, he could use it to good effect. The worst thing of all about it was that we couldn't say anything about the incident but had to take it quietly lest it set tongues wagging about our credulity.

Chapter 8. Wolffgang sees a ghost at the castle. Barthel of the Heath is finished off by the lawyer. Wolffgang's father and his only child die on the same day.

One by one the ladies slipped out of the cemetery and mounted their horses in humiliation and silence. One could have worked their questions into the plot of a play, but we couldn't persuade even one of them to promise us a visit at Dietrich's castle because they knew they would be raked over the coals for their dubious undertaking. They only mentioned to Philipp's wife that they were certain of our prudence and decency and that, therefore, they were sure that they need fear no harm from us. That's why I didn't mention anyone by name or family because I know very well that one can jest with a lady but shouldn't reveal anything that could harm her reputation.

Vague premonitions moved me to start out for my castle as soon as our horses had been brought from the village, but not before I had promised to visit Dietrich very soon. So I galloped through the dust at top speed and reached home the same evening just as darkness was falling.

I found my beloved well again, but my child was very ill and weak, and I spent a night almost sleepless with worry. At midnight I heard a rustling sound next to my window as if a man were walking by in a big fur coat. Since one is much more frightened by this sort of thing at night than in the day, I was alarmed and rose up in bed. I couldn't see anybody in the room even though my night lamp was burning brightly, so I lay down again on my other side thinking it had been a figment of my troubled imagination. Shortly thereafter there was a long sound of knocking at the door; one couldn't have heard anything more distinctly. I thought perhaps it was a servant or a maid who had come to wake me because my child had gotten worse and I asked: "Who is it?" But there was no reply. Then I heard three strokes as if with a switch on my father's picture that hung on the door frame, and I could clearly see dust rise from the picture.

Understandably, this noise gave me quite a fright. I jumped out of bed, hurriedly donned my night furs but still didn't have the courage to open the door at which there had been a knock. So I opened a window hoping thus to overcome my fears when I saw a bright light on a nearby tree and beneath it a woman in a white veil who grew taller and taller until she blew out the light on the top of the tree, then disappeared from sight.

I closed the window and rang for my servant who was as pale as a ghost because he too had seen the woman in white in the inner courtyard. His tale and what I had seen augured ill for the morning and I began to doubt that my beloved little child would get well. Indeed, it died later, to my unspeakable anguish. "Something extraordinary is in this castle and it augurs nothing good," I said to the servant. "Bring your bed in here and sleep in my room the rest of the night." Then I went downstairs and tearfully looked for the last time at the child lying there in great fever, and I felt profound grief that I was to have known it such a short time. Close to tears, I went back and spent the remainder of the night in sorrowful contemplation of the meaning of eternity and how horrifying it must seem to those who can look forward to no consolation in it but must fear ever more affliction.

I welcomed the new dawn more than all the treasures in my world but was barely dressed when I heard a clamor outside my castle. I looked down; it was the lawyer and Barthel of the Heath himself, slashing at one another with the swords and so eager for blood that I could foresee a bad end. Decency and my duty as proper owner demanded the removal of the duelists from my place. I hurried down carrying a heavy sword either to make peace or to drive them off. But I hadn't yet crossed the courtyard when the lawyer sliced the unfortunate Barthel right down to his buttocks. I then had to watch the mortally wounded man suffocate in his own blood and hear him speak blasphemous words as he gave up his restless ghost. "My God," I said to the lawyer. "What have you done?" "I did unto him," he answered, "as he had planned to do unto me. He raced to his own grave when he followed me for four miles and shot my horse out from under me. Now the good fellow lies stretched out here; he got what he asked for. I tried to avoid this and keep a couple of fields between us, hoping he would stop his terrible cursing, but he followed me here and I was so tired from the pursuit that I could only defend myself to the death."

As witness to the incident I took him under my protection. We had hardly gone into the castle when several of Barthel's cronies came running onto the scene with bared daggers, and when they saw their ringleader dead they fired several shots at the windows. I fired back to good effect as two of them fell, keeping their leader company in death as they had in life. The other three I pursued with two horsemen and caught one of them who was set upon and beaten so badly that I doubt he'll ever have a toothache again. I attributed the appearance of the ghost more to this event than to the death of my child and at the same time was glad that the notorious Barthel had got his just desserts after terrorizing the whole area. But I wished he had recognized and repented his evil deeds before he died. It was terrible in what great wrath and fury he died, for no doubt he fell from a cold bath into a hot one, and none of his tricks can get him out of that kettle.

Thus preoccupied with sad and troubled thoughts I cried out inwardly, Oh Wolffgang, you rush from one misfortune into another. Your intuition told you the other day to take up your former life in the tower, and you had a premonition of the responsibility you were taking on. Perhaps these villains died in a state of nonrepentance! Couldn't you have stopped them with less drastic measures? But no. It had to be. Do unto others as you would have others do unto you. What ye give shall ye also receive. We had to use force, how else can we maintain order? If I were the only lenient one I wouldn't avert evil but attract it through my permissiveness. The lawyer agreed and made reference to numerous articles of law, and so Sophia and I were somewhat relieved since her conscience was easily troubled and she worried about the smallest thing.

The lawyer formulated a detailed report and I sent a servant to deliver it to the court in Ollingen and to await instructions as to what should be done with the corpses. The lawyer meanwhile remained in a good mood and stayed for dinner at my house, not at all worried about the incident.

While we were sitting at the table talking about these events, a servant of my father's arrived. My father Alexander was still alive, passing his days devoutly, but this morning while he was on his way to the chapel he had fallen on a stone stairway and was injured so greviously that he appeared to be near death. It seemed as if all possible misfortunes had conspired to afflict me at once, and so I went quickly to my father's castle but found him already dead. The servant had merely wanted to soften the blow and had changed the message. This situation aggrieved me all the more because of the preceding events, and I was quite miserable, by now unable to shrug things off in my usual way. Then, because there was no way around it, I made the necessary arrangements and had the steward swear that he would be loyal, honest, obedient, and prudent as benefits his position.

I locked all the chests, the cellar, and the pantries. In order that the servants wouldn't complain about miserliness on my part, I arranged for the steward to pay their salaries until I returned. I tearfully rode off again having learned how much it hurts to lose parents and children on the same day.

The servant returned from Ollingen with the order that the bodies be left where they lay until the executioner picked them up for burial. This is where matters stood when the lawyer was cited to appear in court to give an account of the fight, something he was more than willing to do. He left on the same evening in order to be in court the next day. I meanwhile came to a clear understanding of the ghost I had seen. The knocks on my late father's picture still distressed me unspeakably whenever I thought of them, but my wife consoled me even though she wasn't free from grief and pain either. I finally came to terms with my fate and diverted my mind with cheerful books; there was nothing anyone could do and no one could undo what had happened. "Well," I said, "we live in the world and must play according to its rules. One cannot always laugh, but one can't always cry either. Wolffgang, you should become a hermit again and everything will work out."

Chapter 9. The secretary of Ichtelhausen comes to the wrong address twice. Alexander is buried. Philipp and Dietrich console the sad Wolffgang in a peculiar manner.

The next day my servant Wastel and I hurried back to my late father's estate where we dressed the body and set the date for the burial. While I was thus occupied, a young fellow came to the house and asked for food to sustain him on his journey. His face was familiar but he didn't recognize me since I wore black. "Aren't you the secretary," I said to him, "formerly in service at Ichtelhausen?" "Yes, I am," he said, his face turning bright red, "but how do you know me?" "I know you well," I said. "Have you finished copying your book yet?" When I said this, he turned around and ran off as fast as he could. I realized then that he had run away from castle Ichtelhausen. I wasn't concerned about the matter because of these more important events and tended to the affairs I had come here for.

When everything was done I rode home. Wastel hadn't forgotten that his foolish talk and stories had often amused me, and I had to laugh when he could hardly open his mouth because of the gusty wind and dust and couldn't hear half of what he was saying because one clump of dirt after another flew into his mouth.

After our return to my castle there was the same secretary who shortly before had begged for food. He was even more frightened here than he had been there, and if I hadn't been blocking the door, he would no doubt have made a flying exit once again. It turned out that my wife had told him to wait for my return because I was looking for a secretary. "Don't be afraid," I said, "in spite of the fact that I know who you are and where you come from. Your punishment at Ichtelhausen was a bit severe. If you are sorry for your mistake and you really want to write, you can stay here this summer to earn your bread."

"I'd like that very much, sir," said the secretary, "especially with such a good master. I well know how I've fared at Ichtelhausen.

I've had to write until my nails almost turned black and hardly got enough to eat for it. You may consider the steward frugal; I know, as do all the servants, that he really brings in little or nothing and what little he takes in is achieved through miserliness and by starving the castle servants. I worked the skin off my hands digging, was beaten like a slave, had to stay in that whole day and night and was supposed to copy a book from a scrap of paper. Sir, let my crime be judged before a court and see whether it would punish me as severely. One day I said I needed to mix some ink. The steward didn't trust me and went to the kitchen with me and told me he would accompany me back to my room and lock me in. Because no one in authority was present, I made the ink and while it was still hot I threw it into the fool's face and ran off."

The story of his sudden departure was amusing to listen to. "I must admit," I said, "that the steward loaded you down with too much work. But you see how it goes. If you can't really work well nowadays, you get stepped on. You made life hard for him too and if you comprehend the ugliness of slander and gossip you must admit that your punishments were far too lenient. Come along now and write some letters. I'll try to straighten out the business at Ichtelhausen." So I led him to my room and dictated the draft for the death notices. He worked so hard that he got all but two done the same evening. Next morning he finished those too, and messengers were sent hither and yon to invite my friends to the funeral. Meanwhile I had mourning dress made for my servants, and the tailor no doubt made a mourning coat for himself on the side. But I shouldn't tarry so long in the description of something that is so painful to relate. For this whole book I haven't used as many drops of ink as the number of tears I shed for my dear father at that time, in spite of the fact that my friends, especially Philipp, did not believe that my sorrow was genuine. Two letters, Philipp's and Dietrich's answer to my painful death notice, will demonstrate:

"Dear Brother, etc.:

You must have had terrible anguish in your heart when you learned in what manner your old father tumbled down the stairs. And probably your eyes are rather red because of the dust that got into them. Most likely you'll have the song "Dearly I Desire" sung at the funeral, and inwardly you'll think "the money to acquire." Oh, you're a big rascal. Anyone who didn't know you would take you for a gosling. As I can tell from your letter, you and the lawyer had quite a rough skirmish; you were just and right. In case you're really sorry that your dear father is dead, I am herewith conveying my condolences, as is customary. I will appear for the funeral procession on the appointed day punctually at the usual hour. In the meantime buy a nice roll of tobacco, for I'm bringing some very beautiful pipes with me. Vale!"

This manuscript, quoted here verbatim, was that of Philipp of Oberstein who was fortunate enough to adjust admirably to even the saddest events. The following is Dietrich's. It went this way:

"Noble, etc., much-honored and sad Friend, etc.:
I doubt that you were as startled when you received the news of your father's death as I was when you poured a barrel of water on me behind the Weather Picture. Your heart most likely pined for his money and treasure just as I did then for a well-heated room. If you are sad nonetheless, remember that you deserve it because of the Weather Picture at Grundstett. Let Philipp's wife sew your mourning dress; she'll stitch horse and camel hair into it so that you'll itch as much as her husband did in the forest. As for me, I suffer with you but am even sadder than you, for I've not lost a rich father. Lawyer Bleifuss is a lucky man; I know how skilled a fighter Barthel was. You should congratulate yourself for your successful defense. For the solemnities you'll have pretty oysters and a fine drink ready for me. One who has such a fine morsel in his kitchen can afford to put a fat roast on the spit. I'll certainly come at the appointed time and will bring along playing cards. Farewell, and give my regards to your wife."

These two had only worldly thoughts on this occasion but all the others answered in a way customary in our area or as they had seen in books. It is not necessary to prescribe what should be written but much better that each follow his own inclinations, for it is not given to everyone to compose a really original letter. It would be folly to give as example a lot of clever phrases and to scold those who cannot imitate them; no one can do everything. People like to be laughed at for not knowing how to write as much as I enjoy being laughed at for not knowing Spanish. And the people who laugh loudest at others are usually those with the most short-comings. Why laugh at your neighbor for not being able to do something? Be happy that you can do it. A soldier who gets some booty and laughs at another who has none is often attacked and loses it.

A house in mourning offers little amusement, and I will turn my pen toward happier material as soon as I have described in short— and reported to the reader in a few words—that the funeral took place without any mishaps. Afterwards we returned to my castle where the rooms were hung with black drapes. On these we had sewn emblems[10] and sayings for the edification of the literate. They had been compiled by the good Lorenz, Philipp's tutor at Ob-erstein, all in all a man of excellent judgment, except that he thought all jokes and pranks beneath contempt.

So that the reader may get an idea of them, I wish to describe the emblems very briefly, for not only did I make note of them in my diary but even had them copied. The first showed a large heap of bones before which stood a fortress on a high mountain. Beneath the bones the inscription: *Nil possumus:* that means: we can do nothing, our strength is as dust. The painter wanted to make us realize the nothingness of man who imagines he can climb tall towers but finally has to learn the *Nil possumus* with these bones.

In the second there was a reaper cutting grain with a large scythe; it bore this title: *Nec una remanebit:* not a single stalk will be left. Which is self-explanatory; all of us are meant.

In the third, three skulls lay next to one another and underneath them the words: *Monstra Regem?* Which of these was the king?

There were twelve lights in the fourth, each shorter than the next. Death was blowing out all of them at once and the title read: *Deleo cuncta:* I extinguish everything. There were others, different ones, but since Lorenz had admittedly collected them from various books, I don't wish to represent them here as new; anyway, a thousand pens have been whittled away on them already.

Translated by James N. Hardin and Gerda Jordan

Notes

1. The name Ollingen is possibly derived from Olling, a small town near Munich. The notes correspond for the most part to those provided by the transla-

tors: James N. Hardin and Gerda Jordan, trans., *The Summer Tales* (New York: Peter Lang, 1984).

2. We often see our likeness in other persons.

3. Seat of Amalia's family where the wedding of Friderich and Amalia has just taken place.

4. Straubing is a city on the Danube in Lower Bavaria.

5. In the original German Grievesfurt is Straubing. It has been changed in the translation to preserve some semblance of Beer's wordplay.

6. In the original Stadtroda in Regensburg, the Bavarian city in which Beer attended the *Gymnasium* (1670–75). It has been changed for the aforementioned reason.

7. Friderich's castle.

8. Weather Picture is a literal translation of *Wetterbild*, the nonsensical name for the so-called oracle that figures in the prank. It has appeared in earlier chapters.

9. Barthel of the Heath has appeared in earlier chapters, notably when he pursued Amalia, Friderich's beloved. He is described as a bachelor nobleman who has lost most of his inheritance and who has made a practice of stirring up trouble. He becomes the leader of a band of rebellious peasants.

10. The emblem is a symbolic drawing with inscriptions. The inscriptions lend the image an interpretation that cannot be derived from the picture alone. Emblems were popular throughout Europe from the Renaissance through the eighteenth century; their imagery was taken up by literature.

Christian Reuter

Christian Reuter, of peasant stock, was born in 1665 near Halle. He was the only one of his nine siblings to attend the *Gymnasium*. At the rather advanced age of twenty-three he began his university studies in Leipzig where he completed around twenty semesters. While in Leipzig a quarrel with his landlady Anna Rosina Müller led him to write the comedy *L'Honnête Femme; or, The Honest Woman of Pliszine* (1695) in which he not only ridicules the mannerisms and habits of the widow Müller but of her entire family. In Act III the landlady's hapless son Schelmuffsky makes his debut in German literature in order to brag of his exploits while on tour. In 1696 the first version of part 1 of *Schelmuffsky's True, Curious, and Very Dangerous Travel Description on Land and at Sea* appeared anonymously followed by a second version the same year and a sequel in 1697. A sequel to the original comedy, *The Honest Mistress Schlampampe's Illness and Death* also appeared in 1696, followed by the opera *Seigneur Schelmuffsky* (1697?) and *The last Monument and Eulogy to the Erstwhile Honest Mistress Schlampampe* (1697). Neither Mistress Müller nor her family were gratified by the publicity and Reuter's literary efforts led to libel suits that eventually resulted in Reuter's incarceration and expulsion from the university and city of Leipzig. After leaving Leipzig Reuter became secretary to the Saxon chamberlain Rudolf Gottlob von Seyfferditz in Dresden in 1700 where he once again tested his literary talents with the comedy *Count Ehrenfried* (1700). Record of Reuter's presence at the Prussian Court in Berlin (1703) exists as well as of the baptism of a son in 1712, but thereafter Reuter vanished from history.

Reuter's novel was nearly forgotten until the early nineteenth century when it was rediscovered by the German romantics who were delighted by the exploits of the consummate talker Schelmuff-sky. Beyond the original impulse to lampoon the Müller family Reuter's novel constitutes both literary satire of contemporary genres, in particular the popular travel description, and social satire of the aspirations of the bourgeois parvenu and would-be cavalier embodied by Schelmuffsky. With his preposterous tales of social success and his inappropriate language and actions Schelmuffsky repeatedly and inadvertently unmasks his humble origins and his delusions of grandeur; at the same time, however, he becomes a master of narration; the creator of himself; a comic figure beloved in German literature; as Wolfgang Hecht has formulated it, a kind of Prometheus.

Schelmuffsky

The First Chapter

Germany is my fatherland, I was born in Schelmerode,[1] at St. Malo I was a prisoner for a whole half year, and I was also in Holland and England. However, in order that I arrange this my very dangerous travel account in a nice, orderly manner I suppose I should begin with my marvelous birth: When the big rat that had eaten my mother's quite new silk dress could not be killed with the broom as it ran between my sister's legs and unexpectedly got into a hole, the worthy lady falls on this account from exertion into such an illness and faint that she lies there for full twenty-four days and can, the devil take me, neither move nor turn. I, who at that time had never yet seen the world and who according to Adam Riese's[2] arithmetic book should have been waiting concealed four full months still became so foolish on account of the cursed rat that I could no longer remain concealed, but looked where the carpenter had left the hole and quickly crawled out to daylight on all fours. Once born, I lay eight full days down at my mother's feet in the bed straw before I could rightly realize where I was. The ninth day I looked at the world with great astonishment, zounds!

How barren everything appeared to me, I was very sick, had nothing on, my mother had stretched out all four limbs and lay there as if she had been struck on the head; I didn't want to cry either because I lay there like a young piglet and didn't want anyone to see me because I was naked, thus I didn't know what to do. I was also of a will to wander back into concealment, but, the devil take me, I couldn't find the way again whence I had come.

Finally I thought, you must really see whether you can cheer up your mother and I tried this by various ways and means; first I took hold of her nose, next I tickled the soles of her feet, now I patted her a little, again I then plucked a hair here and there, again I touched her nipple, but she wouldn't waken from this; finally I took a straw and tickled her left nostril at which she started up hastily and cried: "A rat! A rat!" Upon hearing her say the word *rat* I felt, the devil take me, exactly as if someone took scissors and were cutting out my tongue, whereupon I forthwith began to utter a terrifying ouch! My mother previously had cried out, "A rat! A rat!" now she must have shrieked, "A rat! A rat!" over a hundred times, for she was convinced that a rat was nestling down at her feet. However I was quick to crawl up to my mother very nicely, looked up to her over the cover, and said: "Mother, fear not, I'm no rat, but your dear son; but it's a rat's fault that I appeared so prematurely." Zounds! How happy was my mother when she heard this, that I had been born so unexpectedly that she hadn't known anything of it at all. I just won't tell anyone how she, the devil take me, hugged and kissed me. After she had thus fondled me in her arms a good while, she got up with me, put a white shirt on me, and called in the renters from the whole house who all looked at me most astonished and didn't know what they should make of me because I could chat so nicely already.

Mr. George, my mother's tutor at the time, thought that I was possessed of the evil spirit, otherwise things couldn't possibly be right with me, and he wanted to exorcise the same from me. Thereupon he ran immediately to his study and appeared hugging a big book under his arm with which he intended to exorcise the same from me. He chalked a big circle in the room, wrote a lot of gibberish letters within the circle, made the sign of the cross before and behind him, then stepped into the circle and began to intone the following:

Hocus-pocus black and white,
Leave forthwith as I indite
Schuri muri the little fellow;
Since Mr. George so does bellow.

After Mr. George had spoken these words, I began to speak to him: "My dear tutor, why do you attempt such nonsense and think I am possessed of the evil spirit; if you only knew why I learned to speak so fast and why I was born so prematurely you certainly would not have attempted such a foolish business with your hocus-pocus." Zounds! When they heard me speak thus, how astonished the people in the house were. Mr. George stood there in his circle, the devil take me, so shaking and trembling that everybody around could perceive from the air that the tutor evidently was not in any garden of roses.

But I couldn't stand his pitiful condition any longer and began to relate my astonishing birth and how it was due solely to that rat that had eaten the silk dress that I had arrived so prematurely and could talk so soon. Now after I had told everyone in the house circumstantially the entire incident about the rat they finally believed that I was my mother's son. But Mr. George was ashamed as a dog for trying such silly tricks on my account and believing that an evil spirit must be speaking in me. He was quick to erase his hocus-pocus circle, take his book and walk out of the room silently with his damp and foul-smelling breeches. How then everybody acted, hugging and fondling me, because I was such a beautiful boy and could chat with them right away, that would beggar description, the devil take me, indeed they all insisted right away that the very day amidst a crowd of people I should receive the excellent name of Schelmuffsky. The tenth day after my astonishing birth I gradually learned, although somewhat slowly, to walk by benches, for I was quite sick for neither having eaten nor drunk because Mother's teat was too distasteful to me and I couldn't get used to any other food yet, so that, if it hadn't turned out this way, I should probably have had to die for lack of food and drink. What happened? That very day my mother had placed a big tub full of goat's milk on the stove bench. I come upon it by chance, dunk my finger in it, taste it, and because the stuff tasted very good I seized the whole tub and, the devil take me, drank it all down, after which I became quite lively and strong. When my mother saw that goat's milk agreed with me, she was quick to buy another goat, for she already had one, and so they had to nourish and rear me with nothing but this stuff up to my twelfth year. I may say that the day I turned twelve I had, the devil take me, several yards of bacon on my back, for I had got so fat from the goat's milk. With the beginning of my thirteenth year I likewise learned to nibble down quite gently roasted stuffed birdies and larded young poultry, which eventually also agreed with me very much. As I was now growing older my mother sent me to school, thinking she would now make a lad of me, who in time would exceed everyone in scholarship; indeed at that time I should probably have become something eventually if I had had any desire to learn, but I came out of school just as bright as I went in. My greatest pleasure was the peashooter my grandmother had presented me from the fair at the Ass Mead; as soon as I came home from school I threw my little books under the bench and took my peashooter, ran to the top story, and either shot people in the street on the head or shot sparrows or broke neighbors' beautiful panes of plate glass, and when they clattered, I could laugh right heartily; well, I kept this up day after day, indeed I had learned to shoot the peashooter so accurately that I could kill a sparrow even at three hundred paces. I scared the carrion flock so much that upon hearing my name mentioned they knew what the score was. When now my mother perceived that studying wouldn't sit with me and that she was paying tuition in vain she took me out of school and left me with a genteel merchant with whom I was supposed to become a famous businessman; indeed I probably could have turned out so if only I had desired, for instead of taking notice of the numbers of the goods and of how dearly the yard would have to be sold for a profit, I always had other pranks in mind; and whenever my boss sent me somewhere for a speedy return, I never forgot to take my peashooter along, went up one street, down another, and looked for sparrows or for beautiful, large panes in windows where no one was watching; then I would smash them with a shot and then run along, and when I returned to my master after several hours' absence I would always tell him such nice lie-gends[3] that he never said anything to me his whole life. However, I finally perceived that it wouldn't take much for him to smash my peashooter in two over my back, so I took warning, and pulled out with my pea-shooter, saying I would return. Then he sent word to my mother that I caused him all sorts of trouble with people on account of my peashooter and wouldn't fit into business at all. My mother sent word to the merchant that it was all right, she wouldn't leave me with him again, since I had run away from him and was with her again, perhaps I would show some interest in something better. Well, when my mother answered the merchant thusly, that was water for my mill again and if before I hadn't bedeviled the people in the streets and beautiful windowpanes I really went after them now that I had my own way. When my mother finally saw that complaints kept pouring in and that many people had to have windows replaced, she said to me: "Dear son Schelmuffsky, you're gradually getting better sense and growing nicely, do tell me what I should do with you since you show no interest whatever in anything and day after day do nothing but make enemies of my neighbors with your peashooter and cause me great trouble?" Whereupon I answered my mother, saying: "Dear Mother, know something? I want to get going to see foreign lands and cities, perhaps I shall become a famous fellow through my travels so that later, upon my return, everyone will have to put his hat under his arm before me if he wants to speak to me." My mother liked this proposal and said that if I could accomplish this, I should indeed see something of the world; she would give me some money for the trip to sustain me for a while. Whereupon I was quick to get together what I wanted to take along, wrapped everything in a drill handkerchief, stuck it in my pants pocket, and made ready for the trip; yet I should like to have taken my peashooter too; however, I didn't know how to do this, and feared that it might be stolen or taken en route, so I left same at home and hid it in the top story behind the chimney and set out on my very dangerous trip in my twenty-fourth year. What I now saw, heard, experienced, and withstood abroad by sea and land will be heard in the following chapter with the greatest astonishment.

[Schelmuffsky leaves Schelmerode and immediately meets a count who becomes his traveling companion and the two travel around in the count's sleigh (although it is not winter), finally arriving in Hamburg. They are wined and dined at a Hamburg inn and all are impressed with Schelmuffsky, especially a forward young woman named Charmante. With Charmante at his side Schelmuffsky shows off his prowess dueling and dancing, but his rivals chase him out of Hamburg. He leaves for Sweden.]

The Third Chapter

It was right on garlic Wednesday[4] that I first betook me to sea; now I had thought the ships at Hamburg big that people were wont to sail on at the Jungfernstieg, but I soon perceived that the ones at sea by Altona, the devil take me, were still a thousand times bigger, for people called them great freighters; having taken leave of my countryman, I now embarked on one such and sailed away. Hardly had I sailed a half hour to sea before I became ill with seasickness. Zounds! How I began to vomit, I felt exactly as though, the devil take me, my innards would all have to come out of my body, for there was no end at all, and it kept up three whole days and nights on the ship; the others were all amazed at my having to produce so much stuff; early the fourth day, as I now gradually began to feel a little better, I had the skipper give me a glass of brandy of about twelve measures. I now quickly tossed down same in one gulp, thinking it would cure my stomach again. Zounds! When I got that stuff into my body, how sick I began to get again, and if I had not vomited before, I really threw up after the brandy, with the result that after again regurgitating without surcease four whole days, the devil take me, the following fifth day, the clear goat's milk came up that I had drunk from childhood up to my twelfth year, and that must have caught somewhere in my body for so long; after such was now out of my body, and I had nothing more at all to throw up, the skipper bade me slurp down a good glass full of olive oil, that my stomach hereupon might again settle nicely and accommodatingly, which I proceeded to do, and slurped, the devil take me, well over fifteen tankards of olive oil into me with one gulp.

As soon as I had the stuff in my body, I felt better from that hour on. The thirteenth day around ten o'clock forenoon, it became black as pitch, so that you couldn't even see a stitch, and the captain had to hang out a big lantern on the front of the ship, that he might know whither he was sailing, for he surely didn't dare to trust his compass, it faltered repeatedly. Toward evening then, zounds, such a storm arose at sea that we just thought we should all have to perish. The devil take me, I suppose I can say that it seemed to us exactly in such a storm as if we were being rocked in a cradle as little children; the captain probably would have liked to anchor, but there was no bottom, so he had to take care that he didn't sail his ship onto a reef. The nineteenth day the sky began to clear again gradually, and the storm settled so quickly, that the twentieth day became quiet, with good weather, better than we ourselves wished. Also after this storm the water in the sea became so clear that, the devil take me, you could see all the fish swimming in the sea. Zounds! What sticklebacks! One stickleback there was, the devil take me, as big as the biggest salmon here on land, and pike? The devil take me, they had tongues hanging out of their snouts like big Polish oxen; among others you could also see fish there with horrible, big, red eyes; I will wager that an eye on such a fish was almost bigger than the bottom of a vat here on land in which people are wont to brew good sticky beer. I asked the skipper what they called the fish; he said they just called them big-eyes. At the end of the same month we smelled land, and the following month we got to see the spires of the beautiful towers in Stockholm toward which we were sailing; when now we were still about a mile from the city, we sailed quite smoothly along the shore. Zounds! How beautiful are the meads about Stockholm; people were just haying at this very time, they walked in the grass, the devil take me, up to their arms, it was pure joy to see it; there were probably over six thousand hay doodles that they had already stacked on one mead there. Having now arrived quite near to the city the captain stopped, bade us pay our fare and debark, which we did. Now debarked there on shore, one went this way, another that; I now wandered right into the city and, not wishing to lodge in any common inn, I stayed in the suburb and took my quarters with a fancy gardener who was, the devil take me, quite a solid fellow. Now as soon as I reported to him, requesting quarters, he said yes forthwith; whereupon I immediately told him of my birth and the incident of the rat. Zounds! What a pleasure for the man to hear these things, the devil take me, he was so polite toward me and always kept his little cap under his arm in addressing me, for he called me nothing but Your Grace. Now he also surely perceived that I was a fine fellow, and that there must be something important about me. He had an excellent, beautiful garden; now almost daily the most aristocratic persons from the city drove out to his place for a promenade. Although I suppose I wished to stay there incognito without revealing myself and my position, nevertheless I was soon discovered. Zounds! What *visites* didn't I have from the most aristocratic *dames* in Stockholm; the devil take me, every day I suppose thirty carriages full kept driving into the garden merely in order to see me, for the fancy gardener had probably extolled to the people what a fine fellow I was. Among others, one lady kept driving to the garden, her father was the most aristocratic man of the city, people just called her Mistress Lisette; the devil take me, she was an excellently beautiful female, now she had fallen mortally in love with me, and really gave me to understand that I should woo and marry her. Whereupon answering her very nicely, I said that I was a fine fellow whose eyes showed something of importance, that therefore for the present she could be supplied with no certain answer. Zounds! How the female began to howl and cry as I gave her the gate; well, the devil take me, I didn't know what to do with her. Finally I began to answer her, saying that I was already half and half betrothed to a girl in Hamburg, however I had no post from her whether she was still alive or dead, she should only be patient, in several days I would give her an answer, whether or not I would marry her. Wherewith she was content again, and fell onto my neck and was so fond of me, the devil take me, that I had completely resolved to let *Charmante* go, and hold to Mistress Lisette. Whereupon taking leave of me with crying eyes, she said she would call upon me again early the next morning, and therewith drove into the city to her parents. What happened? The following morning came, I had a good fresh milk prepared, with which I would treat Mistress Lisette in the garden; the forenoon past, the afternoon was likewise almost over, I kept waiting in the garden with the fresh milk, but no Mistress Lisette would come, so that, the devil take me, because I was so crazed, and couldn't contain myself, I let the fresh milk get into my hair and ate it up solely for spite. As I now was putting the last spoonful into my mouth, the gardener's boy ran quickly into the garden, and asked me if I knew the news? As I was now eager to hear what there was, he began, that Mistress Lisette, who had been so long in the garden with me yesterday evening, had suddenly died last night. Zounds! How I started at this post, the last spoonful of milk forthwith congealed in my throat. Yes (the boy continued) and they say the doctor said she must have been sorely grieved about something, otherwise she surely would not have died, since no illness at all was discernible in her. Zounds! How I pitied the female, and there was, the devil take me, surely no one responsible for her death but me for not wanting to marry her. I felt sorry for the female very long, the devil take me, before I could forget her; in her honor I had a poet compose the following lines, and had them cut on her tombstone, which even now may still be read on her grave in Stockholm:

> Wanderer hurried, stay and contemplate this stone
> And guess who here may lie buried all alone:
> For pain of love died Lis', petite on her couchette
> Now guess who lies herein: the lovely child Lisette.

After this little Lisa, the daughter of an aristocratic noble then fell in love with me; her name was Damigen, and she likewise now gave me to understand that she was interested in wooing. The devil take me, she too was an incomparable female. I was obliged to drive around with her every day and ever be with her; now although to be sure I was much given to the noble's daughter, and had likewise given a vain promise of marrying her, nevertheless I had not yet taken the formal step, yet all the little street boys ran around calling that Mistress Damigen was engaged, how well she was doing, that she was getting such an aristocratic fine fellow for a husband, at whom everybody forthwith laughed whenever they saw him. Now the whole city was full of such long-winded chatter. I had quite resolved to marry her, and would have taken her too, if her father had not promised her to another noble without the knowledge and consent of me or her. What happened? Damigen asked me to take her walking through the city of a Sunday that people just might see, for they had heard from the fancy gardener that I was such a fine, excellent fellow from whose eyes nothing common sparkled, so many of them sorely yearned merely to have a look at me. Now I could easily do her the favor of showing her about the city a little. St. Baldwin's day just happened to fall on a Sunday[5] when I went walking with Damigen about the city of Stockholm, leading her by the hand; when the people now saw that I was proudly walking along there with my Damigen, zounds, how they leaned over their windowsills! They kept speaking furtively to one another, and as much as I could hear, first one said:

"Why, he's a wondrously handsome fellow!" Then someone from another house said: "I've never seen the like of him my livelong days!" Again, a pair of little boys stood there, saying to each other: "Hey, you, look, here comes the female who's getting the aristocratic, rich Junker who lodges out there at the fancy gardener's." Then a pair of maids at a corner said: "Oh, people, just think how well Mistress Damigen is doing, she's getting that fellow there who is leading her by the hand, the female doesn't even deserve him." People were now furtively making these and similar remarks to one another. Also, there was such a gawking after us, the devil take me, I can't describe it. When we now came to the market, and tarried there a bit, that I might rightly see the people, that same noble may see this, that I am there conducting Damigen around with complete pleasure whom he was supposed to have as his beloved; however I didn't notice that the fellow will undertake such a foolish thing. As people now were looking at me and my Damigen in great astonishment, he came up from behind, and delivered such a thrust at me, that, the devil take me, my hat flew far from my head, then he quickly ran into a house. Zounds! How I ground my teeth to think that the fellow dared to do such a thing, and if he had not run off, I should have thrust him through the heart with the fifth position, the devil take me, so that he would surely forget to stand up. Also I was of a will to follow him if Damigen had not kept me back; she said it might cause such a big to-do with people and I could find him all right at another time. Damigen having made this suggestion, I donned my hat again in such a nice *manière* that everyone who had seen the thrust delivered to me from behind furtively said to one another there must be something important about me. Even though I now deported myself toward Damigen as if it were of no matter to me, still I could not cease grinding my teeth, so crazed I was that I finally asked Damigen whether, if it pleased her, we shouldn't wander out to the fancy gardener's again and divert ourselves there a bit in the garden. Damigen obeyed me completely, we both walked back again in such a nice *manière* toward the fancy gardener's house where I sat me down in the grass with my Damigen and counseled her how I should go about avenging myself with the noble. Thereafter Damigen entered her coach and drove back into the city to her house. The following day, having inquired where the fellow who had boxed my ears dwelled, I sent the gardener's boy to him

288 · *Seventeenth Century German Prose*

and had him say that I considered him no fine fellow, but rather the most miserable of all lazy louts in the world if he didn't present himself with a pair of good pistols at such and such a time out there on the great mead, and there I would show him I was a fine fellow. What happens when the fancy gardener's boy now rubs these words under the nose of the noble and prattles of pistols, zounds! The fellow is so terrified, he doesn't know how to answer the boy. When now the boy inquires what answer he should bring back then to the aristocratic gentleman, he finally begins to speak, he must indeed admit that he knocked the hat off my head; it had so vexed him to see me leading his dearest to be, Mistress Damigen, by the hand, and he could not stand this at all. Although I was now forthwith challenging him with pistols on account of the ear boxing, he would hardly come, because it was like this with shots, how easily he or I could receive something of them, and how would we then be afterward; and therefore he would not come, but if I would fight him with bare fists, then he would first ask his mother if she would allow this. However, if she should not grant him this, he could give me no *revanche* for the ear boxing. Zounds! When the boy brought me back such an answer from the noble, I should like to have thrust and cut at him immediately. I was quick to consider how I would treat him again. At first I was of a will to knock him down on the street and walk away, but then I thought, where will your Damigen then seek you? Finally I resolved to repay him the thrust doubly in public company, and throw him down weightily with my Spanish stick. I would have done this too, if the fellow had not forthwith made such a great to-do on account of the challenge by pistol, that I was thus requested by high authority to let things be; enough that they all knew that I was a fine fellow, few of the like of whom would scarely be found in the world. Hearing this, that high authority requested me to let him be, and let myself be considered the finest fellow in the world, I should then probably not have troubled myself to think of him again. However I wasn't getting my Damigen either, to be sure her father let me know he well perceived that I was a fine fellow, the like of whom one scarcely found, but he had promised his daughter to a noble, and whoever was not noble dare not imagine that he would get her. Whereupon I let him be informed nicely, that as a matter of fact he had spoken quite rightly in calling me a fine fellow, few of the like of whom were to be met in the world, and indeed I had never yet demanded his daughter, but rather she would have me.

When the old noble questions his Damigen about this, she says yes,
it is true and yet she will not take him whom one would force upon
her; if she should not have me, she would take none at all, and she
would rather do something else than marry someone whom she
couldn't love. But thereupon Damigen's father watched her sharply
and forbade her upon his highest displeasure to drive out to me
again, for he likewise had arranged at all gates that no one should
let her out. If then I thus didn't get to see Damigen again, afterward
the good female was quite unhappy, so that everyone thought ill
of her stern lord and father for denying her to me. Thereafter I
had quite resolved to leave Stockholm again since I already had
looked around there two whole years. Resolved now to betake
myself to ship again the next day, I took one more walk the previous day in the gardener's ornamental park to see if the plums
were soon ripe. While I was examining one tree after another, the
gardener's boy quickly ran up to me, saying that someone stopping
outside by the gate with a beautiful bell sleigh would like to speak
with me. He was wearing a large, green fox fur. Now I could not
think fast who this must be; finally I recalled my brother the count,
wondering whether it must not be he, and quickly ran with the
boy out of the garden; as I came up it was, the devil take me, my
brother the count whom I had left in the lurch in Hamburg.
Zounds, how happy we both were to see each other. I took him
forthwith into the gardener's room and right away had him given
something to eat and drink, for, the devil take me, he was quite
starved, and his horse looked quite meager also; the gardener's boy
forthwith had to ride him out to the meadows in the pasture that
he should have his fill again. Therewith he related to me all sorts
of things, how he had fared in Hamburg, and how Lady *Charmante*
had missed me so when I had had to take flight and leave her so
unexpectedly. He also brought along a letter to me from her which
she had only written me forlorn, that he nevertheless might deliver
it to me, for she had thought I was long since dead, since I had not
written her at all where I was. The contents of the letter were as
follows and versewise:

Charming Youth

Are you still alive? Or do you lie buried?
Send you neither letter nor greeting to your dearest?

Ah the saying is, right in vain for that to have tarried,
Which one kisses in thought must long since be moldy at best.
Are you then dead? So grant I you herewith the most joyous
    pleasures,
Do you still live, my charming sweet? And look now at this
    sheet
Which *Charmante* sends who had t'avoid you with sudden
    measures,
When your hero's bravery did you from the town speed.
Live you still? Then I do please implore, write me back
    importune,
Where you are, no matter may the way dangerous wend,
For you I will implore heaven's goodly, fast fortune,
If forthwith now to your *Charmante* first merely a word to
    send.

When I had read this letter, *Charmante* touched my heart so that
I could not refrain from crying, but bade my brother the count eat,
and went out the door and cried, the devil take me, like a little
boy; being then cried out I asked the gardener to give me quill and
ink, I would answer this letter as fast as possible. The fancy gardener replied that all this could be found above in the summer
room, and if I desired, he would have it fetched down, but if it
pleased me to write up there where I would not be disturbed by
talking, I could do that too. That I accepted, requesting my brother
the count to excuse me while I left him alone a little, and I was
concerned only with answering and sending off the letter. Whereupon my brother the count said I should make no fuss about him,
I might write as long as I would, he would not hinder me. Whereupon I wandered out the door and wanted to run up the stairs as
fast as possible, but failing to notice a broken tread, I fall there
with my right leg into the hole where the step is missing and, the
devil take me, forthwith fragilely break my leg in two. Zounds!
How I began to shriek! They all, including the count, came running
up and asked what had happened to me, but no one could help
me, the leg was simply in pieces. The fancy gardener immediately
sent for the executioner to come and bind me, for he was, the devil
take me, a solid man for healing fractures; he fixed me up again
very nicely, even though he doctored thereon a good twelve weeks.
When now I could step a little on it again, I had to answer *Char-*

mante's letter first of all that was composed very nicely also versewise as follows:

> With the wish first of all for everything dear and good,
> Schelmuffsky's living yet and in very good mood!
> Though twelve weeks ago the right leg he has broken,
> Yet the executioner's healing art will soon give a good token.
> My brother the count safe in his sleigh has come to me here
>   with Godspeed,
> A letter he's brought me from which I now read,
> *Charmante* my dear would like to know, live I yet or be dead?
> The devil take me, for there's yet neither need nor dread.
> I'm living now in Swedish country,
> Would you now like dear child with me to parley?
> With the fancy gardener in Stockholm's sururb I do now
>   reside,
> So soon must you come to my side,
> For here intend I not still longer to repose.
> This is the import of that which I did want as answer fine for
>   you to compose.
> Meanwhile fare well, healthy, pert both late and early
> And I shall remain forever your
>> charming youth
>>> Schelmuffsky.

Now although I had never made any pretension to poetasting,
nevertheless, the devil take me, this letter turned out for me versewise very nicely. I now sent same by the gardener's boy to the
posthouse in Stockholm that it might be dispatched *cito* to Hamburg. Then had hardly four weeks ensued before my dearest *Charmante* showed up too. Seeing me now, zounds, the female fell onto
my neck and hugged me, indeed she almost gobbled up my mouth,
the devil take me. Then she also told me how the Hamburg watch
had searched for me in her bed three times because I chopped so
many fellows to ruin, and how the company at the dancing hall
had missed me so because I was such an excellent leaper. I should
tell her too how I had fared during the time after my forced flight
from Hamburg. That I told her, also how we had had a storm at
sea, and of the various fish I had seen, but, the devil take me, I
told nothing of how I had fared in Stockholm in connection with

the ear boxing on account of Mistress Damigen. Although I now would fain set sail again to have a further look at the world, since my foot again was completely cured, nevertheless I let *Charmante* persuade me to remain another half year in Stockholm to show her this and that. Now there is nothing especial to see there, except that Stockholm is a fine city very pleasantly situated, about which are cultivated beautiful gardens, meads, and excellent vineyards and that, the devil take me, the most beautiful neckar-wine[6] is made there. But of fisheries and such things there are as few as in Hamburg. To be sure they have enough trout there too, but who can always eat the same fish; however there is unprecedented cattle breeding there because of the grazing; there are, the devil take me, cows there of which one may give forty to fifty tankards of milk at one time. In winter they make butter fast too, it looks like the most beautiful spun wax, the devil take me. Having now conducted my *Charmante* everywhere about and shown her this and that in Stockholm, I again prepared for the trip with her and my brother the count, paid for what I had consumed at the fancy gardener's, and we took passage on a ship that should take us to Holland. After we were set with the ship, the count packed his bell sleight with his horse aboard so that, coming to land, he could drive again. It being almost time for the ship to sail away, we took leave of the fancy gardener, thanking again for all favor shown. Whereupon, the devil take me, the man began to cry like a little child, our departure grieved him so. As a final gesture he presented me with a wondrously beautiful flower; even though this flower had coal black leaves, you could nevertheless smell it, the devil take me, at a whole mile's distance. He called it simply violet kohlrabi, and I now took this violet kohlrabi along. Whereupon we now marched away toward our ship; arrived there, zounds, what a crowd likewise bound for Holland was there, the devil take me, there were well-nigh six thousand souls who now came aboard likewise of a will to see Holland. How we now fared miserably at sea will make your hair stand on end when you read the following chapter.

The Fourth Chapter

When we sailed from Stockholm it was just at the time when the cherries and grapes were beginning to color. Zounds! What a crowding and squeezing with so many people aboard. I and my dearest *Charmante*, likewise my brother the count, had a room for our own convenience on the ship because the captain saw that we were persons of quality. But the other six thousand, the devil take me, were obliged to take turns sleeping on pallets of straw. For several weeks we sailed very happily and were all right merry aboard; but then we came to the isle of Bornholm, where there are so many reefs that if a captain doesn't know his way he can very easily capsize. Zounds! What a great storm and turbulence suddenly arose at sea; the wind beat the waves up as high as towers over the ship, and it began to grow dark as coal. As the greatest misfortune of all however he had left and forgotten the compass on an inn table in Stockholm, so that consequently he knew not at all where he was, and whither he should sail. The raging and roaring of the cruel turbulence lasted fourteen full days and nights, the fifteenth day, when we thought things would quiet down a bit, a storm arose again, and the wind drove our ship onto a reef so that it quickly broke, the devil take me, into one hundred thousand pieces. Zounds! What a situation there at sea! In an instant ship, captain, everyone who had been aboard, went down, and if I and my brother the count had not quickly seized a plank upon which we forthwith placed ourselves so that we could float, no other means could have helped us, and we should have had to perish likewise with the six thousand souls; zounds! what a lamentation the people set up in the water, nothing saddens me so up to the present hour as the thought of my dearest of all *Charmante;* whenever I think of that female my eyes still overflow, the devil take me. For I heard her still calling about ten times "charming youth" in the water, but how could I help her, the devil take me, I had all I could do to keep from falling off the plank, not to mention the fact that I should have helped her. It was ever and eternally a pity that that female unexpectedly had to risk her life; the devil take me, not a single soul could save itself except me and the count on the plank. After now viewing this tragedy from our plank at a distance for a while, I and my brother the count paddled it away with our hands and were obliged to float well over a hundred miles before we again came to land; after the lapse of three days we got to see the spires and towers of Amsterdam, toward which we forthwith sailed, and early the fourth day at ten o-clock we landed there with our plank behind the burgomaster's garden, after enduring much danger. Thereupon we walked through the burgomaster's garden ever toward his house, my brother the count had to carry the plank now, and I went ahead; as we now unlatched the garden gate leading into the burgomaster's courtyard, there stood the burgomaster right in the door of his house and watched us come marching up. I shall not tell anyone with what amazement the man looked at us, for we looked as wet as bathed mice, water was still running down the velvet trousers of the count, as though someone were pouring from a vat. Quickly however I related to the burgomaster in two or three words quite nicely how we had suffered shipwreck, and had to float so far before we came to land. The burgomaster who, the devil take me, was a solid, fine man, had great sympathy with us; he led us into his room and had a warm fire lit whereupon I and my brother the count had to step back of the stove into the warm spot to dry ourselves again. Now as soon as the warm stove had helped us a bit, the burgomaster began to ask who we were. I immediately began to tell him quite nicely about my birth and how it had happened that time with the rat. Zounds! What a pair of eyes the man popped open as I told him such things about the rat; hereafter he always kept his little cap under his arm whenever he talked to me, and addressed me as Right Honorable Sir. After this relation, the burgomaster was called out and remained out I suppose a good half hour before he returned; I and my brother the count were very hungry because we neither of us had devoured a bit in four days, therefore because no one was in the room, we looked to see if anything good might be in the burgomaster's warming oven in the warm spot of the stove; the count felt inside and dragged out, the devil take me, a big pot full of sauerkraut, which was probably intended for the servants. Zounds! We took pity on the sauerkraut and wolfed it, the devil take me, clean down. Not long after, I and my brother the count became terribly ill from wolfing such down without bread on an empty stomach. Zounds! We began to throw up and, the devil take me, regurgitated the burgomaster's warming oven abominably full, so that the stench in the room was such that we ourselves could hardly remain there. Hereupon the burgomaster came back into the room, and smelling such, he began to speak to me: "Right Honorable Sir, Your Excellence surely has scorched itself at the stove that it smells so." Zounds!! How was I supposed to answer the aristocratic man quickly at this? I was quick to tell him forthwith in such a nice *manière* how we as a matter of fact had been hungry, had got hold of and wolfed down the pot in the warming oven, and how when the stuff had not agreed with us, we had had to throw it up from us again, and that would be the reason for the present evil odor. Zounds! How the man listened that I could present such in such an adept *manière;* he thereupon calls his housemaid to clean out the warming oven and smoke the room a bit. This being done, he immediately had the table decked and treated me and the count, the devil take me, with right delicate foods. Now as soon as we had dined, some of the most aristocratic dignitaries came to the burgomaster's house and paid me and my brother the count a *visite.* They also invited us to their homes and tendered us great honor so that I may well say Amsterdam is, the devil take me, an excellent city. Right then there was an aristocratic wedding to which they likewise invited me and the count. For a London lord from England was marrying the daughter of an aristocratic dignitary in Amsterdam, and it is now customary there for the aristocratic persons of quality invited to the wedding always to have a wedding *carmen* printed in the honor of the bride and bridegroom and to present them with this, I too wanted to show that I was a fine fellow in this respect. It would soon be St. Gertraute's Day [St. Gertrude's Day] when the flapping stork would return,[7] and since the bride's name was Traute, I would fain take my *invention* from the flapping stork, and the title should read:

The Merry Flapping Stork, etc.

I was quick to sit down with this project and sat well over four hours without hitting upon one line. The devil take me, I couldn't produce one word appropriate for the merry flapping stork; I bade my brother the count try to see if he couldn't produce something by way of emergency since I could hit upon nothing. Now the count said he had recently gone to school where he had learned a bit of poetasting, but he didn't know whether he was still competent, yet he would have a try whether he was. Hereupon the count sat him down, took quill and ink, and began to poetize; what he then scribbled, were the following lines:

In the heavens the lark itself already has presented,
And gradually Mother Flora climbs from her nest;

Yet in her room sleeps Maja firm forthwith and best,
At present little joy is felt or intended.
So will however . . .

When now he had sat with these lines a half hour I suppose, I
peeped over his shoulder at the paper and saw what he had done;
as I now read the stuff I was obliged, the devil take me, to laugh
at my brother the count for such a silly concoction. For instead of
using the flapping stork as he was supposed to, he had scribbled
lark, and in place of Traute he had even used riot of bloom; is a
riot of bloom appropriate for a wedding? And did it have rhyme
topsy-turvy? For "presented" and "nest" rhyme, the devil take me,
as well as a fist on an eye. He wanted to rack his brains with it some
more, but I bade him let it be and sleep instead. Now although I
couldn't concoct anything that day either, nevertheless I sat me
down early the next day with it and would fain make a *carmen* for
the bride with Gertraute and the flapping stork. Zounds! As I
touched the quill, what ideas about the flapping stork didn't I hit
upon, so that, the devil take me, working with it no longer than
half a day, it was done and ran thus as follows:

The Merry Flapping Stork, etc., etc.,

Saint Gertraute's day for us soon now shall ring,
When the merry flapping stork us presents will bring,
Over water and grass he will fly
To bring our bride Traute a gift from the sky,
The devil take me, she'll hold this so dear,
And show it to none ere three-fourths of a year.
To which end then wishes for this ceremony
A body healthy and pert to eternity,
A long life too, late and early,
A person of quality
                            Schelmuffsky

Now as soon as the wedding days were approaching, I and my
brother the count were requested by the father of the bride that
we should do his daughter the great honor of conducting her to
the wedding; whereupon I answered the wedding-father very
nicely, saying that for my part I should fain do this, but I doubted

very much whether my brother the count could be present, because
the rogue had got a cold fever and was confined to his bed. The
wedding-father was very sorry to hear this, and since it couldn't
be, the burgomaster in the meantime had to take his place. When
I now led the bride to the wedding, zounds! What a gawking from
the crowd, they practically crushed one another, the devil take me,
merely because each wanted to see me so badly. For I walked along
very nicely by the bride in my black long, silk cloak with a red,
broad, velvet collar. Now it is the mode in Amsterdam, that persons
of quality wear pure red velvet collars on their black cloaks and
high, pointed hats; the devil take me, I can't say how nicely I
conducted the female to the wedding and how *proprement* the
pointed hat and long cloak with the red velvet collar became me.
When now the wedding was over and the celebration began, I was
quickly obliged to seat me by the bride who sat in the place of
highest honor next to the bridegroom; not until then did the other
aristocratic persons of quality sit down; they all gazed at me in the
greatest amazement, especially those who had not seen me in full,
and they certainly thought to themselves that I must be one of the
finest and most aristocratic fellows in the world (which of course
was true), since one had conferred upon me the high place of
honor. After we now had thus dined for a while, the master of
ceremonies stepped up to the table, stating that whoever of the
persons of quality among the wedding guests had composed a *carmen* honoring the bride or bridegroom should now be so good to
present it. Zounds, how they all reached into the pockets of their
great-coats, each one bringing forth a printed paper and all of a
will to hand them over. But because they noticed me too fishing
around in my trousers, and likewise seeking something, they
thought forthwith that I too would have had something printed
and no one would precede me. Finally I pulled out my *carmen,*
which I had had printed on red satin, from the lining of my trousers. Zounds! How excited the people were, I now presented the
first of all to the bride with a completely nice *compliment.* Seeing
the title of it, zounds, what a face the female made, but now after
perusing it she twisted her eyes in her head, the devil take me, like
a calf, and I know that she surely thought, if only the flapping
stork were already there. The others now I suppose got wind of
the fact that my wedding *carmen* would have to be the best of all,
so the devil take me, almost all put theirs back into their trouser

pockets. To be sure, some turned theirs in, but neither bride nor bridegroom devoted to them one eye, but forthwith placed them under a plate, but, the devil take me, there was such a rush for mine because they all would fain see and read it. Why? In the first place it was of uncommon *invention,* in the second place it was completely nice and charming German. On the other hand the other persons of quality had only used halting words and un-rhymed German for their verses; zounds, what an uproar was aroused among the people after reading my *carmen* they continually put their heads together and kept watching me in the greatest amazement that I was such a fine fellow, and they kept saying furtively to one another that there must be something very important about me. Shortly afterward the bridegroom stood up and began to toast my health. Zounds! How quickly the other persons of quality stood up and made great reverences to me. But I remained seated and looked at the whole line of them with such a nice countenance; the burgomaster, with whom I and my brother the count were lodging, kept laughing so that his belly shook, he felt such a cordial joy that everybody venerated me thusly. Why? Because it was an honor for the man himself to have such an aristocratic person like me occupy his house. My health now having been toasted around the table, I had the master of ceremonies bring me a large water tankard holding, I suppose, twenty-four tankards of the local measure; I bade a servant fill this full of wine and hand to me across the table; the bridegroom, bride, and other wedding guests seeing this, they thereupon opened up their mouths and noses, not knowing what I would do with the water tankard there on the table. But I was quick to stand up in a nice *manière,* held the tankard of wine in my hand and said "Long live Traute the bride." Zounds, how the other persons of quality all bowed toward me. Whereupon I put the water tankard to my mouth and gulped the twenty-four measures of wine clean down in our draft and hurled it against the tile stove so that the pieces flew about. Zounds, how they looked at me, if before they hadn't been amazed at me when they were reading my wedding verses, now they really were astounded to see how I could gulp down the water tankard full of wine so nicely. Forthwith I had the servant fill me another such tankard full of wine and hand to me across the table; like the first one I now gulped this down to the bridegroom's health (his name was Toffel). Zounds! How the dignitaries' daughters, sitting at the other table, all stretched their necks up to me; the females were terribly astounded at me, the devil take me, when they saw that I could drink so nicely. Shortly thereafter, such an unexpected and rapid sleep befell me that I couldn't resist laying my head on the table to listen a bit. Seeing this, the bride bade me lie awhile on her lap, for the table was way too hard, which I did without hesitation. However, I couldn't lie long on her lap, for it was too low for me, my head began to ache from this, and I was quick to lay me on the table again. Whereupon bridegroom Toffel ordered a servant to bring me a cushion from the bride's chamber that I might not lie there so hard. The servant quickly ran and brought the cushion, the bride put it in the corner, saying I should lay me thereon and slumber a little half hour; I was quick to lay me full length on the bench behind the table; to be sure an aristocratic woman of quality was sitting right near me, she was obliged to slide far down that I might not soil her dress with my feet.

Lying now for about half of a quarter hour, zounds, how sick I became and began to groan. The bride, devoted to me above the others, wants to see after me and inquire what my trouble is, but she doesn't perceive, nor do I, that I am so close to throwing up, and there I began to spew, and the devil take me, I spew the bride's bosom quite full, so that it kept on running through below. Zounds, what a stench was there, they were all obliged to take notice and go away; the bride went out forthwith to her room and was of a will to change clothing; the wine had quite dulled my head, I therefore lay there and, the devil take me, I could hardly recollect where I was. The other persons of quality noticing that I am full, they have me taken to my quarters to sleep off the intoxication. Awakening again the following morning I didn't know, the devil take me, what I had done the previous evening; I gathered I was so full because people were saying in the street that the aristocratic foreign gentleman could drink so well and had thrown up so terribly, from which I presumed that I must have drunk too much. It now being time again for the noon meal, the master of ceremonies came and bade me come right soon to the wedding house, for they were all waiting for me with the bridal soup. I was quick forthwith to put myself in order again and sent word by the master of ceremonies that they should only delay the meal a little half hour, I would come right away. But shortly thereafter the bridal carriage with four horses came and fetched me from the burgomaster's house. As soon as I came driving up to the wedding house, bridegroom Toffel was standing in the door with his bride to receive me; likewise they opened the bridal carriage for me to climb out, which I proceeded to do and forthwith leaped out with both feet over bridegroom Toffel, which was right nice to behold, whereupon they led me into the room. Zounds, what great reverences all the persons of quality made to me. Forthwith I was obliged to sit by the bride again, and next to me on the left sat a dignitary's daughter; she too, the devil take me, was a nice girl, for this day they had seated the ladies and gentlemen alternately. Now I didn't know I had thrown up into the bride's bosom yesterday, but Toffel, her bridegroom, told me, and inquired whether I felt better today after yesterday's regurgitation. Zounds, how terrified was I to hear that I had caused such a shameful scene at table yesterday. But hereupon answering Toffel, that was the bridegroom, very nicely, I said that I was a fine fellow, few of the like of whom one would find, and that I had committed a faux pas by spewing the bride's bosom full, it had happened during intoxication, and I hoped that by now she would have had her things washed clean again. Did anyone dare to say a word hereupon? The burgomaster knew all right how things stood with me, and that no one would presume to insult me with impunity; he now kept laughing so that his belly might have burst. Finally I thought, you must tell marvelous things again that they may really open up their mouths and noses and regard you solidly. Forthwith I was quick to begin to relate my marvelous birth and the incident of the rat. Zounds, how the people at the table all looked at me, and especially Toffel the bridegroom. The dignitary's daughter sitting by me appeared, the devil take me, not a hair different to me from my drowned *Charmante;* she whispered probably ten times over the table into my ear, saying I should tell the rat story once more, and wanted to know whether the hole was really big into which it had run after devouring the silken dress. Likewise she indicated an interest in marriage to me, and inquired whether I would take her, her father should forthwith endow her with twenty thousand ducatoons, not to mention the personal possessions that she still had, inherited from her mother. Whereupon answering her very nicely, I said that I was a fine fellow who had already tried his hand at some important things in the world, and who likewise wanted to try further. Thus I could not forthwith come to a decision, but should have to consider a bit. While I was conversing with the dignitary's daughter, Mr. Toffel, the bridegroom, began to inquire why I had not brought along the count? Whereupon I answered very nicely, saying that because he had the common fever and could not stay up, they would have to excuse him this time for being unable to be a wedding guest. Whereupon the noon meal now being ended, the dancing began; zounds, how *galamment* the girls dance in Holland: they place their feet, the devil take me, so nicely, it is an art. Now I too was obliged to dance, as a matter of fact with the dignitary's daughter who had sat at my left at table and spoken of marriage to me. Now at first they just danced ordinary dances as sarabandes, *chiques,* ballets, and such. I went along with all that now. Zounds, how they all looked at my feet because I could place them so nicely. After we had now thus hopped about a good while, a quite nice circle dance was arranged by the cavaliers and their ladies, which I also was obliged to dance. The idea was this: The cavaliers or young bachelors had to form a circle, and each man in the circle had to have a lady stand on his shoulders and cover his face with her skirt so that he couldn't see; this done, the music to the dance of death began, and the young bachelors had to dance accordingly. Zounds, how *propre* was the dance. Now I had the dignitary's daughter, who had fallen in love with me, standing on my shoulders and danced very nicely with her around in the circle. Zounds, the female was so heavy that, the devil take me, I grew quite tired on this account, yet no cavalier dared to stop dancing until his lady had fallen down. This circle dance now ended, they all begged me to dance solo. Now I could easily grant them the favor of dancing solo. I was quick to give the musicians two ducatoons, saying: "*Allons,* gentlemen, how about playing the Leipzig ditty once?" Zounds, how the fellows began to scrape their fiddles. Whereupon I now began just with cross capers and leaped up, the devil take me, several fathoms high so that the people concluded surely that something was going to spring out of me. Zounds, how people came running in to the wedding house from the street, they were watching me there in amazement. Having now danced off the Leipzig ditty, I was now obliged, with this same dignitary's daughter, who would become my dearest, to stroll about the city of Amsterdam a little in order to cool me off a bit. I fell in with this proposal and walked around a little in the city with this female because I hadn't really got a good look at her yet.

Now she led me all around, wherever there was something to see. I was likewise obliged to accompany her to the Amsterdam Stock Exchange, which, the devil take me, is built *proprement*. Here she likewise showed me the tombstone of deceased Admiral Reyter established as a perpetual memorial because Reyter was such an excellent hero at sea and is always still very much mourned in Amsterdam. The dignitary's daughter having now shown me this and that, she said, turning to me, that I really should take her and that if I should fain not remain in Amsterdam with her, then she would pack her bundle and wander off with me wherever I wished, even though her father should know nothing thereof. Whereupon answering her, I said I was the finest fellow in the world, it might work out, but couldn't be arranged so quickly, I would surely consider ways and means and report to her soon. Whereupon I returned to the dancing place to see where my future dearest might be who had run away from me so fast on the street; I wore my eyes out looking for her, but couldn't get to see her. Finally an old woman began to address me, saying: "Your Grace, whom are you looking for?" Answering her now, I asked whether she had not seen the female who had sat on my left at table. "Yes, Your Grace," the old woman continued, "I saw her; however, her father ordered her home and gave her a terrible scolding for succumbing to the great boldness of permitting such an aristocratic gentleman to conduct her around the city so that people would now have something to gossip about, and Your Grace wouldn't take her anyway." The old mother having thus informed me, I inquired further whether she might not return soon. Whereupon she answered me by stating that she doubted her return here very much, for her father (as she had heard) had told her: "Stubborn girl, don't show yourself again to the aristocratic gentleman." Zounds, how such business vexed me, that I should not get to see the female, and when she really didn't return, I presented my wedding gift to Mr. Toffel, the bridegroom, as well as to bride Traute, and took a quite nice leave of them, as well as of the other persons of quality and ladies, and kept on toward the burgomaster's house. The same day they now sent the bridal carriage with four horses twenty to thirty times again, begging me please to present my aristocratic person at the celebration just this one evening still, even though I shouldn't desire to return for the other days. But the devil take me, I didn't return, but kept sending the bridal carriage back to the wedding house empty again. Mr. Toffel, the bridegroom, informed me by the burgomaster he should not hope that one of the wedding guests would have offended me and that I should just let him know what was wrong with me. He would be responsible for everything. However, the devil take me, no one, except the old woman, learned what my trouble was, that I was so angry on account of the dignitary's daughter whom I should not get to see again. I was also of a will forthwith to sail again the same day, if my brother the count had not begged me so sorely not to leave him in his indisposition, but to delay until he had thrown off his fever again, after which he would travel with me wherever I wished. So to favor my brother the count, I stayed in Amsterdam two whole years still, spending my time mostly in gambling houses where every day there was always excellent company of aristocratic ladies and cavaliers. The elemental fever now having left my brother the count completely, I went with him to the *banco,* we drew new bills of exchange, and, boarding a ship, were of a will to have a look at India in which country the Great Mogul resides.

Translated by Wayne Wonderly

Notes

1. Schelmuffsky, Schelmerode: *Schelm* is the German word for rogue or rascal. Schelmuffsky is supposed to sound Polish. An English equivalent for Schelmuffsky might be Rogoski. *Rode* is a common component of German place names. An English equivalent for Schelmerode might be Roguesborough. The notes are indebted in part to Ilse-Marie Barth, ed., *Schelmuffskys war hafftige curiöse und sehr gefährliche Reisebeschreibung zu Wasser und Lande,* by Christian Reuter (Stuttgart: Philipp Reclam June, 1964). The introduction is partially based on information gleaned from Wolfgang Hecht, *Christian Reuter* (Stuttgart: J. B. Metzler, 1966).
2. Adam Riese's arithmetic book: Adam Riese (1492–1559) wrote a number of textbooks for arithmetic.
3. In German the word is *Lügente,* a combination of the word for lie *Lüge* and the word for legend *Legende.* Reuter was certainly not the first to make this play on words in the seventeenth century.
4. In Leipzig on the Wednesday before Whitsunday people ate garlic as they thought it particularly healthful to do so at this time of year.
5. St. Baldwin's Day: Valentine's Day. February 14, 1692, fell on a Sunday.
6. The Neckar is a river in one of the wine regions of Southwest Germany. This numbers among the many illogical details of Schelmuffsky's narrative.
7. St. Gertraute's [Gertrude's] Day is March 17. She is associated with the return of spring and is the patron saint of captives, sailors, and travelers. The return of spring is marked by the return of the storks. Of course the stork was also said to deliver babies.

ACKNOWLEDGMENTS

Every reasonable effort has been made to locate the owners of rights to previously published translations printed here. We gratefully acknowledge permission to reprint the following material:

From *The Meeting at Telgte* by Günter Grass. Copyright © 1979 by Hermann Luchterhand Verlag GmbH KG, Neuwied und Darmstadt. English translation copyright © 1981 by Harcourt Brace Jovanovich, Inc. Published by arrangement with Harcourt Brace Jovanovich, Inc.

From *The Travels of Olearius in Seventeenth-Century Russia* translated and edited by Samuel H. Baron with permission of the publishers, Stanford University Press. © 1967 by the Board of Trustees of the Leland Stanford Junior University.

From *A Woman's Life in the Court of the Sun King: Letters of Liselotte von der Pfalz, 1652–1722* (translated and introduced by Elborg Forster). The Johns Hopkins University Press, Baltimore/London, 1985.

From *Pia Desideria,* translated by T. G. Tappert, copyright © 1964 Fortress Press. Used by permission of Augsburg Fortress.

From *Simplicius Simplicissimus,* by permission of the translator George Schulz-Behrend.

Reprinted from Johann Jacob Christophel von Grimmelshausen: *The Runagate Courage,* translated by Robert L. Hiller and John C. Osborne, by permission of University of Nebraska Press.

Reprinted by permission of the publisher, from *Christian Reuter's "Schelmuffsky,"* translated by Wayne Wonderley. © 1962, 1990 The University of North Carolina Press.

THE GERMAN LIBRARY
in 100 Volumes

Wolfram von Eschenbach
Parzival
Edited by André Lefevere

Gottfried von Strassburg
Tristan and Isolde
Edited and Revised by Francis G. Gentry
Foreword by C. Stephen Jaeger

German Medieval Tales
Edited by Francis G. Gentry
Foreword by Thomas Berger

German Mystical Writings
Edited by Karen J. Campbell
Foreword by Carol Zaleski

German Humanism and Reformation
Edited by Reinhard P. Becker
Foreword by Roland Bainton

German Theater before 1750
Edited by Gerald Gillespie
Foreword by Martin Esslin

Eighteenth Century German Prose
Edited by Ellis Shookman
Foreword by Dennis F. Mahoney

Eighteenth Century German Criticism
Edited by Timothy J. Chamberlain

Sturm und Drang
Edited by Alan C. Leidner

Immanuel Kant
Philosophical Writings
Edited by Ernst Behler
Foreword by René Wellek

Friedrich Schiller
Plays: Intrigue and Love and Don Carlos
Edited by Walter Hinderer
Foreword by Gordon Craig

Friedrich Schiller
Wallenstein and Mary Stuart
Edited by Walter Hinderer

Johann Wolfgang von Goethe
*The Sufferings of Young Werther
and Elective Affinities*
Edited by Victor Lange
Forewords by Thomas Mann

Johann Wolfgang von Goethe
*Plays: Egmont, Iphigenia in Tauris,
Torquato Tasso*
Edited by Frank G. Ryder

German Romantic Criticism
Edited by A. Leslie Willson
Foreword by Ernst Behler

Friedrich Hölderlin
Hyperion and Selected Poems
Edited by Eric L. Santner

Philosophy of German Idealism
Edited by Ernst Behler

G. W. F. Hegel
*Encyclopedia of the Philosophical Sciences in Outline
and Critical Writings*
Edited by Ernst Behler

Heinrich von Kleist
Plays
Edited by Walter Hinderer
Foreword by E. L. Doctorow

E. T. A. Hoffman
Tales
Edited by Victor Lange

Georg Büchner
Complete Works and Letters
Edited by Walter Hinderer and Henry J. Schmidt

German Fairy Tales
Edited by Helmut Brackert and Volkmar Sander
Foreword by Bruno Bettelheim

German Literary Fairy Tales
Edited by Frank G. Ryder and Robert M. Browning
Introduction by Gordon Birrell
Foreword by John Gardner

F. Grillparzer, J. H. Nestroy, F. Hebbel
Nineteenth Century German Plays
Edited by Egon Schwarz in collaboration with
Hannelore M. Spence

Heinrich Heine
Poetry and Prose
Edited by Jost Hermand and Robert C. Holub
Foreword by Alfred Kazin

Heinrich Heine
The Romantic School and other Essays
Edited by Jost Hermand and Robert C. Holub

Heinrich von Kleist and Jean Paul
German Romantic Novellas
Edited by Frank G. Ryder and Robert M. Browning
Foreword by John Simon

German Romantic Stories
Edited by Frank Ryder
Introduction by Gordon Birrell

German Poetry from 1750 to 1900
Edited by Robert M. Browning
Foreword by Michael Hamburger

Karl Marx, Friedrich Engels, August Bebel, and Others
German Essays on Socialism in the Nineteenth Century
Edited by Frank Mecklenburg and Manfred Stassen

Gottfried Keller
Stories
Edited by Frank G. Ryder
Foreword by Max Frisch

Wilhelm Raabe
Novels
Edited by Volkmar Sander
Foreword by Joel Agee

Theodor Fontane
Short Novels and Other Writings
Edited by Peter Demetz
Foreword by Peter Gay

Theodor Fontane
Delusions, Confusions and The Poggenpuhl Family
Edited by Peter Demetz
Foreword by J. P. Stern
Introduction by William L. Zwiebel

Wilhelm Busch and Others
German Satirical Writings
Edited by Dieter P. Lotze and Volkmar Sander
Foreword by John Simon

Writings of German Composers
Edited by Jost Hermand and James Steakley

German Lieder
Edited by Philip Lieson Miller
Foreword by Hermann Hesse

Arthur Schnitzler
Plays and Stories
Edited by Egon Schwarz
Foreword by Stanley Elkin

Rainer Maria Rilke
Prose and Poetry
Edited by Egon Schwarz
Foreword by Howard Nemerov

Robert Musil
Selected Writings

Edited by Burton Pike
Foreword by Joel Agee

Essays on German Theater
Edited by Margaret Herzfeld-Sander
Foreword by Martin Esslin

German Novellas of Realism I and II
Edited by Jeffrey L. Sammons

Friedrich Dürrenmatt
Plays and Essays
Edited by Volkmar Sander
Foreword by Martin Esslin

Hermann Hesse
Siddhartha, Demian, and other Writings
Edited by Egon Schwarz in collaboration with
Hannelore M. Spence

German Essays on Art History
Edited by Gert Schiff

Max Frisch
Novels, Plays, Essays
Edited by Rolf Kieser
Foreword by Peter Demetz

Gottfried Benn
Prose, Essays, Poems
Edited by Volkmar Sander
Foreword by E. B. Ashton
Introduction by Reinhard Paul Becker

German Radio Plays
Edited by Everett Frost and
Margaret Herzfeld-Sander

Hans Magnus Enzensberger
Critical Essays
Edited by Reinhold Grimm and Bruce Armstrong
Foreword by John Simon

All volumes available in hardcover and paperback editions at your bookstore or from the publisher. For more information on The German Library write to: The Continuum Publishing Company, 370 Lexington Avenue, New York, NY 10017.